P9-EDK-071

Valuation of Wildland Resource Benefits

Also of Interest

Public Lands and the U.S. Economy: Balancing Conservation and Development, edited by George M. Johnston and Peter M. Emerson

Conflict and Choice in Resource Management: The Case of Alaska, John S. Dryzek

The Individual vs. the Public Interest: Political Ideology and National Forest Policy, Richard M. Alston

Natural Resource Administration: Introducing a New Methodology for Management Development, edited by C. West Churchman, Spencer H. Smith, and Albert H. Rosenthal

Alaska's Rural Development, Peter G. Cornwall and Gerald McBeath

†*A Wealth of Wild Species: Storehouse for Human Welfare,* Norman Myers

The Forest Service, Michael Frome

The U.S. Fish and Wildlife Service, Nathaniel Pryor Reed and Dennis Drabelle

†*The National Park Service,* William C. Everhart

†Available in hardcover and paperback.

A Westview Special Study

Valuation of Wildland Resource Benefits
edited by George L. Peterson and Alan Randall

Roughly two-thirds of the United States is wildland—land not used for industrial, urban, or agricultural purposes. How can a price be put on this vast resource, which includes forests, range, and recreational areas as well as wilderness? What concrete value can be placed on an asset that provides almost limitless tangible—and intangible—benefits? This collection of essays provides a comprehensive review of the most advanced techniques in the valuation of wildland benefits, a field within natural resources economics that is gaining widespread attention as pressures on U.S. wildlands reach critical levels and debate over their proposed uses and costs grows. The contributors discuss concepts, methods, and problems in wildland benefit valuation, offering critical perspectives on the role of benefit-cost analysis as a decision-making tool in the formation of public land policy. They emphasize benefits rather than costs because, in their judgment, the difficult problems are concentrated on the benefits side. Included in the book is a sophisticated, yet realistic view of the proper role of information in the evaluation of the economic costs and benefits of wildland management plans.

Dr. George Peterson is currently project leader for Valuation of Resource Benefits, U.S. Forest Service. Formerly, he was a professor of urban and regional planning at Northwestern University. **Dr. Alan Randall** is a professor of agricultural economics at the University of Kentucky.

Published in cooperation with the
U.S. Department of Agriculture, Forest Service,
Rocky Mountain Forest and Range Experiment Station

Valuation of Wildland Resource Benefits

edited by George L. Peterson
and Alan Randall

Westview Press / Boulder and London

A Westview Special Study

Published in 1984 in the United States of America by Westview Press, Inc., 5500 Central Avenue, Boulder, Colorado 80301; Frederick A. Praeger, Publisher

Library of Congress Catalog Card Number: 84-51044
ISBN 0-8133-0018-5

Composition for this book was provided by the editors
Printed and bound in the United States of America

10 9 8 7 6 5 4 3 2

Contents

List of Figures

Chapter 1

Chapter 2

Chapter 6

Chapter 7

Chapter 11

Chapter 12

Chapter 13

Contributors

Dr. Alex Anas
Department of Civil Engineering
Northwestern University
Evanston, IL 60201

Dr. Ellsworth T. Bartlett
Department of Range Science
Colorado State University
Fort Collins, CO 80523

Dr. Perry J. Brown
Chairman, Department of Resource
Recreation Management
Oregon State University
Corvallis, OR 97331

Dr. Sanford L. Gray
Department of Economics
Colorado State University
Fort Collins, CO 80523

Dr. William F. Hyde
Duke University
Durham, NC 27706

Dr. George Peterson
Project Leader
Rocky Mountain Forest and Range
Experiment Station
Forest Service—USDA
240 West Prospect
Fort Collins, CO 80526

Dr. Alan Randall
Department of Agricultural Economics
University of Kentucky
Lexington, KY 40506

Dr. William W. Shaw
School of Natural Resources
University of Arizona
Tucson, AZ 85721

Dr. William Vogely
Department of Mineral Economics
Pennsylvania State University
University Park, PA 16802

Dr. Elizabeth Wilman
Resources for the Future
1755 Massachusetts Ave., N.W.
Washington, D.C. 20036

Dr. Robert A. Young
Department of Economics
Colorado State University
Fort Collins, CO 80523

Acknowledgments

We are grateful to Hal Worth for his energetic and well-organized leadership in initiating the process that led to this book. We also want to thank John Krutilla, whose keen insights and broad experience were helpful in planning and critiquing the effort.

Chapter 1
The Valuation of Wildland Benefits: An Overview

Alan Randall and George L. Peterson

The wildlands of North America are diverse and include a wide variety of terrains, and climates. Their common characteristic, which makes them wildlands, is that human influence has been more limited there than on other lands. The definition of wildlands excludes land used for industrial, urban, and agricultural purposes. However, wildlands are more than just wilderness. Wildlands also include forest, range, and recreational lands which are being put to some commercial uses.

Wildlands provide a wide variety of services for people. Commercial enterprises may utilize its timber, range, and mineral resources to produce marketable products. The scenic, fish and wildlife, hydrological, and ecological resources of wildlands may be used by public agencies and private businesses to provide recreation and tourist activities. Wildlands serve as catchment areas for many major watersheds, providing water for a wide variety of downstream uses. Wildlands also play a significant role in purifying air and water.

In addition to providing such tangible benefits, wildlands are valued because they are special kinds of places. They preserve a wide variety of natural ecosystems. Wildlands may be the last hope for saving rare, threatened, and endangered species and ecological communities. For people, wildlands are an educational and spiritual resource, contributing to their sense of history, oneness with nature, and spiritual wholeness.

Much of the wildlands in the United States are in the public domain. These public lands have perhaps the greatest assurance of remaining in a relatively wild condition. There are privately owned wildlands, and the interactions between public wildlands and neighboring private property are important. Nevertheless, public ownership predominates and is a major influence on the management of wildlands.

Legislation and administrative practice require that these public wildlands are managed and conserved in the public interest. Thus, public land managers must determine which of the conflicting demands from various sectors of the public will be served, and to what extent current demands are to be restrained for the benefit of future generations, all within the bounds of the possibilities determined by nature. The concept of multiple use—that, wherever appropriate, several uses will be simultaneously served and no particular use is granted an automatic presumption of priority—is well established. Increasing emphasis is being placed on economic costs and benefits of wildlands. Benefits and cost are to be explicitly considered when making wildlands management decisions.

The Resources Planning Act, which governs the management of much of America's wildlands, requires consideration of economic costs and benefits in making land management decisions. Other legislation affecting the use of wildlands also encourages the consideration of economic benefits and costs. For many years, starting with the Flood Control Act, explicit consideration of the economic benefits and costs has been required for water resources projects. More recently, the National Environmental Policy Act has required that economic impacts be considered, the Endangered Species Act as amended permits exemptions in cases where the economic argument for exemptions is strong, and Executive Order 12,291 requires explicit consideration of economic benefits and costs before regulatory programs are initiated or reauthorized. In addition, the "watchdog" agencies, most notably the Office of Management and Budget, are strongly pressuring the land management agencies to justify their programs in terms of economic benefits and costs.

However, there are problems associated with increasing the role of benefit cost analysis (BCA) as a decision aid. Some individuals in the public land management agencies and various clientele groups are unfamiliar with the theory and methods involved in BCA. Others are opposed to an expanded role for BCA. They contend that it is based on an unacceptable normative theory of public policy, and that its empirical methods are inadequate to evaluate complex issues in public land management.

Because of these concerns and lack of consensus, this review was made of the state-of-the-art in wildlands benefit estimation. The contributors to this review shared an immediate, pragmatic goal: to provide a comprehensive, judicious, and accessible review of what is known about analysis of wildlands benefits. Many of the contributors also had a deeper, perhaps more philosophical concern: to convey a sophisticated yet realistic view of the proper role of information about the economic costs and benefits of alternative wildlands management plans.

While this volume focuses on methods to estimate wildlands benefits, it does so in the context of economic benefits. The underlying theoretical framework is that of benefit cost analysis. Here, we emphasize benefits rather than costs because, in the judgment of the authors and the Forest Service administrators who commissioned this work, the difficult problems are concentrated on the benefits side.

Benefit Cost Information in the Public Decision Process

Benefit cost analysis (BCA) can be viewed as an information system—or, perhaps more aggressively, a decision tool—for public policy. This suggests two fundamental questions: (1) What kind of policy-relevant information does BCA convey? If it is used as a decision tool, in what directions would it mold public policy? What kind of philosophy of government would it implement? (2) How is an information system, or a decision tool, used in the process through which public policy decisions are made? Both of these issues are addressed in this section. The answers that emerge are in one sense definitive: What BCA is, and how it is used, are crucial in defining the appropriate theory, empirical methods and reporting procedures for BCA. In another sense—are the philosophical bases for BCA consistent with enlightened theories of the relationship between government and citizens, and with sound policy decision-making practice?—no definitive answers are possible. Reasonable individuals can disagree about what constitutes enlightened theory of government and sound decision-making practice. Exposure of the fundamental issues is, nevertheless, surely helpful in focusing the discussions and controversies surrounding the role of BCA.

Normative Theories of the Relationship Between Individual and Government

A wide variety of normative theories of the relationship between established authority (government) and the individual can be found, especially if one's horizons extend beyond modern western societies. Our purview here, however, is confined to three variants of social contract theory that have been influential in shaping the political institutions of modern democracy.

Social contract theory originated about three centuries ago, at a time when Europe was beginning to emerge from monarchical and feudal institutions. It inverted the previously dominant political philosophy, and emphasized not the duties of the individual to society and its institutions but the fundamental rights of individuals. Society is seen, in social contract theory, as a human artifact that comes into existence when individuals, recognizing that anarchy is intolerable, choose rationally to delegate some rights to established authority. Within social contract theory, the major issues concern the limits to governmental authority over the individual and the rights of citizens vis-a-vis a government that has misused or exceeded its authority.

Social contract theory was perhaps at its zenith at the time of the American Revolution and helped shape both the institutions of American democracy and the competing political philosophies that remain influential to this day. It is useful to briefly examine three variants of social contract theory: (1) philosophical individualism, which provides an ethical justification for voluntarism and its derivatives, voluntary exchange in the market and the unanimity rule in political choice; (2) Rousseau's "general will" approach, which permits taxation and regulation to modify economic activities and redistribute income, in the public interest; and (3) utilitarianism, one version of which establishes the benefit cost criterion as a public decision rule. This examination serves to clarify the nature of the benefit cost criterion as a public decision rule and to identify its ethical implications and compare them with those of alternative approaches. Whether one likes, or does not like, the ethical bases of a benefit cost decision rule, one inescapable conclusion emerges. The benefit cost criterion is not an alien intruder from the economic area into the political environment. Rather, it is directly derived from one particular, utilitarian, political philosophy.

Individualism, the Market and Pareto-Safety

To philosophical individualists, the rights of the individual are fundamental and unquestionable. Established authority and, by extension, each application of its powers must continually be justified. In the viewpoint of the purest individualist, the purview of governmental authority must be strictly limited to those tasks necessary to maintain order.

The individualistic tradition emphasized the possibilities of conflict resolution via trade. Since trade is a voluntary activity, it follows that no one would knowingly participate in a trade which would leave him worse off. While it is a big step from one-on-one voluntary exchange to complex organized markets, individualists tend to attribute the desirable characteristics of voluntary exchange to market behaviors in general.

Individuals bring to the market their preferences; their endowments, which include income, wealth and property, but also native talents, acquired skills, and time; and their production functions, which specify their capability to produce goods and services for exchange in the market or for direct use within the household. Together, the endowments and production functions define the constraints on individual capacities to achieve satisfaction through the market. In the process of exchange, the relative prices (values, in this sense) of different kinds of goods and services are established. Resources are acquired by those who can put them to the most efficient use, and final goods and services accumulate in the hands of those who most value them. The relative prices established in the process of trade serve to direct inputs and efforts to the most productive uses while rewarding those who make the most effective use of their productive endowments. Incentives arise for saving, investment of capital, and investment in developing one's own human capacities. From this perspective, markets are seen as remarkably effective institutions for harnessing individual aspirations and resolving conflicts among individuals.

Markets themselves are social creations, and require continuous social investment to ensure their smooth functioning. Property rights must be defined—those that are defined to be exclusive and transferable encourage efficient exchange—and enforced. This alone requires a considerable legal, administrative, policing and judicial apparatus. Since definition of rights is, itself, a social act, some kind of legislative system must be maintained for that purpose. Property rights must be defined so as to reflect the aspirations of the individuals who compose society, and occasionally extended or redefined as emerging patterns of scarcity or technological development create new possibilities for conflict. A national defense establishment is essential to protect society and its individual members from intrusion, plunder, and enslavement. Even this rather minimal social overhead is costly, so revenues must be generated and expenditures monitored. Since society will function more smoothly if it is able to rely on substantial voluntary obedience to the law and compliance with procedures for gathering tax revenues and assembling a militia in time of threat, even the individualistic society will invest in programs designed to enhance the loyalty of its citizens. Even the "minimal government" is a substantial and powerful organization.

The voluntarism of the marketplace ensures Pareto-safety—that only those changes are acceptable which make no one worse off in his own judgment—in that sphere. In principal, pure individualists would prefer to see the protections of Pareto-safety extended to the political arena. Thus, one observes concerns with unanimity rules for voting in legislative bodies and optimal taxation strategies (defined so that each individual contributes to each public program on the basis of true willingness to pay; in concept this kind of taxation system would lead to unanimous approval of the optimal package of optimally sized programs). Such procedures have proved elusive, in practice. The individualistic response has been to seek to limit the scope of government (i.e., to maintain the "minimal government") and establish institutions that restrict the capacity of the government to act in arbitrary ways.

While the individualistic vision has its obvious attractions, some qualifications are essential. Markets may fail to provide collective goods (i.e., those that are nonexclusive and/or nonrival) efficiently, and efficient systems to collectively provide and finance them remain elusive. There is no assurance that income and wealth are equitably distributed in the market. Further, if distribution could be shown to be inequitable, that would imply that resources are inappropriately allocated, since the distribution of endowments clearly influences resource allocation.

The "General Will" and the "Public Interest, Market Failure" Model

Rousseau's version of the social contract posits that, in an environment of political equality, deliberative bodies are capable of identifying and interpreting "the general will" and establishing policies and programs to implement it. Under this view, there is no compelling need to minimize the size and power of government, so long as government serves the public interest. Government may seek to establish and promote conceptions of what is good for society. It may attempt to rectify the failures of markets, not merely by seeking to perfect the structure of property rights, but by direct public investment and regulation. To ensure political equality and promote the general will, considerable regulation of individual activities for the "public health, welfare, safety, and morals" may be justified. Goods viewed as especially meritorious—conceivably anything from environmental quality to educational and cultural amenities—may be provided at public expense and paid for through coercive taxation. A considerable variety of regulations, taxes, and subsidies may be used to modify the rules and incentives directing market behavior, in order to influence market outcomes. While almost all of the above-mentioned governmental activities have their distributive consequences, direct policies of coercive redistribution may also be implemented. Governmental activity to all of these ends is permissible, so long as it serves the public interest.

The Samuelson (1947) social welfare function (itself under intense attack since Arrow's 1951 monograph) may be interpreted as an attempt to formalize the idea of the "general will" and incorporate it into the body of economics. Market failure concepts have an active history in economics, beginning with the writings of Marshall and Pigou.

In the political arena, some conflict between individual aspirations and the general will is inevitable. However, public interest theorists place their faith in constitutional procedures and majority institutions to maintain a delicate balance between public and private interest. Since establishing and maintaining this balance is easier said than done, a considerable government apparatus is seen as necessary to adjudicate various kinds of conflicts. All public interest theorists see substantial roles for the legislative, administrative, and judicial branches. Some tend to place their faith in an increasingly professional and planning-oriented civil service. Others, reflecting the philosophy of participatory democracy, favor programs to cultivate freedom of information and to open many avenues through which citizens and interest groups may state their case before legislative, administrative and judicial bodies.

Those of an individualistic persuasion are deeply skeptical of the notion of a public interest, and impute no special authority to majority opinion. The individualist sees majorities as merely successful coalitions imposing their will upon less successful coalitions. Clearly, Pareto-safety, a cornerstone of individualistic social philosophy, has a more limited role under public interest theory. It applies to transactions protected by private property rights, and to the constitutional prohibition against taking of property without due process, but is not compelling in cases concerning, for example, regulation, taxation and redistribution.

One may observe that the individualist is critical of the public interest approach because it fails to provide individuals the same kind of protections in the political arena that they (are presumed to) enjoy in the marketplace. On the other hand, adherents of the public interest approach favor a strong public sector specifically because they believe it provides an essential counterbalance to the myopia and inequity of the market.

Utilitarianism and the Potential Pareto-Improvement

At the individual level, Benthamite utilitarians and individualists are in complete agreement about what is good: What the individual wants is good for the individual. Where collective choices were required and individuals differed about what was good, Bentham suggested that the option promising the greatest good for the greatest number should be socially preferred. This utilitarian criterion entailed obvious difficulties in cases where trivial good for each of many was opposed to very great good for each of a few.

A solution to this problem was proposed, more than a century later, by Nicholas Kaldor and John Hicks. If those who would gain from a proposed change could compensate those who would lose, to the full extent of their perceived losses, change would be acceptable. Note that this criterion differs from Pareto-safety in one, very crucial, way: it requires only the possibility of compensation, whereas Pareto-safety requires that compensation actually be paid. Thus, the Kaldor-Hicks criterion became known as the "potential Pareto-improvement". It boils down to the criterion that change is acceptable if the sum of money-valued gains (as judged by the gainers) exceeds the sum of money-valued losses (as judged by the losers). In other words, change is acceptable when its benefits exceeds its costs regardless of the identity of gainers and losers. Obviously, it permits collective action that imposes harm on individuals while helping others, and is indifferent to whether the gainers are those already well off and the losers already badly off or vice-versa.

The Benefit Cost Criterion as a Utilitarian Social Decision Rule

As we have shown, the benefit cost (BC) criterion can be strictly derived from utilitarian theories of the proper relationship between government and citizens. Therefore, it cannot be claimed that the BC criterion is economic (or, worse, commercial) in its origins and thus has no proper place in public political affairs. Those who are uncomfortable with the BC approach must find some other basis on which to attack it.

It can, of course, be attacked on the grounds that the theory of government that it implements is not a good theory of government. While BC is utilitarian in origin, some modern utilitarians argue that alternative versions of the utilitarian ideal are much to be preferred. Non-utilitarians find even greater fault with the BC criterion as a social decision rule.

The BC criterion has direct links to the individualistic and public interest approaches, but also deviates from them at crucial points. The BC criterion draws its concept of value from individualism: market prices that emerge from voluntary transactions, or those prices that would be established if markets were complete and efficient. However, the individualistic prohibition of collectively sanctioned actions that injure nonconsenting minorities is entirely absent from the BC criterion. As previously indicated, the concept of the public interest may find expression in the social welfare function. The BC decision rule can be interpreted as a specific form of social welfare function: one that weights dollar-valued gains and losses equally without regard to the identity of gainers and losers. Many adherents of the public interest model would find this a rather peculiar expression of the public interest.

Public Policy Decision Processes

How is BC information brought to bear on public policy decisions? The answer depends, in large part, on the decision processes, themselves. BCA is a formal, rigidly structured information system, oriented towards "the bottom line": Is the particular proposal qualified for implementation or not; and, if qualified, where does it rank among other qualified proposals? Clearly, it is well adapted for use in a technocratic policy decision environment. Once the technical apparatus for routine and systematic performance of BCA is in place, decision-making itself could be formalized and systematized.

However, public decision processes in the United States deviate substantially from the technocratic model. Two alternative models are instructive. So, we briefly develop their implications.

The more conventional model (which we call the "linear" model) focuses on the role of senior officials in public agencies. Within his/her area of responsibility, each is viewed as the decision maker (D), who decides issues and resolves conflicts on behalf of society. The public interest is assumed to be revealed to D (in large part through the political process, but D's own ethical sensibilities play a role). There is a venerable tradition that D should be insulated from direct involvement in the political arena. "Politicizing the managers" is resisted (Behan 1981a, 1981b, Box 1982).

D maintains a staff, including scientific and technical experts, whose function is to identify alternatives, to predict the performance of each, and to establish the relevant constraints. At D's request, they may perform analyses to identify the combination of strategies that would maximize an objective function specified by D. Perhaps sensitivity analyses may be requested. These information-gathering and analytical tasks are to be performed competently and using the best that science and technology have to offer. However, they are to be confined strictly to matters of fact, and the scientists' and technicians' values are not to intrude. Upon receipt of the relevant information, D selects the policy that he or she believes will best serve the public interest, and supervises its implementation.

In this model, BCA is among the kinds of analyses that, if requested, may be performed by the disinterested technicians. However, the role of BCA and the BC criterion differs from that under the technocratic model. D is not necessarily bound to request a BCA, and is most definitely not obligated to abdicate the decision-making role to a formal criterion. Instead, D, would decide the importance attached to the BC criterion on the same basis as all other issues are decided: his/her vision of the public interest.

An alternative model, the "diffuse" or pluralistic model of the policy decision process takes a very different perspective. While many individuals and interest groups are seen as influential, it is seldom possible to identify a D who makes decisions for society in the public interest. Even top-level managers in public agencies are seen as participating in the decision-making process, rather than dominating it. Those within government have their own personal views of the public interest as well as views of their self-interest and the interest of their agencies. Those outside of the government sector have a wide variety of private interests and preferences about public affairs. All participants, public and private, seek to allocate their endowments to maximize their own satisfactions. In so doing, they allocate their resources across the private and public sectors. Participants will be observed both maximizing within the current rules and institutions and maximizing by attempting to influence rules and institutions (through behaviors designed to change institutions or to preserve preferred institutions which are under attack).

Rather than a single decision locus the diffuse model recognizes many points at which ultimate decisions may be influenced: legislatures, administrative agencies (often there are several exercising jurisdiction over various aspects of a particular decision problem), the judiciary, and the wide variety of hearings, quasi-judicial procedures, etc. through which legislatures and administrative agencies may be influenced.

In the diffuse model, information plays a multiplicity of roles. Within public agencies and organized private interest groups, an apparatus gathering, interpreting, analyzing and disseminating information will be maintained. To each organization, information serves roles in (1) informing the organization so as to permit it to determine its preferred strategy and (2) attempting to persuade others of the merits of that strategy. Given the latter persuasive role of information, a wide variety of kinds and qualities of information competes in the public arena for attention: fact-oriented and in varying degrees accurate and inaccurate, and the value or goal-oriented and in varying degrees conventional, radical, and eccentric.

Under the diffuse model, members of the scientific and technical community serve a public role as generators and disseminators of information, and also as reviewers and critics thereof. Public and peer criticism are essential for quality control with respect to information. The diffuse policy process is thus dependent on openness of the flow of information and access to criticism. Desirable properties can be claimed for this kind of decision process to the extent that only that information that withstands criticism influences and deserves to influence eventual policy decisions.

BCAs may be performed, circulated, reviewed, critiqued and accorded varying degrees of credibility and influence. Rather than a decision rule, or a policy tool, BCA serves as an information system. Since the "bottom line" is not necessarily decisive, attention may be drawn to other aspects of the BC statements. Many users of BC information may be more interested in what it reveals about the prospects for particular program components and clientele groups than whether the total undertaking would generate a potential Pareto-improvement.

To summarize, the technocratic, linear and diffuse models of the policy decision process have quite different implications for the policy role of BCA. The present authors lean towards the diffuse model, and therefore tend to see BCA as an information system (and by no means the only acceptable information system) rather than a formal tool for systematizing, and perhaps to some extent dehumanizing, public resource allocation decisions.

Benefit Cost Information and Wildlands Management

Much of America's wildlands are in the public domain. Further, the public lands are of the most immediate interest in the policy context because public policies can be most readily brought to bear on the management of public lands. While some states are significant owners of public lands, the federal government is the largest public land holder. The following is most directly applicable to the management of federal lands.

Immediate responsibility for management of public wildlands has been given to specific federal agencies. Such agencies typically maintain a staff of professional land managers, and also scientific and technical personnel, and ultimately are responsible to the current administration. These agencies also are responsible to the Congress, which makes laws establishing basic policies and procedures, which the agencies must carry out, and the judiciary, which may review the performance of the agencies in terms of their compliance with relevant law.

Management decision options are embedded in a complex web of existing laws: civil law, constitutional law, and a broad range of public laws. Public laws include generally applicable federal laws, laws specifically addressed to the role and function of land management agencies, and more broadly applicable resource management and environmental laws, such as the National

Environmental Policy Act and the Endangered Species Act. Relevant laws include those which require land management agencies to do certain things and those which restrict the options available to the agencies.

There are considerable and significant interactions between the private sector and the public land managers. Management policies and strategies pursued on the public lands may affect the well-being of those who own nearby private lands. Important kinds of public land uses involve private exploitation of natural resources. Grazing, timber harvest, and minerals exploration and extraction fall into this category. Recreation facilities may involve private concessions on public lands. Where the public agencies are entirely responsible for provision and operation of recreation facilities, they directly serve the recreationist public. Accordingly, a considerable variety of individuals and groups will have a diversity of self-interests and personal visions of the public interest with respect to management of the public lands.

Interested individuals and groups may gain access to the system at many points. They may make their viewpoints known to the professional managers or to political appointees. They may work through other political channels, attempting to persuade legislators and/or the political arm of the administration of the validity of their positions. Under a considerable variety of laws and administrative procedures, they may present their cases in administrative or judicial hearings. Finally, they may make their cases through the public media, in an effort to influence public opinion and, ultimately, legislative processes and administrative procedures.

All of these considerations suggest that the discretion of the professional land managers in the public agencies is limited. Nevertheless, they are required to establish management policies and make day-to-day decisions concerning the disposition of land resources. Where these decisions arouse little controversy, they may go unquestioned. However, decisions pertaining to conflicts where there is much at stake may become controversial and, thus, may cause political and/or judicial review.

As indicated earlier, legislation and administrative actions have, in recent years, been aimed at influencing public land management in the direction of economic efficiency. Explicit consideration of economic benefits and costs in a BCA framework has long been required for water resources projects under the Flood Control Act. More recently, Executive Order 12,291 has expanded the domain of BCA to include regulatory initiatives. The Endangered Species Act, as amended, provides that economic benefits be a major consideration in deciding petitions for exemption. Under the National Environmental Policy Act, economic impacts of proposed undertakings are considered along with other kinds of impacts.

In legislation specifically addressed to public lands management, the Resources Planning Act and the National Forests Management Act place considerable emphasis on economic efficiency. This legislation mandated the development and use of FORPLAN, a linear programming model for planning the management of the national forests.

The increased prominence of the economic efficiency goal on the public land management agenda should not be interpreted as dominance. Other economic concerns are recognized and receive attention. Executive Order 12,291 calls for an accounting and exposure of the distribution of costs and benefits. The economic impacts addressed in NEPA are addressed as much, or perhaps more, to local and regional economic impacts as to national economic efficiency. The water resources planning process begun under the Flood Control Act has long since been expanded to require, in addition to BCA in a national economic development context, analyses of beneficial and adverse impacts on regional economic development and environmental quality (U.S. Water Resources Council 1973). More generally, current public land management procedures emphasize multiple uses and the service of multiple objectives, in principle.

There is, in practice, some inevitable tension among these goals. Some uses are incompatible, and, if certain desired uses are to be served, some parcels of land must be assigned exclusively to special purposes. Further, many agencies are required by legislation to provide particular services, and such mandates may well conflict with multiple use principles and with the goal of economic efficiency.

The protagonists in these kinds of conflicts—who often include persons within and outside the land management agencies—share a tendency to equate the terms "economic" and "commercial." Those who would prefer that the public wildlands support more commercial production of raw materials often look to efficiency concepts and benefit cost analyses for support. Those who are convinced that the public wildlands do, and should, provide a special kind of environment devoted to values that are not well served in the commercial world often look askance at benefit cost analysis. They suspect it imposes a commercial value system on public operations that often enjoy a legislative mandate to serve particular purposes without any special regard for things commercial.

The concepts of social benefits and costs are quite different from commercial revenues and expenditures. Benefit cost analysis is a test for potential Pareto-improvements and, as such, is logically quite different from the kind of feasibility study a prudent private firm would undertake before committing itself to a major capital investment.

BCA as an Evaluative Tool

The potential Pareto-improvement is a criterion for choice at the societal level. BCA is an empirical framework for evaluating alternatives according to the criterion. Thus, it is primarily an evaluative tool. Present arrangements projected into the future (i.e., the "without project" state) are compared with one or more alternative "with project" states. That which is more efficient—in that it generates the greater total net value of output evaluated given the "without project" distribution of endowments—performs better under the BC criterion. It has the higher benefit/cost ratio and the greater net present value.

As Randall makes clear later in this book, the "without" project and "with" project states are complex, and must first be defined in terms that owe more to the natural sciences than to economics. The relationships between "natural systems inputs," the attributes of the environment and the flows of services it can provide must be quantified. Then, the impacts of human endeavors on this complex system must be estimated to permit development, in physical terms, of "without" and "with project" scenarios. Only then does economics enter the picture, to predict the uses that humans would make of the "without" and "with project" environments and to estimate the economic benefits and costs of the various alternative proposals.

The accuracy of economic estimates depends on the capacity of the natural sciences to generate reasonably reliable estimates of relationships that, in many cases, remain quite elusive.

Assuming that the "without" and "with project" states have been defined in physical terms—i.e., as vectors of services—the next task is valuation. This proceeds according to the potential Pareto-improvement criterion. Benefits are valued at willingness to pay (WTP) and costs at willingness to accept (WTA), both of which depend, ultimately, on individual preferences and endowments. As the "new consumption theory" (Lancaster 1966, Becker 1965, Stigler and Becker 1977) emphasizes, consumption technologies and preferences together affect WTP and WTA. Consumption technologies reflect acquired knowledge and skills in using the environment to obtain satisfactions. To put it basically, one values more highly those things one learns to appreciate.

Markets, where they are well developed and reasonably competitive, provide useful evidence of WTP and WTA. Where markets are not well developed, the economist must invest ingenuity and effort in attempts to impute WTP and WTA from more tenuous kinds of evidence.

Finally, individual WTP and WTA are summed algebraically, according to the potential Pareto-improvement criterion.

This brief overview merely touches upon several important points, which are developed later in this volume. Nevertheless, it provides sufficient background to introduce the major criticisms that have been leveled at BCA as an evaluative tool. These criticisms are:

1. BCA gives a misleading impression of precision. This criticism applies to both the physical and economic data used in BCA. The last three decades have witnessed substantial improvements in the theory and practice of BCA. Yet there is much more work to be done, and this criticism remains valid to some extent. It has its greatest validity where the evaluation task involves complex and little-known natural relationships and the time horizon is long. The BC analyst can counter this criticism by considering a range of estimates of imprecisely known relationships and conducting sensitivity analyses.
2. Where markets are incomplete or in some way distorted, value data are incomplete and unreliable. Actually, great strides have been made in extra-market valuation. However, some problems remain.
3. Given that the better physical and economic data concern routine commercial uses, while data on the benefits of preservation strategies is often sparse, BCA is biased towards commercial production of raw materials from wildlands resources. In principle, this need not be so. Nevertheless, it is important in practice to make every effort to reduce what might otherwise be an imbalance.
4. The "consumer sovereignty" basis of WTP and WTA is inappropriate for evaluating the amenity and preservation uses of wildlands because

people just don't know enough about these uses to make wise judgments. This is a difficult and subtle issue. The concept of consumption technology clearly suggests that people can learn to increase their satisfaction from using these amenities and that more fully developed consumption technologies will be reflected in higher WTP and, ultimately, greater benefits from strategies that emphasize amenities and preservation. The recreation resources specialists (for example) within the public land management agencies may play a part in developing consumption technologies which enhance appreciation of natural amenities.

The economist must be alert for any evidence that values assigned to natural amenities are increasing at a faster rate than values from raw materials uses, and must use such evidence in projecting the future flow of benefits.

5. Because individual WTP and WTA are determined by, among other things, individual endowments, BCA takes a conservative approach to valuation in that it implicitly accepts the status quo distribution.
6. The aggregation rule (that individual gains and losses are to be summed algebraically) and the decision rule (that a proposal is acceptable if its benefits exceed its costs without regard to the identity of gainers and losers) may be philosophically unacceptable. This criticism—which is necessarily valid if one accepts philosophical premises opposed to the potential Pareto-improvement—has already been discussed at some length.

BCA as a Planning and Management Tool

BCA provides a complete framework in which to systematically identify, quantify, and evaluate the efficiency consequences of proposed actions. While its major contributions to planning and management come at the evaluative stage, its usefulness is not confined to that stage. The completeness of its scope and its systematic framework often serve to identify otherwise overlooked considerations, and to suggest alternatives that might not otherwise come to the attention of planners and managers.

Nevertheless, there are considerable limitations of BCA as a planning and management tool. While BCA makes use of a wide range and variety of management-related information, the BCA process is directed towards the bottom line. Its compulsion for aggregation and monetization tends to compress, summarize, and, in the process, hide or obscure many of the considerations crucial for effective design, planning, and management. For example, much of the excellent work elucidating the attitudes and preferences of recreationists, and the relationships of these to underlying trends in society, is of great potential value to designers, planners, and policy-makers to help them plan ahead to provide services to meet emerging demands. The kind of information this work provides, however, may not be directly displayed in a benefit-cost analysis but, rather, subsumed under projections of willingness to pay for various services.

More generally, planners and managers—who are responsive not only to the goal of economic efficiency but also to legislative and executive mandates to provide particular services and serve particular objectives—must be concerned with the consequences of alternative actions. Consequences can be defined in many dimensions, and the contribution to economic efficiency is one way of looking at consequences. But, it is not the only way. Planners and managers often need a different and more disaggregate view of consequences than a typical BC statement provides.

The Economic Theory of Benefit-Cost Analysis

Benefit-cost analysis is a complete and coherent framework for the evaluation of alternative plans of action. It provides an empirical test for potential Pareto-improvements.

Efficiency in General Equilibrium

In general, the best proposals according to the BC criterion are characterized by efficiency. The concept of economic efficiency in general equilibrium may be explored with a simple diagrammatic model.[1] Consider an economy that consists of two individuals, called 1 and 2; two ordinary rival commodities, called *B* and *W* (for bread and wine); and two inputs, called *L* and *D* (for labor and land). The production functions are:

$$B = h_b(L_b, D_b) \text{ and } W = h_w(L_w, D_w)$$

where L_b is the amount of labor devoted to the production of bread, D_b is the amount of land devoted to the production of bread, and L_w and D_w are defined similarly, for wine.

It is assumed that the production technology remains constant throughout the analysis, and that all units of each of *B, W, L,* and *D* are homogeneous in quality.

The utility functions are:

$$U_1 = f_1(B_1, W_1) \text{ and } U_2 = f_2(B_2, W_2),$$

where U_1 is the level of utility enjoyed by the consumer 1, B_1 is the amount of bread consumed by 1, W_1 is amount of wine consumed by 1, and U_2, B_2, and W_2 are similarly defined for consumer 2. The utility functions are assumed to remain unchanged during the course of the analysis; that is, the tastes and preferences of each individual do not change.

It is assumed that the marginal productivity of each input in the production of each output is positive but diminishing, and the marginal utility of each consumer from the use of each commodity is positive but diminishing. Thus all isoquants derived from the production functions and all indifference curves derived from the utility functions will be convex to the origin.

Now, assume the total availability of resources is fixed, so that $L_b + L_w = L$ and $D_b + D_w = D$.

First, consider efficiency in production. The fixity of resources permits formation of an Edgeworth box, a rectangle with height *L* and width *D* (fig. 1).

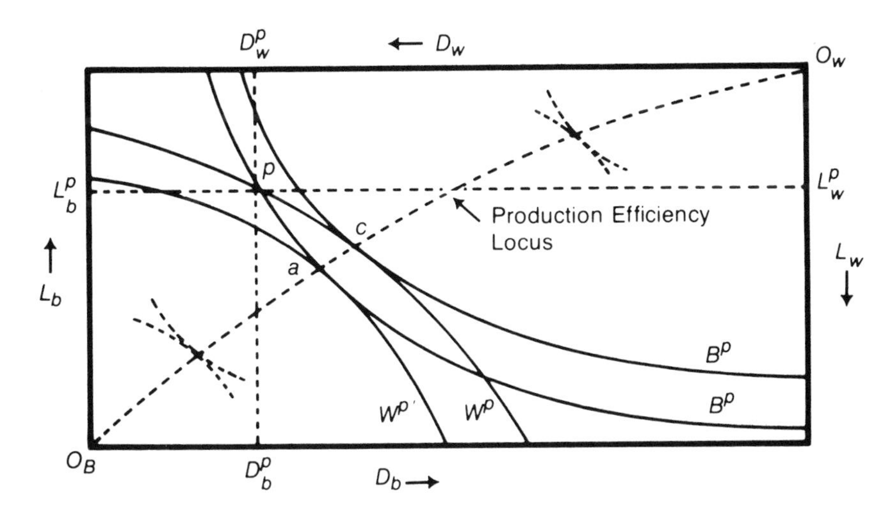

Figure 1. Efficiency in production.

Within the box are isoquants, e.g., B^P, B^{P1}, W^P and W^{P1}. Clearly, the resource allocation identified by the point p is inefficient there is a locus, ac, of points at which more of at least one commodity and no less of the other can be produced using the same quanity of resources. In general, the dashed line from O_b to O_w passing through a and c is a locus of tangencies, i.e., efficient combinations of inputs. At any point on the production efficiency locus, the rate of technical substitution (RTS) of inputs is equal to their price ratio (fig. 2). Formally,

$$(\text{RTS}_{D,L})_B = (\text{RTS}_{D,L})_W = P_D/P_L. \quad [1]$$

However, at each point on that locus, the mix of products is different. A uniquely efficient solution for this model economy has not been identified yet, and no more progress can be made until the preferences of the consumers are considered.

The production efficiency locus can be mapped into commodity space, to form the efficient production possibilities curve (fig. 3), which identifies all of the possible combinations of B and W which can be produced by efficiently allocating L and D. If some point, d, on that curve is arbitrarily selected, one may ask the question: How would the consumers distribute the specific product mix B^d, W^d among themselves? Form a consumption Edgeworth box with dimensions B^d, W^d. The locus of points of tangency between indifference curves for the two consumers is the consumption efficiency locus. That locus may be mapped into utility space, to become a utility possibilities curve, which identifies the possible combinations of utility for 1 and for 2 from efficiently distributing B^d and W^d (fig. 4). Notice that, while mutually beneficial trades may be made from points off the consumption efficiency locus or utility possibilities curve, movements along this locus or curve cannot be consensual, because one individual is made better off at the expense of the other.

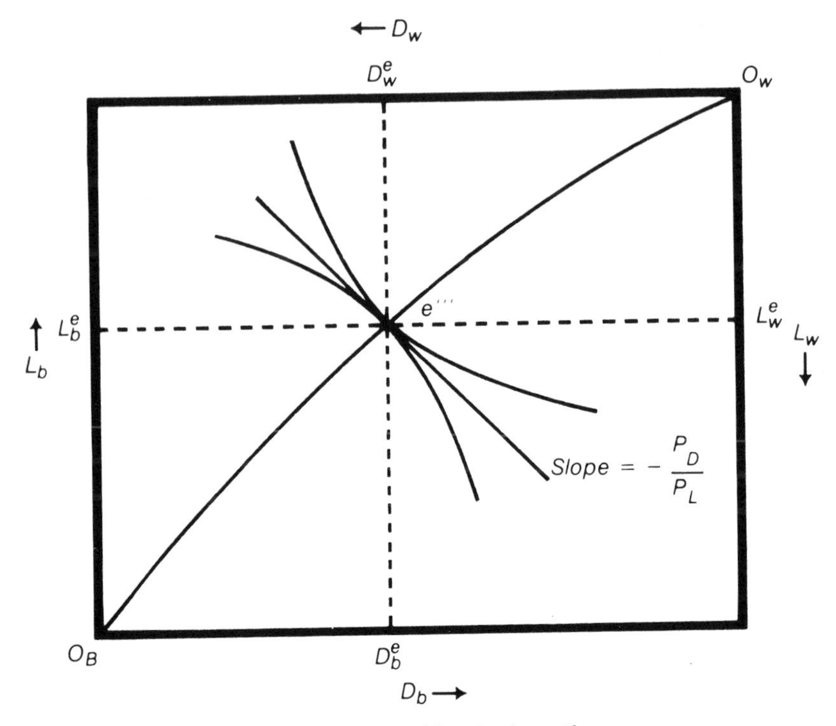

Figure 2. Efficient resource combination and input price ratio.

Remember that the product mix B^d, W^d was selected arbitrarily for further analysis. If some other product mix was selected, that would change the dimensions of the consumption box and generate a different consumption efficiency locus and a different utility possibilities curve (fig. 5). For completeness, the analysis shown in figures 3 and 4 must be repeated for every possible product mix. Then the envelope curve that connects the outermost segments of the various utility possibility curves can be found. This envelope is called the Grand Utility Frontier (GUF).

All points on the GUF are Pareto-efficient. That is, starting from any point on the GUF, it is impossible to change resource allocation or commodity distribution so as to make one party better off without in the process making someone else worse off. Thus, the search for efficiency in general equilibrium has not resulted in a uniquely efficient solution. Rather, we are left with a locus of efficient solutions, each with different distributional consequences.

If, however, there were some basis to select a particular efficent solution (say, *e* in fig. 5), the necessary conditions could be derived for efficient commodity distribution and efficient product mix (fig. 6). Commodities are efficiently distributed when the rate of commodity substitution (RCS) is equal for both consumers and equal to the commodity price ratio. Formally,

$$(\mathrm{RCS}_{W,B})_1 = (\mathrm{RCS}_{W,B})_2 = P_W/P_B. \qquad [2]$$

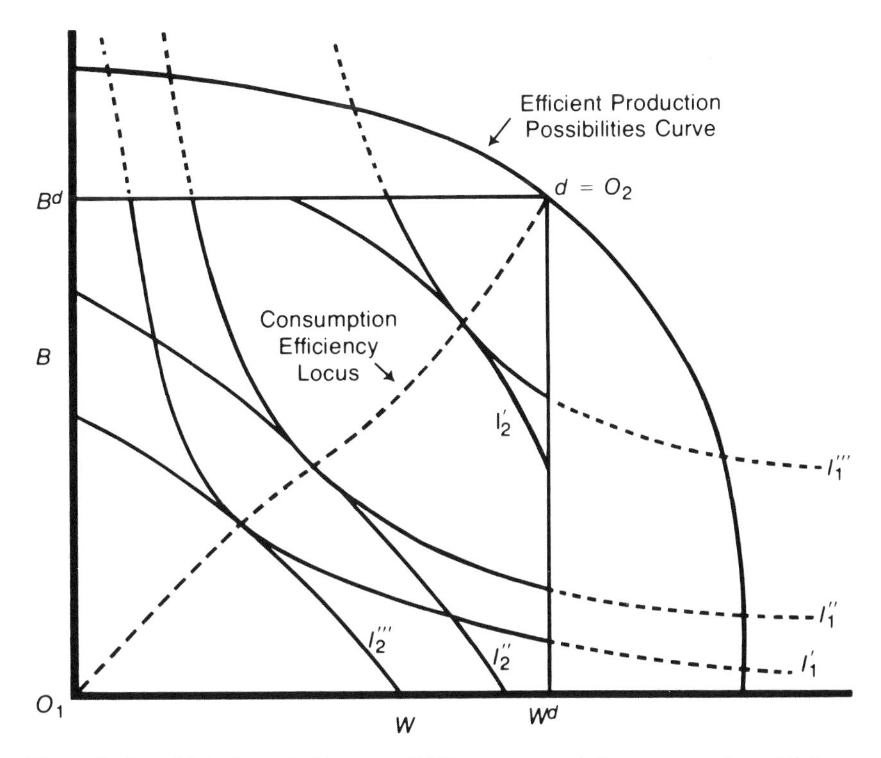

Figure 3. The efficient production possibilities curve and the consumption efficiency locus.

The efficient product mix is attained when the rate of product transformation (RPT) equals the commodity price ratio. That is,

$$(\text{RPT}_{W,B})_1 = P_W/P_B. \quad [3]$$

Consumption and production are efficiently coordinated when equations [2] and [3] are combined, through their common price ratio:

$$(\text{RCS}_{W,B})_1 = (\text{RCS}_{W,B})_2 = \text{RPT}_{W,B} = P_W/P_B. \quad [4]$$

Equations [1] and [4] together identify the necessary conditions for Pareto-efficiency.

From this simplified analysis, several conclusions can be made.

1. In general equilibrium, efficiency is a complex concept involving all of the following: efficient allocation of resources in production; efficient distribution of commodities among consumers; and coordination of production and consumption, as both production and preference relationships help determine the efficient product mix.
2. Efficiency for ordinary, rival goods can be defined (as shown) in terms

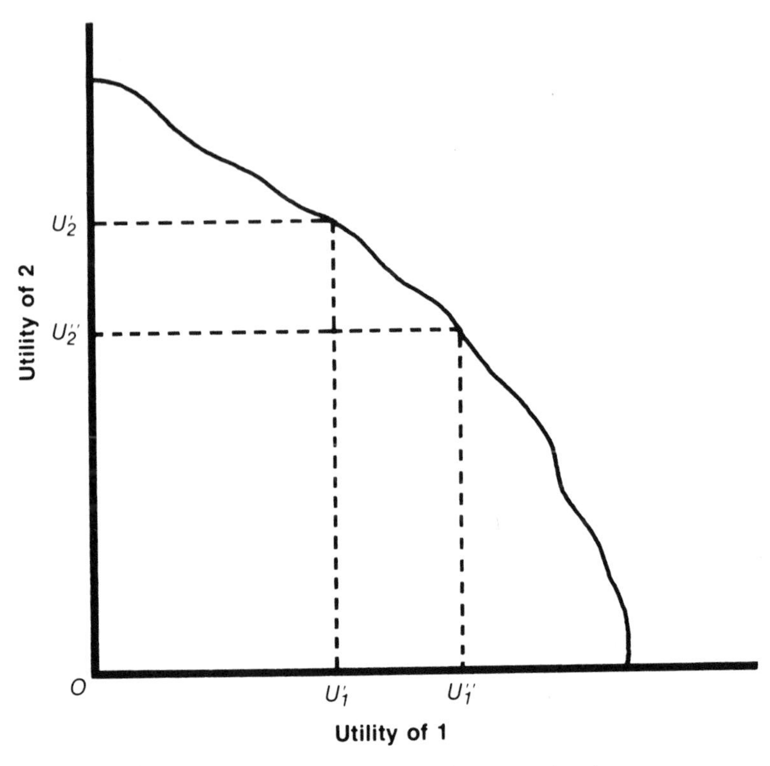

Figure 4. The utility possibilities curve for the product mix B^d, W^d.

of necessary relationships among production possibilities, preferences and price ratios at the margin. When nonrival goods are involved, the analysis becomes more complicated, and the conditions under which efficient outcomes emerge are more restrictive.

3. While most conceivable organizations of an economy are demonstrably inefficient, there remain (at least in concept) an infinity of efficient solutions, arrayed along the GUF.
4. Each efficient solution is different in terms of its distributional consequences.
5. Voluntary agreement to change the economy from one efficient solution to another is inconceivable when technology and preferences are static.
6. Starting with an inefficient situation, unimpeded voluntary exchange will result in movement toward efficiency. The bounds upon the solutions that are attainable are determined by the individual utility levels at the initial situation. Changes which, even though they represent improvements in efficiency, would make someone worse off cannot be voluntarily achieved.
7. In concept, a system of ideal markets will generate a Pareto-efficient

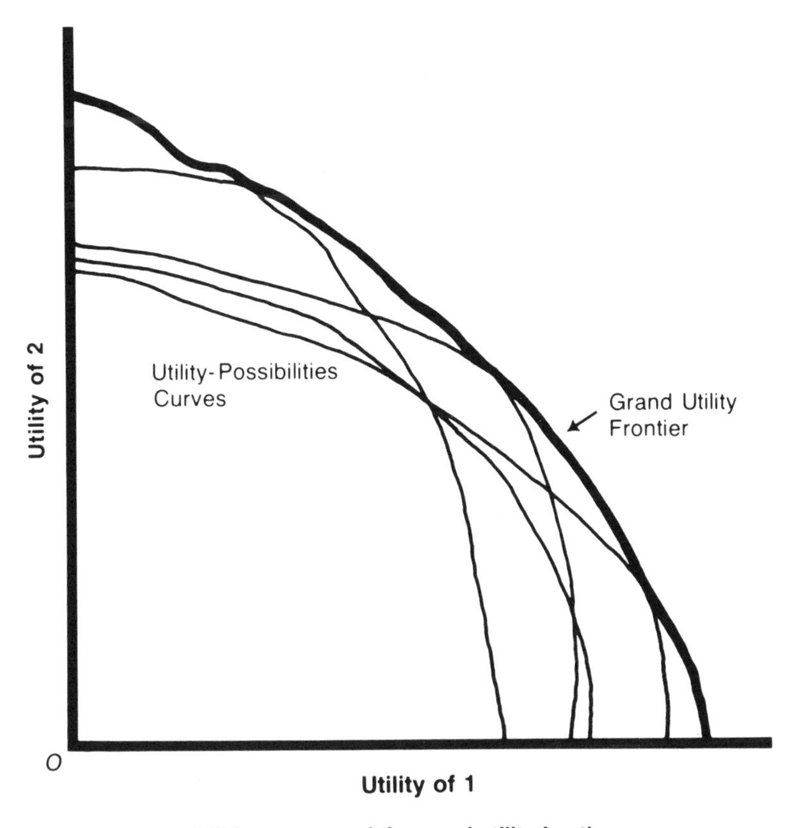

Figure 5. Utility possibilities curves and the grand utility frontier.

equilibrium. Which particular efficient equilibrium, of the many candidates arrayed along the GUF, depends on the initial distribution of endowments.

Market Failures: Nonexclusiveness and Nonrivalry

A system of ideal markets will, as indicated, generate an efficient equilibrium. Two conditions necessary for the outcome are that property rights be nonattenuated (Cheung 1970) and the array of goods and services be limited to those which are rival. The violation of these conditions is usually called nonexclusiveness and nonrivalry, respectively.

Where resources, goods and amenities are nonexclusive, there is no way to exclude those who do not contribute (e.g., by paying) from using or enjoying them. Conversely, there is no incentive for economizing in consumption, restraint in resource use, or investment in producing nonexclusive goods. Nonexclusiveness is a symptom of incomplete (i.e., attenuated) property rights. The individualistic solution to this problem is to establish a nonattenuated system of property rights. However, this is not always easy. There are some resources—examples include ambient air; water in lakes, streams

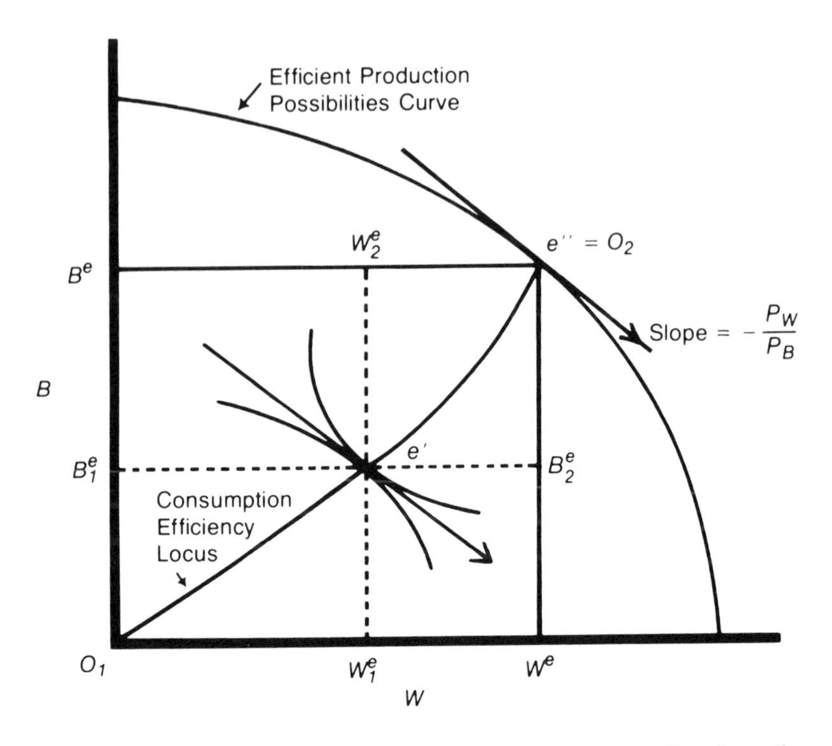

Figure 6. Efficient product mix, commodity distribution and commodity price ratios.

and oceans; scenery; and some kinds of fish and wildlife populations—for which the costs of exclusion exceed any benefits that could be derived. In these cases, there is no real alternative to some form of public or collective management of nonexclusive resources and provision of nonexclusive goods and services.

Nonrival goods (the term "public goods" is often used, but we prefer the designation, nonrival) have the characteristic that consumption by one individual does not diminish the amount available for others. Examples include atmospheric visibility, and radio and television signals. The class of nonrival goods is substantially expanded when one admits congestible goods: those goods which exhibit nonrivalry until some considerable number of consumers are using them, after which point congestion sets in. Many of the important classes of benefits provided by wildlands are congestible, e.g., campsites, hiking trails, boating ramps, hunting and fishing places, and scenic overlooks. The problem with nonrival and congestible goods is that ordinary exclusion—exclusion of those persons who do not pay the going price for use—is insufficient to assure efficiency. A more demanding kind of exclusion, in which those who do not pay their own personal valuation for use are excluded, is required. Because it is difficult for others, "outsiders," to detect and verify an individual's personal valuation, this kind of exclusion is very difficult to implement.

It is important to observe that a wide variety of goods and services that are collectively produced and consumed are nonrival or congestible. These include quite simple goods like highways and bridges, but also less tangible things, such as ecological diversity and stability, the continued existence of endangered species, and the personal benefits derived from living in a community where one's aspirations and values are compatible with those of others.

One characteristic of congestible goods is that the per capita cost of serving users declines as the number of users increases, often over a considerable range, until congestion begins to increase costs at a faster rate than increases in capacity utilization decrease them. Thus, many so-called decreasing cost industries (the "natural monopolies") involve congestible goods and services.

Some rather elaborate schemes have been developed to encourage accurate revelation of individual preferences for nonrival goods. The idea is, simply stated, to effectively penalize false revelation so that true revelation of preferences is the least costly strategy for each individual. These devices are called "incentive-compatible mechanisms" (Groves and Ledyard 1977, Tideman and Tullock 1976). They are potentially useful in research to determine valuations for nonrival goods, but have not as yet been systematically incorporated into public decision processes.

Markets may thus fail to perform efficiently, even in societies which do all that can be done to encourage efficiency in exchange, where nonrivalry exists and/or the costs of exclusion are prohibitive. It is important to note that nonrivalry (or congestibility) and nonexclusion may occur separately or together. When they occur together, the problems they induce are additive.

Finally, externality is often identified as a source of market failures. Externality is usually defined as a situation in which the actions of one party affect the well-being of another party who has no influence over the first party's decisions. However, Cheung (1970) has shown that externality does not cause inefficiency when property rights are nonattenuated. Thus, externality is a symptom of inadequate property rights. As Randall (1983) argues, those problems often blamed on externality are, in fact, attributable to nonexclusiveness and/or nonrivalry. The concept of externality adds nothing to this diagnosis or solution.

These concepts of market failure have several implications for wildlands management and BCA in that context. First, wildlands resources and the goods and amenities they provide include many that are nonrival or congestible and even more that are nonexclusive. Nonexclusiveness arises from two different causes; in some cases, the costs of exclusion are prohibitive, while in others, government has preferred not to establish exclusive and marketable property rights, for various social and political reasons. Where these sources of market failure pertain, markets will not generate efficient equilibrium solutions.

Second, many proposals for wildlands management actions spring from a desire for public solutions to market failure problems. It is important to remember that the desirability of these solutions must be demonstrated, not merely assumed. The existence of market failure is not sufficient evidence to prove that government would do better.

Third, where nonrivalry and nonexclusiveness are involved, markets provide incomplete and often misleading evidence about the value of resources, goods, and amenities. BC analysts are obliged, in these cases, to use considerable ingenuity and effort to estimate benefits and costs without access to direct market observations.

The Distinction Between Actual and Potential Pareto-Improvements

A Pareto-improvement is a change that makes at least one person better off while making no one worse off. Thus, Pareto-efficiency could be characterized as the state which prevails after all possibilities for Pareto-improvements have been exhausted.

Starting at the inefficient point, *a* (fig. 7), the curvilinear triangle *abc* represents the zone of (actual) Pareto-improvements, and the segment *bc* of the GUF represents the set of efficient solutions which are Pareto-improvements. Using Pareto-safety as the social decision criterion, there is no basis for preferring any point on *bc* to any other. Note that the triangle, *abc*, contains no points which would make anyone worse off than at *a*.

The potential Pareto-improvement asks only whether the aggregate gains from a proposed change exceed the losses. The identity of gainers and losers is presumed inconsequential. This criterion can be represented on figure 7 by first substituting "dollars to individual 1" for U_1, and "dollars to individual 2" for U_2 and then drawing a straight line of slope -1 through point *a*. It can immediately be seen that the potential Pareto-improvement represents one very simplistic form of social welfare function, one in which money-valued gains and losses are weighted equally, regardless of the circumstances of individual gainers and losers.

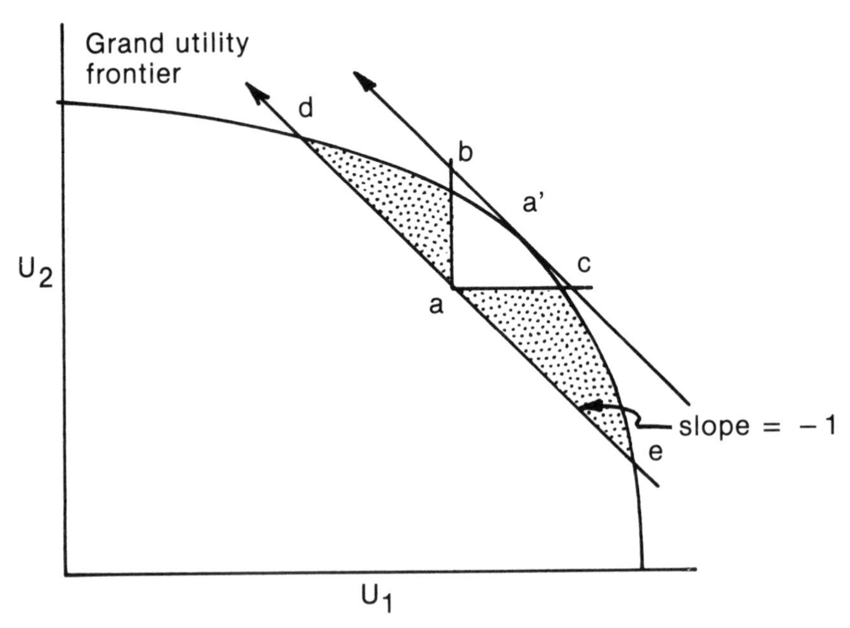

Figure 7. Actual and potential Pareto-improvements and the maximum value of social product.

The zone of potential Pareto-improvements includes not only *abc* but two additional areas, *abd* and *ace*. The first of these additional areas, *abd*, is characterized by gains to individual 2 at the expense of 1; while the second, *ace*, involves gains to 1 at the expense of 2. These shaded regions (fig. 7) could not be attained, starting at *a*, through voluntary processes. They could be attained through policies implemented by government institutions. However, the philosophy of such policies are subject to opposing views.

Finally, while the actual Pareto-improvement criterion identifies a locus, *bc*, of attainable efficient states but makes no distinction among them, the potential Pareto-improvement identifies a unique situation that it calls optimal. This occurs at point *a*' (fig. 7), where a tangency occurs between the GUF and a straight line of slope -1. At this point, the dollar value of social product is at a maximum.

National Economic Development

If the potential Pareto-improvement criterion is indifferent to interpersonal redistributive effects of public projects, it is equally indifferent to interregional redistributive effects. Benefits and costs are algebraically summed without regard to the region in which they accrue. BCA is thus entirely concerned with the effects of proposed undertakings on national economic development (NED).

The logic underlying the treatment of regional economic impacts in BCA is quite subtle. Increases in regional productivity contribute to the national economy. The problem is that local and regional decreases in economic activity detract from the national economy. The kinds of regional impacts which benefit one place while reducing the economic productivity at some other place have both benefits and costs. If the increase in regional productivity at favored locations is exactly equal to the decrease elsewhere, then the net NED impact of this interregional transfer of activity is zero. Its benefits are exactly equal to its costs.

If, however, the increase in economic productivity in the favored region exceeds the loss elsewhere, a net benefit is accrued and is reflected in the NED account.

In practice, the economic inquiries that gather data for BCA are usually concentrated in the immediately impacted region. It is usually too costly to examine all other regions to try to determine their economic costs caused by a transfer of activity to the project region. Instead, a rule-of-thumb, soundly based on economic theory, is invoked. If resources, including labor, are fully employed in the impacted region, the net NED benefits of those activities which are increased only indirectly by the project are zero. Under full employment, then, the net value of project or program outputs is included in a benefit-cost analysis; the regional impacts of service activities "induced by or stemming from" (Eckstein 1958) project outputs are valued for NED analyses, at zero in the net. Thus, a heavy burden of proof is placed on the inclusion of these kinds of indirect benefits in a benefit-cost analysis. As McKean (1958) argues, even in times of unemployment in the impacted region, a positive contribution from induced activities to NED can occur only when unemployment is persistent and resources are immobile.

Present Value and Discounting Procedures

Benefits in the distant future count for less than benefits due immediately. There are two reasons for this. First, individuals act, in aggregate, as though they prefer current consumption to that in the future. Thus, positive rewards for saving and positive costs for borrowing are necessary to equilibrate the pattern of consumption over time. Second, given that alternative investments offering a positive return on capital are available, investors will consider only those opportunities which promise a competitive positive return. From the first reason emerges the concept of the rate of time preferences (RTP); from the second reason emerges the notion of marginal efficiency of capital (MEC). Because the capital used by investors ultimately comes from (somebody's) savings, these two influences are equilibrated in the market for capital. In perfect and unrestricted capital markets, RTP = MEC at the margin, and both are equal to the rate of interest, *r*.

Benefits and costs accruing in future time periods are discounted at the rate, *r*, to determine their present value. Formally, the present value (PV) at time $t=0$ of a stream of revenue $R = (R_1, \ldots R_t, \ldots, R_T)$ accruing at times $t = 1, 2, \ldots T$ is

$$PV(R) = \sum_{t=0}^{T} \frac{R_t}{(1+r)^t} \cdot \qquad [5]$$

Undertakings with projected impacts over many time periods are expected to make a positive contribution to NED if (and only if) their net present value—i.e., the present value of benefits minus that of costs—is greater than zero. If that criterion is met, it is necessarily true also that the ratio of present-valued benefits to cost exceeds one.

In the context of ordinary public investments, the conceptual validity of the present value concept and its implementation via discounting is sound. However, the selection of the appropriate discount rate, *r*, is not on such firm footing. Capital markets equating RTP = MEC = *r* are not observable. Instead, many different rates of interest are observed, reflecting different degrees of risk that the lender will be unable to meet the repayment schedule, and the effects of government efforts to promote some kinds of investments in production equipment and consumer durables via preferential treatment in capital markets. Further, some kinds of distortions are generally prevalent and affect any observed interest rate: experienced and anticipated inflation, and taxes in investment income and capital gains.

In principle, nominal interest rates (*m*) are adjusted for anticipated inflation (*a*), so that $m = r + a$. However, anticipated inflation can be forecast only imperfectly (recently experienced inflation provides clues, but no more). In times of uncertainty about future inflation, *m* tends to be adjusted upward to reflect both the expected *a* and the uncertainty which attaches to *a* and thus to *m* in future periods.

Interest rates cannot be equal for savers and borrowers in a world where transactions costs are positive. The nominal interest rate for savers, m^s, must be less than that for borrowers, m^b, by an amount equal to transactions costs,

t. That is, $m^b = m^s - t$. The distortionary influence of personal and corporate taxes is considerable. A saver is rewarded with m^s minus any taxes; a borrower needs to earn at least m^b to make it worthwhile to invest borrowed funds; and a corporation needs to obtain better than m^s plus corporate taxes if it is to compete for savings.

These various complications take a good deal of unraveling and are subject to much debate. The state-of-the-art analysis (Lind et al. 1982) suggests that, for most public investments, the appropriate discount rate, r, will lie in the range from 0% to 6%, while for many typical investments, that range can be narrowed to 2% to 4%. These rates assume a is zero and, therefore, are appropriate when future benefits are valued as though no general inflation is expected.

All of the above is based on investment theory; therefore, this implicitly assumes that public undertakings are generically similar to private investments which generate ordinary income and typically reach maturity in one generation or less. Events, several generations in the future, have trivial influence on present values, even at (positive) discount rates of 4% or less. Yet, it is unsatisfying to conclude that the possibility of drastic ecological disturbance several generations from now should have only minor influence on decisions made today. When considering events which may drastically restrict the opportunities of future generations, it seems that discounting theories based on the logic of ordinary investments are simply out of their depth. Perhaps it is not the responsibility of a book on valuation of wildlands benefits to resolve these issues. However, attention should be drawn to them.

Net Benefits: The "With and Without" Principle

As Randall (Ch. 2) emphasizes, the typical project or program promises (or threatens, as the case may be) nonmarginal changes in a complex environment. In the absence of the undertaking, there will be several things happening, some beneficial and some harmful. If the proposal is implemented, there will also be several things happening, but some of them will be different. Projects and programs cannot create something out of nothing. Rather, they change an existing system for better or worse.

In Chapter 2, Randall conceptualizes the environment as a functioning system in which the activities of humankind interact with the natural system to influence environmental attributes and the services produced by the environment. These services are demanded, directly or indirectly, by people, who value them. The process through which the existing environment acquires a present value or capital value, is outlined in equations [1-4] of that chapter.

Consider some proposed project which would disturb that environment at some cost, changing its attributes and its productivity of services. The net present value of such a project is the PV of the environment with the project minus the PV of the environment without the project, minus the costs of converting the environment to the "with project" state.

Benefit Valuation in General Equilibrium

General equilibrium theory treats the whole economy as a huge interactive system. Given constraints on resource availability and on the supply of money, a significant disturbance initially affecting prices or quantities in any sector will eventually influence prices and quantities throughout the economy. Those sectors closely linked with the sector initially impacted may experience significant adjustments. More insulated sectors may experience delayed and cushioned effects. General equilibrium analysis painstakingly traces all of these adjustments until a new equilibrium for the whole economy is attained.

At the opposite end of the spectrum lies the most partial of partial equilibrium analyses—that which examines only the most immediate effects of the initial disturbance. Clearly, general equilibrium analysis is conceptually superior. However, difficulties may arise in specifying such systems. The computational requirements for their solution can be enormous. The inherent complexity of such systems can lead to imprecision through the compounding of errors. Thus, the choice among levels of complexity in economic analysis is, itself, a typical economic problem. The greater completeness of general equilibrium analysis must be balanced against its higher cost and greater complexity.

General and partial equilibrium analyses represent not a dichotomy but the endpoints of a continuum. In practice, applied economic analyses usually follow the "rule of reason": adjustments are traced, starting with the most significant, until those remaining unanalyzed seem not worth the effort.

Subsequent chapters in this volume develop three approaches to economic valuation: general equilibrium, and two versions of the partial equilibrium approach, one based on economic surplus and the other on market price.

Economic surplus is generally the correct measure of value. However, as Randall (Ch. 2) demonstrates, there are some limited circumstances in which the market price is an exact measure of unit value, and a broader range of circumstances in which price is a serviceable approximation thereof.

Economic surplus constructs have been developed for general and partial equilibrium analyses. As Anas points out, in Chapter 5, in a fully closed general equilibrium system, all values are reflected in consumers' surpluses. In an incomplete general equilibrium system, economic surplus will be expressed as the sum of consumers' surpluses and land rents.

Thus, the various definitions of economic value developed in subsequent chapters—economic surplus in general and partial equilibrium, and unit price—are not fundamentally different. In fact, they represent the same basic theory of value. Differences in approach are not theoretical but pragmatic. In the judgment of the various authors, different degrees of complexity are appropriate for benefit evaluation in general and for different specific valuation tasks.

Most of the authors represented here have, for purely pragmatic reasons, chosen to work with value definitions which are, in varying degrees, partial equilibirum. Nevertheless, the arguments of Anas (Ch. 5) provide a useful antidote to complacency with partial equilibrium analyses. He points out the interactions between public land policy and the private land market and emphasizes the inadequacy of partial equilibrium approaches. While it is likely that Anas (Ch. 5) underestimates the difficulties in empirically implementing a general equilibrium valuation model in an environment where nonmarketed services predominate, the kinds of analyses he suggests may well foreshadow future advances in benefit estimation.

Economic Surplus

Economic surplus is associated with several other terms—consumer's surplus, producer's surplus, rent and quasi-rent are the most commonly mentioned. It is important at the outset to carefully distinguish among them.

First, it is generally true that the value of an increment or decrement in the quantity provided of some service is equal to the associated change in economic surplus.

Second (as Anas notes in Ch. 5), in a fully closed general equilibrium system, all welfare impacts are ultimately reflected as changes in consumers' surpluses. In a less completely closed system, one may usefully distinguish consumer's surplus and economic rent as the two components of economic surplus. Rent is the residual which accrues to fixed resources. Resources that are fixed and scarce will generate rents for their owners.

The concept of producers' surpluses is usually defined as the excess of revenue above the costs of production or, diagrammatically, the area above the supply curve and below the price line. Producers' surpluses has been a source of confusion in the literature, but its role is now clarified (Mishan 1968). In long-run equilibrium, all producers' surpluses will be reflected in economic rents to fixed resources. In short-run or disequilibrium situations, quasi-rents may accrue to producers able to benefit from these temporary market dislocations.

Thus, in competitive equilibrium situations, the various producers' surpluses and rents reduce to economic rent, and economic surplus is the sum of consumers' surpluses and economic rents.

On publicly owned wildlands, economic rents seldom accrue to the landowner, for political and institutional reasons. Those rents which might otherwise accrue are often transferred to the direct and derived users of wildlands services. Thus, the value to consumers of wildlands services is typically the sum of consumers' surpluses, plus payments to the public management agencies for access, use permits, etc. Where these user charges are set so as to cover the agencies' out-of-pocket operating costs but not generate land rents, the aggregate consumers' surpluses is an excellent approximation of benefits.

For these reasons, subsequent discussion focuses on consumers' surplus, as does the formal development by Randall (Ch. 2). In cases where economic rent is an important empirical issue, the analysis of economic rent is symmetrical to that of consumers' surpluses (Currie et al. 1971).

As is the case with most of microeconomic theory, economic surplus concepts are most readily explicated and implemented in partial equilibrium framework. However, as Anas (Ch. 5) notes, general equilibrium formulations are feasible in concept (e.g., Harberger 1971, Willig 1979) and may be empirically implemented in simplified versions (Just et al. 1982).

This volume follows the partial equilibrium formulation developed by Randall (Ch. 2) and Randall and Stoll (1980) and Brookshire et al. (1980). This formulation is well adapted to benefit estimation for programs and projects affecting the flows of services from environmental systems because it focuses directly on changes in the quantity of services provided. Textbook formulations typically examine the welfare impacts of price changes. However, by focusing on quantity changes, a benefit estimation framework can be developed which is appropriate for considering changes in the level of provision of all kinds of goods, including those which are for any reason unpriced.

Randall (Ch. 2) considers an individual who enjoys some initial level Q^0 of an environmental service and Y^0 of a composite commodity representing all other goods and services. What is the value to that individual of increments or decrements in the level at which Q is provided? The potential Pareto-improvement criterion establishes value on the basis of voluntarism. Thus, value under the potential Pareto-improvement criterion is the same as it would be under a Pareto-safety rule. This means it is assumed that the individual is assured of retaining Q^0 and Y^0, if he desires. The value to that individual of an increment in Q, therefore, is the amount he is willing to pay (WTP) for it. The value of a decrement in Q is the amount of compensation which would induce that individual to voluntarily accept that decrement (WTA). In a market situation, the individual would purchase increments in Q if they were priced equal to or less than his WTP; he would sell decrements in Q if he were offered an amount equal to or greater than his WTA.

WTP for increments and WTA for decrements are identically equal to the Hicksian compensating measures of consumer's surplus. For an individual, these measures can be read from a total value curve, which is an indifference curve passing through the individual's initial levels Q^0 and Y^0 (Randall, Ch. 2, fig. 1).

In addition to the Hicksian compensating measure of consumer's surplus, there are other measures of value—the Hicksian equivalent measure of consumer's surplus, Marshallian consumer's surplus, and the market price. It is important to establish the relationships between these various measures. The equivalent measure, which is identically equal to WTP to avoid decrements in Q and WTA to forego promised increments, assumes the individual is assured not the initial levels of Q and Y, but the proposed levels instead. Therefore, equivalent measures of consumer's surplus can be read, not from a total value (TV) curve passing through the initial situation, but from a TV curve passing through the proposed level of provision.

The Marshallian measure of consumer's surplus differs from the Hicksian measures in that it is not based on indifference curves and compensated demand curves, but on ordinary, uncompensated Marshallian demand. To evaluate a change in the quantity of Q, the Marshallian consumer's surplus is the integral beneath the ordinary demand curve and between the initial and proposed quantities of Q. Marshallian consumer's surplus is not a conceptually justifiable measure of value. However, circumstances have been defined in which it provides an acceptable approximation of the Hicksian compensating measure, and formulas have been developed to permit estimates of the Hicksian measure from data in Marshallian form (Willig 1976, Randall and Stoll 1980, Randall, Ch. 2). This approach to benefit estimation is especially convenient for cases in which secondary data permitting estimation of ordinary demand curves is readily available, while direct observation of WTP and WTA would be expensive and time consuming.

There is an important limiting case, in which unit price is a precise measure of value. When the resource service at issue, Q, is a perfectly divisible good traded at the unit price, p, in infinitely large markets with zero transactions cost, WTP = WTA = $p \times Q$ (where Q indicates the number of units by which Q is to be increased or decreased). In this case, the good Q has the essential characteristics of currency and is valued not so much for what it is but for what it will buy. The conditions defining this limiting case seldom apply in the real world. However, there are many examples of ordinary marketed goods where these conditions are not grossly violated. For example, many of the livestock, timber and minerals products derived from wildlands are subsequently traded in reasonably competitive markets with fairly low transactions costs. Policy or management decisions affecting relatively small areas of wildlands will have trivial impacts on the market price of these products. In cases like these, the use of market price as a value indicator in benefit estimation introduces errors which are tolerably small.

Kinds of Value from Wildlands Services

As Randall (Ch. 2, eq. [3]) indicates, wildlands services are valued by people because they generate utility directly or indirectly. Various categories of value have been conceptually defined.

Use value.—This economic value is derived from using wildlands in any way—as a source of raw materials, medicinal products, aesthetic satisfaction, personally experienced and vicarious adventure, etc. Clearly, the concept of use includes raw materials and amenity uses. Use value may be derived from present and expected future use.

Option value.—When risk attends the demand for use and/or the supply of ecosystem services, expected values from future use must be modified to include risk discounts and premia (Bishop 1982, Graham 1981).

Quasi-option value.—If more information is expected to be revealed with the passage of time, delay in deciding the disposition of some wildlands ecosystem may result in a better decision. Quasi-option value is the value gained in this way. In an age when the expectation of technological progress has been institutionalized, it is reasonable to expect that, for example, the list of species known to provide pharmaceutically useful chemical compounds will grow with the accumulation of research results over time. For any species there is some positive, if unknown, probability that new uses generating positive value eventually will be discovered. With extinction, however, that probability drops to zero, as does the expected value of the resulting benefits. Quasi-option value can be considered the value of preserving options, given the expectation of growth in knowledge (Arrow and Fisher 1974).

Existence value.—This is the value enjoyed from just knowing that something exists. Because the concept of existence value is susceptible to misinterpretation, a few clarifying comments may be helpful (see Randall and Stoll (1983) for a more complete development of these points).

Existence value for a resource (in order to distinguish it from use value) must be derived without combining it with any other good or service in order to produce any activity other than "just knowing it exists."

The level of existence value depends on consumption technology, which may be enhanced by skills and information acquired by past use. Many of the activities of the various nature lobbies are designed to enhance consumption technologies and thus increase existence values for species, habitats, etc.

Existence values are not confined to unique natural phenomena threatened with irreversible damage. In principle, anything may have existence value. However, value at the margin depends on demand and supply. It is likely that the existence value, in total, for cattle exceeds that for condors. However, the existence supply of cattle is very large, while that for condors is quite small. Thus, the loss in existence value from the destruction of a few condors likely far exceeds that from the loss of a few cattle. Other things being equal, existence values will be higher at the margin for those things which are rare, and of more immediate interest for those things which are threatened with convulsive shock.

Because existence values are independent of current use, expected future use, and the avoidance of risks related to future use, they must be derived from some form of altruism. Three relevant kinds of altruistic motives are possible—philanthropic, in which the resource is valued because one's contemporaries may want to use it; bequest, in which the source of value is that future generations may want to use the resource; and intrinsic, in which the individual human cares about the well-being of nonhuman components of the ecosystem. Such caring may be limited in its extent and selective in its application, and because it is extended unilaterally, it similarly may be withdrawn.

Methods of Benefit Estimation

Where the services produced by the wildlands environment are sold directly in large and reasonably competitive markets, benefit estimation can be based on observed prices and Marshallian demand relationships without introducing substantial error. Where the quantities involved are trivial when compared with the size of the total market, the value of output may be taken as the quantity multiplied by the unit price. Where the quantities involved are sufficiently large to influence market price, the Marshallian consumers' surpluses may be estimated from the ordinary demand curve, and then used to approximate the Hicksian compensating measure of value.

However, it is only rarely that the goods and services produced by publicly owned wildlands are sold directly in competitive markets. Some wildlands services are unpriced, while the charges for other kinds of services are institutionally established and may deviate considerably from the prices which would be determined in competitive markets. While livestock, timber and minerals products often are sold in fairly competitive markets, these products seldom are directly produced by the public wildlands. Rather, wildlands services—for example, mineral ores, standing timber and range suitable for grazing—are provided on the public wildlands and used by the private sector as inputs into the production of marketable commodities such as refined minerals, timber, and livestock products. Where institutional and political considerations enter into the establishment of charges for the rights to extract minerals, harvest timber or graze, markets in finished resource commodities do not necessarily reveal the value of the right to exploit raw materials. Subsequent chapters by Hyde, Bartlett, and Vogely detail the appropriate methods for inferring the value of these kinds of wildlands resource services, and discuss some of the difficulties which are encountered in their application.

There are many other kinds of wildlands services which are directly demanded by their users (e.g., the environmental amenities which contribute to the enjoyment of recreation, sight-seeing, and nature study). Typically, these services are unpriced, or user charges are institutionally established. User charges typically are designed to recover some portion of operation and maintenance expenditures, and thus bear no relationship to the demand for these services or the total cost of providing them. In many instances, because these user charges are too low to effectively restrain demand in peak periods, other rationing devices are used. These kinds of charges or prices reveal very little of substance about the values users place upon environmental services.

For environmental services that are unique or highly specialized, and for which available substitutes are few and quite imperfect, total value may exceed the values which accrue to on-site users. A considerably expanded user audience may be reached through written or broadcast descriptions, pictures, etc. Option values and expected consumers' surpluses may be generated by individuals who are not currently users but would pay something to preserve the particular environment in order to retain an option for future use. Some who have no prospects of future on-site use may, nevertheless, obtain genuine value from merely knowing that the environment continues to exist at a desirable level of quality. These off-site use values, option values, expected consumers' surpluses, and existence values are seldom reflected, directly or indirectly, in observable prices.

Nonmarket Benefit Estimation

When observable prices or user charges do not exist or are uninformative with respect to benefit values, the benefit-cost analyst must find other methods of estimating benefit values. Two basic categories of methods are currently in use: those which use markets in related goods to infer the value of the unpriced good; and those which construct hypothetical or experimental markets in which individuals can reveal their valuations for the good or service. Although various nomenclatures have been suggested for classifying these various methods, none has been universally accepted. Randall (Ch. 4) suggests a classification based on the underlying approach to valuation theory. The two basic approaches are via the income compensation function and via the expenditure function. These methods obtain equivalent results under certain, well-specified conditions. Nevertheless, the approaches are a little different, and each suggests different techniques for implementation.

Income Compensation Approaches

The income compensation approaches seek directly to determine the amount of money compensation, paid or received, which will restore the initial level of an individual who experiences an increment or decrement in the level at which a nonrival good is provided. This amount of compensation, WTP if paid or WTA if received, is defined by the indifference curves (Randall, Ch. 4, eq. [4]). Since indifference surfaces are not ordinarily available for direct observation, estimation methods using these approaches usually involve the researcher in conscious contrivance of situations in which experimental subjects or survey respondents reveal relevant points on their indifference surfaces.

These contrived situations, often called contingent markets, must perform satisfactorily in terms of several considerations.

1. They must conform to an acceptable theory of economic value in the context of benefit cost analysis.
2. Salient dimensions of the policy situation—e.g., the proposed increment or decrement in environmental services, its location and time dimensions, and the conditions under which citizens will gain access to and enjoyment of the service—must be effectively communicated to respondents or experimental subjects.
3. The realism and relevance of the contingent market must be effectively communicated, without overloading the perceptual system of the respondent or experimental subject.
4. The contingent market should carry no excess "baggage." That is, while it should contain sufficient stimuli to realistically communicate the policy context, nonessential stimuli of a kind which may divert attention to extraneous issues must be avoided. While this principle seems obvious enough, it is by no means a simple practical task to design contingent markets that simultaneously satisfy conditions 3 and 4.
5. Contingent markets must encourage accurate revelations of preferences. In this context, two basic problems may arise. First, contingent markets record the results of decisions made by respondents or subjects, and effective decision making requires some considerable investment on the part of the decision makers. If respondents or subjects perceive the cost of a poor decision in a contingent market as being significantly lower than such costs in a real-world situation, they might underinvest in decision making when using a contingent market. If that happened, the preference information thus obtained might be of poor quality.

   Second, if the incentive structure of the contingent market is incomplete and if respondents or subjects believe that the results obtained in these markets will be used to determine actual policy, they may develop and use strategies designed to influence policy in directions favorable to themselves. This kind of strategic behavior is confined to cases in which the contingent market and the actual policy context exhibit nonexclusiveness and/or nonrivalry. For such cases, the principles for design of incentive-compatible devices have been developed (Groves and Ledyard 1977, Tideman and Tullock 1976). Incentive-compatible devices are systems of incentives—usually multipart taxes—that effectively penalize all strategic behaviors, so as to make truthful revelation of preferences the least costly strategy.

   However, perfectly incentive-compatible contingent markets can seldom be designed in practice, and there is now considerable evidence that many respondents and subjects forego strategic behavior in the absence of perfect incentive-compatibility (Smith 1980). Thus, incentive-compatibility is best treated as desirable but not a necessary condition for an effective use of contingent markets.

Given the concerns that must be addressed in design of contingent markets, it is not surprising that many alternative formats have been used in published research, and the proliferation of formats appears to be accelerating if one is to judge from unpublished research and work in progress. The rather basic concept of a survey to elicit WTP and WTA information has been implemented in a considerable variety of ways—single questions directly asking WTP (Hammack and Brown 1974); a single question stating a dollar amount and seeking yes/no answers which permit estimation of consumers' surpluses values via a logit analysis (Bishop and Heberlein 1979); iterative yes/no questioning designed to converge upon the individual's maximum WTP or minimum WTA (Randall et al. 1974); a single question asking WTP, with the answer to be selected from a check list (Schulze et al. 1981); and a single WTP question to be answered by respondents who have access to a "payment card" indicating typical expenditures on a variety of publicly provided goods. Surveys have been conducted by mail, telephone, and in person, in both one-to-one and group situations. Obviously, the various question formats are not equally amenable to implementation in each kind of survey, e.g., the iterative yes/no bidding routine requires interaction between enumerator and respondent, and thus cannot be administrated in an ordinary mail survey.

While one would expect some differences in the performance of these various formats, there has been little systematic testing for such differences. Randall et al. (1981) report a pilot study permitting such comparisons, but definitive conclusions may need to await replication of the effort with larger sample sizes. Brookshire et al. (1982a) obtained some empirical evidence providing tentative, but not definitive, support for Randall's contention that the iterative yes/no bidding routine has desirable performance characteristics. The Water Resources Council (1979) approved the use of contingent valuation methods for estimating recreation benefits, and expressed a preference for the iterative routine administrated in personal interview surveys.

While there is little empirical evidence about the relative performance of these various formats, there is some evidence comparing the results of contingent valuation exercises with those obtained via travel cost, hedonic land value, and experimental market methods. In summary, the empirical evidence suggests that results of contingent valuation exercises are often quite comparable with those obtained by other methods. Where the results of contingent valuation methods deviate from those of other acceptable methods, these deviations are likely to be on the low side for WTP and the high side for WTA (see, e.g., Bishop and Heberlein 1979, Brookshire et al. 1982b). If, as the theory suggests, increments in goods or amenities are valued at WTP and decrements at WTA, the effects of these deviations would be conservative. The net benefits of programs that introduce change would be underestimated. If, as often occurs in practice (U.S. Water Resources Council 1979), WTP to avoid a decrement is used to approximate WTA, the effect of these deviations is to underestimate the costs of change.

Economic researchers have not confined themselves to refinement of WTP and WTA survey methods. Rae (1983) developed a contingent ranking mechanism which permits calculation of an individual's WTP for a particular increment in amenity levels. Basic data are responses indicating how that person would rank a variety of alternatives that vary in terms of both amenity levels and cost of access. The more complicated analysis required with this kind of method may be acceptable if it could be demonstrated that individuals rank an array of alternatives varying in two or more dimensions more accurately than they state their WTP or respond to yes/no questions expressed in terms directly interpretable as WTP.

Within the economics profession, experimental methods and explorations in the theory of incentive-compatible mechanisms are both currently attracting increased attention. Much of the published experimental work with incentive-compatible mechanisms uses "induced" preferences, that is, subjects are in fact told what their preferences are (Smith 1980). This work is, therefore, unhelpful in eliciting WTP and WTA information. Nevertheless, it may lead to future advances toward development of incentive-compatible mechanisms for estimating amenity benefits.

Some conclusions can be suggested. Methods based on the income compensation approach may be implemented in a wide variety of circumstances to estimate the benefits of nonmarketed goods, services and amenities. There is some evidence that these techniques are reasonably reliable, and that any inaccuracies are likely to result in underestimates of WTP and overestimates of WTA. Given the proliferation of methods that use the income compensation approach, some will probably perform better than others, but the empirical evidence on this point is very incomplete. It is likely that the next decade will witness the devotion of considerably more effort to income compensation approaches, in both the development of modified methods and the systematic performance testing of new and old methods.

Expenditure Function Approaches

If the amenity level influences the demand for some ordinary marketed good, it is possible that observations from the market in such goods can be used to generate information about the economic value of relevant nonmarketed amenities. While this idea is simple enough, the necessary analytics are by no means simple, even when developed in their most basic form (see Freeman 1979, Randall, Ch. 4).

One proceeds from ordinary demand information, via duality theory, to the expenditure function. The derivative of the expenditure function with respect to the price of an ordinary good yields the Hicksian compensated demand curve for that good, from which precise estimates of consumer's surplus may be obtained. If the demand for an ordinary good is a function of the level of provision of some nonmarketed amenity, the derivative of the expenditure function with respect to that amenity yields the inverse compensated demand curve for that amenity. This compensated demand curve can be used to estimate the change in consumer's surplus resulting from a change in amenity levels. In this way information about the demand for some ordinary good can be used to estimate the economic benefits from providing a nonmarketed amenity.

There are complications, as Freeman (1979) and Randall (Ch. 4) indicate.

If the ordinary marketed goods and the nonmarketed amenity are separable in the utility function, there is no hope of successfully using these methods. Where utility functions are nonseparable, there are genuine prospects of success. However, the mathematics required for solution are often complex, and it often may be necessary to place additional restrictions upon the system in order to obtain a complete solution. One commonly invoked restriction is weak complementarity (Maler 1974). When the relationship between the ordinary marketed good and the nonmarketed amenity exhibits weak complementarity, the demand for the ordinary good shifts as the amenity level changes, and the integral between ordinary demand curves approximates the benefits from the change in amenity levels. This assumption provides the basis for such techniques as the travel cost method for estimating recreation benefits and land value method for estimating the benefits of air, water, and view quality and similar residential amenities.

The valuation possibilities offered by perfect substitution (Maler 1974) have long been recognized. For example, if household water filters are effective substitutes for improved quality of pipeline water, information on the demand for filters may be useful in estimating the benefits of improved water quality.

If some ordinary marketed good is a perfect substitute for a nonmarketed environmental amenity, while the amenity and all other marketed goods are independent in the utility and demand functions, amenity benefits may be simply imputed. The marginal demand price of the amenity reduces to the price of the marketed substitute multiplied by the substitution ratio. Where the good and the amenity are less than perfect substitutes, and the proposed change in amenity level is nonmarginal, the necessary adjustments are intuitively obvious, if not always analytically straightforward.

Despite its obvious appeal, this method has been used relatively little. Many environmental amenities come to the attention of policy makers because they have no good substitutes. Where the amenity is unpriced, but its marketed substitute is notably expensive, the issue of market clearance must be faced. It cannot be assumed that all of the amenity would be demanded if it were priced at the cost of its expensive substitute. For example, wetlands may provide tertiary treatment of waterborne wastes. However, tertiary treatment is expensive and very little of it is currently provided. In this circumstance, it would be improper to value the waste treatment services provided by wetlands as though such services would be demanded without limit at a price as high as the cost of tertiary treatment.

In the past decade, hedonic methods have attracted considerable attention. Rather than the homogeneous goods customarily analyzed by economists, consider a class of goods like "house," "automobile," or "vacation trip" in which different members of the class may possess different characteristics. If one of these characteristics is the amount of some amenity enjoyed along with the good, it may be possible to use the hedonic price function for the class of goods to generate information about the benefits of the amenity. The early hedonic analyses were able to identify only marginal implicit prices for characteristics, rather than inverse demand curves; and even this limited success was attained only under quite restrictive assumptions. However, there has been a recent upsurge of activity in hedonic price analysis, and researchers are attempting to make the method less restrictive and more adaptable. For example, Freeman (1974) suggested a two-stage analytical process that would permit identification of amenity demand curves rather than mere marginal amenity prices. Researchers attempting two-stage estimation have encountered difficulties, but these eventually may be surmounted.

Hedonic price analyses rely on the weak complementarity assumption. Thus, there is an obvious kinship between weak complementarity approaches and hedonic approaches. The simplest travel cost approaches are not hedonic, because they use single-site models that do not permit site characteristics to vary. However, the estimation of multi-site models opens the door to hedonic analyses. All land value methods make use of variation in locational amenities and site characteristics. The simple, one-stage hedonic analyses, which estimate marginal prices for amenities, may be characterized as "bargain basement" applications of the weak complementarity assumption. Two-stage procedures to identify amenity demand schedules would more completely implement the weak complementarity approach.

Finally, we must draw attention to the recent advances in the theory of benefit estimation in cases where the choices are discrete (Small and Rosen 1981) and in applicable statistical methods (Domencich and McFadden 1975).

Certain applications of the expenditure function approach have become routine; e.g., the travel cost method of estimating demand for recreation sites and the hedonic land value method of estimating the value of neighborhood amenities (including environmental quality). While the travel cost method suffers from some unresolved problems—most obviously the treatment of travel time, and the violations of weak complementarity inherent in multi-purpose trips—it remains, in many circles, the preferred method for estimating recreation benefits. Recent development of a hedonic travel cost method (Brown and Mendelsohn 1980) provides some promise of effectively adapting travel cost methods for valuing the environmental amenities enjoyed along with the recreation site.

Surveying the recent literature on expenditure function approaches, one must be impressed by the ingenuity and analytical rigor which has been committed to the effort. Considerable progress has been made, and it is reasonable to expect such progress to continue unabated.

The Alternative Approaches Compared

Income compensation and expenditure function approaches are based, in principle, on the same theory of economic value. Both kinds of methods will, in principle, precisely identify potential Pareto-improvements. However, each approach takes a different route. Income compensation approaches use a very direct analysis but with data that may be questioned on account of its genesis under hypothetical or experimental conditions. Expenditure function approaches use as data the records of actual transactions subject to the incentives of the marketplace. However, the analytical route is less direct, and results may be influenced by assumptions and restrictions imposed during the analysis.

Economists have tended to accord the expenditure function methods the presumption of validity but, in the judgment of the present authors, the income compensation methods seem to be gaining credibility. The stock of these latter methods has been boosted by (1) their acceptable performance in direct empirical comparisons with expenditure function methods, (2) a growing awareness of the theoretical difficulties of expenditure function methods, and (3) the theoretical and experimental work with incentives that has undermined the belief that income compensation methods would surely fall victim to strategic responses.

Even practitioners who are a little insecure about the reliability of income compensation methods are increasingly using them, because of their superior adaptability. Since these approaches involve the creation of contingent or hypothetical markets, the valuation task does not depend on identifying some closely related marketed good, and the increments and decrements that can be evaluated are not limited to the currently observable range. User values can be estimated for a broader array of amenities and for a wider range of amenity levels. Further, the so-called non-user benefits (option value and the various existence values) must currently be evaluated with income compensation approaches, or not at all.

Estimating Wildlands Benefits

The wildlands environment is conceptualized as a complex system producing services which are valued by people (Randall, Ch. 2). Inputs from the natural system are combined with inputs controlled by people, to determine the attributes of the environment and the flow of services it can provide. These services are valued, in varying degrees, by individuals, and these individual valuations are ultimately reflected in the costs and benefits attributed to programs which change the flow of services.

To evaluate a proposed program which would change the wildlands environment by changing some of those inputs controlled by people, it is necessary to specify what may be called the production and demand systems for services. While this book is most directly concerned with human preferences and demands for services, the benefit estimation exercise becomes meaningless if the production relationships are ignored. Further, the production system is interactive. Randall (Ch. 2) referred to the "with project" stream of services, which he characterized as the vector S^P, and the "without project" stream of services, S. The attempt to manipulate one specific service almost invariably results in changes (often reductions) in the availability of other kinds of services.

Some aspects of the production and demand system for wildlands services can be presented schematically (fig. 8). The natural wildlands system is presented as a complex interaction of geological, hydrological, atmospherical, and biological systems. The interaction of this system with human demands in an environment of ultimate scarcity converts some of the system's attributes into valued resources: for example, timber, mineral deposits, range, water, wildlife populations, habitat, land forms, atmospheric visibility, and the biological processes are valuable in waste assimilation and the cleansing of air and water. No attempt is made here to diagram the complicated processes through which the natural wildlands system provides these valuable resources.

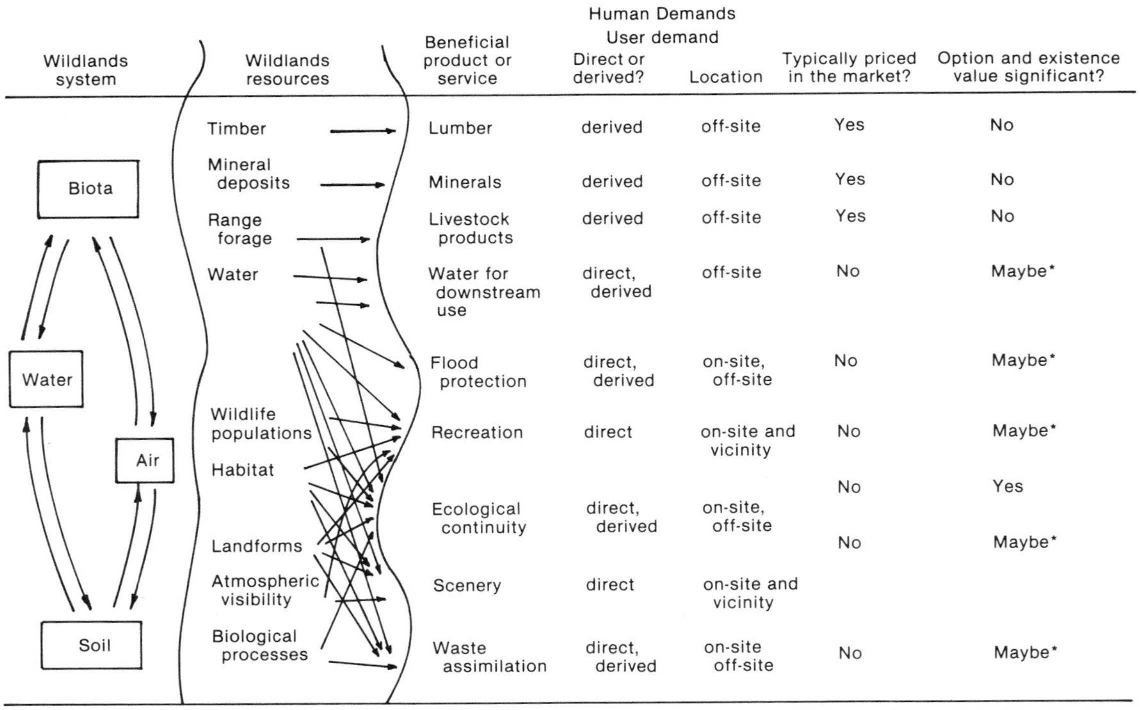

Wildlands system: Biota, Water, Air, Soil

Wildlands resources: Timber; Mineral deposits; Range forage; Water; Wildlife populations; Habitat; Landforms; Atmospheric visibility; Biological processes

Beneficial product or service	Human Demands: User demand — Direct or derived?	Location	Typically priced in the market?	Option and existence value significant?
Lumber	derived	off-site	Yes	No
Minerals	derived	off-site	Yes	No
Livestock products	derived	off-site	Yes	No
Water for downstream use	direct, derived	off-site	No	Maybe*
Flood protection	direct, derived	on-site, off-site	No	Maybe*
Recreation	direct	on-site and vicinity	No	Maybe*
			No	Yes
Ecological continuity	direct, derived	on-site, off-site		
			No	Maybe*
Scenery	direct	on-site and vicinity		
Waste assimilation	direct, derived	on-site off-site	No	Maybe*

* The possibility of significant option and existence value is real, and should be considered in benefit estimation.

Figure 8. Major categories of wildland benefits.

Each of these resources contributes to the production of one or more kinds of products or services demanded by people. This figure presents only a partial and very simplistic model of the process through which resources contribute to the production of goods and services. For example, it is noted here that the timber resource is central to the production of lumber, while many kinds of resources—water, wildlife populations, habitat, land forms, and atmospheric visibility—contribute to the production of recreation services. However, only the most direct contributions are diagrammed.

Competitive relationships among product and service categories are highly important but are not shown (fig. 8). These kinds of relationships may arise from simple competition for limited resources (e.g., the competition between livestock products, recreation, and ecological continuity which arises when domestic livestock and wildlife compete for the same land and vegetation resources) and from more overtly antagonistic relationships (e.g., the adverse effects which certain timber harvesting practices have on water run-off and stream siltation and, in turn, on water quality and flood protection).

To correctly specify the "with project" stream of services, S^P, all of these various complementary and competitive relationships among service categories must be considered and taken into account.

Given an adequate specification of the "with project" and "without project" streams of services, the next task is valuation of proposed changes in the amounts of various services provided. Subsequent chapters in this book address benefit estimation for many of the major categories of services identified in figure 8. The authors of these chapters implicitly subscribe to the same theory of economic benefit evaluation. However, individual authors vary in their judgments as to just how much simplification is permissible in order to expedite data collection and the analytics of benefit estimation. For the most part, these differences reflect general agreement among economists that some kinds of services (e.g., ecological continuity and the survival of endangered species) require more complicated analytical constructs for benefits estimation than others (e.g., marginal changes in the output of fairly homogeneous timber or minerals products). However, there are some genuine differences of opinion about the appropriate trade-offs between simplicity and analytical validity. Anas argues strongly for the broad implementation of at least limited general equilibrium concepts. At the other extreme, Hyde has confined his analysis of timber benefits to the most simple price and quantity relationships.

While our authors subscribe to the same implicit theory of economic benefit valuation, some differences of opinion emerge about the significance to be attached to economic benefits. Brown and Shaw argue strongly for a broader concept of benefits than economics permits.

An overview of benefits estimation procedures for the major categories of wildlands services follows.

Raw Materials

Lumber, minerals, and livestock products have so much in common economically that it is convenient to discuss them together. Demands for these products are derived from user demand for various kinds of finished goods or final products. Final demand is usually expressed where people live and shop, that is, usually at some place removed from the wildlands site. Final products are typically priced in organized markets, and option and existence values are unlikely to be significant as long as the quantities influenced by the program under evaluation remain small relative to the total stocks of the resource in question. Because the demand for raw materials is derived from final demands adequately expressed in organized markets, the benefit estimation is considerably simplified.

For raw materials benefit estimation, the present value of benefits is equal to the capital value to society of resources capable of producing these raw materials. Conceptually, this is identical to the social capital value of a land resource capable of yielding minerals, timber and/or range forage, or, alternatively, the market-determined capital value of a land resource in private ownership plus the present value of consumers' surpluses attributable to the raw-material-producing resource. Anas carefully develops the net rent concept of land value and its relationship with consumers' surpluses and total net economic value.

Where programs affecting raw materials production on public lands involve quantities that are small relative to the total markets, consumers' surpluses can be ignored, and total value will be adequately represented by land-resource values. However, because the public lands represent a significant proportion of all lands which could yield these raw materials, and because these lands are not traded in the market, it is necessary to use some method to infer their capital value. It would be a simple matter to infer capital value from market information about the annual rents of resource-bearing land, but annual rental markets do not exist.

Because annual rents represent the annualized value of the residual which remains from receipts after out-of-pocket costs have been accounted, information about the competitive price of the right to exploit the resource, properly adjusted to reflect costs encountered by the owner of resource-bearing lands, could be easily adapted for benefit estimation. However, markets in the right to exploit the raw materials resources deviate in varying degrees, from the competitive ideal. Even where competitive bidding is the norm, a resource manager seeking to make decisions about the use of wildlands, at that stage, will seek appraisals of the value of raw materials resources rather than offer them irrevocably for competitive bid. For these various reasons, benefit estimation relies on a process of inference. The existence of competitive markets in final products is not sufficient to resolve the benefit estimation problem, although it surely helps.

Vogely (Ch. 6) details the application of the land rent model Anas (Ch. 5) in estimating minerals benefits. Observing that markets in minerals tend to be organized on a world-wide scale, Vogely makes use of the notion that the perfectly elastic supply of imports ensures that changes in domestic production will not affect the level of consumers' surpluses. Thus, he correctly views the benefit estimation task as that of estimating the net economic rent to domestic resources.

Vogely notes that for some minerals—sand, gravel, and construction stone—for which markets tend to be local, the opening of new deposits for extraction may generate some consumers' surpluses. It would also be necessary to consider consumers' surpluses in the case of any mineral subject to import restrictions or prohibitions. If, for example, imports of a strategic mineral were prohibited for national security reasons, a significant augmentation of available resources might increase total consumers' surpluses.

In dealing with timber resources, Hyde (Ch. 7) takes a somewhat more restricted view. In his judgment, for wildlands benefit estimation, the most relevant timber valuation problem is that of estimating in a short-run context the value of an existing stand of harvestable timber. He assumes that the outcome of the wildlands use decisions will not appreciably shift the national supply curve for lumber. For decisions concerning the use of a particular parcel of land, this assumption is reasonable. However, where policies with respect to timber management and harvesting are under consideration at the national level, the possibility of significant supply shifts as a direct result of policy must be considered. If national timber markets are to some extent isolated from markets in other countries, policy decisions may influence the level of both resource rents and consumers' surpluses.

It is also important to note that Hyde focuses entirely on the value of the right to harvest timber. This approach is defensible if one is considering only the value at harvest of an existing stand of timber. If, however, one considers post-harvest land uses, including the possibility of reforestation, the value of a given stand of timber begins to diverge from the long-run residual or rent value of timber-bearing land. In this broader context, costs of replanting and management must be subtracted from the value of the right to harvest, in order to estimate residual values. Further, the value of the right to harvest is influenced by the optimal harvest strategy, which differs depending upon whether one is considering harvest of a single existing stand or the time-to-harvest period in an optimal long-term rotation.

Discussing the value of range forage, Bartlett (Ch. 8) confronts the problem of inferring benefits in a situation where grazing permit fees are administratively determined. If grazing permits were exchanged in competitive markets, their value in exchange would be a close estimate of the annual rent or residual value of grazing land after management and livestock-related costs had been met. In the absence of competitive markets in grazing permits, Bartlett surveys the kinds of evidence which may be gleaned from the markets in alternative livestock feedstuffs, private grazing leases, and privately owned land where there is an expectation that a purchaser would also have access to grazing permits for federal lands. For various well-documented reasons, Bartlett finds ambiguities in each of these kinds of evidence. In the end, he expresses some preference for computer programming (usually linear programming) analyses of the livestock production process. These analyses yield, among other things, an imputed or "shadow" price representing the marginal value of an additional unit of range forage. In preferring this benefit estimation method, Bartlett perhaps reflects majority opinion among range economists.

There are, however, two quite different points to be made. First, it is the rental value of range forage which is of interest in benefit estimation. If the derived demand curve for range forage is perfectly elastic, then the value of the marginal unit of range forage will be equal to the average rental value of all units; otherwise, it will not. Second, linear programming and related computer programming techniques, while thoroughly respectable, are fundamentally synthetic analyses. The economics of a grazing system are modeled, and inferences thus derived necessarily pertain to the performance of the model itself rather than to the performance of the real system under study. This is not necessarily a devastating criticism of such techniques. It does, however, provide cause for caution in their use.

It seems quite possible that some technique which analyzes the behavior of the real-world system more directly may eventually replace linear programming for this purpose. The hedonic price analysis method, now widely used in urban economics, permits analysis of the sale price of real property in order to infer the market value of its individual and neighborhood attributes and characteristics. Future developments may permit adaptation of hedonic price techniques to analyze ranch real estate sales data in order to estimate value of range forage.

Nonmarketed Resource Services

The remaining kinds of wildlands products and services shown in figure 8 mostly are in the nonmarketed category. The term nonmarketed is used as a shorthand expression to cover a wide variety of situations in which markets are non-existent, incomplete, or institutionally restrained from reflecting the free interplay of supply and demand. To say that a wildlands product or service is nonmarketed is not intended to suggest that markets provide literally no information as to its value. On the contrary, the fundamental premise of that class of benefits estimation techniques termed the expenditure function approaches is that value estimates for nonmarketed goods and services can be derived from information generated in the markets for some related commodities. To label a good or service nonmarketed does not necessarily imply that markets tell nothing of its value; rather, the implication is that, at best, existing markets provide incomplete or indirect information.

The wildlands products and services in the nonmarketed category are a diverse group, in terms of both physical and economic characteristics. Many of them exhibit the physical characteristic of nonrivalry, which has the rather important economic implications addressed earlier in this chapter. Nonexclusiveness is a common characteristic, sometimes because the costs of specifying, transferring and enforcing exclusive property rights would exceed any benefits which could be thus obtained, and in other cases apparently reflecting political beliefs that private property institutions are inappropriate for some special kinds of amenities.

These goods and services vary in the extent to which markets are absent. For many kinds of amenities, there are no direct markets. However, there are cases in which markets in, for example, land reflect the economic value of environmental amenities consumed jointly with the other services that land provides. In still other cases, wildlands products are transferred from the public sector to private users in exchange for fees. The problem here is that the level of fees may be determined administratively rather than competitively.

For products and services in the nonmarketed category, user demands may be direct and/or derived. Many kinds of environmental amenities may be demanded directly and enjoyed on site. Derived demands, however, are not trivial. Water for agricultural and industrial uses, waste assimilation, and even ecological continuity may be demanded as an input into production processes which yield final goods. Ecological continuity includes possibilities such as the yet-unidentified but potential contributions of some biological species to the production of pharmaceutical products. In addition to user demands, the possibility of significant option and existence values must be seriously considered in each case.

As to the location of demand, the whole range of possibilities is pertinent to at least some cases. User demands for amenities are usually expressed on-site or on privately owned and developed land in the vicinity. Nevertheless, amenity enjoyment via descriptions or pictorial representations is a form of use (by our definition), and demand for it may be expressed far off-site. Derived demands are usually expressed off-site, and option and especially existence demands may be expressed in places very distant from the wildlands site.

This considerable array of possibilities with respect to kinds of demand, the location of demand, and the ease with which value information can be extracted from markets in final products or related goods and services virtually ensures that non-market benefit estimation will be performed somewhat eclectically. A considerable variety of techniques is used, various adaptations to the more standardized techniques exist, and the advantages and disadvantages of particular methods depend on the particular circumstances. Accordingly, care must be exercised in defining the categories of nonmarketed goods and services, and estimating the benefits attributable to individual categories, so that subsequent benefit aggregation yields an accurate picture of total benefits; omissions and double-counting are both to be assiduously avoided.

The basic concepts of economic benefits apply across the broad array of wildlands products and services: to the raw materials and to the various different categories of nonmarketed services and amenities. Economic benefits are defined as aggregate net consumers' surpluses (Randall, Ch. 2), or net land rents (Anas, Ch. 5). As Anas points out, in a fully closed general equilibrium system all land rents are ultimately reflected as consumers' surpluses. Thus, at the conceptual level, there is complete consistency in the definition of economic benefits. In dealing with particular applications, however, the authors of the subsequent chapters exercise their own best judgments as to the most effective methods of empirically implementing benefits concepts, and the level of complexity which is appropriate given that more complete conceptual systems are empirically implemented at greater cost and sometimes with reduced reliability.

Among the nonmarketed products and services, the status of water for downstream use is perhaps most complex. Water in lakes and streams exhibits the characteristic of a nonexclusive and nonrival amenity, contributing to recreation, scenic enjoyment, ecological continuity, etc. Its economic benefits in these kinds of uses may be appropriately conceptualized using theoretical and empirical constructs similar to those used in benefit evaluation of air quality and scenic beauty. In contrast, water for agricultural and industrial uses is an input into production processes which ultimately yield final goods, and its benefits may be appropriately conceived along the lines of the raw materials model. Gray and Young (Ch. 9) carefully consider the value of water in various raw materials and amenity uses, paying attention to its quality aspect and giving some consideration to option and existence values.

In the wildlands benefits context, however, water is an enormous topic. Wildlands management decisions may contribute, positively or negatively, to its quantity and quality. Undisturbed catchment areas may provide waste assimilation services, effectively cleansing water for later uses. Alternatively, decisions with respect to the timing of timber harvest, the extent of minerals extraction, and the techniques used in timber harvesting and mining may influence run-off, soil erosion, and sedimentation in streams and lakes.

Increased erosion adversely affects water quality and contributes to stream siltation, reducing the capacity of stream channels to handle the run-off from intense precipitation. These effects, combined with increased run-off as a consequence of devegetation and soil disturbance, threaten water quality and may increase the frequency and the severity of flooding. Flooding is an important and rather special case: water as a discommodity. The beneficial service which wildlands can provide in this respect is protection from flood damage, and the economic benefits of that service are equal to the value of flooding losses avoided. Flood protection benefits are not specifically addressed in any of the subsequent chapters. Nevertheless, whenever the possibility exists that a proposed project or program would influence the quantity and quality of water run-off from a wildlands area, beneficial or adverse impacts on flood protection should be explored, and valued in economic terms. There is a considerable literature on economic estimation of flood protection benefits. Guidelines for evaluating this category of benefits have been published by the Water Resources Council (1979).

Values arising from beneficial impacts of land management practices on water yield and quality are carefully addressed by Gray and Young. Nevertheless, the design of this volume (which includes separate treatments of, e.g., minerals, timber and water values) leaves to the BC practitioner the task of establishing the linkages between resource extraction, land use, and water quantity and quality, first in physical and eventually in economic terms.

For the amenities service—recreation, scenic visual amenities, ecological continuity, and waste assimilation (which is ultimately reflected in improved quality of water and air)—benefit estimation is almost always an exercise in nonmarket valuation. In almost every case, value information cannot be obtained directly from markets. In addition, there are many cases in which basic physical quantity relationships are not systematically recorded but must be established in a research exercise.

The discussion of scenic and visual benefits (Randall, Ch. 10) provides a perspective which is equally appropriate for estimating several other kinds of amenity benefits. There is a chain of cause and effect, which starts with some action (a project undertaking or a policy initiative) that changes the attributes of the wildlands environment, thus influencing the flow of services it provides. These impacts are (at least potentially) capable of objective measurement with appropriate instruments, etc. Objectively measurable impacts, however, are not directly reflected in changes in benefit levels. Rather, because amenities (which are multi-dimensional and qualitative in many dimensions) are involved, changes in benefit levels are most directly related to humanly perceived impact than to objectively measured impact. Preferences are expressed across perceived amenity levels, and the economic value of changes in amenity levels is defined as WTP for preferred amenities or WTA for less preferred amenities. This chain of inference from action to impact, perception, and economic valuation often may require an explicit research effort at each of its stages. The recent literature includes several attempts at multi-disciplinary, integrative analysis of the whole process from action to economic valuation (see Randall's literature cited).

Economic valuation of benefits requires considerable ingenuity. Using the various income compensation approaches, contingent or experimental markets are contrived in which representatives of the population (survey respondents or experimental subjects) may express their WTP or WTA for relevant changes in amenity levels. Alternatively, various expenditure function methods—the travel cost methods for estimating recreation benefits, the land value and hedonic price analysis techniques by which air and water quality and neighborhood amenity values may be inferred, and various adaptations such as the hedonic travel cost method (Brown and Mendelsohn 1980) and the multi-site travel cost method (Wilman, Ch. 13)—may be used to infer amenity values from data generated in markets for related goods and services.

In addition to use value, the possibility of significant option and existence values must be considered, for many kinds of amenity services. Given the current state-of-the-art, techniques for estimating option and existence values seem confined to the income compensation approaches.

Finally, Randall directly confronts the dilemma which arises when amenity benefit estimation techniques are imperfect or limited in application. Although estimates of benefits may be unreliable, failure to estimate the particular category of benefits is often interpreted as an implicit statement to the effect that such benefits are zero. Given the substantial existing evidence that individuals value amenities and are willing to make economic sacrifices to obtain them, "implicit zero valuation" of amenities would be fundamentally misleading and, if widely practiced, would tend to systematically bias wildlands management decisions toward production of raw materials. Randall points out that, in the absence of acceptable measures of benefits, it is often possible to marshall real evidence to the effect that amenity services are produced and demanded. Such evidence should be gathered and displayed in all cases where an amenity service is being provided, however, current techniques do not permit accurate benefit estimation.

For scenic and visibility benefits, Randall endorses integrative analyses; finds value in social science studies elucidating the relationships between impact, perception and preference; regards income compensation function methods as most widely applicable in estimation of use, option and existence values for scenic visual services, but considers the particular circumstances in which expenditure function approaches may be applicable; and insists that, where complete economic estimates of benefits are impossible, other kinds of evidence that amenities are produced and demanded should be assembled and displayed.

Three of the subsequent chapters address recreation benefits, each from a different perspective. Brown (Ch. 11) and Shaw (Ch. 12), in separate chapters, examine the consequences of decisions pertaining to recreation and wildlife amenities, respectively. While the other chapters focus quite specifically on economic benefits in a national economic development context, Brown and Shaw draw attention to a broad range of beneficial consequences some of which are entirely consistent with the concept of economic benefits and others of which are not. Shaw is concerned that the economic model of benefits starts with individuals placing values on those things they perceive to be good. Considering how little is currently known about complex ecological relationships, vital but unrecognized environmental services may go unvalued. Shaw also expresses the opinion that economists, taken as a group, have a tendency to overestimate the effectiveness of existing economic techniques of benefit estimation.

Brown explicitly deviates from the economist's model of net benefits, seeking instead an all-encompassing categorization of beneficial consequences. He recognizes that his concept of consequences, if directly adapted to benefit estimation, may involve gross rather than net benefit concepts and the possibility of multi-counting of benefits. He takes a planning perspective, and insists that consideration of consequences should be not merely an evaluative procedure, but also an integral part of management planning. In this context, detailed information about human perception of amenity levels, preferences, and their relationship to broad trends in society play a larger role. Knowledge of these things is more essential to management and planning for the future than it is to evaluation of specific proposals.

The Brown and Shaw chapters do not provide prescriptions for estimating economic benefits. But, that is not what their authors intended. These chapters serve the useful purpose of broadening our perspective on the consequences of wildlands allocation decisions, while raising some pertinent questions about the efficacy and completeness of current economic methods.

The chapter by Wilman (Ch. 13), is firmly in the economic tradition. However, it does not seek to offer a broad perspective on the economics of recreation benefit estimation. Instead, Wilman offers an introduction to the travel cost method of estimating recreation site values, and some innovative extensions of the multi-site travel cost model, which suggest the possibility of adapting travel cost methods for valuing differences in recreation amenity levels. The latter sections of this chapter may be of particular interest to professionals in the field of recreation benefit estimation.

In figure 8, two further categories of non-marketed wildlands services are identified: ecological continuity and waste assimilation.

Shaw's paper on wildlife benefits addresses the contribution of wildlife populations and habitat to recreation and to ecological continuity. Economic theorists such as Fisher (1982) can readily demonstrate that traditional models of optimal resource extraction, when modified to admit the possibility that continuity provides economically valuable services, may generate results favoring continuity. When both extraction and continuity generate benefits, the economic efficiency argument is no longer unambiguously in favor of extraction. While there can be no quarrel with Fisher's theoretical development, pragmatists must agree with Shaw that much more work is needed before reliable empirical estimates of the economic value of ecological continuity can be routinely made.

None of the authors has explicitly addressed the economic benefits from waste assimilation service provided by wildlands. It is clear that such services may be provided; catchments with good vegetative cover and wetlands serve to help purify water, while forest and other densely vegetated habitats oxygenate and purify the air. Water quality and air quality have attracted some attention (in chapters by Gray and Young, and Randall, respectively). Economic methods for estimating benefits of improvements of water and air quality have been addressed. What has not been explicitly considered in the remainder of this volume is the production side: the parameters which define the productivity of wildlands in improving water and air quality. There has been relatively little research on these questions. Nevertheless, benefits cost analyses of wildlands management alternatives must give consideration to the possibility that alternative proposals may influence the levels of waste assimilation benefits.

The various authors represented in this book have identified a wide variety of beneficial services provided by wildlands resources, uses which people make of these services, and methods of benefit valuation. Some of the main conclusions they have reached are summarized in the table, which considers the categories of value generated, issues of rivalry and exclusiveness, and appropriate benefit estimation methods.

Organization of This Book

The remaining chapters of this volume are organized into two major sections. In the first, three chapters by Randall develop a conceptual model of economic benefits, discuss the role of BCA in the public policy decision process, and breifly summarize the theory of nonmarket estimation techniques. The chapter by Anas develops a general equilibrium interpretation of land market theory, developing the relationships between productivity, land rents, and consumers' surpluses in a general equilibrium context.

In the second major section, eight chapters summarize the state-of-the-art of benefit estimation for particular categories of wildlands services. While there is much to learn from taking an integrative perspective of these chapters as a group, one should not lose sight of the individualized perspectives of the various authors. Here, one may obtain access to a variety of sometimes contrasting viewpoints on: the appropriate level of economic analysis; the preferred techniques and methods; and, in the chapters by non-economists Brown and Shaw, some fundamental limitations of economics as a thought system for conceptualizing and measuring wildlands benefits.

Literature Cited

Arrow, K. 1951. Social choice and individual values. John Wiley and Sons, New York, N.Y.

Arrow, K., and A. C. Fisher. 1974. Environmental preservation, uncertainty and irreversibility. Quarterly Journal of Economics 55:313-319.

Bator, F. M. 1957. The simple analytics of welfare maximization. American Economic Review 47:52-59.

Becker, G. S. 1965. A theory of the allocation of time. Economic Journal 75:493-517.
Behan, R. W. 1981a. Multiple use management: Kudos and caveats. Presented to Workshop on Political and Legal Aspects of Range Management, National Academy of Sciences, Jackson Hole, Wyo., September 13-15.
Behan, R. W. 1981b. RPJA/NFMA: Time to punt. Journal of Forestry 79:802-805.
Bishop, R. C. 1982. Option value: An exposition and extension. Land Economics 58:1-15.
Bishop, R. C., and T. Heberlein. 1979. Measuring values of extra-market goods: Are indirect measures biased? American Journal of Agricultural Economics 61:926-930.
Box, T. 1982. Professionalism, politics and land managers. Presented to Symposium on Politics vs. Policy: The Public Lands Dilemma, Utah State University, Logan, Utah, April 21-23.
Brookshire, D. S., R. G. Cummings, M. Rahmatian, W. D. Schulze, and M. Thayer. 1982a. Experimental approaches for evaluating environmental commodities. U.S. Environmental Protection Agency Grant No. CR 808-893-01, Draft Final Report.
Brookshire, D. S., A. Randall, and J. R. Stoll. 1980. Valuing increments and decrements in natural resource service flows. American Journal of Agricultural Economics 62:478-488.
Brookshire, D. S., M. Thayer, W. D. Schulze, and R. C. d'Arge. 1982b. Valuing public goods: A comparison of survey and hedonic approaches. American Economic Review 72:165-177.
Brown, G., and R. Mendolsohn. 1980. The hedonic-travel cost method. Final report prepared for Division of Program Plans, U.S. Department of Interior, University of Washington, Seattle, Wash.
Cheung, S. N. S. 1970. The structure of a contract and the theory of a nonexclusive resource. Journal of Law and Economics 15:49-70.
Currie, J. M., J. A. Murphy, and A. Schmitz. 1971. The concept of economic surplus and its use in economic analysis. Economic Journal 81:741-799.
Domencich, T. A., and D. A. McFadden. 1975. Urban travel demand. North-Holland, Amsterdam.
Eckstein, O. 1958. Water resources development: The economics of project evaluation. Harvard University Press, Cambridge, Mass.
Fisher, A. C. 1982. Economic analysis and the extinction of species. Presented to AAAS Symposium on Estimating the Value of Endangered Species of Plants, Washington, D.C., January 3-8.
Freeman, A. M. 1979. Approaches to measuring public goods demands. American Jounral of Agricultural Economics 61:915-920.
Freeman, A. M. 1974. On estimating air pollution control benefits from land value studies. Journal of Environmental Economics and Management 1:74-83.
Graham, D. A. 1981. Benefit cost analysis under uncertainty. American Economic Review 71:715-725.

Groves, T. E., and J. Ledyard. 1977. Optimal allocation of public goods: A solution to the free-rider problem. Econometrica 45:783-809.
Hammack, J., and G. M. Brown. 1974. Waterfowl and wetlands: Toward bioeconomic analysis. Johns Hopkins University Press, Baltimore, Md.
Harberger, A. C. 1971. "Three basic postulates for applied welfare economics: An interpretive essay." Journal of Economic Literature. 9:785-797.
Just, R. E., D. L. Hueth, and A. Schmitz. 1982. Applied welfare economics and public policy. Prentice-Hall, Englewood Cliffs, N.J.
Lancaster, K. J. 1966. A new approach to consumer theory. Journal of Political Economy 74:152-157.
Lind, R. C., K. J. Arrow, G. Corey, P. Dasgupta, A. Sen, T. Stauffer, J. E. Stiglitz, J. Stockfisch, and R. Wilson. 1982. Discounting for time and risk in energy policies. Resources for the Future, Inc. Johns Hopkins University Press, Baltimore, Md.
Maler, K. G. 1974. Environmental economics: A theoretical inquiry. Johns Hopkins University Press, Baltimore, Md.
McKean, R. N. 1958. Efficiency in government through systems analysis. John Wiley and Sons, New York, N.Y.
Mishan, E. J. 1968. What is producer's surplus? American Economic Review 58:1269-1282.
Rae, D. A. 1983. The value to visitors of improving visibility at Mesa Verde and Great Smoky National Parks. p. 217-234. *In* Managing Air Quality and Visual Resources at National Parks and Wilderness Areas. R. D. Rowe and L. G. Chestnut, editors. Westview Press, Boulder, Colo.
Randall, A. 1981. Resource economics—An economic approach to natural resource and environmental policy. Grid Publishing Inc., Columbus, Oh.
Randall, A. 1983. The problem of market failure. Natural Resources Journal 23:131-148.
Randall, A., J. P. Hoehn, and G. S. Tolley. 1981. The structure of contingent markets: Some results of a recent experiment. Presented to American Economics Association annual meeting, Washington, D.C.
Randall, A., B. C. Ives, and C. Eastman. 1974. Bidding games for valuation of aesthetic environmental improvements. Journal of Environmental Economics and Management 1:132-149.
Randall, A., and J. R. Stoll. 1980. Consumer's surplus in commodity space. American Economic Review 70:449-455.
Randall, A., and J. R. Stoll. 1983. Existence value in a total valuation framework. p. 265-274. *In* Managing air quality and visual resources at national parks and wilderness areas. R. D. Rowe and L. G. Chestnut, editors. Westview Press, Boulder, Colo.
Samuelson, P. A. 1947. Foundations of economic analysis. Harvard University Press, Cambridge, Mass.
Schulze, W. D., D. S. Brookshire, E. G. Walther, and K. Kelley. 1981. The benefits of preserving visibility in the National Parklands of the Southwest. Methods Development for Environmental Control Benefits Assessment, U.S. Environmental Protection Agency, Washington, D.C.
Small, K. A., and H. S. Rosen. 1981. Applied welfare analysis with discrete choice models. Econometrica 49:105-130.

Smith, V. L. 1980. Experiments with a decentralized mechanism for public goods decisions. American Economic Review 70:584-599.
Stigler, G. J., and G. S. Becker. 1977. De gustibus non est disputandum. American Economic Review 67:76-90.
Tideman, T. N., and G. Tullock. 1976. A new and superior process for making public choices. Journal of Political Economy 84:1145-1159.
U.S. Water Resources Council. 1973. Water and related land resources: Establishment of principles and standards for planning. Federal Register 38:174, Part III, September 10.
U.S. Water Resources Council. 1979. Procedures for evaluation of national economic development benefits and costs in water resources planning (level C): Final rule. Federal Register 44:242, Part IX, December 14.
Willig, R. D. 1976. Consumer's surplus without apology. American Economic Review 66:587-597.
Willig, R. D. 1979. Consumer's surplus without apology: Reply. American Economic Review. Vol. 69:469-474.

Footnotes

[1]*The analysis presented in this section is adapted from Bator (1957). Figures 1-6 are reproduced from Randall (1981) with permission from John Wiley and Sons, Inc.*

Table: Categories of wildlands benefits, characteristics and methods of benefit estimation

Resource Product or Service	Kinds of Value[a]	Rival/ Nonrival[b]	Exclusive/ Nonexclusive[c]	Methods of Benefit Estimation[d]
Lumber	Use, RM	R	E	M
Minerals	Use, RM	R	E	M
Range forest	Use, RM	R	E	M; linear programming analysis for synthetic firms; EFM(?)
Water for downstream use	Use, RM	R	E, NE	M
	Use, D	R	E	M
	Use, A	NR, C	E, NE	EFM, ICM
Flood Protection	Use, RM (Protection of property)	NR	NE (except through locational choice)	M, EFM, ICM
	Use, A (Preservation of human health and safety)	NR	NE (except through locational choice)	EFM, ICM
Recreation	Use, A	C	E, NE	EFM, ICM, M
	Option, A	NR	NE	ICM
	Existence, A	NR	NE	ICM
Ecological continuity	Option, RM	NR	NE	ICM
	Quasi-Option, RM	NR	NE	ICM, M(?)
	Existence, RM	NR	NE	ICM
	Use, A	C	E, NE	ICM, EFM
	Option, A	NR	NE	ICM
	Quasi-Option, A	NR	NE	ICM, EFM (?)
	Existence, A	NR	NE	ICM

Table: Categories of wildlands benefits, characteristics and methods of benefit estimation—Continued

Resource Product or Service	Kinds of Value[a]	Rival/ Nonrival[b]	Exclusive/ Nonexclusive[c]	Methods of Benefit Estimation[d]
Scenery	Use, A	C, NR	E, NE	ICM, EFM
	Option, A	NR	NE	ICM
	Quasi-Option, A	NR	NE	ICM, EFM (?)
	Existence, A	NR	NE	ICM
Waste assimilation	Use, RM	R	E, NE	M, EFM
	Quasi-option, RM	NR	NE	ICM, M (?), EFM (?)
	Use, A	C, NR	E, NE	EFM, ICM
	Option, A	NR	NE	ICM
	Quasi-Option, A	NR	NE	ICM, EFM (?)
	Existence, A	NR	NE	ICM

[a]*RM:* *raw materials*
D: *direct consumption commodities*
A: *amenities*

[b]*R:* *rival*
NR: *nonrival*
C: *congestible*

[c]*E:* *exclusive*
NE: *nonexclusive*

[d]*M:* *estimation based on economic analysis of data generated by markets in raw materials or final products*
ICM: *income compensation methods of nonmarket valuation*
EFM: *expenditure function methods of nonmarket valuation*

Chapter 2
The Conceptual Basis of Benefit Cost Analysis

Alan Randall

Benefit cost analysis (BCA) emerged as a response to the idea that there should be some analysis of the benefits and costs of public investments—perhaps, a public sector counterpart of the feasibility studies which prudent private investors perform before undertaking long-term development projects. Before long, however, rather clear distinctions were developed between financial and economic-efficiency analysis, and between private and social concepts of efficiency. BCA clearly was oriented toward the economic rather than the financial and toward social rather than private concepts of efficiency.[1] The idea was to pretest public programs proposed for national economic development purposes to see whether they were in fact likely to make positive contributions to that goal. BCA was designed to evaluate proposed programs, identifying those which would move the national economy in the direction of social efficiency.

Given the purposes for which BCA has evolved, the conceptual task involves defining social efficiency (a state) and, then, developing a test capable of identifying and ranking changes which would move the economy toward that state. What are the necessary and sufficient conditions for a socially efficient state, and for a change to be an unambiguous improvement in terms of social efficiency? These questions are most readily answered for model economies in which there are a manageably small number of homogeneous, perfectly divisible, rival, and exclusive resources and commodities. In these circumstances, the necessary conditions can be expressed entirely in terms of marginal equalities between various rates of substitution (and transformation) and price ratios.

However, in many wildlands management contexts, BCA evaluates nonmarginal changes to complex environments. The resources, goods and amenities involved are varied, seldom homogeneous, and often include the indivisible or lumpy, the nonrival, and the nonmarketed and, therefore, unpriced or inefficiently priced. Clearly a simple, marginal economics of efficiency provides an inadequate base for BCA in such situations. For this

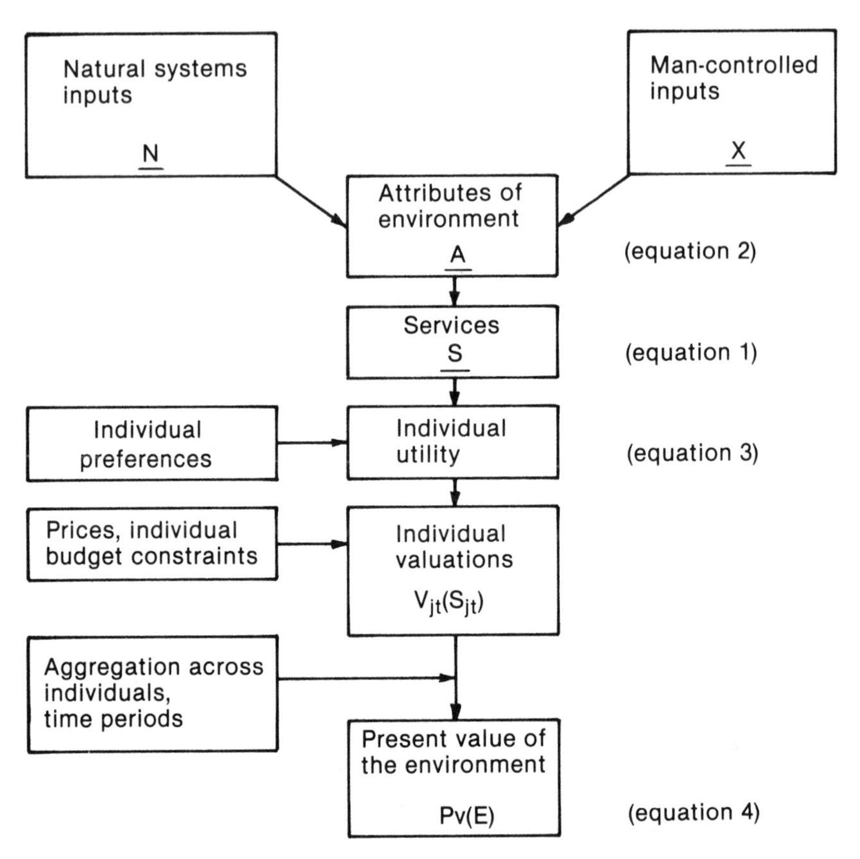

Figure 1. Economic valuation of a complex environment: A schematic exposition of equations [1-4].

reason, a general conceptual basis for BCA is developed; the familiar results of marginal analysis emerge, as a special case, from the more general conceptual model.

Net Benefits of Nonmarginal Changes in Complex Environments

In this section a general model is developed for valuing net economic benefits of human-induced changes in complex environments. Mathematical exposition is used for two reasons: first, to permit a degree of conceptual precision; second to suggest the vast array of information from the earth sciences, biology and economics which is needed to establish the parameters and relationships which underly the benefit and cost estimates. A schematic representation of the relationships developed in equations [1-4] is presented in (fig. 1).

Consider a complex environment, E, producing a vector of services $S = (s_1,\ldots,s_k,\ldots,s_m)$, valued by people. The services (or goods, or amenities) are likely to be diverse—e.g., support services for human, animal and plant life; aesthetic services including atmospheric visibility, landscape amenities, and diversity of flora and fauna; recreation opportunities; waste disposal services; and streams of water, timber and mineral resource-products for use as inputs in producing final consumption goods—and many of them are likely to be nonmarketed. The supply of each of these services in any time period, t, is a function—uniquely determined by geological, hydrological, atmospheric and ecological relationships—of the attributes, $\boldsymbol{A} = (a_1,....,a_r,....,a_s)$ of the environment.

$$\begin{aligned} s_{1t} &= f_1 (\boldsymbol{A}_t) \\ &\vdots \\ s_{mt} &= f_m (\boldsymbol{A}_t) \end{aligned} \qquad [1]$$

People enter the system as modifiers of resource attributes. They may do this directly, e.g., by reassigning land to other uses, diverting water, removing vegetation, disturbing soil for mining, etc. They may also modify the resource as a side effect (expected or unexpected) of some other decision, e.g., disturbing land elsewhere for cultivation or mining, deposition of wastes in water upstream, etc. For each kind of resource attribute,

$$\begin{aligned} a_{1t} &= g_1 (N_t,X_t) \\ &\vdots \\ a_{st} &= g_s (N_t,X_t) \end{aligned} \qquad [2]$$

where N is a vector of "natural systems inputs," e.g., geological, hydrological, atmospheric and ecological, and X is a vector of human-controlled inputs and activities, including harvesting effort.

Both N and X are subject to scarcity, and the attribute production functions are determined by the laws which govern natural systems and by human technology. The production system for environmental services is now complete, if it is remembered that the level of demand for some kinds of services, s_k, influences the level of X and that interactions between X and N are possible and likely. For example, the attempt to enjoy high levels of waste assimilation services involves high levels of pollution inputs, which may modify N, the 'natural' characteristics of the system.

Now consider the value of resource services. Each individual, j, enjoys utility in each time period, t:

$$U_{jt} = U_{jt} (S_{jt},Z_{jt}) = U_{jt} (S^a{}_{jt}, Z^b{}_{jt} (S^b{}_{jt}), Z^a{}_{jt}), \qquad [3]$$

where $\boldsymbol{Z}$ is a vector of valued goods and services which are not directly produced by the environment E (for example, $\boldsymbol{Z}$ includes things bought at the local shopping center); and the service vector $\boldsymbol{S}$ is divided into S^a which are enjoyed directly, and S^b which are inputs into the production of other goods and services; and the vector $\boldsymbol{Z}$ of other goods and services is divided into Z^a which are produced in processes bearing no immediate relationship to S, and Z^b for which S^b are inputs. This formulation permits both direct and derived demands for S.

By minimizing the individual's expenditure, subject to the constraint that his utility must be maintained at a level equal to or greater than that which he enjoys with the existing environment, E, Hicksian compensated demand curves for each of the services, s_{kt}, can be derived.[2] From these, the individual's total net valuation, V_{jkt}, of each s_{kt}, and thus his V_{jt} of the vector S_{jt} of services he enjoys, may be calculated.

The capital value of the environment E is obtained by summing the net values of service flows, discounted at the rate, r, across time periods and individuals:

$$\mathrm{PV}(E) = \sum_t \sum_j V_{jt}\,(S_{jt})/(1 + r)^t\,. \qquad [4]$$

Thus, the environment, E, is seen as a capital good acquiring value to the extent that the services it provides are valued by people. These services are determined by the environment's attributes, which are themselves determined by the characteristics of the natural system and by the activities of people (fig. 1). If that environment were to be disturbed—that is, if the X vector of human-controlled inputs were to be modified—its attributes could change, changing the S vector of services it provides and its capital value.

Consider a project P, which would change X to X^P, thus converting the environment, E, to some "with project" state, E^P, at some conversion cost, $C^P = \sum_t C_t^P/(1 + r)^t$. The proposed project would replace the "without project" stream of services, S, with some "with project" stream, S^P. The net present value of such a project is:

$$\mathrm{PV}(P) = \mathrm{PV}((E^P - C^P)\text{-}E) = \sum_t \frac{(V(S_t^P) - C_t^P - V(S_t))}{(1 + r)^t} \qquad [5]$$

where $V(S_t^P) = \sum_j V_{jt}\,(S_{jt}^P)$ and $V(S_t) = \sum_j V_{jt}\,(S_{jt})$.

Thus, $\mathrm{PV}(E^P)$ is calculated by summing the net discounted value of "with project" services across service types, individuals and time periods, while $\mathrm{PV}(E)$ is calculated by handling "without project" services similarly. Remember that the basic value data, the V_{jkt} (s_{jkt}), were derived by constraining the individual's utility at the "without project" level. Thus, the net present value of the project, P, can exceed zero if and only if the sum of individual welfare gains from its implementation exceeds the sum of individual welfare losses. In other words, BCA implements the *potential Pareto-improvement criterion* and the benefit cost test is an empirical test for Potential Pareto-improvements.[3]

Benefit Cost Analysis and the Market

Voluntary exchange among individuals in markets satisfies the actual Pareto-improvement criterion. Individuals endowed with rights to keep what they have engage in voluntary exchange only if they believe they will receive something of greater (or, at least equal) value to themselves than they give up.

Buyer's best offer must at least equal seller's reservation price. Thus individual gains exceed (or, are at least equal to) individual losses for each and every individual. Trade which does not satisfy that condition will not take place.

However, the potential Pareto-improvement criterion is a "what if?" test. *If* those who would gain from implementation of the project *P*, *could* offer enough to buy the acquiescence of those who would lose, the project passes the test. But, the gainers are not required to buy the project's implementation from the losers. The losers, therefore, are not assured of compensation for their losses. The benefit cost criterion values S^P and S as a market would—i.e., PV(E^P - C^P) is identical to the buyer's best offer for the project, and PV(E) is identical to the seller's reservation price for the "without project" state—but gainers are not required to compensate losers, as they would be in a market.

A General Model for Valuation of Single Period Service Flows

Having constructed a general conceptual framework for BCA, the fundamental valuation problem is considered next. What is the value to an individual of one time-period's flow of a single environmental service? For notational convenience, drop the subscripts identifying the individual and time period, and let $\boldsymbol{Z}$ represent the vector of all goods and services except for the single service Q which is of particular interest. The utility function [3] may then be rewritten as:

$$U = U(Q,\boldsymbol{Z}) \qquad [6]$$

If $\boldsymbol{P}$ is the vector of prices for $\boldsymbol{Z}$, and Y is the individual's income, the utility function is expressed as:

$$U = U(\boldsymbol{P},Q, \mathrm{Y}) \qquad [7]$$

Alternatively, if Y is the numeraire value of $\boldsymbol{Z}$, the utility function, implicit in prices, may be expressed as[4]:

$$U = U(Q,Y) = U(\boldsymbol{P}(Q,Y)) \qquad [8]$$

In general, it is conceivable that a project or program could directly and simultaneously change $\boldsymbol{P}$, Q and Y (or Y). However, it is useful to focus on a more restricted analysis at the outset. As Mishan (1977) argued, most public investments or regulatory initiatives do not change income directly; instead, they change individual utility by first modifying prices or quantities. While most authors (including Mishan 1977, Willig 1976) focus on the $\boldsymbol{P}$ vector, this author believes it is often useful to focus initially on Q. That is, the individual is most immediately affected, as a result of a public project, by a change in the flow of services the impacted environment provides him.

Consider an individual who enjoys the levels Q^0 and Y^0 of the service and the "all other goods" numeraire. His initial welfare level is $U(Q^0, Y^0)$, at the origin (fig. 2). To the right of the origin, the level of provision of Q to the individual increases; to the left of the origin, it decreases. From the origin, a movement up the vertical axis indicates a decrease in the numeraire.[5] The total value (TV) curve, or bid curve, is of positive slope, given that the service is a commodity and the individual is not satiated in the range under consideration. For decreases in Q, the TV curve lies in the southwest quadrant; for increases in Q, it lies in the northeast quadrant. If it is possible to define the quantity of the service in unidimensional, cardinal terms, the assumption of diminishing rates of commodity substitution is sufficient to ensure the curvature shown.[6]

The TV curve is an indifference curve (between a commodity, Q, and a discommodity, reductions in Y), passing through the individual's initial state. That is,

$$U(Q^0, Y^0) = U(Q^-, Y^+) = U(Q^+, Y^-) \, . \qquad [9]$$

Starting at the origin, $Y^0 - Y^-$ is the individual's willingness to pay (WTP) to obtain an increment in the level of provision of the service from Q^0 to Q^+. Willingness to accept (WTA), i.e., $Y^+ - Y^0$, is the amount of money which would induce the individual to accept voluntarily a decrease in the level of provision of the service from Q^0 to Q^-. WTP is the total value to the individual of an increment from Q^0 to Q^+; WTA is the total value to the individual of a decrement from Q^0 to Q^-. Restating equation [9],

$$U(Q^0, Y^0) = U(Q^-, Y^0 + \text{WTA}) = U(Q^+, Y^0 - \text{WTP}). \qquad [10]$$

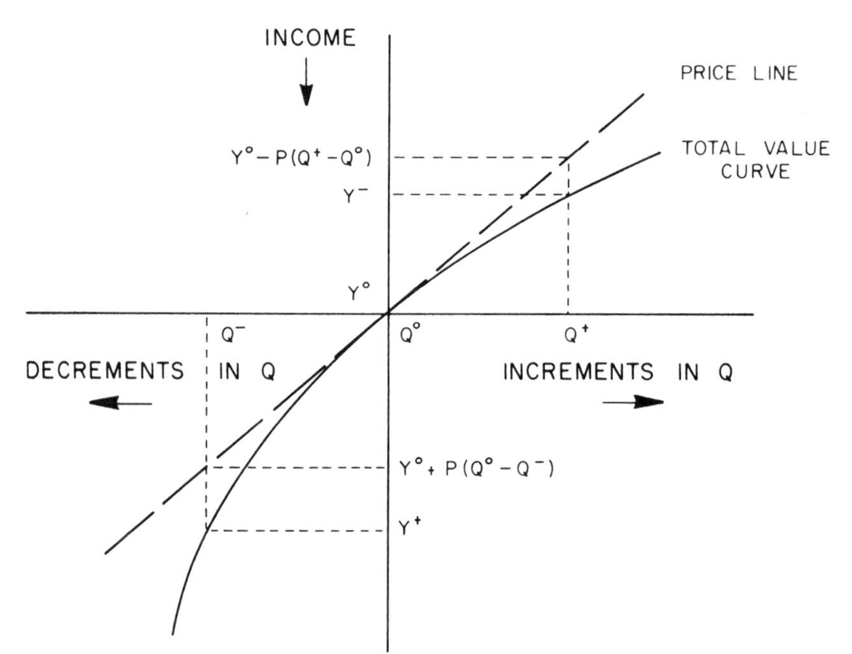

Figure 2. The total value curve and the price line.

WTP, WTA, Economic Surplus and Market Prices[7]

By derivation, WTP and WTA represent the total value to the individual of a given increment or decrement, respectively, in the level of *Q* provided. In market terms, WTP is the individual's best offer to buy the increment, taken as a "lump"; and WTA is the same individual's reservation price to sell the decrement, similarly conceived. How do WTP and WTA relate to the more customary measures of value, economic surplus and market price?

Hicks (1943) showed that there are four measures of consumer's surplus,[8] none of which is conceptually identical to the Marshallian measure. These are now usually called equivalent surplus (ES), equivalent variation (EV), compensating surplus (CS), and compensating variation (CV) (Currie et al. 1971). The surpluses differ from the variations in that the latter are calculated after the consumer has made optimizing adjustments in his consumption set, while the former do not permit such adjustments. In BCA, the choice between variations and surpluses turns upon the question of whether post-change optimizing adjustments are feasible. Where such adjustments are feasible, the variations are used; otherwise the surpluses are used.

The difference between the Hicksian compensating and equivalent measures of consumer's surplus is considerably more significant. The equivalent measure is defined as the amount of compensation, paid or received, which would bring the consumer to his subsequent welfare level if the change did not take place. The compensating measure is defined as the amount of compensation, paid or received, which would keep the consumer at his initial welfare level if the change did take place.

Thus, the compensating measures are consistent with the potential Pareto-improvement criterion, and may be estimated (as in fig. 2) from a total value curve passing through the individual's initial state. WTP^C (where the superscript indicates the compensating measure), willingness to pay to get an increment in *Q*, is the appropriate measure of individual benefits. WTA^C, willingness to accept compensation and permit a decrement in *Q*, is the appropriate measure of individual costs (or negative benefits).

Because there are also equivalent measures of WTP and WTA, care must be taken to avoid confusion. WTP^E, willingness to pay to avoid a threatened decrement in *Q*, and WTA^E, willingness to accept compensation in lieu of a promised increment in *Q*, are equivalent measures, are not consistent with the potential Pareto-improvement criterion, and cannot be estimated from a total value curve passing through the individual's initial state (Randall and Stoll 1980b).

Value data are often available in some form other than WTP^C or WTA^C. Instead, the analyst may be confronted with value data in the form of WTP^E, WTA^E, Marshallian consumer's surplus (*M*), or market prices. Following some recent theoretical work (Willig 1976, Randall and Stoll 1980a and b), the formal relationships between these various value measures have been elucidated, and conversion factors permitting approximations of WTP^C and WTA^C from data in other forms are now available. The important results are summarized immediately below.

In general, when comparing any two levels of *Q* (e.g., Q' and Q'', where $Q'' > Q'$ and *Q* is a non-inferior good),

$$\mathrm{WTP}^C = \mathrm{WTP}^E \leq M \leq \mathrm{WTA}^E = \mathrm{WTA}^C, \qquad [11]$$

where WTP^C is to get an increment from Q' to Q'', WTP^E is to avoid a threatened decrement from Q'' to Q', WTA^E is to forego a promised increment from Q' to Q'', and WTA^C is to permit a decrement from Q'' to Q'.

At this point, note that the potential Pareto-improvement is a conservative criterion. It is entirely possible that a proposed project may just fail the potential Pareto-improvement test (which measures benefits at WTP^C and costs at WTA^C), while just passing a (conceptually invalid) benefit test which used WTA^E as the measure of benefits and WTP^E to measure costs. That is to be expected. The potential Pareto-improvement requires that proponents of change be (at least) able to compensate those who prefer the status quo, if that were required.

Two questions remain. Under what conditions are WTP and WTA equal, and when WTP < WTA, can the bounds on the difference be rigorously defined? Again, the answers provided below assume Q is a non-inferior good.

When the resource service, Q, is a perfectly divisible good traded at the unit price p in infinitely large markets with zero transactions costs,[9] WTP = WTA = $p \cdot \Delta Q$ *(where* ΔQ indicates the number of units by which Q is to be increased or decreased). In this case, the good Q has the essential characteristics of currency, and is valued not so much for what it is but for what it will buy. The price line (fig. 2) replaces the total value curve as the basis for valuation.

When transactions costs are positive, WTP < WTA. The difference between WTP and WTA is empirically trivial when unit transactions costs amount to a small fraction (e.g., one-tenth) of the unit price of the good. However large transactions costs may be, the difference between WTP and WTA never exceeds that in the case following this one.

All of this means that increments in goods which are homogeneous, divisible in production and rival in consumption, and traded in relatively inexpensive and competitive markets may be valued at unit price multiplied by quantity change, with only a small loss of precision.

If, instead, Q is a lumpy good which can be held only in the amounts Q'' and Q', WTP is always less than WTA. However, the relationship between the magnitudes of WTP, M, and WTP is theoretically tractible, which permits rigorous derivation of empirical bounds on differences between these measures. Where ζ is the price flexibility of income for Q (i.e., $\frac{\partial P(Q,Y)}{\partial Y} \frac{Y}{P(Q,Y)}$) and $\zeta M / Y^0$ is small (e.g., ≤ 0.05),

$$\mathrm{WTA} - \mathrm{WTP} = \frac{\zeta M^2}{Y^0} \qquad [12]$$

provides a serviceable approximation. That is, for lumpy goods which are valued by the individual at only a small fraction of his total budget, [12] provides an adequate basis for estimating WTP^C or WTA^C from data in the form of WTP^E, WTA^E, or M. For cases where the budget share of Q is large and ζ is not constant, rigorous (but more complicated) bounds on WTA-WTP are provided (Randall and Stoll 1980b).

The pragmatic import of this is that where Q is a normal good which accounts for a small share of the individual budget, the difference between WTA and WTP is fairly small and easily estimated. However, where Q is a superior good accounting for a large budget share, WTA is much larger than WTP. In this case, it is important that the correct compensating measure of economic surplus be used in valuation. The rigorous bounds permit estimation of the correct value measure from other, sometimes more readily available, measures.

Summary and Concluding Comments

A general framework for benefit cost evaluation of management alternatives for complex environments is developed above. Production and demand systems for environment services are conceptualized and the value of the environment, as a capital good, is defined as the net present value of its service flows. Proposals to modify the environment are evaluated, in a benefit cost analysis, by the potential Pareto-improvement criterion.

A conceptual basis for the individual valuation of specific service flows is then developed. Benefit and cost items must be evaluated in terms of the Hicksian compensating version of economic surplus. The relationships between WTP, WTA, economic surplus and market price are summarized and conclusions are drawn concerning the appropriate value concepts for use in empirical applications.

Discussion of consumer's surplus concepts is confined to a simple, partial equilibrium case, in which the first-round effects of a change in quantity of an environment service are evaluated. This simple case is often the case of interest in empirical application of BCA. However, the reader should be aware of the considerable literature which addresses more complex cases—the general equilibrium case (Harberger 1971); the multi-product case (Willig 1979); the discrete choice case, in partial and general equilibrium contexts (Small and Rosen 1981); and the case of several alternatives, each of which differ in terms of both price (or quantity, one presumes) and income (Hause 1975, Silberberg 1978, Chipman and Moore 1980).

This paper serves as a starting point for two subsequent papers which take quite divergent paths—Chapter 3, which examines BCA as an information system; and Chapter 4 which develops the conceptual basis for empirical techniques of valuing non-marketed goods, services and amenities.

Literature Cited

Bradford, D. F. 1970. Benefit cost analysis and the demand for public goods. Kyklos 23:775-791.

Chipman, J. S., and J. C. Moore. 1980. Compensating variation, consumer's surplus, and welfare. American Economic Review 70:933-949.

Currie, J. M., J. A. Murphy, and A. Schmitz. 1971. The concept of economic surplus and its use in economic analysis. Economic Journal 81:741-799.

Harberger, A. C. 1971. Three basic postulates for applied welfare economics: An interpretive essay. Journal of Economic Literature 9:785-797.

Hause, J. C. 1975. The theory of welfare cost measurement. Journal of Political Economy 83:1145-1182.

Hicks, J. R. 1943. The four consumers' surpluses. Review of Economic Studies 11:31-41.

Mishan, E. J. 1977. The plain truth about consumer's surplus. Zeitschrift fur Nationalokomie 37:1-24.

Mishan, E.J. 1968. What is producer's surplus? American Economic Review 58:1269-1282.

Randall, A., and J. R. Stoll. 1980a. Consumer's surplus in commodity space. American Economic Review 70:449-455.

Randall, A., and J. R. Stoll. 1980b. Economic surplus and benefit cost analysis. Agricultural Economics Research Report 35. University of Kentucky, Lexington, Kentucky.

Silberberg, E. 1978. The structure of economics: A mathematical analysis. McGraw-Hill, New York, N.Y.

Small, K. A., and H. S. Rosen. 1981. Applied welfare economics with discrete choice models. Econometrica 49:105-130.

Willig, R. D. 1979. Consumer's surplus without apology: Reply. American Economic Review 69:469-474.

Willig, R. D. 1976. Consumer's surplus with apology. American Economic Review 66:587-597.

Footnotes

[1]*Some objections to BCA fail to recognize these elementary distinctions.*

[2]*Some readers may be more familiar with Marshallian demand curves, which are derived by maximizing utility subject to a budget constraint. However, Hicksian demand relationships permit more precise specification of consumer's surplus values.*

[3]*A Pareto-improvement is a change which makes at least one person better-off while making no one worse-off. A potential Pareto-improvement is a change which chould be a Pareto-improvement if those who gain were to compensate those who lose. Thus, any change in which the gainers value their gains more highly than the losers value their losses is a potential Pareto-improvement.*

[4]*Note that in general* $Y \neq Y$ and when Q is a priced commodity $Y > Y$. However, the case where Q is unpriced to the individual and Y [5] Y is often of interest in BCA.

[5]*The orientation of the Y axis may seem a little strange at first. However, it permits easy reading of total value (TV) which is positive for increments in Q and negative for decrements.*

[6]*If "quantity" is multidimensional, or if it cannot be accurately defined in cardinal terms, no prior assumption can be made concerning the curvature of the TV curve (Bradford 1970).*

[7]This section summarizes results developed in detail in Randall and Stoll (1980a and b).

[8]Benefits and costs are properly valued as economic surplus, i.e., the value of a good or service in excess of its factor costs (the latter not including resource rents). Economic surplus may be partitioned into consumer's surplus and "producer's surplus" or resource rents (Mishan 1968), but the relative size of these two subsets is a distributional issue which, for given levels of output and demand, does not affect the magnitude of economic surplus. Mishan (1968) and Currie et al. (1971) show that the analytics of consumer's surplus and producer's surplus are identical. Thus, discussion is put in terms of the customary consumer's surplus language; all of the results obtained can be easily generalized to economic surplus.

[9]These conditions never can be strictly satisfied. They may be approximated, however, in the markets for some minerals, timber and agricultural products.

Chapter 3
Benefit Cost Analysis as an Information System

Alan Randall

Benefit cost analysis is an empirical test for potential Pareto-improvements. Thus, it emerged from one particular attempt to give empirical substance to the utilitarian dictum, "the greatest good for the greatest number." To consider the appropriateness of the benefit cost criterion as a decision rule for society, it is necessary to place utilitarianism in perspective among modern theories of democratic government.

The Social Contract

While the notion of social contract has little modern currency—it has been rejected as logically unsatisfying, and unnecessary to the theory of democracy—much that is important in the modern theory of democratic government has its origins in the writings of the three great contractarians, Hobbes, Locke, and Rousseau. All three wrote as though directly or indirectly influenced by Machiavelli. The contract theorists argued that, because society is a human artifact, the rights of people cannot derive from duties of one man toward another and towards society. Instead, the rights of people and of the sovereign derive from a single fundamental right: the birth-right of each person to preserve himself and to choose freely the means to his self-preservation. For Hobbes, there was nothing fundamental about society; rather, individuals would rationally choose to voluntarily submit themselves to some kind of social order simply because the alternative, anarchy, was intolerable. While people originally consent to be governed, in Hobbes' philosophy the sovereign is virtually unconstrained thereafter, and all future generations are bound to the sovereign by the original act of consent.

Locke made a major break by assigning sovereignty to the individual. Government, deriving its authority from the people, must act only in the public good. The people may resist and replace a government which has violated this trust, but they must immediately install a new government.

Some commentators have seen in Locke's social contract not merely a rationale for the replacement of governments which have violated the public trust, but strict limits to the authority of any government. That is, individuals are guaranteed some rights and a government invading or denying these rights would exceed its rightful authority. Thus, Locke is seen as a founder of philosophical individualism, and an important contributor to modern theories of politics and economics. Locke's social contract points forward to the bills-of-rights emphasis in contemporary democratic theory and to the voluntary exchange notion of economic freedom and justice.

Rousseau treated individual rights as axiomatic rather than "natural." Although he used the social contract notion, it was not really essential to his scheme of things. His starting point was that all people are bound to the realization of equality, without which politics and justice are contradictions in terms. Governments expressing the "general will" must legislate only laws which are addressed to the common good of the society's members and which extend the same rights to, and impose the same duties on, each citizen. When the citizen finds himself under the sway of a law that does not meet with these requirements, the social contract has been violated and its obligation lapses. Rousseau further modified the contract concept by requiring that no citizen be excluded from the deliberations which produce expressions of the "general will' and that each citizen, on coming of age, has the option of consenting to existing institutions or withdrawing from society. Although Rousseau was unclear about the requirements for transition from one government to the next, his philosophy foreshadows the modern emphasis on political equality and consitutional government. While Locke emphasized sovereignty of the individual, Rousseau stressed the active participation of citizens in the political process as an indispensible condition for "government by consent." These emphases, along with the concept of the "general will," are precursers to modern "public interest" theories of government.

Individualism

Modern individualism, as expressed by, for example, the political economist Buchanan (1975 and 1977), emphasizes Pareto-safety in economics and politics. Pareto-safety is the criterion that no change which harms any individual can be considered an improvement. In economic activity, this criterion is satisfied by voluntary exchange among individuals whose expectations are secured by nonattenuated property rights.[1] Assuming the individual is the best (the only) judge of his own well-being, no one would voluntarily enter a trade which would make him worse-off. It is important to note that voluntary exchange protects the individual from coercion in the static environment. However, it does not protect the individual from the dynamic consequences of his prior choices or of changes in technology, supply, and demand. Thus, protection from direct coercion in exchange does not exempt the individual from the discipline of the market place.

In the political sphere, Pareto-safety can only mean that a proposed change must enjoy unanimous consent if it is to be implemented. The idea of the "general will" is explicitly denied. All that matters is the individual, and no individual should be coerced into accepting political change which is not in his interest. The more sophisticated individualistic philosophers have recognized that Pareto-safety protects the status quo. Thus, it is just only to the extent that the status quo itself is just. This led Buchanan (1977) to adopt Rawls' (1971) "veil of ignorance" procedure[2] for establishing a just starting point for a subsequent political regime of Pareto-safety. Clearly, this is a device more helpful to conceptualization than to political practice.

Individualist philosophy suggests that a just process for making social decisions would have the following characteristics. Rights to life, liberty, and property would be specified at the individual level. Property rights would be nonattenuated, to encourage the resolution of conflicts via trade. Such a system of pervasive property rights would extend the Pareto-safe protections of the market over the largest possible array of human activities. Even pure public goods would be brought into the arena of voluntary exchange via incentive-compatible mechanisms (Tideman and Tullock 1976, Groves and Ledyard 1977).[3] Having thus minimized the need for government, the individualists visualize a strictly limited state, with constitutional restrictions upon its authority and functions. Such a government would be bound to respect individual rights, and could impose its decisions upon minorities only to fulfill the most pressing societal needs (obvious examples being national defense and the maintenance of internal law and order). In all other situations, government should do everything it can to maximize opportunities for voluntary exchange and to seek to incorporate minorities into a political consensus by compensating those who would otherwise be made worse-off by political decisions.

"Public Interest" Theories of Government

"Public interest" theories of government posit that there is a "general will" and that, in an environment of political equality, deliberative bodies are capable of identifying and interpreting that will, and of establishing policies and programs to implement it. To ensure political equality and to promote the "general will" over the interests of a powerful but selfish few, some considerable regulation of individual activities for the "public health, welfare, safety, and morals" may be justified. There is no compelling need to minimize the scope of government as long as government serves the interests of the general public. Thus, programs to promote economic activity, to rectify "market failure" (i.e., to internalize externalities and to provide public goods and "merit" goods), and to promote equality of economic opportunity, may all be seen as enhancing the general welfare and thus within the purview of government.

Some conflict between individual aspirations and the "general will" is inevitable, but "public interest" theorists believe that individuals will be adequately protected by constitutional procedures and majority institutions. "Public interest" theorists, nevertheless, recognize that majority institutions may be susceptible to selfish behavior by interest groups and coalitions. Thus, they see the necessity for a broad array of legislatures, committees, courts and tribunals, and an increasingly professional and planning-oriented bureaucracy (civil service), to ensure the continued dominance of public interests over private interests in the political sphere.

Utilitarianism and the Potential Pareto-Improvement

Bentham, who was influenced by the social contract theorists and the early classical economists, popularized the notion that human motivations were the pursuit of pleasure and the avoidance of pain. It is as a result of his influence that the word "utility" acquired two meanings—its customary meaning of usefulness and, in technical economics, its association with individual satisfactions and thus individual preferences. In early neoclassical economics, individual utility was thought to be, at least in principal, measurable on some cardinal scale.[4]

While the difficulties of the cardinal concept of utility were mostly theoretical in the case of individual choice, they became crucial for political philosophy when the analysis was expanded to collective choice. Bentham thought that the proper criterion for collective choices was "the greatest good for the greatest number." That sounded fair enough, but entailed obvious difficulties in the quite plausible case where very great good to each of a few might be directly opposed to rather trivial good for each of many. However, if cardinal utilities could be summed across individuals, that could provide one solution to the problem.

As it turned out, that avenue proved to be a dead end. Much later, about 1940, the concept of the potential Pareto-improvement emerged. If the gainers from some proposed change could compensate those who would otherwise lose, the potential Pareto-improvement criterion would find that change acceptable even if compensation did not actually occur. Thus, market prices served as the value indicators, but the Pareto-safety protection of voluntary exchange was held to be unnecessary. Here, at last, was an empirically applicable criterion by which the utilitarian concept of "the greatest good for the greatest number" could be implemented. BCA is strictly a test for potential Pareto-improvements.[5]

Decision Criterion or Information System?

If the benefit cost criterion—that change is justified when its benefits exceed its cost, regardless of the identity of the gainers and losers—was to be adopted as the universal criterion for collective decisions, individual rights would be completely subordinated to the rights of the collective. Resource reallocation could then legitimately proceed with government taking from the inefficient and giving to the efficient (as opposed to the exchange process in which the efficient purchase those resources from the less efficient). Thus, philosophical individualists would be implacably opposed to such a collective rule. They favor efficiency, of course, but prefer that it emerge spontaneously from individual transactions rather than be deliberately imposed, without regard to the consequences to individuals, by governments armed with benefit cost analyses.

"Public interest" theorists would not be happy with such a decision rule either. Political equality is unlikely to be best served by a value system based entirely upon price and an interpersonal aggregation method which algebraically sums individual gains and losses. Further, it is conceivable and likely that the "general will," on occasion, would require some sacrifice of economic efficiency in the service of other social well-being goals. Many observers regard much of the existing body of regulatory, public resource management and redistributive laws as specific instances in which society has chosen to quite deliberately do some things inefficiently. Thus, it has been argued, to submit such laws to BCA would be a logical error.[6] A full-fledged "public interest" conception of the role of government would reject the benefit cost criterion as a decision rule. It is ultimately a unidimensional rule when surely the "general will" is multidimensional.

The preceding discussion has been naive, in that it has treated the benefit cost criterion as a single social decision rule in a society without other rules or laws. American society, of course, has a vast array of rules and laws, institutionalizing private property rights over a broad domain of objects, as well as a limited public sector planning apparatus, a more expansive regulatory and judicial regime, and a public treasury with powers to tax and spend. Thus, institutions responsive to notions of individualism and the "public interest" are firmly established in their relevant domains and coexist in the same modern mixed economy. If the benefit cost criterion was to be institutionalized as a social decision rule, it would be superimposed upon (or somehow integrated into) this matrix of existing institutions.

As an example, consider a structural water resources project approved on the basis of the benefit cost criterion. Assume the project will use structural materials provided by the private sector, some river bottom land, and a segment of a flowing stream. The structural materials will be obtained through the market. From the sellers' prospective, the exchange will be voluntary and Pareto-safe. The land will be acquired through the power of eminent domain; the farmers will be compensated at the fair market value of their land, but that compensation will be less than Pareto-sate. The funds to purchase structural materials and compensate farmers whose land is taken are gathered through coercive taxation of the general public, few of whom can expect to benefit directly from the project. Recreationists who enjoy the free-flowing stream segment are without property rights and will lose stream amenities without compensation. They, along with any disgruntled taxpayers and farmers whose land has been condemned, under current institutional arrangements, may press their cases in various public forums. Some may value this opportunity, while others would prefer institutions which granted them more explicit rights to the status quo. But, it is unlikely that any would prefer a change to a situation in which the final decision was made on the basis of the benefit cost criterion alone.

The point is that adherents of neither individualistic nor "public interest" philosophies of government are likely to find much merit in the institutionalization of the benefit cost criterion as a social decision rule. In fact, it is likely that adherents of both kinds of political philosophies would find little to recommend any formal decision rule. Decision rules are, after all, the domain of the technocrats, while individualists would rather place their trust in individuals, and "public interest" theorists would rather place theirs in the citizenry.

If one takes a more pragmatic, and less philosophical, view of the political process, one observes that an enormous variety of individual and group interests are represented and that conflict resolution is pursued simultaneously or sequentially in a variety of arenas. Institutions offering themselves as places for conflict resolution include: electoral politics; legislative and administrative institutions at the federal, state and local levels; a wide variety of special purpose multi-governmental organizations: the judicial system, with its courts and professional advocates; the public information media; and markets, large and small, but all subject to law. A wide variety of specialized individual and group interests seek representation, along with the less differentiated general public. Even those who staff the institutions of government have their own individual and group interests and cannot be entirely disinterested in the final outcomes of conflict resolution processes.

In this kind of public decision process, information plays a central role. It is used by all participants in the process, both to inform and to persuade. Many divergent kinds and qualities of information—positive and normative, and to varying degrees complete or incomplete and accurate or inaccurate—compete for attention. The scientific and technical communities have a role in the public decision process to the extent that they are recognized as having a comparative advantage in the generation and dissemination of complete and accurate information.

In this context, BCA is viewed as an information system. Because it is an empirical test for potential Pareto-improvements—that is, a particular way of empirically implementing utilitarian concepts—BCA is a fundamentally limited information system. The information it generates takes its place among the wide variety of informational inputs which eventually influence ultimate decisions. This argument suggests, in a sentence, that benefit cost information is important but not necessarily dominant in public decisions.

When resource allocation concerns are pertinent to the policy issue at hand, many participants in the public policy process have a genuine interest in the kind of information which is generated by competent BCA. Some respond to a personal or group interest in national economic development, while the interest of others in BCA lies in its persuasive powers—if one's pet project appears favorable in the light of BCA, that may help persuade others to support its implementation. The scientific and technical communities, in this context, are both generators of benefit cost information and guardians of its quality.

Recognition of this limited public role of BCA in no way undermines the importance of complete and accurate benefit cost analysis. While an empirical test for potential Pareto-improvements has a limited role, it is nevertheless essential that such a test be as complete, accurate, and faithful to the relevant economic theory as is feasible. In the public decision process, the role of the scientific and technical communities lies in the generation of information and its quality control. That role must be played in BCA, as elsewhere, with ingenuity and dedication to scientific standards.

Information Quality in Benefit Cost Analysis

The general conceptual model for benefit cost analysis (Ch. 2, eqs. [1-5]) is simple enough, in principle, and serves as a useful guide for organizing one's thinking. However, at every step, the path from concept to empirical application is enormously complex. Merely to identify the elements of S, the vector of goods, services, and amenities provided by a complex environment, may be an overwhelming task. Those elements which are inputs into the organized production of marketable commodities (e.g., timber products, livestock grazing, minerals, etc.) may be fairly well-defined and routinely recorded. For publicly-owned recreation sites, management agencies now routinely record visitor-days. However, a few recent studies (e.g., Schulze et al. 1981, Majid et al. 1983) have found that, for some kinds of relatively scarce environmental resources, the values generated through visitation are swamped by the values generated by a larger population who in some way appreciate the environment without actually visiting. That is, existence services to nonvisitors are, in some environments, considerably larger than recreation visitor services. Yet, existence services, themselves, have a somewhat nebulous character, and recent attempts at precise definition of such services have produced less than impressive results. Environmental services, such as ecosystem diversity and the integrity of hydrological systems, may be recognized in principle, but tend to escape precise definition and quantification. Further, in the context of exponentially growing scientific and technical knowledge, there is the possibility that currently unrecognized services will acquire significant value in the future.

If the mere identification and measurement of environmental services is a difficult task, specification of the production system for services [eqs. 1 and 2] is considerably more challenging. Yet, it is a crucial step in the evaluation of wildlands management alternatives. Management alternatives are implemented via deliberate manipulation of the X vector of human-controlled inputs. Again, more is known about the production systems for commercial services and recreation visitor days than about those for less well-defined kinds of environmental services.

In terms of readily available information, there is a similar situation with respect to the demand system for environmental services [eqs. 3 and 4]. Markets generate considerable information about the demand for those services which are traded commercially. Nevertheless, difficulties in BCA may arise in cases where prices are determined administratively rather than in competitive markets. There is now a considerable reservoir of empirical information about the demand for recreation services, but much of the emphasis has been placed on estimating the value of a visitor-day at a specific site under narrowly defined partial equilibrium conditions. Relationships among substitute sites are less well understood; general equilibrium demand systems have seldom been attempted; and off-site values (e.g., option value, quasi-option value, and existence value) have received empirical consideration in only a few recent studies.

As the discussion of value measures—market price, economic surplus, willingness to pay, etc.—makes clear (Ch. 2 and 4), value estimation is technically more demanding at the conceptual and empirical levels for those goods which are neither divisible nor traded in large, competitive markets. Equations [4] and [5] in Chapter 2 implement the potential Pareto-improvement aggregation rule (the implications of which have been discussed at length above), and apply the customary discounting formula, which opens the door to the long standing debate about the appropriate discount rate (see, e.g., Baumol 1968, Sjaastad and Wisecarver 1977) and the validity of discounting concepts (Ferejohn and Page 1977).

Having taken a closer look at the general conceptual model for BCA, it must be concluded that many of its elements are poorly specified and elusive in measurement, and that many crucial production and demand relationships are unknown. Further, it seems certain that more and better information is available with respect to the kinds of services which customarily enter commerce, and those which are now routinely recorded by management agencies. Not only is the necessary information matrix incomplete, it is systematically more complete with the respect to the kinds of things which come to the attention of, for example, accountants than the kinds of things which concern ecologists. While all aspects of BCA are susceptible to incomplete and inaccurate empirical analysis, the information base for evaluating marketed goods is inherently richer and less costly to assemble than that for nonmarketed services.

BCA is an empirical test for potential Pareto-improvements and, thus, a fundamentally limited information system. Nevertheless, the information it is capable of providing is useful, and therefore, valuable, in the public decision process. If, however, the information base in not merely incomplete but more complete with the respect to some kinds of goods and services than other kinds, the threat of systematic bias exists. Such bias may distort the outcome of public decisions, in extreme cases rendering the information value of BCA negative. In such a context, it is imperative that effort be specifically channeled toward redressing imbalances in the information base for applied BCA.

Strategies for Limited Information Situations

Formal BCA reduces a large amount of information which varies in kind and in quality to a single number—a benefit/cost ratio or a net present value. Services for which no value data are available are treated as making zero contribution to benefits, costs, and net present value, unless care and effort are expended specifically to correct such misinterpretation. Consideration of several strategies for BCA in limited information situations follows.

Valuation of nonmarketed goods and services.—Substantial progress has been made, in the past two decades, in developing, refining, and validating techniques for valuation of nonmarketed goods and services. In general, the absence of value information revealed in organized markets is no longer sufficient reason to exclude nonmarketed benefit and cost items from formal BCA. Effort and ingenuity should be directed toward value estimation for nonmarketed goods and services. This involves quantification of production relationships, the selection of a valuation method from among the several kinds now available, data collection, analysis, and some attempt at validation (which may involve comparison of value estimates obtained with more than one technique).

It has been argued above, that given the inherently richer data base for valuation of marketed goods, effort should be specifically channeled toward economic evaluation of nonmarketed goods and services. However, there are some limits on the amounts of talent and funding which can reasonably be directed to this. In addition, the prospects for success are better for some categories of goods and services than for others; and, in problem cases, the difficulty is as likely to lie in the absence of physical and biological data as in failure to develop appropriate economic valuation methods. It must be expected that economic value data, comparable with that available for commercially marketed goods and services, will remain unavailable for some nonmarketed services which, nevertheless, are vitally important considerations in selection of appropriate management plans. In such cases, it is essential that all obtainable information be documented. This implies in some cases the careful assembly and display of information which falls short of conveying dollar value numbers.

Documentation of positive value.—It is often possible to document that environmental services are being provided and are of unambiguously positive value. For example, in research in progress at the Universities of Chicago and Kentucky, a wide variety of convincing empirical evidence has been assembled, demonstrating that people in aggregate make the kinds of choices which necessarily imply that they place positive value on atmospheric visibility. Given the current state-of-the-art, it is not always possible to take the next step: to estimate benefits in dollar terms. Nevertheless, careful documentation that visibility values are real and positive serves effectively to counter the erroneous implication that those things which cannot be reliably valued in dollar terms are without value.

Documentation of positive production of services.—As a last resort, it may be possible to document that certain kinds of environmental goods and services are being provided in positive quantities. This kind of information also serves to correct the tendency to ignore those things which cannot be incorporated in a single benefit cost or net present value.

In general, the analyst's operating rule should be to value in economic terms those goods and services which can be valued; failing that, to document that observable behavior necessarily implies a positive valuation for particular services; and failing even that, to document that production of environmental goods and services is demonstrably positive. All of these various kinds of evidence have their place in the final display of results from BCA.

Sensitivity analysis.—Where uncertainty exists with respect to technical coefficients and value estimates, sensitivity analysis is appropriate. Benefit and cost estimates are based upon the "best" estimates of coefficients and prices, but the range of values these parameters might possibly take is recognized. The arithmetic is reiterated, using the end points of this range and perhaps several intermediate values. The purpose is to determine whether the final conclusions are sensitive to assumptions about technical and price parameters for particular environmental services. When uncertainty is unequally distributed across the vector of services, particular attention should be addressed to sensitivity analysis where the uncertainty is the greatest. Clearly, the BCA exercise is inconclusive if sensitivity analysis demonstrates that benefits of the proposed change exceed its costs under some plausible technical and price assumptions but not under others.

Inverse sensitivity analysis.—There may be environment services which are recognized as significant, but for which it is impossible to make plausible estimates of crucial technical or value coefficients. In such cases, inverse sensitivity analysis should be used. Rather than determining how alternative estimates affect benefit cost outcomes, inverse sensitivity analysis asks "how large would an unquantified benefit or cost item need to be, in order to reverse the conclusion of a BCA which omits that item?" Inverse sensitivity analysis is a useful indicator of the robustness of benefit cost conclusions in cases where particular benefit and/or cost items are admittedly unquantifiable.

While BCA is a fundamentally limited information system, it remains important that it be conducted as competently, completely, and accurately as feasible. If this is not done, a potentially useful information system may be rendered useless or even harmful. Completeness and accuracy require first that all benefit and cost items be recognized and documented to the extent possible. After this, all items should be expressed in comparable dollar values. However, if this second step is not always possible, the first step remains essential. Thus, an important part of the BCA exercise involves the careful assembly and display of information, some of which falls short of conveying dollar number values.

Literature Cited

Baumol, W. J. 1968. On the social rate of discount. American Economic Review 58:788-802.

Buchanan, J. M. 1975. The limits to liberty: Between anarchy and leviathan. University of Chicago Press, Chicago, Ill.

Buchanan, J. M. 1977. Freedom in constitutional contract. Texas A & M University, College Station, Tex.

Ferejohn, J., and T. R. Page. 1978. On the foundations of intertemporal choice. American Journal of Agricultural Economics 60:269-275.

Groves, T. E., and J. Ledyard. 1977. Optimal allocation of public goods: A solution to the free-rider problem. Econometrica 45:783-809.

Majid, I., J. Sinden, and A. Randall. 1983. Benefit evaluation of increments to existing systems of public facilities. Land Economics 59:377-392.

Rawls, J. 1971. A theory of justice. Harvard University Press, Cambridge, Mass.

Sagoff, M. 1981. Economic theory and environmental law. Michigan Law Review 79:1393-1419.

Schulze, W. D., D. S. Brookshire, E. G. Walther, and K. Kelley. 1981. The benefits of preserving visibility in the national parklands of the southwest. Methods Development for Environmental Control Benefits Assessment, 8. United States Department of Interior, Environmental Protection Agency.

Sjaastad, L., and D. Wisecarver. 1977. The social cost of public finance. Journal of Political Economics 85:513-547.

Tideman, T. N., and G. Tullock. 1976. A new and superior process for making public choices. Journal of Political Economics 84:1145-1159.

Footnotes

[1]*Nonattenuated property rights have the following characteristics: they are completely specified, enforced, transferable, and in no way inconsistent with the requirements for Pareto-efficiency. Structures of property rights having these characteristics encourage efficiency through trade.*

[2]*Individuals, each of whom has his own position to protect, are unlikely to reach unanimous agreement about a just or fair distribution of endowments and rights. Therefore, Rawls explored the kind of agreement which might be reached within a group of people who "know everything in general and nothing in particular," that is, who know the broad possibilities and limits for society but not the particular position they themselves occupy within society. In Rawl's terms, one could imagine this occurring if people withdrew behind a "veil of ignorance."*

[3]*Incentive-compatible mechanisms generally use a complex system of taxes designed to make true revelation of preferences the least-cost strategy for the individual. Thus, the "free-rider" effect is eliminated and markets in public goods can be made efficient.*

[4]*Not until Hicks' indifference curve analysis was a theory of consumer choice based on strictly ordinal preferences.*

[5]*The potential Pareto-improvement is a conceptual application, and BCA is an empirical application of utilitarian principles. However, that is not to say that utilitarian concepts necessarily lead to the potential Pareto-improvement and BCA.*

Two points are important here. First, while BCA is based on values derived from the notion that the individual is the proper judge of his own well-being, some utilitarians including John Stuart Mill were careful to distinguish "higher" and "lower" pleasures and to argue that what people want does not always make them happy. Second, summation of either cardinal utilities or dollar-valued gains and losses across individuals is only one of many possible solutions to the problem of aggregating welfare changes across individuals. Simple summation makes the problem tractable, but entails the specific assumption that society considers the satisfactions of its members to be perfectly substitutable across individuals.

BCA is a utilitarian device, but is a particular kind of one. Not all utilitarian thinking leads in the direction of BCA.

[6]*Sagoff (1981) makes such a case.*

Chapter 4
Theoretical Bases for Non-Market Benefit Estimation

Alan Randall

Many of the services produced in complex environments are not marketed directly. Air quality, hydrosystem and ecosystem stability, and visual aesthetics are just a few examples. Other services, e.g., recreational access, often are administratively priced at levels bearing no systematic relationship to market-clearing prices. In these cases, value information, in forms consistent with theoretically valid concepts, is not directly observable in organized markets. For this reason, considerable ingenuity has been devoted in recent years to devising and implementing non-market methods for value estimation. In this chapter, the theoretical bases for the "mainstream" non-market valuation methods are developed in terms compatible with the general model for benefit cost analysis presented in a previous chapter.[1]

The "mainstream" methods attempt to estimate benefits in terms interpretable as measures of welfare impact, i.e., the change in economic surplus. Nevertheless, several different approaches to this common task have been developed. There is not, as yet, any simple system for classifying these methods which has gained universal acceptance. A classification system is proposed here based on the chosen theoretical approach to valuation. Under this classification, income compensation approaches are those which seek to measure welfare change directly in terms of compensation requirements to restore some reference level of utility. Expenditure function approaches use data on expenditures for related goods to infer the value of the non-market good in question.

One of the important outcomes of the mathematical analysis presented is that both approaches yield, at least in concept, identical measures of benefits. The choice of benefit estimation technique then, revolves around practical issues: the reliability of obtainable data, and the inaccuracies which may be introduced when necessary analytical assumptions diverge from reality.

Following the mathematical introduction to each group of approaches, the applied methods which have been developed for implementation are introduced and briefly discussed.

The Income Compensation Approach

Working with the utility function implicit in prices, $U = U[P(Q,Y)]$ (Ch. 2, eq. [8]), the income compensation function, $\mu(Q|Q^*, Y^0)$, represents the least amount of the numeraire the individual would require with Q to achieve the same level of utility as with Q^* and Y^0 (Hurwicz and Uzawa 1971). A system of partial differential equations may be derived for various reference levels, Q^*, of Q,

$$\frac{\partial \mu(Q|Q^*,Y)}{\partial Q} = P\,[Q,\mu(Q|Q^*, Y^0)] \quad [1]$$

For a change from Q'' to Q', where $Q'' > Q'$, the Hicksian equivalent measure of the welfare impact upon the individual—in this case, his WTP to avoid the change—is

$$\text{WTP} = \int_{Q'}^{Q''} P\,(Q,\mu(Q|Q', Y^0))\, dQ. \quad [2]$$

The compensating measure for the same change is

$$\text{WTA} = \int_{Q'}^{Q''} P\,(Q,\mu(Q|Q'', Y^0)\, dQ \quad [3]$$

that is, both WTP and WTA are defined as areas under (different) Hicksian compensated demand curves for Q. WTP and WTA may be directly observed using any technique which permits estimation of (relevant points on) the respective indifference surfaces passing through

$$\begin{aligned} U'(Q',Y^0) &= U'(Q'',Y^0 - \text{WTP}), \text{ for WTP and} \\ U''(Q'',Y^0) &= U''(Q',Y^0 + \text{WTA}), \text{ for WTA.} \end{aligned} \quad [4]$$

Because indifference surfaces are not directly observable in the ordinary course of events, estimation methods using this approach necessarily involve the researcher in conscious creation of opportunities to observe [4]. Ideally, markets could be created in which individuals would reveal their Lindahl prices for nonmarketed, nonrival environmental services.[2] But, that ideal thus far has been unattainable. A variety of methods has been proposed and tested in prototype form, each having some but not all of the desirable characteristics of the elusive Lindahl-price-revealing market.

Bishop and Heberlein (1979) established an experimental market in which they purchased away from licensed hunters the right to hunt Canada geese. Real money and real goods (goose permits) changed hands. Within their experimental population, different strata received different-valued offers, to be accepted or rejected. Thus, WTA was not directly observed. However a logit analysis permitted estimation of aggregate consumer's surplus for the experimental population.

Bohm (1972) experimentally observed WTP to watch television programs, examining the effect of various alternative incentives on WTP. Again, money changed hands and the goods were delivered.

Groves and Ledyard (1977) identified, in concept, the general characteristics of "incentive-compatible mechanisms," that is, markets or market-like situations in which each individual's optimal strategy is to reveal his true Lindahl price for nonrival goods.[3] The earlier-circulated Clarke Tax (Tideman and Tullock 1976) is a special case of the more general Groves-Ledyard formulation. In general, these mechanisms will yield true Lindahl prices in situations where real money prices (and the necessary side-taxes) are collected and the goods are delivered.

Unfortunately, most research contexts involving nonrival environmental goods do not permit the goods to be delivered. In these cases, the researcher is confronted with a cruel dilemma: to obtain value data, incentive-compatibility must be sacrificed; alternatively, individual valuations can be "induced" (in effect, the individual is told what his valuation for the good is) and the role of incentive-compatibility in facilitating group agreement about provision of nonrival goods can be explored. To choose the first approach exposes the research to the possibility of obtaining value data distorted by strategic behavior, while to choose the latter sacrifices the goal of gathering value data. Both approaches have been pursued, and the latter approach has generated some evidence which is supportive of the former approach.

During the 1960s, surveys in which respondents were asked if (and sometimes how much) they would be willing to pay for various (carefully, or loosely, defined) environmental amenities gained currency. Among what mostly amounted to rather unimpressive opinion-pollstering, the work of Davis (1963) stood out. During the 1970s, a series of articles (notably, Randall et al. 1974, Brookshire et al. 1980, Schulze et al. 1981) formally developed the conceptual bases and the implementation methods for a direct asking approach consistent with the income compensation function approach to estimating changes in economic surplus. Hypothetical markets are established, in which respondents reveal their valuations of nonrival environmental goods. Such valuations are contingent upon the existence of the hypothetical markets described (hence, the general term, contingent valuation, for this kind of research). Randall preferred to collect value data via an interative bidding routine administered face-to-face, while others (e.g., Hammack and Brown 1974, Gramlich 1977, Bishop and Heberlein 1979) used various one-shot questions (Maximum WTP? Minimum WTA? Would you buy if the price was $\$x$?) in mail surveys.

While contingent valuation methods are not incentive-compatible,[4] there is a body of psychological evidence to the effect that strategic behavior is likely to be encountered only infrequently (Hebert et al. 1979). Smith (1980), working with induced valuations, and using an experimental approach in which various kinds of incentives (some incentive-compatible, and some not) were compared, found that often only a few members of his samples behaved strategically in the absence of incentive-compatibility. Thus, it appears that contingent valuation methods cannot be dismissed simply on the charge of susceptibility to strategic bias.

Following a somewhat different approach, based on the farm production economics tradition of decision analysis under uncertainty (Anderson et al. 1977), Sinden (1974, 1978) estimated indifference curves from which value information for environmental amenities can be generated. While Sinden developed some methods of internally validating his results, it remains true that perfect devices for observing Lindahl prices for goods which cannot be delivered within the experiment are still unavailable.

The Expenditure Function Approach[5]

An alternative formulation of the empirical valuation problem starts with a utility function of the form $U = U(Q,Z)$ (Ch. 2, eq. [6]). Maximizing utility subject to the budget constraint $\sum_i p_i z_i = Y$, generates a set of Marshallian demand functions

$$z_i = z_i\,(\boldsymbol{P},Q,\ \mathrm{Y}) \qquad [5]$$

The possibility that Q is an argument in the demand for private goods suggests that market data—i.e., prices and quantities taken—for z_i may be used to reveal the welfare impact of changes in Q. To explore this possibility, first the theoretical equivalence of the expenditure function and income compensation function approach is established. Then, implementation of the expenditure function approach is considered.

The utility maximization problem yields ordinary demand equations [5]. The dual of the same problem minimizes expenditure, $\sum_i p_i z_i$ subject to the constraint that utility must be at least equal to some specified level, U. Solution of the dual problem yields the expenditure function. Considering a proposed change from Q'' to Q', where $U'(Q',Z) < U''(Q'',Z)$, the relevant expenditure functions are, respectively

$$\begin{aligned} &E'\ (\boldsymbol{P},Q,U'),\ \text{and} \\ &E''\ (\boldsymbol{P},Q,U''). \end{aligned} \qquad [6]$$

The derivative of any expenditure function with respect to any price, p_i, yields a Hicksian compensated demand function for z_i. For the expenditure functions (eq. [6]), the compensated demand functions are

$$\begin{aligned} Z_i^{h'} &= \frac{dE'}{dp_i} = E'_{p_i}\,(\boldsymbol{P},Q,U'),\ \text{and} \\ Z_i^{h''} &= \frac{dE''}{dp_i} = E''_{p_i}\,(\boldsymbol{P},Q,U''). \end{aligned} \qquad [7]$$

The inverse Hicksian compensated demand curves for Q are given by

$$\begin{aligned} -\frac{dE'}{dQ} &= E'_q\,(\boldsymbol{P},Q,U')\ \text{and} \\ -\frac{dE''}{dQ} &= E''_q\,(\boldsymbol{P},Q,U''). \end{aligned} \qquad [8]$$

Thus, the equivalent and compensating measures of the welfare impact of the proposed change are respectively,

$$\text{WTP} = -\int_{Q'}^{Q''} E'_q\,(P,Q,U')\,dQ, \text{ and} \qquad [9]$$

$$\text{WTA} = -\int_{Q'}^{Q''} E''_q\,(P,Q,U'')dQ. \qquad [10]$$

Equation [9] is, of course, equivalent to equation [2], and equation [10] is equivalent to equation [3]. This alternative formulation, however, offers the prospect of empirically estimating WTP and WTA without directly observing (relevant points on) indifference curves in (Q,Y) space. Instead, under favorable conditions, it should be possible to estimate WTP and WTA via appropriate manipulation of readily accessible market data for private goods, z_i, expressed in forms suitable, initially, for estimating [5]. Several techniques have been developed which use this approach. Examples include methods which analyze travel costs incurred in recreation site visits, property values, and hedonic prices.

Now, consider the theoretical prerequisites for successful application of these methods.

If utility functions are separable.—When the utility functions are strongly separable in Q, i.e.,

$$U(Q,Z) = U_z\,(Z) + U_q\,(Q), \qquad [11]$$

the demand functions for z_i will all be of the form

$$z_i = z_i\,(P,Y), \qquad [12]$$

that is, completely independent of the level of Q. Certain commonly used functional forms for utility functions (e.g., the Cobb-Doublas and CES forms) have this property, and Freeman (1979) argued that some important classes of environmental services may in fact be separable. While Freeman mentioned various unpriced amenities of urban living and the option value of unique natural resources, even better examples may be the so-called non-user values (existence and intrinsic values) which, by definition, arise from enjoyment of natural resource services without the simultaneous use of any complementary inputs.

In the case of strong separability, empirical valuation methods based on the expenditure function approach are without any prospects, and valuation is performed via the income compensation approach or not at all.

When utility functions are nonseparable in Z and Q.—In many cases, demands for z_i may not be separable from Q, as in equation [5]. If such a system of demand equations has been estimated, and it satisfies the Slutsky conditions for integrability, it may be possible to solve for the underlying expenditure function. If so, equations [9] and [10] can be estimated and the value of Q at the margin, or the welfare impact of $Q'' - Q'$, can be estimated. Unfortunately, it is generally necessary to impose additional conditions on the problem in order to solve the system completely (Maler 1974). However, there are two kinds of assumptions—each of which is benign, i.e., consistent with reality, in some particular cases—which permit satisfactory solution: weak complementarity, and perfect substitution.

Weak complementarity occurs if, when the quantity z_i demanded is zero, the marginal utility of Q is zero (Maler 1974).[6] In such cases, when Q increases the demand for z_i shifts out, and the value of $Q'' - Q'$ is approximated by the integral between $z_i\,(\boldsymbol{P},Q'',Y)$ and $z_i\,(\boldsymbol{P},Q'\,Y)$, to the extent that the integral between Marshallian demand curves approximates the integral between Hicksian compensated demand curves (Willig 1976, Randall and Stoll 1980).

The assumption of weak complementarity provides the basis for the travel cost method of valuing recreation amenities (Clawson and Knetsch 1966, Stevens 1966, Burt and Brewer 1971) and the land value method of valuing increments in air quality, view quality, and other residential amenities (Freeman 1974, Brown and Pollakowski 1977). It should be noted, however, that Maler (1977) expresses doubts as to whether the weak complementarity assumption is generally satisfied in the housing market and (by extension) in other markets frequently used to provide the basic data for implementation of these methods.

If some good, z_i, can be identified which is a perfect substitute[7] for Q, while Q and $\boldsymbol{Z}^j$ (z_i is not in $\boldsymbol{Z}^j$) are independent in the utility and demand functions, the marginal demand price of Q reduces to the price p_i of z_i multiplied by the substitution ratio between z_i and Q (Maler 1974). If the elasticity of substitution between z_i and Q is less than infinite, this method would underestimate the value of Q.

There are some obvious limitations to the applicability of this concept. First, many kinds of environmental services become policy-relevant simply because they have no good substitutes. Where existing substitutes are markedly expensive, the issue of market clearance must be faced. If the environmental service were unit priced at p_i multiplied by the substitution ratio, would the market clear, i.e., would all of Q be demanded? This must be demonstrated, not merely assumed.

Hedonic prices.—Assume first that z_i and Q are not strongly separable in the utility function. Second, assume that z_i can be defined in terms of a vector of characteristics $\boldsymbol{C}_i = (c_{il},\ldots\ldots,c_{in})$. Third, assume that a purchaser, j, of z_i can vary $\boldsymbol{C}_i$ by choosing a particular unit, z_{ij}. That is, z_i is not the customary homogeneous good, but a class of goods like "house" or "automobile" such that different members of the class may possess different packages of characteristics. Finally, suppose that one of the characteristics in $\boldsymbol{C}_i$ is c_{iq}, the amount of Q enjoyed along with z_i. Therefore, as the consumer selects, for example, a particular house or car, the amount of residential air quality he enjoys along with his house or the amount of safety associated with his car is also determined. For any unit of z_i, say z_{ij}, its price $p_{z_{ij}}$, is

$$p_{z_{ij}} = p_{z_i}\,(c_{ijl},\ldots,c_{ijq},\ldots,c_{ijn}), \qquad [13]$$

where p_{z_i} is the hedonic price function for z_i. If p_{z_i} can be estimated from observation of the prices $p_{z_{ij}}$ and the characteristics c_{ij} of different z_{ij}, then the price of any z_{ik} $(k \neq j)$ can be calculated given knowledge of its characteristics. The implicit price of the characteristic, c_{ijq}, for individual j can be found by differentiation:

$$p_{c_{ijq}} = \frac{dp_{z_i}}{dc_{ijq}} . \qquad [14]$$

Under favorable conditions, it is possible to use information in the implicit price function to identify the demand for c_{iq}, that is, the demand for Q if Q is enjoyed only as a characteristic of z_i. Assume the individual purchases only one unit of z_i (or, if more than one unit, only identical units) and the utility function is separable in z_i and Z^j (z_i is not in Z^j) so that the marginal rate of substitution between any pair of characteristics of z_i is independent of Z^j. Then, depending on the form of the hedonic price function (Rosen 1974), it might be possible to estimate the inverse demand curve[8] for Q. In such a case, the integral between the inverse demand curves for Q'' and Q' would approximate (Willig 1976, Randall and Stoll 1980) the integral between the appropriate Hicksian compensated demand curves.

In the brief period since Rosen's (1974) publication, many attempts to use hedonic price functions in valuing non-marketed goods have been initiated. Applications have included aspects of residential amenities (e.g., Harrison and Rubenfeld 1978, Abelson 1979) and work-place safety (Thaler and Rosen 1975).

Comparing Two Kinds of Empirical Methods

The value estimation methods briefly discussed (and summarized in the Appendix) can be classified into two quite different kinds, those conceptually based on the income compensation function, and those based on the expenditure function. While the formal equivalence of the two conceptual approaches is easily demonstrated, the strengths and weaknesses of the two kinds of empirical valuation methods derived therefrom are almost opposites. Expenditure function approaches start with market-generated price and quantity data for some z_i and, by using various more or less benign assumptions and various more or less contrived mathematical manipulations, may eventually arrive at value estimates for associated nonrival environmental goods. With income compensation approaches, the analysis is usually straightforward and consistent with the relevant theory, but the data come from "markets" which are in some ways contrived and seldom incentive-compatible. Thus, it is not plausible to argue on conceptual grounds that either class of technique is perfect, or that either one should be summarily dismissed in favor of the other.

In every case, the reported applications of these various methods include some kinds of evidence for the success of the undertaking. Plausible value estimates are obtained and, for example, estimates may be replicated within or across studies; or it may be demonstrated that (some of) the variation in individual valuations is explained by estimated economic relationships with robust coefficients of the expected sign. The body of such evidence is quite impressive. There seems little doubt that, in appropriate applications, experimental methods, contingent valuation, travel cost, property value, and hedonic price studies—to name only the more common methods—can cast considerable light on the economic value of nonrival environmental goods.

However, the "crucial experiment"—that is, one which tests a refutable hypothesis to the effect that estimated values are (are not) equal to the real values—is seldom permitted. In this situation, demonstrations that the results obtained with one kind of method are consistent with those of another provide supportive, but not conclusive, evidence of reliability. Various researchers have attempted such comparisons, with considerable success. Knetsch and Davis (1966) and, more recently, Bishop and Heberlein (1979) reported that contingent valuation estimates of WTP for recreational amenities are consistent with those obtained with the travel cost method.[9] Brookshire et al. (1982) reported that contingent valuation estimates of WTP for visual air quality in a residential environment are consistent with hedonic prices estimated from the market in residential land.

It seems that both classes of methods will continue to be used and to be the focus of attempts at improvement and refinement. Among the expenditure function methods, there has been considerable recent progress in hedonic analysis. Recent developments in the theory and application of discrete choice models (Small and Rosen 1981) are suggestive of a new wave of progress.

While it seems likely that economists will always be uneasy with contingent valuation and similar approaches, given their lack of incentive-compatibility, they probably will be used increasingly. For recreation benefit evaluation in the context of federal water resource projects, the contingent valuation method has been approved, along with the travel cost method (U.S. Water Resources Council 1979). Further, there are many valuation contexts in which there is currently no available option representing the expenditure function approaches: e.g., where the levels of provision of Q under consideration go beyond the currently observable range; where the relationship between z_i and Q in consumption cannot be satisfactorily rendered in a model capable of solution for consumer's surplus values of Q; and where—the extreme example of the problem just mentioned—Z and Q are strongly separable in the utility and demand functions. In cases like this, income compensation function approaches remain feasible. For example, Greenley et al. (1981) used contingent valuation methods to estimate the option price of preventing an irreversible degradation of in-stream water quality.

Literature Cited

Abelson, P. W. 1979. Property prices and the value of amenities. Journal of Environmental Economics and Management 6:11-28.

Anderson, J. R., J. L. Dillon, and J. B. Hardaker. 1977. Agricultural Decision Analysis. Iowa State University Press, Ames, Ia.

Bishop, R. C., and T. Heberlein. 1979. Measuring values of extra-market goods: Are indirect measures biased? American Journal of Agricultural Economics 61:926-930.

Bohm, P. 1972. Estimating demands for public goods: An experiment. European Economic Review 3:111-130.
Brookshire, D. S., A. Randall, and J. R. Stoll. 1980. Valuing increments and decrements in natural resource service flows. American Journal of Agricultural Economics 63:478-488.
Brookshire, D. S., M. A. Thayer, W. D. Schulze, and R. C. d'Arge. 1982. Valuing public goods: A comparison of survey and hedonic approaches. American Economic Review. 72:165-77
Brown, G. M., and H. O. Pollakowski. 1977. Economic valuation of shoreline. Review of Economics and Statistics 69:273-278.
Burt, O. R., and D. Brewer. 1971. Evaluation of net social benefits from outdoor recreation. Econometrica 39:813-827.
Clawson, M., and J. L. Knetsch. 1966. Economics of outdoor recreation. Johns Hopkins University Press, Baltimore, Md.
Davis, R. K. 1963. Recreation planning as an economic problem. Natural Resources Journal 3:239-249.
Freeman, A. M. 1974. On estimating air pollution control benefits from land value studies. Journal of Environmental Economics and Management 1:74-83.
Freeman, A. M. 1979. Approaches to measuring public goods demands. American Journal of Agricultural Economics 61:915-20.
Gramlich, R. W. 1977. The demand for clean water: The case of the Charles River. National Tax Journal 30:183-194.
Greenley, D. A., R. G. Walsh, and R. A. Young. 1981. Option value: Empirical evidence from a case study of recreation and water quality. Quarterly Journal of Economics 95:657-673.
Groves, T. E., and J. Ledyard. 1977. Optimal allocation of public goods: A solution to the free-rider problem. Econometrica 45:783-809.
Hammack, J., and G. M. Brown. 1974. Waterfowl and wetlands: Towards bioeconomic analysis. Johns Hopkins University Press, Baltimore, Md.
Harrison, D., and D. Rubenfeld. 1978. Hedonic housing prices and the demand for clean air. Journal of Environmental Economics and Management 5:81-102.
Hebert, J., R. Shikiar, and R. Perry. 1979. Valuing environment via bidding games: A psychological perspective. Battelle Pacific Northwest Laboratory, Richland, Wash.
Hurwicz, L., and H. Uzawa. 1971. On the integrability of demand functions. *In* Preferences, Utility and Demand. J. S. Chipman et al., editors. Harcourt Brace Javanovich, New York, N.Y.
Knetsch, J. L., and R. K. Davis. 1966. Comparisons of methods for recreation evaluation. *In* Water Research, A. V. Kneese and S. C. Smith (eds.). Johns Hopkins University Press, Baltimore, Md.
Maler, K.-G. 1977. A note on the use of property values in estimating marginal willingness to pay for environmental quality. Journal of Environmental Economics and Management 4:355-369.
Maler, K.-G. 1974. Environmental economics: A theoretical inquiry. Johns Hopkins University Press, Baltimore, Md.
Meyer, P. A. 1979. Publicly vested values for fish and wildlife: Criteria for economic welfare and interface with the law. Land Economics 55.

Randall, A., B. C. Ives, and C. Eastman. 1974. Bidding games for valuation of aesthetic environmental improvements. Journal of Environmental Economics and Management 1:132-149.
Randall, A., and J. R. Stoll. 1980. Consumer's surplus in commodity space. American Economic Review 70:449-455.
Rosen, S. 1974. Hedonic prices and implicit markets: Product differentiation in pure competition. Journal of Political Economy 82:34-55.
Schulze, W. D., R. D. d'Arge, and D. S. Brookshire. 1981. Valuing environmental commodities: Some recent experiments. Land Economics 57:151-172.
Sinden, J. A. 1978. Estimation of consumer's surplus values for land policies. Australian Journal of Agricultural Economics 22:175-193.
Sinden, J. A. 1974. A utility approach to the valuation of aesthetic and recreational experiences. American Journal of Agricultural Economics 56:61-72.
Small, K. A., and H. S. Rosen. 1981. Applied welfare economics with discrete choice models. Econometrica 49:105-130.
Smith, V. L. 1980. Experiments with a decentralized mechanism for public good decisions. American Economic Review 70:584-599.
Stevens, J. B. 1966. Recreation benefits from water pollution control. Water Resources Research 2:167-182.
Thaler, R. H., and S. Rosen. 1975. The value of saving a life: A market estimate. *In* National Bureau of Economic Research Studies in Income and Wealth 40, N. Terleckyj, editor.
Tideman, T. N., and G. Tullock. 1976. A new and superior process for making public choices. Journal of Political Economy 84:1145-1159.
U.S. Water Resources Council. 1979. Procedures for evaluation of national economic development benefits and costs in water resources planning (level c): Final rule. Federal Register 44 (242, Part ix) December 14.
Willig, R. D. 1976. Consumer's surplus without apology. American Economic Review 66:587-597.

Footnotes

[1]Randall, Chapter 2.

[2]*Because nonrival goods are, by definition, available in the same quantity for all once provided for any, ordinary prices will not efficiently allocate these goods. Lindahl prices are individualized prices which, for each consumer of a nonrival good, represent his money-valued marginal utility for the good (or, his consumer's surplus from its consumption). If each member of the community paid his Lindahl price for a nonrival good, and the aggregate payments covered the costs of providing it, the good could be provided in a way which leaves no one worse off.*

[3]*Incentive-compatible mechanisms typically use a complex system of taxes designed to make true revelation of preferences the least-cost strategy for the individual. Thus, each will voluntarily pay his Lindahl price, ensuring efficiency in the market for a nonrival good.*

[4]*The absence of incentive-compatibility means the absence of a powerful incentive to respond truthfully. Perhaps the term "incentive-perverse" could be used to suggest powerful incentives to respond untruthfully. "Incentive-neutral" would then suggest no in-built incentives for or against truth-telling. Presumably, an individual with a positive*

but weak preference for truth-telling would respond truthfully to an incentive-neutral contingent valuation device.

While few contingent valuation devices have been developed which are truly incentive-compatible, many lie somewhere between incentive-neutrality and incentive-compatibility.

[5]*This section makes considerable use of Freeman's (1979) excellent review.*

[6]*Examples frequently noted in the literature include: if a recreational site is not visited, no utility is derived from the trip; if one does not fish in a certain lake, one does not care about the quality of the water therein; unless one owns residential land in a particular several-block neighborhood, one does not care about the quality of amenities there. These examples suggest that weak complementarity may often be a serviceable assumption, but that the analyst should be alert for violations.*

[7]*Examples of substitutes include: dredging and sediment control; wetlands and sewage treatment works; pollution removal and effluent control. Again, the analyst should be alert for the possibility that substitution is less than perfect.*

[8]*If the hedonic price function is linear, it is not possible to identify an inverse demand curve for Q. However, the marginal implicit price can be interpreted as marginal WTP for small changes in Q. If the hedonic price function is nonlinear, identification of the inverse demand curve for Q depends on model specification and functional form.*

[9]*There does appear to be a problem, however, with contingent valuation estimates of WTA, in cases where compensation for diminished amenities seems "fair" but is nevertheless not customary (see Bishop and Heberlein 1979, and Meyer 1979).*

APPENDIX: A Listing and Classification of Mainstream Methods of Valuing Non-Marketed Goods and Services

Method	Areas of Application
Income Compensation Approach	
Experiments: buy or sell	Exclusive goods and services, e.g., Hunting licenses. (Bohm, Bishop and Heberlein).
Experiments with induced preferences	Testing of the performance of various market structures for nonrival goods, e.g., incentive-compatible, incentive-neutral, etc. (Bohm, Smith).
Contingent Valuation	
1. Willingness to pay, accept a) mail survey, group administration or personal interview b) single question, iterative bidding, checklist or payment card.	Application unlimited, but reliability depends in part on realism (Brookshire et al. 1980, 1982, Davis, Hammack and Brown, Gramlich, Greenley et al., Meyer, Randall et al., Schulze et al.).

APPENDIX: A Listing and Classification of Mainstream Methods of Valuing Non-marketed Goods and Services—Continued

Method	Areas of Application
2. Willingness to buy, sell a) mail survey, group administration or personal interview b) state price and seek buy/not buy or sell/not sell response.	(Bishop and Heberlein).
3. Utility function estimation	(Sinden)
Expenditure Function Approaches	
Travel Cost	Access to sites for, e.g., recreation (Burt and Brewer, Clawson and Knetsch, Stevens).
Property Value	Amenity values, e.g., air quality, water quality, noise abatement, view amenities (Abelson, Brown and Pollakowski, Freeman 1974, Harrison and Rubenfeld, Maler).
Hedonic	Amenity values, where amenity level can be conceptualized as characteristic of a marketed good (Abelson, Brown and Pollakowski, Harrison and Rubenfeld, Rosen, Thaler and Rosen).
Cost of the least-cost Alternative	Where least-cost alternative is a perfect substitute for an environmental good.

Chapter 5
Land Market Theory and Methodology in Wildland Management

Alex Anas

Introduction

This paper provides an analysis of the application of land market theory and methodology to the valuation of prices and unpriced benefits obtainable from wildlands as a result of public land management policies and strategies. First, concepts of land market theory and methodology are reviewed: what it is, how it has been applied within urban economics, and land economics in general and how it relates to questions of wildland allocation, management, and benefit evaluation. This review is intended to familiarize the reader with the scope of land market theory and methodology. Second, the relationship between determining the price of wildlands and the social benefits of wildland programs is discussed. It is demonstrated that the accurate measurement of land price changes must precede the evaluation of the social and other benefits of wildland programs. Third, innovative public strategies and policies for wildland management and allocation are examined. They revolve around the issue of how to use land value taxation to provide cost efficient management and allocation of wildlands.

In the context of this paper "wildland" refers to land areas of any size which are in a natural or undeveloped state while having many potential uses such as mineral exploration and excavation, agricultural, forestry, rangeland, recreational development, urban development, preservation as scenic wildland or wildlife habitat, etc. Although some wildland in the United States may be privately owned, most is owned by state or federal government. Because of the predominance of government ownership and control, the management of public wildlands affects the value and future development potential of privately owned wildlands, of agricultural and urban lands, and of the welfare of society in general, and specifically the users of wildland such as certain groups of recreationists, hunters, etc.

Government control over wildlands can take many forms. The government can sell certain wildland parcels or acquire privately owned land parcels in order to promote their return to a wild state. In other words the government may have a policy of diminishing or augmenting the available supply of public wildlands. Sale of public wildland is a policy which raises a complex set of questions. How much public wildland should be sold to private owners? Which parcels should be sold? At what price should the parcels be sold? What restrictions, if any, should be placed on the development of the sold parcels? Is it preferable to sell or to lease these parcels? Is it preferable that the government itself participate in the development or commercial/economic exploitation of these parcels?

In addition to these questions a different set of questions concerning the sale policy also can be raised. How will the sale of public wildlands and their subsequent development affect the use of these lands and the use of other lands still in a wild state? How will the sale of public wildlands influence the price and development of adjoining or competing lands in private uses such as agriculture, urban, commercial, or wild?

These questions are relevant, not only in the case of the sale of public wildlands, but also in any other public program influencing the disposition and modification of these lands. These answers are essential for an accurate benefit/cost analysis and evaluation of wildland programs.

This is not meant to imply that the government should engage in a widespread policy of wildland sales. However, any decision regarding public wildlands, including keeping them in the public domain, requires detailed knowledge of the opportunity cost of such a decision. This can be ascertained only by asking: What would happen if these lands were in the free market instead of in the public domain? If, after answering this question, it is decided that the relevant lands should be in the free market, this still does not mean that the lands should actually be sold. It could mean instead that the relevant public agency should imitate the market and treat the land the same way it would be treated in the market, except when there are significant other factors which call for special treatment.

This chapter is organized into six major sections. The first section reviews the scope and purpose of land market theory as developed by agricultural and urban economists and points out its usefulness within the framework of wildland valuation, management, and allocation. The second section discusses the arithmetic involved in the computation of the price of a wildland parcel, based on the net present worth concept. The use of this concept for land use sequences, cases involving multiple uses with and without externalities, and the role of uncertainty are discussed. The third section discusses how land price changes in wildland and adjoining, non-wildland parcels must enter the computation of traditional valuation and benefit measures such as consumer or producer surplus. It is argued that neglecting this practice can result in gross errors in the determination of the total benefits of a wildland management program. The fourth section reviews hedonic estimation (via multivariate regression analysis) and linear programming models of land allocation as two methods for estimating the market price and allocation patterns of wildland areas. The fifth section discusses the use of publicly owned wildlands as land banks and points out the applicability of value capture and joint development policy as a means for recapturing the costs of certain public investments in wildlands which increases the prices of adjoining land parcels. Finally, in the last section, the major conclusions of this chapter are summarized and recommendations for data collection and future research are outlined.

Land Market Theory and Its Relevance to Wildland Valuation, Management and Allocation

Land market theory begins with the work of von Thunen (1826) who attempted to explain the workings of an agricultural land market. Much later, Alonso (1964) extended von Thunen's theory to the urban land market in an effort to explain the structure of land prices and land use densities in an idealized urban form. Alonso's work is roughly contemporaneous with that of Muth (1969) and Mills (1967) who extended land market theory to a general equilibrium context in which the interaction of several land use sectors, such as manufacturing, housing and transportation, are examined in detail. During the 1970s, the work begun by Mills gained wide recognition, and the field of urban economics achieved maturity because of numerous contributions to land use and land market theory.

Land market theory aims to achieve three objectives. First, it is a conceptual structure designed to explain and predict the prices of various land parcels in a land market in a way which takes into account the location and various other characteristics of those parcels. For example, agricultural land market theory will predict the price of a parcel of farmland as a function of that parcel's location relative to major markets, the soil's fertility, the cost of transporting materials to and from the farm, etc. Second, land market theory will explain and predict the type of land use under certain market conditions. In this context, agricultural land market theory will explain why certain parcels are observed to be in corn cultivation while others are in wheat cultivation and still others remain uncultivated. Urban land market theory will explain why certain areas of a city are residential while others are commercial, and why the density of development measured in floor space per acre terms declines as one moves away from major urban centers. Thus, land market theory will explain or predict changes in land prices, land uses, and land use intensities (or densities) over periods of time. Agricultural land market theory should be able to explain certain crop rotation patterns and changes in cultivation patterns, while urban land market theory should explain certain patterns of urban redevelopment, such as the transition of land from agricultural to suburban housing to high density urban to commercial etc. In summary, the goals of land market theory are to explain and predict the price, use, development density of land parcels and changes in price, use, and density over time.

The past two decades of research and theoretical development in land market theory have yielded many useful findings which are too lengthy to be reviewed here. Nevertheless, the basic assumptions and findings (or propositions) of land market theory can be usefully summarized before examining applicability of these results to wildland issues.

There are some basic assumptions of land market theory. It is assumed that the land market is perfectly competitive, which means that there are many landowners each controlling a parcel of land or land holdings of several parcels which are small compared to all the land in the market. Perfect competition also implies that there are many buyers competing for the purchase of land parcels. In this respect, land market theory does not differ from any other economic market theory in which there are many buyers and sellers. An important difference is that each parcel in the land market is essentially a unique commodity different from any other parcel because of its location and other characteristics. Even though unique, each land parcel easily can be substituted with many other parcels. This assures a perfectly competitive land market.

Starting with the above assumptions, land market theory obtains several results. First, it is concluded that each seller (landowner) will sell his land parcel to the highest bidding buyer. Second, each buyer, because of competition with other buyers, is forced to bid the maximum possible amount that he can afford per acre of land. Third, and by implication of the first result, each land parcel is allocated to the highest bidding use. Fourth, and by implication of the second result, the market price of each parcel is equal to the highest possible amount that can be afforded for that parcel. In other words, the land use that is willing to bid (pay) the highest possible amount for a land parcel is the use that will occupy that parcel in a competitive market equilibrium outcome. The only way one land use can displace (or replace) another land use at a given location is if economic changes enable the replacing use to raise its bid price above that of the replaced use. The above results comprise the principle of economic efficiency as embodied in land market theory.

Another important result established in land market theory deals with the presence of externalities such as congestion in traffic, pollution, neighborhood externalities, etc. It has been shown that when such externalities are present, there is still a competitive market equilibrium which obeys all of the above properties. Each land parcel is still allocated to the highest bidder. The only problem caused by externalities is that this competitive equilibrium is not Pareto-efficient, whereas if there are no externalities, then the competitive equilibrium is Pareto-efficient. This result is just a reflection of a similar result from general economic theory. Land market theory also demonstrates that when externalities do exist, controls such as tolls, taxes, zoning ordinances, etc., must be imposed on the market so that when the market operates subject to these controls, a Pareto-efficient equilibrium is achieved. Public ownership of some land is one way to control the land so as to achieve a Pareto-optimum. In many cases, much simpler controls, such as taxation or zoning, can be found.

To see how land market (or bid rent) theory is useful for examining questions related to wildlands, we may imagine a hypothetical land price profile in a region centered around a city. Land prices are highest at the CBD (the downtown or central place of the area) and decline as one moves away from the CBD toward the suburban areas. This decline occurs because land uses located away from the CBD have lower bid rents than land uses located near it, because they must incur higher costs of transportation to and from the CBD. Just beyond the suburban center, the highest bidding uses are agricultural. Further away from the center of the region, land is in a wild state with a price of zero, because there is no land use that can afford a positive price for land at those locations. Thus, these land parcels are in their natural (uncultivated, undeveloped) states. Private landowners in a competitive market would rent or sell their lands to the highest bidding use. Thus, a privately owned land parcel would not be observed to be in a wild state unless its price is indeed zero (i.e., no non-wild use can pay a positive price for it now or in the foreseeable future). The same is not true for publicly owned wildland parcels. If the governments owning these parcels manage them solely on the basis of efficiency of the the competitive land market, they would follow a strategy of holding only those parcels the price of which is indeed zero and selling or renting the remaining parcels to the highest bidding use. Alternatively, the government could hold these lands but develop them in their "best" (i.e., highest bid) use, thereby imitating the behavior of the highest bidding land use. In reality various public welfare and political considerations prevent governments from following a strategy of land market efficiency. Therefore, much of the wildlands held in the public interest have a positive price, implying that they have some present or future development value.

It should be emphasized that in a simple two-dimensional illustration, only one attribute, distance from the CBD influences the price of land. Including many attributes, changes nothing about the principle. For example, if the natural beauty of the land increases greatly as one moves away from the city, or if there are spots of beauty, or environmental amenities, prices will be higher around these locations. In principle it is even possible that prices in some wild areas, kept for future development will be higher than prices in some of the developed areas. Once attributes other than distance are introduced, land prices need not decline with distance. However, the pattern of land prices which decline with distance is quite commonly observed due to the importance of transportation cost.

There are three types of publicly held wildland parcels. In general, there are some wildland parcels, the price of which is truly zero. These are those parcels which at the current time have no foreseeable development potential. Society suffers no cost if such parcels are held in the public interest. There is a second category of wildland parcels, the price of which is not zero, reflecting a future development potential for such parcels. These are those parcels which are currently wild but if released to the market would become developed at some future date. Their price is the present value of their expected future development. Society suffers an economic inefficiency if these parcels are still kept wild beyond the future date when they would be developed. The third category is those parcels which have been held out of the market beyond the date when they should have been developed. Clearly, such parcels have a positive price in general, because there are profits to be made in developing them even after the optimal date. For this third category of parcels, it should be determined whether the opportunity cost of postponing or forever ruling out their development is justified by the flow of the social services these parcels provide in their wild state. This question is central to wildland management and provides the crux of a benefit cost analysis approach to evaluating any program dealing with the disposition of wildland parcels.

The presence of externalities affecting the development of certain wild parcels does not necessarily mean that such parcels should not be developed.

Rather, the presence of certain externalities simply means that those parcels can be developed efficiently only if their development, whether done by the private market or the public agency, is properly controlled (taxes, zoned, etc.), so as to assure Pareto-efficiency.

Land market theory does not imply that all wildlands which are visited and used by people at their expense should be developed. Clearly, there are wildland areas which are visited by people for hunting, fishing, recreation, etc. While it may be true that people would pay a fee to visit these lands, and while great benefits may be derived by the visitors, it may not be economical to put any development on these lands because the profit that would be made from any such development may not be positive, given the costs of the development. If it is positive and the land is privately owned, it would be clearly developed unless it is more profitable (in present value) to develop the same land in the future. Development should be defined very generally. For example, fencing a piece of land and placing a ticket booth for entering and using it constitutes development. But even this simple type of development sometimes can be unprofitable in a free market. People from a city can travel long distances to use and enjoy wildlands, but such land may be not developed because it is deemed that its development will yield negative profits, even though it can yield substantial benefits measurable as a consumer surplus.

Land market theory remains unincorporated into natural resource economics. A well known book in this area is by Krutilla and Fisher (1975). It is evident from this book that resource economics has not been influenced by developments coming after those of Ely and Wehrwein (1940) such as the works of Alonso (1964), Mills (1967), and Muth (1969). The popular perspective adopted by natural resource economists is to treat public lands as public goods and to apply the economic analysis of public production as developed by Musgrave (1959) and others. If appropriately viewed, this perspective is entirely compatible with land market theory. To see this, consider a wildland area where certain recreational services are produced by the appropriate public agency. The benefits generated from such public production should be greater than the benefits that could have been generated by private (market) production. However, this probably is not true for all publicly owned wildlands. In particular, if there are no externalities and the market is competitive, then there is no economic reason for public instead of private ownership. The public goods/public production approach, therefore, is just one way of dealing with externalities. The opportunity costs of public production are manifest in private production. They must be computed by asking "what would occur if the land was in private production?" Then the land would be in the highest bidding private production use, and the economic surplus generated in this situation should be compared to the economic surplus generated from public production. If there are no externalities and the market is competitive, it should not be possible that public production can do better than private production. If there are externalities, then public production may be one way of doing better.

An aspect of land market theory which is not embraced by natural resource economists is general equilibrium land market analysis. Introduced by Mills (1967), general equilibrium analysis is now an integral part of land market theory. The basic error that resource economists make when they ignore general equilibrium analysis is to fail to measure the impact of wildland management programs on the adjacent land markets. In contrast to this, urban and agricultural land economists normally examine these impacts (at least in theory). A wildland management program normally will influence adjacent economies and land markets. The total economic surplus benefit measure should include the benefits which occur in the adjacent lands.

Determination of the Price of Wildlands

In the preceding section, the price of a land parcel was defined as the highest possible amount that any land use in a competitive market could afford to pay for that parcel. The maximum amount that a land use could afford to pay is that amount which absorbs all of that land use's profits from maintaining the land in that use. Thus, in a competitive market, landowners can set prices which are high enough to absorb all profits which result from the development of a particular land parcel.

This definition of land price can be made more precise by taking into account the role of time. The profits from a land development do not occur instantaneously, but instead, are distributed in the form of monthly or annual cash flows. Thus, the price of a land parcel at any given point in time must equal the present value of the stream of profits that can be realized from that parcel beginning with the current point in time. If this principle is followed then the bid price for any land parcel can be computed by knowing the sequence of land uses that will occupy that parcel, the revenues and costs that will be incurred during each time period, and an appropriate money discount rate or interest rate for discounting future profits. The "present value of profits" is also referred to as the "net present worth."

The Net Present Worth Concept for a Single Use

To demonstrate the arithmetic involved in the application of the "net present worth" (NPW) concept, first consider the simplest case: that of a wildland parcel which is placed into a non-wild use at the present time period and is expected to remain in that use forever. Let Π_{it} denote the profits that result from the land parcel in use i in year t. Then,

$$\Pi_{it} = R_{it} - C_{it} \qquad [1]$$

where R_{it} is the revenue from keeping the parcel in use i in year t, and C_{it} is the cost of keeping the parcel in use i in year t. For example, if the ith use is "forestry", then R_{it} denotes the revenues generated from an annual harvest, and C_{it} denotes the cost of cultivating, maintaining and preserving the forest during year t. Assuming that the interest rate is denoted by r, "the present value of profits" or "the net present worth" at the current time is,

$$\mathrm{NPW_i} = \Pi_{i0} + \frac{\Pi_{i1}}{(1+r)} + \frac{\Pi_{i2}}{(1+r)^2} + \ldots$$

$$= \sum_{t=0}^{\infty} \frac{\Pi_{it}}{(1+r)^t} = \sum_{t=0}^{\infty} \frac{R_{it} - C_{it}}{(1+r)^t} . \qquad [2]$$

The quantity NPW_i is the "net present worth" of the land parcel which results from placing this parcel into the ith use, and thus the price that would be paid for this parcel in a competitive market situation by the competitive developers of the ith use. Any such developer who wishes to occupy the parcel must forego all future profits (i.e., accept zero or normal profits) by paying the net present worth of these profits to the current landowner.

Net Present Worth With Land Use Sequences

The example given is not very realistic, because it assumed that the land parcel would remain in the same use for perpetuity. In reality, the development of a wildland parcel can involve sequential switching of the parcel from one use to another over time, assuming that there are no multiple uses of the parcel during the same time period. The case of multiple uses at the same time is examined in the next subsection.

Some possible sequences for initially wildland parcels may be the following:

(1) wild - forestry
(2) wild - forestry - mining
(3) wild - forestry - recreational development
(4) wild - forestry - recreational development - commercial development.

In sequence (1), the land parcel is initially in a wild state. Although the parcel may contain valuable timber resources, there is no cultivation of these resources by private or public uses. Eventually, the parcel becomes ripe for development, and organized timber production ensues. This can happen at a future time when the price of timber increases sufficiently or the cost of harvesting or transporting the harvested timber decreases. In other words, a switch to timber production occurs at such time as the forestry use becomes profitable but not before then.

In the second sequence, the increased demand for timber may encourage extensive harvests until a point is reached where the exploitation of the parcel for mineral extraction is more profitable. Alternatively, the switch may occur because the market price of mineral products has increased so much that foregoing the remaining timber production potential becomes feasible in view of the heightened mineral production revenues, and the switch to mineral production occurs even though some future timber production potential still remains. It is assumed that mineral extraction requires clearing of all forests prior to such extraction, but this may not always be the case. Cases where this is not necessarily true will be discussed in the next subsection.

In the third sequence, a land parcel is eventually allocated to timber production, but in view of increasing demands for on-site recreation, it is allocated to recreational development at a later date. At such a date, the exploitation of the forest for timber stops and its development for recreational enjoyment begins.

Finally, in the fourth sequence, recreational development is followed by commercial development, because excessive urbanization pressures around the site increase the rent paying ability or bid price of hotels, motels, and other commercial activities.

Many other sequences not elaborated on here can be constructed and discussed. The key point is that each sequence involves one or more switches from one land use to another more profitable land use. At the time of switching, the current value of profits from the new (replacing) land use (or the remaining part of the sequence) must exceed the present value of profits that would be derived were the old (replaced) land use or any other land use to continue for the foreseeable future.

To give an example of the land price calculations for the case of a land use sequence, consider the case of wildland followed by forestry. Suppose that the switch to forestry is to take place in the third period. Then the net present worth of the sequence s is,

$$NPW_s = \frac{R_{i3} - C_{i3}}{(1+r)^3} + \frac{R_{i4} - C_{i4}}{(1+r)^4} + \ldots, \qquad [3]$$

where i denotes the forestry use, R denotes annual revenues, and C denotes annual costs, the costs and revenues of the wildland use in the first two periods being zero. If a switch from forestry to recreational development is to occur in the fifth period, then the net present worth of such a sequence s is,

$$NPW_s = \frac{R_{i3} - C_{i3}}{(1+r)^3} + \frac{R_{i4} - C_{i4}}{(1+r)^4} + \frac{R_{j5} - C_{j5}}{(1+r)^5} + \frac{R_{j6} - C_{j6}}{(1+r)^6} \qquad [4]$$

That the switch to recreational development occurs in the fifth period automatically implies,

$$\frac{R_{j5} - C_{j5}}{(1+r)^5} + \frac{R_{j6} - C_{j6}}{(1+r)^6} + \ldots \geqq \frac{R_{i5} - C_{i5}}{(1+r)^5} + \frac{R_{i6} - C_{i6}}{(1+r)^6} + \ldots. \qquad [5]$$

where j denotes recreational development (the replacing use) and i denotes forestry (the replaced use). That the switch does not occur in the fourth period implies

$$\frac{R_{j4} - C_{j4}}{(1+r)^4} + \frac{R_{j5} - C_{j5}}{(1+r)^5} + \ldots \leqq \frac{R_{i4} - C_{i4}}{(1+r)^4} + \frac{R_{i5} - C_{i5}}{(1+r)^5} + \ldots. \qquad [6]$$

From the above discussion the following pricing principle emerges. The "best use" of a wildland parcel and the price of that best use can be determined by enumerating all possible land use sequences for that parcel, the revenues and costs for each year in each sequence, and then selecting the land use sequence with the highest net present worth.

Contemporaneous Multiple Uses of a Land Parcel and Externalities

The preceding discussion of land use sequences applies only to cases where each land parcel is in only one use at any given time but is switched from one land use to another over time (such as from year to year). This is not always the case, because two or more land uses can coexist in a parcel at a given time. For example, the parcel may be used for recreation during the winter and for limited forestry during the summer. In this case, because the two land uses alternate within a year, they may be considered to be coexisting in a time framework where the unit time period is the year. Another type of coexistence occurs when two land uses occupy adjacent locations. For example, commercial fishing and water recreation may be jointly pursued on a river and its banks. The very nature of these activities is such that the definition of parcels cannot be designed so as to have only fishing or only water recreation on any given parcel. Instead, it may be preferable to consider the land and water involved in these activities as an input in a joint production process involving two outputs, "fishing" and "water recreation". The principle of land price determination is not affected by this situation. The price of the parcel would still be the present worth of the stream of net profits from the parcel resulting from the combined fishing and recreation uses. The only difficulty may be that the joint production function is more complex than the single production functions for fishing and water recreation. It is probably the case, in this example, that fishing and water recreation are competitive with each other. Therefore, a parcel in joint use can produce less fishing than could be produced if that parcel were devoted strictly to fishing and less water recreation than would be produced if it were devoted strictly to water recreation. In contrast, the net profits from the joint use may be higher than the net profits from any single use, thus requiring that the parcel remain in the "highest bidding" joint use. The competitiveness or interference between the two uses may be simply a result of land scarcity, because some of the land must be devoted to fishing facilities, less land will be available for recreation facilities. But the interference can also be the result of an externality, the pleasurability of water recreation is diminished because of the presence of large numbers of fishing craft.

An externality occurs whenever one land use places an unpriced cost or burden on another land use situated on the same or an adjoining parcel. For example, mining activity in a certain parcel may diminish the aesthetic value or recreational enjoyment that can be derived from adjacent parcels. In such a case, to determine the price of an adjacent parcel, the presence of the mining activity in the nearby parcel must be considered, because it may affect the profitability of adjacent parcels in other uses. Thus, when positive or negative externalities are present, it is generally infeasible to compute the land price of each parcel by treating it in isolation from its neighboring parcels. Rather, a larger region which contains all the externalities must be defined, and the land prices of each parcel within this region must be determined by noting that the net profits of the different parcels are interdependent.

Another important way in which externalities enter the problem of wildland pricing is through the interdependence between wild and adjoining non-wild lands. For example, a wilderness area used for water recreation, hiking, camping, canoeing, etc., may be adjacent to a small urban center and a surrounding agricultural area. Expansion of the various recreation activities in the wilderness area will have a generally positive effect on the economy of the small urban center, creating new land developments in hotels, motels, parking and other commercial establishments oriented towards the recreationists. In addition to these positive externalities, negative externalities such as noise, pollution, etc., from the increased number of visitors, and some taking of agricultural land may be expected. Land prices in the urban center and the adjacent agricultural area will inevitably change. This leads to another important principle. This principle states that when a particular wildland parcel or larger area is considered, the surrounding non-wild land which serves as the "spillover" or "externality shed" of the wild area must be considered.

The Role of Expectations and Uncertainty

Any net present worth calculation requires substantial information about the future stream of costs and revenues. Bidders and developers do not know all the detail that appears in the arithmetic, but they intuitively estimate or speculate on the net present worth of any given parcel. If the market is truly competitive and the spirit of entrepreneurship keen, then good (or market-wise) developers do a successful estimation of the net present worth of parcels on which they bid. Some less experienced developers take a risk and overbid, while those who are risk-averse fail to bid enough and are culled out of the market. Those who overbid are also culled out eventually as they experience negative profits. In an intensely competitive market, only the market-wise developers or speculators (bidders) remain. It may be said of these bidders that they have accurate expectations of the future, which means that they can anticipate net present worths without getting bogged down in the detailed computations that would be undertaken from the analytical point of view. Expectations of the future take into account not only the net present worth when this is fairly straightforward to compute, but also when future costs and revenues are highly uncertain, as they frequently are.

Two types of uncertainty must be distinguished. The first is the pure uncertainty about the future. For example, the price of timber or the costs of timber farming five years from now cannot be known with certainty, simply because the future is always unpredictable to some degree. In such cases, one may conceive of an "expected price of timber five years from now" and proceed to calculate this using probability distributions. This approach is tenuous at best, because often the probability distributions themselves are unknown and must be subjectively estimated.

The second type of uncertainty refers to an inherent lack of knowledge about the physical properties of the land parcels even at the current time. A good example of this type of uncertainty can be encountered in the case of mineral exploration and excavation. Typically one is not fully knowledgeable about the type, richness, extent, and extraction costs associated with mineral deposits. The land use activity of mineral exploration is intended to incur costs in the hope of obtaining better information about the nature of the hidden deposits and thus reducing the uncertainty involved. Determining the bid price for a parcel's use in mineral exploration or extraction is complex and requires careful expected value calculations and highly subjective probability distributions. This may be an area in which there is no large number of market-wise entrepreneurs and in which the possibility for error is substantial.

Land Prices and the Social Benefits of Wildland Management Programs

Traditionally applied economists set out to measure the benefits of public investments or public management programs by evaluating the demand for the products and services created by these investments or programs and subsequently deriving appropriate measures of user utility (or benefit) from the evaluated demand. The best known and most commonly used such measures are the "consumer surplus" and "producer surplus" measures which purport to be measures of consumer utility in monetary terms or producer profit derived by making certain restrictive assumptions about the shape of the consumer's utility function.

If a market is truly competitive, what is called "producer's surplus" is absorbed as land rent (Mishan, 1968). But if the market is not fully competitive, then land rent can be less than profit, and the remaining part of profit can be called a "producer surplus." Thus, markets are competitive, then total economic surplus can be measured in two parts as "consumer surplus" and "land rent." If the market is not fully competitive, then three parts are needed: "consumer surplus," "producer surplus", and "land rent."

The application of consumer surplus benefit measures to wildland products and services is straight-forward. The demand function for the proposed individual or joint wildland uses such as water recreation, fishing, hiking, etc., must be measured. Measuring the demand in this context means determining the functional relationship between the number of visitors or visitor-hours at a wildland site and all the attributes and prices of the site. The demand function for the site must be a multidimensional (or multiattribute) function, otherwise demand responsiveness can be measured only partially and very naively. To illustrate how this sort of analysis should be done, an example follows.

The Boundary Waters Canoe Area (BWCA) consists of 2 million acres of federally held land and lakes in northern Minnesota, used heavily by recreationists who enter and exit this system at nearly 70 points, controlled by the U.S. Forest Service. A management objective of the Forest Service is to control the extent of congestion that occurs within the lake system and presumably maximize the consumer surplus of the users of the system. This can be done by allocating and distributing campsites within the system, by imposing entrance fees at certain entrance sites, by imposing quotas on the frequency of visitors at certain entrance sites (this is the implemented alternative), or by opening new entrance sites.

Consider the last alternative. If this is done, certain land developments will occur in the area around the new entrance site. Land prices there will increase, and certain industries such as lodging, canoe rental, parking concessions, etc. will move in. If the Forest Service measures the consumer surplus resulting from only the reduced congestion within the system, a gross error is possible. It is necessary to also measure the change in consumer surplus resulting from the possible reduction of parking fees, lodging costs, etc. from the other entrance points from which visitors have been diverted, and it is necessary to take into account all the attributes and prices that enter these consumer surplus measures. Finally, the land rent increases at the entrance site and possible decreases at competing sites also should be measured. Any profits remaining to developments after rent can be counted as producer surplus. It is possible that while opening a new entrance point could increase consumer surplus because of reduced congestion at the new and old entrance points and within the system, the land rent decrease at the other points may entirely counterbalance the consumer surplus gain. This cannot be determined unless a general equilibrium analysis of the whole system is performed.

There is considerable debate as to whether land price changes observed in the land market are accurate measures of the benefits of public investment programs which created those changes. Rothenberg (1967), Strotz (1968), Lind (1973), and Pines and Weiss (1976) have attempted to come up with useful formulas allowing the land economist to estimate benefits from land price changes. The conclusion of this debate is that land price changes (i.e., the aggregate change in land prices) can disagree with the aggregate change in benefits, such as a consumer surplus measure, in both sign and magnitude (see Pines and Weiss 1976). It appears from these findings that, although land price changes at a particular site are of the utmost importance in reaching a correct measure of total benefits, they are not themselves a measure of total benefit.

Land prices are a measure of part of the total benefits from a site. The aggregate change in land prices is the landowner's surplus or deficit and thus a measure of the benefits (wealth gain or loss) accruing to that particular group of market participants. In cases where the land is publicly owned, a public decision to keep the land in a wild state involves an opportunity cost which is precisely equal to the net present worth that land would have in an alternative scheme which allowed its development, such as a scheme which would place that land in its perfectly competitive "market" use. This foregone source of public income can be considered a social loss, but to reach a better assessment of this loss one must also consider just how this public income would have been reinvested had it been available. In a similar way, when a wildland management program alters the price of adjoining non-wildland, then the change in the price of this land is a surplus or deficit for the owners of those land parcels.

Generally, when the public sector holds more than the optimal amount of land in a wild state (i.e., by holding parcels with a competitive market price greater than zero), then it is reasonable to expect that the aggregate prices of adjoining non-wild parcels will be higher, because by over-holding land the public sector creates a land scarcity around the wild area. Conversely, when the public sector holds only all or some of those lands with a competitive market price equal to zero, then the prices of the adjoining wildland parcels are not changed from what they would be in a competitive market.

From the preceding discussion, the basis for a particular form of benefit-cost analysis well suited to wildland management emerges. Suppose the government wishes to evaluate the benefits and costs of holding some land in a wild state. Such a strategy will potentially alter the prices of adjoining lands and will result in an opportunity loss from keeping the land in a wild state. The net land value change resulting from the strategy may be positive or negative. This net change is equal to the aggregate net change of the adjoining lands plus the foregone price of the land kept in a wild state. This net change can be compared to the benefits flowing from the wildland program itself. These benefits may be measured as the consumer and producer surpluses of the various groups using the wildland, and the consumer and producer surpluses of the user groups using the adjoining lands. Thus, the net benefits of holding the land in a wild state (assuming land price and consumer and producer surplus measures are to be treated additively) can be computed as,

$$\begin{matrix}\text{NET}\\ \text{BENEFIT}\end{matrix} = \begin{matrix}\text{TOTAL}\\ \text{CONSUMER}\\ \text{SURPLUS}\end{matrix} + \begin{matrix}\text{TOTAL}\\ \text{PRODUCER}\\ \text{SURPLUS}\end{matrix} + \begin{matrix}\text{TOTAL}\\ \text{LAND PRICE}\\ \text{SURPLUS}\end{matrix} \qquad [7]$$

where,

$$\begin{matrix}\text{TOTAL}\\ \text{CONSUMER}\\ \text{SURPLUS}\end{matrix} = \sum_{i} \begin{matrix}\text{CONSUMER}\\ \text{SURPLUS OF}\\ \text{iTH WILDLAND}\\ \text{USER GROUP}\end{matrix} + \sum_{j} \begin{matrix}\text{CONSUMER}\\ \text{SURPLUS OF}\\ \text{jTH ADJOINING}\\ \text{USER GROUP}\end{matrix}$$

$$\begin{matrix}\text{TOTAL}\\ \text{PRODUCER}\\ \text{SURPLUS}\end{matrix} = \sum_{i} \begin{matrix}\text{PRODUCER}\\ \text{SURPLUS OF}\\ \text{iTH WILDLAND}\\ \text{PRODUCER GROUP}\end{matrix} + \sum_{j} \begin{matrix}\text{PRODUCER}\\ \text{SURPLUS OF}\\ \text{jTH ADJOINING}\\ \text{PRODUCER GROUP}\end{matrix}$$

$$\begin{matrix}\text{TOTAL}\\ \text{LAND PRICE}\\ \text{SURPLUS}\end{matrix} = \begin{matrix}\text{AGGREGATE}\\ \text{CHANGE IN}\\ \text{ADJOINING}\\ \text{LAND PRICES}\end{matrix} - \begin{matrix}\text{FOREGONE LAND}\\ \text{PRICE OF THE SITE}\\ \text{KEEPING THE SITE}\\ \text{IN A WILD STATE.}\end{matrix}$$

If the market is fully competitive, there will be no producer surplus, it all will become the land price surplus. If the market is not fully competitive, the producer surplus is the area above the supply curve and the price line less land price (or rent).

Two points are worth noting. First, these benefit measures are only approximations. If one had a complete fully closed general equilibrium model of the economy, only consumer surplus computed from this model would be needed. This is because in a closed system, land rent (and producer surplus, if any) becomes income, income makes utility and utility is measured as consumer surplus. Because such closed analysis is generally too difficult, the framework described serves as a first approximation of true benefits. Second, the "loss in aggregate land price from keeping the land in a wild state" or keeping it in public ownership is the land price which is foregone because of public ownership. If the land were in the private market, this foregone land rent would be realized as benefit. Typically, public ownership is justified when the higher consumer surplus part of benefits exceeds the foregone land price, but this cannot happen in those cases for which there are no externalities and the land market is competitive, unless the loss in land price is offset by imposing appropriate consumer charges or tolls and counting them as benefits.

It also should be noted that the additivity of these different benefit measures is highly questionable. For example, the consumer and producer surplus measures of different groups can be added only by making the restrictive assumption that producer and consumer benefits are measurable in money terms and that the benefits of the different groups should be weighed equally. Adding land price surpluses to the consumer and producer surpluses has the implication that the gains of landowners (private and public) should be weighed equally with the benefits of user and producer groups. Politically incongruous conclusions can result from such additivity assumptions. Most decision makers and politicians are unlikely to assume additive benefits across diverse user, producer, and landowner classes. Such decision makers would prefer to observe an itemization of the different benefits in disaggregate format and to reach decisions by subjectively combining or synthesizing the various benefits into an overall welfare rule.

The above framework of consumer, producer, and land price surplus computations provides a basis for comparing the benefits of any two public programs for wildland management. To do this one would have to compute the consumer and producer surplus differences between the two programs and the total land price difference between the two programs. Thus, any number of public programs can be comparatively assessed and ranked in relative terms. The more fundamental question is whether absolute comparisons among public programs also are possible. One answer to this question may be found by assuming that the baseline policy is a situation in which there is no government control or ownership of wildlands. Thus, one can seek to find the aggregate consumer, producer, and land price surpluses for the hypothetical case in which all wildland currently controlled by the public sector is assumed to be allocated to the highest bidding use in a competitive market. This may be viewed as a "minimum interference" or "complete deregulation" situation and should correspond to a scenario of "maximum land market efficiency." Then, any government program which restricts or dictates the use of some wildland is a deviation from this benchmark case and can be evaluated relative to it.

A few comments are in order about this benchmark case of "maximum land market efficiency." First, this case is substantially dissimilar to most real policy alternatives precisely because the public sector does control a great deal of wildland with a positive price. To achieve this case, all of this publicly controlled land would have to be released into the competitive market. Second, precisely because of this great difference between the current wildland control pattern and the minimum or no control pattern, the benchmark benefits of the no-control pattern are difficult to estimate because they reflect drastic changes from the status quo. Third, if all the publicly owned or controlled land in the United States were to be released into the private market, the very size and geographic distribution of these land holdings would introduce great interdependencies among the different locations within the country. As a result, to correctly evaluate the no-control option, one would have to treat the entire nation or very large regions of it as a unit. In contrast, if one deals with policies and wildland management programs which deviate only marginally from the status quo, then one can isolate small regions of the national landscape so that each of these subregions can be dealt with in isolation. In conclusion, it is easy to imagine that the "minimum interference" or "no public control" option is difficult to evaluate in practice and unrealistic or infeasible as a policy option. One such benchmark is the current (status quo) situation. The improvement resulting from any policy or public program deviating from the status quo can be evaluated with relative ease, especially if one considers policies and programs with small (marginal) impacts. These, in the final analysis, are the politically feasible programs and policies.

Estimating the Price of Wild and Adjoining Lands and Simulating Wildland Markets

The prediction and analysis of the prices of real estate is a well established methodology that has been widely used by urban economists. This methodology is generally known as "hedonic price estimation." Hedonic price estimation allows the analyst to predict the sale price of real estate parcels by statistically inferring this price from recently sold real estate parcels in the same local market or from real estate which has not sold but the price of which is known or preestimated through other means. An alternative to hedonic estimation is the direct estimation of the net present worth of a land parcel by performing the necessary cost-revenue computations discussed previously. In some situations, hedonic estimation is often the more economical and reliable approach, but there are situations where a direct estimation procedure would be more appropriate.

A distinction must be made between partial equilibrium and general equilibrium estimation of land prices. Hedonic estimation is essentially a partial equilibrium method. It is assumed that the land market is in an equilibrium (or steady) state and that the prices of land parcels can be related to the characteristics of those parcels and are not affected by adjustments in other sectors of the economy. In contrast, there are situations where these assumptions are not true. For example, when a government policy releases large tracts of land into the market, thus greatly increasing the supply of land, the prices of land parcels may change drastically and are not easy to explain simply as a function of the land parcel characteristics. In this case, the government policy may have the effect of altering the assumed functional relationship between land prices and land parcel characteristics. To take these effects into account, certain general equilibrium estimation techniques may be applied.

Hedonic Estimation and Shortcomings

Examples of the hedonic estimation techniques as applied to land and housing price analysis in urban economics may be found in Kain and Quigley (1975), Straszheim (1975), Wheaton (1977), Lerman et al. (1977), Anas

(1982), and others. The following equation serves as the basis of hedonic estimation. Let P_j be the sale price of the jth land parcel, then

$$P_j = a_0 + \sum_{i=1}^{I} a_i X_{ij} + \epsilon_j \qquad [8]$$

is a linear equation which estimates the sale price P_j. This estimate is related linearly to i = 1...I characteristics (or attributes) of the jth land parcel. Typical attributes which must be included in hedonic estimation are the date of the sale, the land area of the parcel, the quality and quantity characteristics of any existing land use, commercial activity or public improvements situated on the parcel, the parcel's proximity to key locations and important surrounding sites, the visual attractiveness, pollution, noise, and other aesthetic and environmental qualities prevailing at the site. All such characteristics entered into the hedonic equation must be quantitatively measured as the X_{ij}'s, and any unknown or unobserved characteristics are captured by the error term ϵ_j. The coefficients a_0 and a_i, $i = 1...I$ measure the contribution of one unit of the ith attribute to the sale price P_j. For example, if the kth attribute is land area, then a_k is the price per square foot of land area, and a_k X_{kj} is the part of the price (or value) of parcel j that is due to its land area. In this way, hedonic estimation not only determines the price of a parcel but also breaks this down into the value added (or subtracted) by each characteristic of the parcel.

The hedonic equation can be estimated using multivariate regression techniques. To do so one must observe the sale prices and characteristics of $j = 1...N$ parcels, where N, the number of parcels, must be at least several times larger than I, the number of characteristics. The regression coefficients a_0 and a_i, $i = 1...I$ and the variance of the error term ϵ_j then can be estimated. Once a hedonic equation is estimated from actual sales, it can then be used to predict the sale prices of unsold land parcels. To do so one must observe the $i = 1...I$ characteristics of an unsold parcel, enter these into the right side of the hedonic equation, and compute

$$\hat{P}_j = a_0 + \sum_{i=1}^{I} a_{ij} X_{ij} \qquad [9]$$

net of the error term ϵ_j for the jth parcel. This is an estimate of P_j, the actual sale price which would occur if the parcel was actually sold. In this way, a properly conducted hedonic estimation study provides the analyst of land markets with an ability to track and forecast the behavior of market prices in an urban or agricultural land market in which there are many separately and competitively owned land parcels. It must be added that the hedonic equation need not be a linear function of parcel characteristics but can be specified as a more complex nonlinear function. Such nonlinear functions can be estimated using appropriate econometric techniques but with higher cost and computational effort. The concern here is not the statistical methodology of hedonic estimation, but rather, the applicability of hedonic estimation to wildlands. Suppose one wishes to estimate the prices of certain publicly held wildland parcels. To do so one must be able to identify a sufficient number of privately owned and previously sold land parcels which are similar to or located in the same general area (i.e. the same geographic market). One must then estimate a hedonic equation from these sales and use this equation to predict the price for which the publicly owned parcels would sell if they were released into the market. The difficulty is that there may not be a sufficient number of privately owned land parcels which are similar in their characteristics to the publicly owned parcels. Thus the equations estimated from the privately owned parcels may give biased predictions for the publicly owned land. This can easily occur in cases where the publicly owned land has unique aesthetic and visual features which cannot be found in the surrounding private lands. To minimize this type of problem, the analyst must take care to measure and identify the attributes of land parcels in as generic terms as possible. For example, the relevant attributes of a forest parcel may be the fertility of the soil, the type and quantity of current trees on the parcel, the topography or slope of the parcel, its location relative to major timber markets, the presence of any known underground mineral deposits, the degree of rainfall at the site, measures of the recreational potential of the site for hiking, camping, hunting, etc. These are examples of sufficiently generic attributes which are rather easily identified. An attribute which may be more difficult to identify in generic terms may be the presence of a unique vista point or unique scenic view. In such cases, an attempt may be made to measure this feature in generic terms by identifying certain attributes such as "percent of view consisting of mountain range", "percent of view consisting of green, sky, barren soil" etc. Photographic analysis or other methods may be used to derive these measures but it is understood that these aesthetic attributes are in principle quite difficult to measure and quantify compared to the more traditional, physical and geographic measures.

Because of this difficulty of identifying parcels similar to public parcels but exchanged in the free market, hedonic estimation must be applied with care. In many situations, the direct estimation of land prices via the net present worth method may prove superior to hedonic estimation, as in cases involving publicly owned wildland parcels.

General Equilibrium Estimation and Linear Programming Models for Land Allocation

Wildland management programs which drastically change the supply of land in the market cannot be adequately evaluated via hedonic estimation. They need to be subjected to general equilibrium estimation. The general equilibrium problem in land market analysis is that of land allocation among a number of competing uses (or land use sequences) according to the market principle of highest bidder. Linear programming is a commonly used and appropriate tool for simulating the outcome of such general equilibrium allocations. Two linear programming formulations have been applied in land market theory. The first is the Herbert-Stevens (1960) model which seeks to allocate land parcels to the highest bidders. A second model is that of Mills

(1972) which allocates land parcels among uses in such a way as to minimize the total cost of land allocation. Although the Mills model seeks to minimize total cost, it can be shown through the duality theory in linear programming that it is generally consistent with the highest bidder principle in land market analysis. Although these two models have been developed and applied in the contexts of housing and urban land use allocation, they are generally applicable to wildland allocation with only minor modifications in their basic assumptions. The Herbert-Stevens model is representative of the concept of allocating uses to parcels so as to maximize the aggregate net present worth of the entire land. The Mills model is representative of the concept of allocating uses to parcels so as to minimize the aggregate cost of land development.

To implement aggregate net present worth maximization, a wildland use planner must first decide on a reasonable division of the wildland into $i = 1 \ldots I$ zones (or parcels), each parcel being of varying size and containing, for example, L_i acres. One must then estimate the bid rent or net present worth per acre for each land use sequence, j, and for each parcel, i. This gives the bid rents per acre, R_{ji}. The net present worth (or bid rent) maximizing allocation then can be formulated as

$$\text{Max} \sum_i \sum_j R_{ji} X_{ji} \qquad [10]$$

subject to:

$$\sum_j X_{ji} \leqq L_i , \; i = 1 \ldots I$$

$$X_{ji} \geqq 0 \text{ for each } i \text{ and } j.$$

where X_{ji} are the unknowns (or variables) of this linear program and measure the amount of land in each zone allocated to the jth land use sequence. The constraint equations state that the land allocated to all the uses in a particular zone cannot exceed the total land available in that zone, and that negative amounts of land cannot be allocated. The linear program's solution will determine X^*_{ij} for each j and i, thus deciding how much land in each zone must be allocated to each use in order to maximize aggregate net present worth. The market price of each land parcel, i, will be determined as being equal to the bid rent of the highest bidding land use sequence. The linear program can be extended by adding other constraints to reflect the presence of certain physical or policy restrictions on the adjacency of land uses and, more important, the fact that the total number of acres allocated to a land use over the entire region should be no more than a certain number. Such a constraint is relevant if, for example, the demand for the services or goods provided by each land use is limited or because of policy impositions on the mix of different land uses.

The aggregate cost minimization approach results in a different linear programming formulation. Namely,

$$\text{Min} \sum_i \sum_j C_{ji} X_{ji} \qquad [11]$$

subject to:

$$\sum_j X_{ji} \leqq L_i \,, i = 1 \ldots I$$

$$\sum_i X_{ji} = N_j \,, j = 1 \ldots J$$

$$X_{ji} \geqq 0 \text{ for each } i \text{ and } j$$

where C_{ji} is the cost of allocating one acre of parcel i to land use sequence j, the first set of constraints state that no more than the available L_i acres can be allocated in parcel i, and the second set of constraints state that N_j acres of land must be allocated to land use sequence j across all parcels i.

Both of the above formulations are intended for cases in which the adjacency of different land uses does not create any externalities. In other words, the net present worth of land use sequence j in site i R_{ji} or the cost C_{ji} do not depend on the type or size of adjacent land uses. If such interdependencies do exist because of externalities, then the above linear programming formulations are inadequate and appropriate non-linear formulations must be specified to deal with these cases. Mills' model of urban land use can deal with some of these externalities by approximating these interactions as linear.

The Discrete Choice Approach and General Equilibrium Estimation

Another approach for directly estimating land prices and other prices which enter demand is the general equilibrium discrete choice approach first developed by Anas (1980, 1982). Discrete choice models first appeared in the area of travel demand (Domencich and McFadden 1975) and housing choice (Quigley 1976). In the discrete choice approach, one estimates a demand function in which the choice alternatives are discrete instead of continuous. In travel demand, these are modes of travel. In housing, they are types of housing or specific dwelling units. In wildland related choices, the discrete alternatives should be specific sites for which demand exists as demand for fishing, hunting, hiking, camping, picking berries, etc. The consumer's choice is both among alternative sites and among alternative activities at the sites.

In discrete choice models, the demand function is estimated as a probability function: what is the probability that a random consumer from a population of similar consumers will choose to visit a certain site and engage in a certain activity there, given all the prices he must pay to do so and all the quantitative and qualitative attributes which he will enjoy when he visits that site? From this probability function the expected number of visitors that will be generated by a given population can be computed.

From 1962, since the work of Warner, to the current time all applications of discrete choice modeling focused on one thing—how to estimate the probability functions from choices observed to occur. Thus, estimating demand functions from a discrete choice viewpoint is now well understood in economics. Williams (1977) first developed the consumer surplus measure from a discrete choice function, and Small and Rosen (1980) refined this derivation.

The application of discrete choice models to general equilibrium problems is recent. Anas (1982) developed and empirically tested multinominal logit models of discrete choices for the demand and supply sides of the Chicago housing market. The demand side is the choice of housing location and travel mode, and the supply side is the landlord's decision to rent or keep vacant dwelling units. Anas solved for an equilibrium allocation of households to dwellings under the assumption that demand equals supply at each location. He computed the consumer surplus resulting from policy changes in transit travel times, and costs and resulting from equilibrium changes in housing prices.

Similar discrete choice analyses can be applied to wildland "markets." It is possible to estimate the demand functions, generate the distribution of visits among the sites, specify the site characteristics determined by site management, equilibrate demand and supply at each site and in this way find the equilibrium changes in market prices at each area surrounding each site.

For example, the BWCA problem discussed earlier can be most directly handled in this way. The problem with the application of discrete choice problems to issues dealing with natural resources is that resource economists are not yet familiar with these methods. Consequently, talent must be imported from travel and urban economists.

Public Strategies and Policies for Wildland Management and Allocation

Wildland as a Land Bank

Normally, the public sector controls substantial wildland holdings which would have a positive price if released into the land market. It is important to understand that this situation keeps the prices of adjoining lands artificially inflated to some degree. A release of some of these wildlands into the market tends to reduce the prices of adjoining lands, and an augmentation of the wildland supplies through new acquisition tends to inflate the prices of adjoining lands. Thus, public wildland holdings have the characteristics of a "public land bank." Regardless of the potential use of wildland parcels in the provision of goods and services, one of their most important uses is their role as a land bank. Public strategies may call for the government to release certain wildland parcels into the market, solely in order to counteract price inflation in adjacent lands. The opposite strategy of increasing wildland supplies may also be pursued solely in order to increase the prices of certain adjoining land prices and thus provide a subsidy or compensation to adjoining landowners.

By controlling the location, timing, and extent of wildlands to be released into the market, the public sector can have a powerful tool for regulating land price dynamics in the private market and indirectly for regulating the prices of many goods and services produced from these private lands.

Value Capture and Joint Development

The "value capture" idea is an approach to land use policy recently popularized by Sharpe (1974) and Hagman and Misczynski (1978). The central concept in value capture is that increases in market land prices created because of certain government actions or public investments are taxable in the public interest. Conversely, decreases in land prices caused for the same reasons justify compensation payments to the owners. Although value capture policy has been discussed primarily for the case of transportation and especially mass transit investments (Sharpe 1974; Anas 1981, 1982), the basic idea is equally applicable to wildland related government policies and investments.

For example, suppose that the government decides to develop certain wildland parcels adjacent to a small urban area, for recreational use. The government will proceed to designate these areas as suitable for camping, boating, hiking, or whatever other use is appropriate. Facilities suitable for these activities will be provided in time, and the adjacent urban center will receive a boost in its economy in the form of new jobs, hotels, and other developments secondary to the recreational development. The prices of land and real estate within the urban center will increase somewhat to reflect the effect of these secondary benefits. If a value capture policy is implemented, the increase in the adjoining land and real estate can be taxed away by the government. The revenues collected in this way can be used to reimburse the public sector for the costs of the recreational developments and for the costs of any compensation due to displaced, relocated, or adversely affected parties. The value capture idea thus provides a rationale for wildland management. When the government decides to develop or market certain wildland parcels, it can choose to do this judiciously and in a way which deliberately tries to create a land value surplus in the adjoining lands. This surplus can then be taxed away and used as government revenue or to defray the costs of the developments initially undertaken.

The concept of "joint development" is a natural derivative of the value capture idea. According to this concept, the land value surplus created by the public program or investment can be maximized if the government participates in or controls the secondary developments spurred by the original investment. In the example given, this may be achieved if the government sets aside some of the wildland for hotel development and leases or sells this land to hotel developers, thereby directly capturing the profits from these secondary developments.

Examples may be given where the value capture/joint development idea is not applicable because the government action has the effect of depressing rather than enhancing adjacent land prices. But even in such cases, the positive economic impacts on adjoining lands and urban centers can in many cases exceed the negative impacts, thus leaving a net taxable surplus in land values.

Conclusions, Data and Research Needs

Wildland management programs should be evaluated by measuring the consumer surplus derived from the services generated by the management program and the land rent changes generated by the management program. If the markets influenced by these programs are not fully competitive, a producer surplus measure also should be quantified.

If the wildlands in question do not generate or are not subject to any significant externalities, the principle of the highest bidder provides the basis for achieving efficiency in the allocation of public wildland parcels. To achieve such efficiency, the governmental authorities can either sell wildland parcels which yield a positive market price, or the relevant agencies can proxy (replace) the highest bidding developers and develop these parcels in their best uses. If this efficiency principle is followed, the government will at no point hold undeveloped any wildland which has a positive price unless this price is extracted through user charges and special taxes.

When externalities are present, there are possibly many strategies for wildland allocation. One strategy is to release the land into the market and allow its development but with appropriate restrictions, taxes, ordinances placed on it so that its development is efficient. Another strategy is to keep it in the public domain and develop it efficiently in this domain. Generally defined, "development" can include some very simple forms of fencing, ticketing, policing, etc. Development occurs when there is a positive profit per acre. When there is no such profit, development is not economical and not efficient. In this case, the land remains in a wild state but still can be used and yields benefits measurable as consumer surplus.

When the government maintains ownership of wildland parcels which would be positively priced, there is an unrealized land rent. If there are no externalities, the unrealized land rent loss outweighs the consumer surplus benefits generated by having the land in public ownership. If externalities are present, however, this is not necessarily the case.

Traditional valuations of the benefits of wildland programs are incomplete because they ignore the portion of benefits resulting from land rent changes but deal instead with consumer surplus only (see Krutilla and Fisher, 1975). Two divergent improvements are necessary. First, consumer surplus measures should be derived from multi-attribute, multi-price demand functions. Second, the consumer surplus and land rent changes not only of the directly affected wildlands but also of the adjoining lands should be considered. If the land market is less than fully competitive, a producer surplus should be defined and measured as well for directly affecting and adjoining wildlands.

Any two wildland management programs (including the status quo) can be compared by evaluating the difference between each of the benefit components—consumer surplus, land value and producer surplus (if any).

The market prices of wildland parcels can be evaluated by applying the arithmetic of the "net present worth" method. This method requires the pre-estimation of a stream of annual revenues and costs for each land use sequence that can feasibly occupy a parcel and appropriate discounting of the annual profit stream to the present time.

The market price of a wildland parcel also may be estimated statistically via the application of "hedonic estimation" techniques which utilize multivariate regression analysis. Data scarcity problems and the uniqueness of wildland parcels complicate the applicability of this technique. Appropriate care is needed in implementing it.

When public programs require extensive changes in the supply of wildlands, market prices are better estimated by general equilibrium methods which involve solving linear programming or nonlinear programming problems. Linear programs are adequate in cases which do not involve land market externalities whereas nonlinear programs are generally called for when land market externalities are significant.

Another general equilibrium method for simulating wild and public land markets is to adopt the discrete choice demand function approach developed by Anas (1982) and tested in urban economics.

Public wildlands have a potential use as land banks. In this regard, their timely release into the market can act as a policy for regulating price inflation in privately held adjacent lands.

The potential benefits of many wildland management programs can be increased if value capture taxation of adjoining lands is coupled with government initiated joint development and/or public-private partnership schemes.

Data and Research Needs

Many of the concepts and techniques discussed would greatly benefit from an extended data collection program which would yield an easily accessible, detailed and comprehensive data base on wildlands. This data base should have the following characteristics.

Its units should consist of individual small wildland parcels which should be geocoded.

A survey should determine and code the soil fertility, current and past land use, climactic, topographic, geologic, mineral and other known features of each parcel.

Each parcel should be cross referenced with adjacent and neighboring wildland parcels.

A survey should determine the current land use, price, and other characteristics of non-wild public and private land parcels adjoining the wildland parcels.

This data set should be put in machine readable form.

In addition to the above data set on wildland and adjoining parcels an attempt must be made to obtain exhaustive data on the production cost characteristics of each land use type as well as on the unit prices of the goods and services produced by each land use. These data will enable the direct estimation of land prices via the net present worth method.

Future research should focus on the following areas.

1. Development of multiattribute demand and supply functions in which land prices and other attributes enter jointly and development of consumer surplus and producer surplus measures from these functions. Disaggregation of these demand and supply functions by land use type.
2. Testing of the adequacy of hedonic estimation versus the direct estimation of the prices of wildland.
3. Testing of the linear programming models discussed in this chapter.
4. Selected case studies of the impact of wildland management programs on adjoining lands and evaluation of the value capture potential of such programs.
5. Careful development of a list of joint development and public/private action programs which can increase the value capture potential of adjoining lands.

Literature Cited

Alonso, William. 1964. Location and land use. Harvard Press, Cambridge, Mass.

Anas, Alex. 1980. A probabilistic approach to the structure of rental housing markets. Journal of Urban Economics 7:225-247.

Anas, Alex. 1981. Development and testing of an operational simulation model for analyzing the effects of transportation on housing values. Phase I Report for research contract DOT-RC-92028, United States Department of Transportation, FY 1979 University Research Program. Northwestern University, Evanston, Ill.

Anas, Alex. 1982. Residential location markets and urban transportation: Economic theory, econometrics and public policy analysis with discrete choice models. Studies in Urban Economics. Academic Press, Inc., New York, N.Y.

Domencich, T., and D. McFadden. 1975. Urban travel demand: A behavioral analysis. North Holland.

Ely, R. T., and Wehrwein, G.S. 1940. Land economics. MacMillan, New York, N.Y.

Hagman, D., and D. Misczynski (eds.). 1978. Windfalls for wipeouts: Land value re-capture and compensation. American Society of Planning Officials, Chicago, Ill.

Herbert, John D., and Benjamin Stevens. 1960. A model for the distribution of residential activity in urban areas. Journal of Regional Science 2:21-36.

Kain, John, and James Quigley. 1975. Housing markets and racial discrimination: A microeconomic analysis. National Bureau of Economic Research, New York, N.Y.

Krutilla, J. V., and A. C. Fisher. 1975. The economics of natural resources. The John Hopkins University Press, Baltimore, Md.

Lerman, S. R., D. Damm, E. Lerner-Lam, and J. Young. 1977. The effect of the Washington METRO on property values. Center for Transportation Studies Report No. 77-18. M.I.T., Cambridge, Mass.

Lind, R. C. 1973. Spatial equilibrium, the theory of rents and public program benefits. Quarterly Journal of Economics 87:188-207.

Mills, Edwin S. 1967. An aggregative model of resource allocation in a metropolitan area. American Economic Review 57:197-210.

Mills, Edwin S. 1972. Markets and efficient resource allocation in urban areas. The Swedish Journal of Economics 74:100-113.

Mishan, E. J. 1968. What is producer's surplus? American Economic Review 58:1269-1282.

Musgrave, R. A. 1959. The theory of public finance: A study in public economy. McGraw-Hill, New York, N.Y.

Muth, Richard F. 1969. Cities and housing. University of Chicago Press, Chicago, Ill.

Pines, David, and Yoram Weiss. 1976. Land value improvement projects and land values. Journal of Urban Economics.

Quigley, John. 1976. Housing demand in the short run: An analysis of polytomous choice. Explorations in Economic Research.

Rothenberg, J. 1967. Economic evaluation of urban renewal: Conceptual

foundation of benefit cost analysis. Studies of Government Finance, The Brookings Institution, Washington, D.C.
Sharpe, Carl. 1974. A value capture policy. Volumes I-IV, Technical Report TST-75-82-85. United States Department of Transportation, Washington, D.C.
Small, K. A, and H. S. Rosen. 1981. Applied welfare economics with discrete choice models. Econometrica, 49(1):105-130.
Straszheim, Mahlon, 1975. An econometric analysis of the urban housing market. National Bureau of Economic Research, New York, N.Y.
Strotz, Robert. 1968. The use of land rent changes to measure the welfare benefits of land improvements. *In* Haring (Ed.), The New Economics of Regulated Industries. Los Angeles: Economic Research Center, Occidental College.
von Thunen, J. H. 1826. Der Isolierte Staat in Beziehung auf Landwirtschaft und Nationalokonomie, Hamburg.
Warner, S. L. 1962. Stochastic choice of mode in urban travel: A study in binary choice. Northwestern University Press, Evanston, Ill.
Wheaton, William, C. 1977. A bid rent approach to housing demand. Journal of Urban Economics 4(2):200-217.
Williams, H.C.W.L. 1977. On the formation of travel demand models and economic evaluation measures of user benefit. Environment and Planning 9:285-344.

Chapter 6
Valuation of Mineral Resources

William A. Vogely

This chapter examines the valuation of mineral resources that may be contained in the earth's crust of the wildland. First, the theoretical concept of resource value accruing to the resource in the ground is examined. Second, various characteristics of resources are identified which will determine the methodology that can be used to assign a value. Third, the production function is described for mineral resources as a necessary background for evaluation. Last, concepts contained in the literature are reviewed.

Theory of Resource Value

Mineral deposits in the earth's crust are the result of geologic processes. The entire crust consists of mineral elements plus organic matter. Mineral deposits are concentrations of minerals sufficiently high so that the deposit is distinguishable physically from the surrounding, common rock. Such occurrences can be classified according to the scheme developed jointly by the U.S. Bureau of Mines and U.S. Geological Survey as indicated in figure 1. This classification scheme for mineral occurrences has both a geologic and an economic axis, based upon the degree of geologic knowledge concerning the occurrence and the economic characteristics of the occurrence in terms of its production potential under prevailing technological and economic conditions. Thus, at least theoretically, the earth's crust in any area can be described in terms of the mineral occurrences classified according to this diagram. Note, however, the only known mineral occurrences are those that have been identified, lying to the leftward portion of the classification figure. And of those identified resources, the economic value of the resource in place increases as the costs of development relative to price of that resource decrease.

The value of a resource in place is expressed by the amount of the pure economic rent accruing to that resource in production. In figure 2, the economic rent concept is illustrated. The cost line in figure 2 is the total cost of developing and producing the mineral contained in the deposit, including

RESOURCES OF (commodity name)

[A part of reserves or any resource category may be restricted from extraction by laws or regulations (see text)]

AREA: (mine, district, field, State, etc.) UNITS: (tons, barrels, ounces, etc.)

Cumulative Production	IDENTIFIED RESOURCES			UNDISCOVERED RESOURCES	
	Demonstrated		Inferred	Probability Range (or)	
	Measured	Indicated		Hypothetical	Speculative
ECONOMIC	Reserves		Inferred Reserves		
MARGINALLY ECONOMIC	Marginal Reserves		Inferred Marginal Reserves		
SUB-ECONOMIC	Demonstrated Subeconomic Resources		Inferred Subeconomic Resources		

Other Occurrences	Includes nonconventional and low-grade materials

Figure 1. Major elements of mineral-resource classification. Source: U.S.G.S. Circular 831.

the rate of return on capital investment required to cause the investor to maintain operation or to undertake the initial investment in the long run. The marginal deposit, that is the deposit which just covers cost, bears no economic rents. All deposits which are of higher quality because of the physical characteristics of the deposit, or perhaps locational and other kinds of advantages, provide a return at market price greater than the cost as defined. Thus these deposits earn a rent. Regardless of the distribution of that rent between the landowner, the producer, the government, and whomever else stakes a claim, it is the size of the rent which determines the value of the deposit. Because the rent can be actually received only through the process of production, which for most deposits extends over many years, the relevant valuation of the deposit in the ground is the time stream of rents discounted to a present value by an appropriate discount rate. This gives a figure that is the amount that a firm would be willing to pay for the right to mine the deposit, given the expectations of that firm with respect to future prices, costs, and discount rate. Thus, the value of a mineral deposit in the ground is the present value of the discounted economic rents.

Note that this valuation of the mineral resource as it occurs under the surface of the wildlands is independent, except indirectly, of the consumer surplus or consumer benefits from the development of a new resource. If the resource is large enough so that it shifts the long-run supply curve sufficiently to the right to cause the current marginal producer to lose his market, then there would also be a benefit arising from decreased prices to consumers for the commodity. However, the increase in consumer surplus from such an action would decrease the value of the economic rents to be obtained from all deposits. As indicated below, such a situation is highly unlikely for any of the

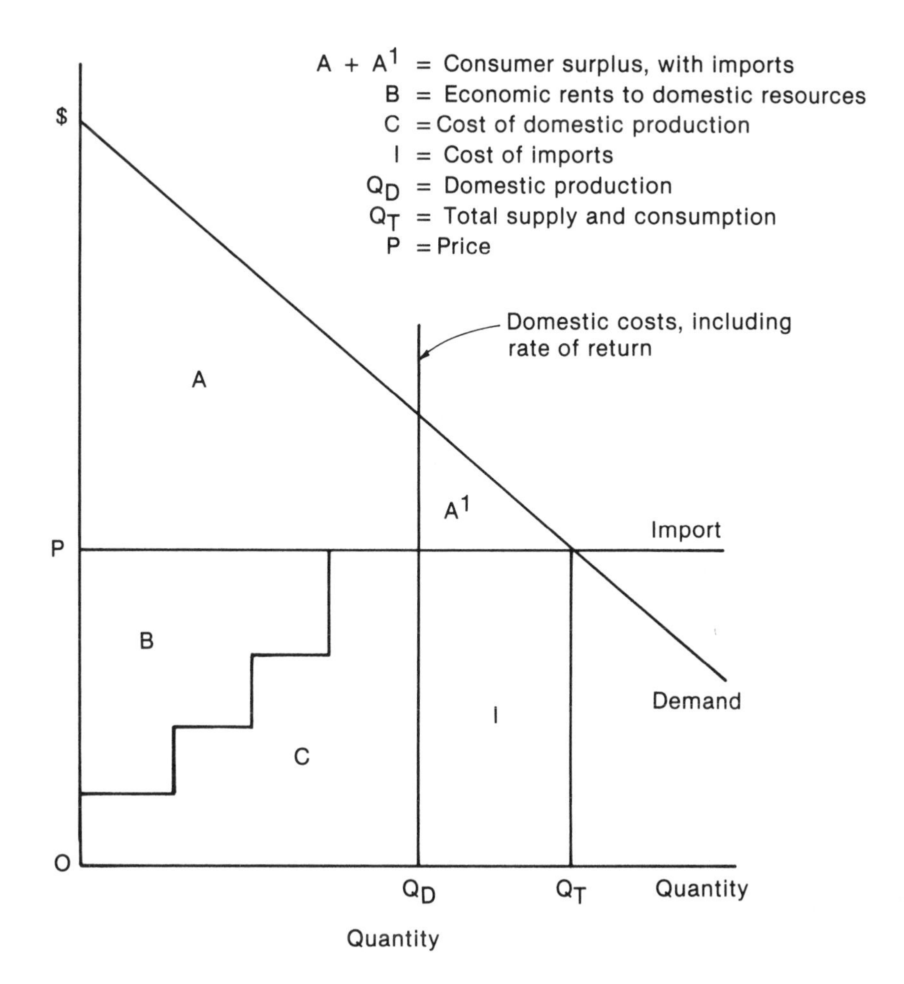

Figure 2. Supply and demand diagram illustrating value and cost concepts.

mineral commodities which are traded and marketed worldwide. It might be significant for locally produced minerals. Figure 2a, based on figure 2, shows graphically the valuation of a new deposit. The new deposit replaces imports at a cost saving equal to the economic rent, thus creating a value to society. Consumers are unaffected.

The theory of resource value is very simple to state but that value is extremely difficult to measure. The value of a resource in the ground is the net present value of the sum of the rents that that resource would earn were it developed plus, in some cases, the consumer surplus flowing to consumers of the resource product through a decrease in equilibrium price. Because, at the time of valuation, the size of the economic rents in the future and thus their present value is dependent upon quite uncertain estimates as to future prices, costs, technologies, etc., a precise determination of the value of these rents is virtually impossible. Such values will be determined by a market if the area

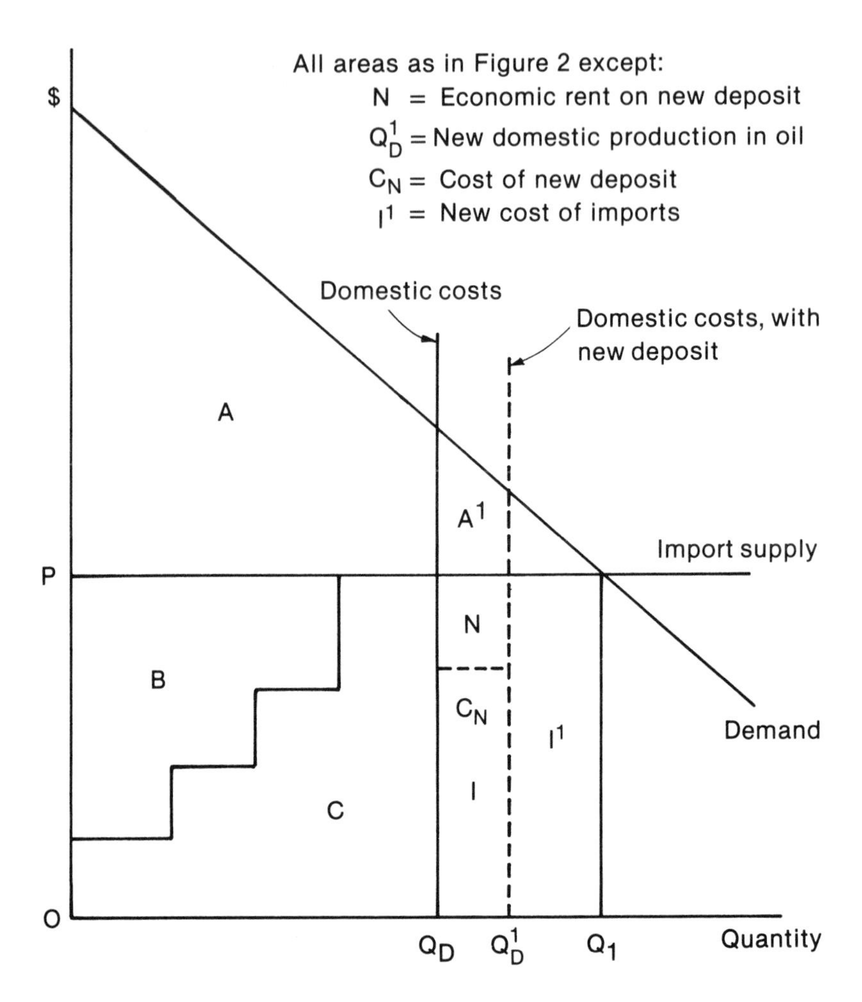

Figure 2a. The value of a new domestic deposit which earns economic rent.

can be offered for competitive bidding for exploration. However, lacking such a market-determined value, the determination of value becomes a complex estimation procedure.

Characteristics of Deposit Which Affect Valuation Technique

The first major element in the classification is whether or not the deposit has been identified, and if it has been identified, whether it has been demonstrated or inferred. For demonstrated deposits, the proper valuation procedure is to conduct a cost analysis for the production of the resource from the deposit. Such cost analyses for all identified and demonstrated deposits of some 33 minerals in the United States eventually will be conducted by the U.S. Bureau of Mines under their minerals availability system.

If such a deposit exists on the wildland in question, then the evaluation either has already been done under the minerals availability system analysis, or the methodology for so doing it is described in publications of the U.S. Bureau of Mines.

The analysis presented by the Bureau of Mines or developed using their technology will determine the cost of production, including a normal rate of return for providing the primary product of the resource. To estimate the economic rents involved in the development and production of the deposit, an estimate of future price for the product of the deposit at the deposit site and an estimate of the production profile through time must be developed. Note that the value of the product at the site is not only dependent upon its cost of production (which is obtained from the U.S. Bureau of Mines methodology) but also from its location, because the price of the material will be established on a world level or a national level, and the product of the specific deposit must absorb transportation costs involved in marketing the product. Once these estimates are made, then the calculation of the value of the deposit simply rests upon the choice of a discount rate to discount the rent stream through time to a present value.

If a deposit is identified but inferred, the estimating procedure becomes more uncertain and more complex. To assign a cost to an inferred deposit involves major assumptions concerning the physical characteristics and extent of that deposit and the kinds of technologies which can be used to produce and win the mineral values. Such estimates are highly unique to each deposit, but can be performed by mining engineers with the help of a geologist using the same techniques used for the demonstrated resources. The valuation which occurs from such an analysis, however, clearly is much more uncertain than the valuation of the demonstrated deposits.

There are also differences in valuing identified resources depending upon the characteristics of the minerals contained in the deposit. If those minerals are fuels, metals, or major chemical minerals that are marketed in national markets or international markets, the deposit will be a price taker, i.e., its development will not affect the overall supply and demand situation for that commodity, and evaluation can proceed on the basis of the economic rents generated by the specific deposit. However, if the mineral contained is one that is locally marketed, such as sand and gravel or construction stone, the analyst must determine not only the cost of production from the deposit, but also the price at which the product can be sold on the local market. Then, there will be two elements in the valuation—(1) the economic rent, if any, flowing to the deposit, and (2) the consumer surplus, if any, flowing from the availability of the material locally rather than being transported in from a more distant source. Critical to this estimation are costs of transportation of the material to the site of use.

The problem of estimating the value of the undiscovered resources is much more difficult and subject to uncertainty. There are techniques, described later, for making broad area and small area resource appraisals whereby the upper portion of the diagram will be estimated as a single number. These estimates are very uncertain and impart very little real information. Certainly there is not sufficient information to permit a calculation of cumulative economic rents and current values of economic rents. However, there is an alternative construct here which may be able to provide an estimate for any given piece of wildlands. This is to determine the price that would be paid for the right to explore the lands for mineral deposits on the assumption that found deposits could be produced. The first step in making such an evaluation would be to obtain a geological description of the piece of wildland and an indication of whether it is geologically suitable for the occurrence of minerals and which minerals they would be. The next step would be to simulate or estimate the valuation of these resources, perhaps by using government geologists to determine the minimum bid that the government would require if the lands were to be leased under competitive situations. Techniques have been developed within the U.S. Geological Survey and the Bureau of Mines to determine these minimum bids; these techniques could be applied to a specific piece of wildland. However, if the interest is in a very large area of wildland, such as the wilderness areas in Alaska, then a broad area appraisal conducted according to techniques described in the literature review section could be done; but the result would only be a series of guesses as to the ultimately recoverable resources in the upper right box. Such information would not provide the ability to evaluate on the basis of economic rents or on the basis of leasing for exploration.

Mineral Production Functions

The production of minerals is a multistage process. The first step of the production function is exploration wherein a deposit is discovered within the earth's crust. Following the initial identification of the existence of a deposit, further investments are required to determine whether the deposit is economically worth developing. Next a feasibility study is made. If results are positive, the site is placed under development. During the development phase, the mine and the mill, in the case of metals, and the development drilling and infrastructure in the form of gathering systems, etc., in the case of petroleum and natural gas, are put in place. The next stage involves the actual production from the deposit, the product of which moves for further processing either to smelters and refineries or other processes appropriate to the commodity under concern. The stages beyond production are usually conducted off of the site, and therefore need not be examined.

The opportunity cost or spillover effects of these various stages are significantly different. Exploration requires access to a very large area that will be evaluated by various geological, geochemical, and geophysical techniques. Some of these techniques, such as overflights, do not impact on the surface at all. Others, such as core drilling in the case of metallic and nonmetallic deposits and drilling to target rocks in the case of oil and gas exploration, involve disturbance of the surface area in the form of clearing the site where actual drilling takes place, and providing transportation facilities to that site.

Once a prospect is identified, the area of work shrinks considerably, but the degree of disturbance of the surface increases. Gathering material for a feasibility study requires drilling additional holes to delineate the deposit to determine its productivity in terms of content of minerals and to determine its characteristics in terms of designing a productive facility.

If the deposit is then developed for production, the area contained in the project and auxiliary areas for access and dumping of waste become solely devoted to the project in the case of metal mining, although some multiple use is possible in the case of petroleum and natural gas, where the amount of surface involved is relatively small.

The implication of this production function for valuation of mineral resources from wildlands is that these lands have differing values according to the stage involved. Exploration, to be successful, requires the examination of a large area which has geologic potential for the occurrence of a valuable deposit. Within this large area of exploration only a very small area will contain valuable mineral deposits. Thus, the land involved decreases dramatically as the exploration stage gives way to the delineation stage. A second characteristic of the development of the exploration stage is that the lands maintain their value for exploration through time. In other words, lands are not explored once with all values being found. They are explored time and time again as the technology of exploration changes, as the target mineral changes, and as the value of various minerals change through time. For example, the state of Nevada was explored intensively by prospectors searching for gold in vein deposits at the time of the booming mineral developments with the opening of the West. It is being explored intensively again today for a different kind of gold deposits, the disseminated deposits, and major finds are still being made on the land.

Upon discovery of a mineral deposit, the dedication of the land area over the deposit becomes pronounced, and in the appraisal stage there will be substantial alteration of the surface of the land. If the appraisal stage results in the existence of a mineral deposit, then the economic rents or value flowing from that deposit can be determined on the basis of the appraisal information. At that point, the valuation can be determined according to the theory of resource value, i.e., the economic rents existing for that deposit. At that stage, the exploration expenditures leading to the initial discovery of the deposit should not be subtracted from the economic rents, because they are sunk costs undertaken to discover the deposit and cannot be ascribed solely to that deposit. For this reason, there are two separate valuation of the wildland areas—one for exploration and one for delineation and development of identified deposits.

Literature Review

There is virtually no literature specifically on the issue of valuation of mineral deposits for land use decisions. The literature which exists is of three types. First, there is literature of a directly applied nature for the use of mine managers and firms making investments which describes the feasibility study and the economic determination of whether or not a deposit should be developed. At this level there are virtually no theoretical issues, although the application of new techniques for apppraisal such as geostatistical inference is an important frontier of knowledge. The objective is to minimize the cost of making the decision as to whether or not the deposit should be developed.

The techniques developed for this purpose would be applicable to determining the value from wildlands in the case of identified and demonstrated deposits. It also could be used on a more estimated basis for identified and inferred deposits. From the point of view of the manager of these lands, as contrasted to that of a firm seeking to develop a deposit, the valuation procedure is best done according to the procedures developed by the U.S. Bureau of Mines as part of their mineral availability system.

The second class of literature deals with the appraisal of mineral resources by relatively small areas. These appraisal techniques, which involve estimation of resource potential by various techniques, have been used in the United States for resource appraisals for public policy purposes. The literature in this area derives mainly from the recent interest in petroleum resources and uranium resources, although there have been other attempts covering many other commodities.

The third area of interest is the global world picture for availability of resources which has little implication for any specific area of wildlands. Nevertheless, these techniques are of interest.

The Material Availability System (MAS).—The materials availability system is described in Berg and Carillo (1980), and Davidoff (1980).

The minerals availability system has as its priority to include coverage on 23 commodities. They are (in order of priority) copper, aluminum, chromium, cobalt, manganese, phosphate, zinc, lead, nickel, platinum, iron, tin, potash, fluorine, tungsten, asbestos, titanium, columbium, tantalum, mercury, gold, silver, and molybdenum. An additional 10 commodities are of second priority. They are pyrite, beryllium, lithium, magnesium, rare earths, sulphur, thorium, zirconium, and vanadium. Eventually, coverage will be extended to all nonfuel mineral commodities. Note that this system does not include any of the fuels including uranium. The materials availability system work flow indicates the kind of data that will be contained. Figure 3, shows this flow and specifically identifies the two sections which are described in Berg and Carillo (1980) and Davidoff (1980). This involves identification of a deposit and then a determination of the characteristics of the deposit, its

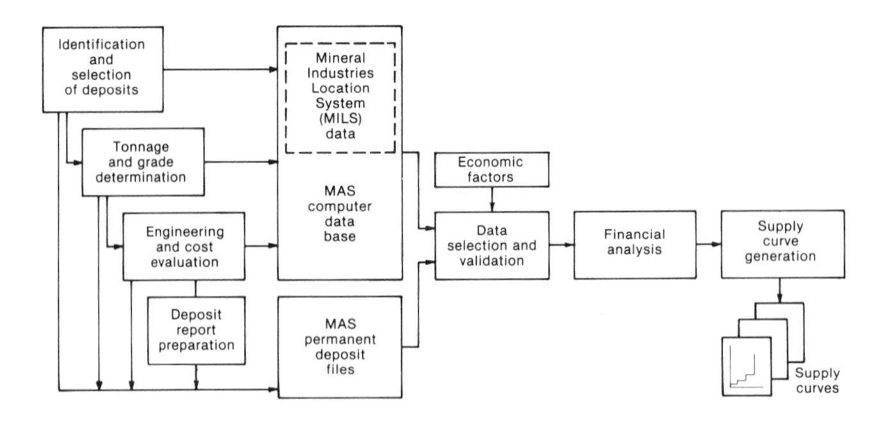

Figure 3. Minerals availability system work flow. Source: Davidoff (1980).

engineering cost, the economic factors involved, a financial analysis, and finally, a statement of the availability of a mineral in terms of costs.

The minerals industry location system (MILS) contains information on more than 135,000 mineral locations and processing plants in the United States. The information included is the name, location, commodity, type of operation, bibliography, and cross-references for each property or prospect. The system has available computer-drawn map overlays at various scales showing clustering of MILS locations. This provides an overview for a wildland assessment as to activities which have occurred in the geographic area of the wildland under consideration. Figure 4 is reproduced from Berg and Carillo (1980), and indicates the kind of information available for each deposit. From this information, maps such as the example given (fig. 5) show the clustering of these deposits for Wallace, Idaho which indicate the existing identified deposits in the areas concerned with the evaluation.

The MILS make it possible to access the MAS computer database to determine the cost evaluation and financial analysis of these deposits. The supply system described in Davidoff (1980) includes a financial analysis program which can be applied to evaluate a known deposit at assumed rates of return. Then this cost analysis can be compared to projected prices to determine economic rents, the evaluation sought for the wildland work. As an example

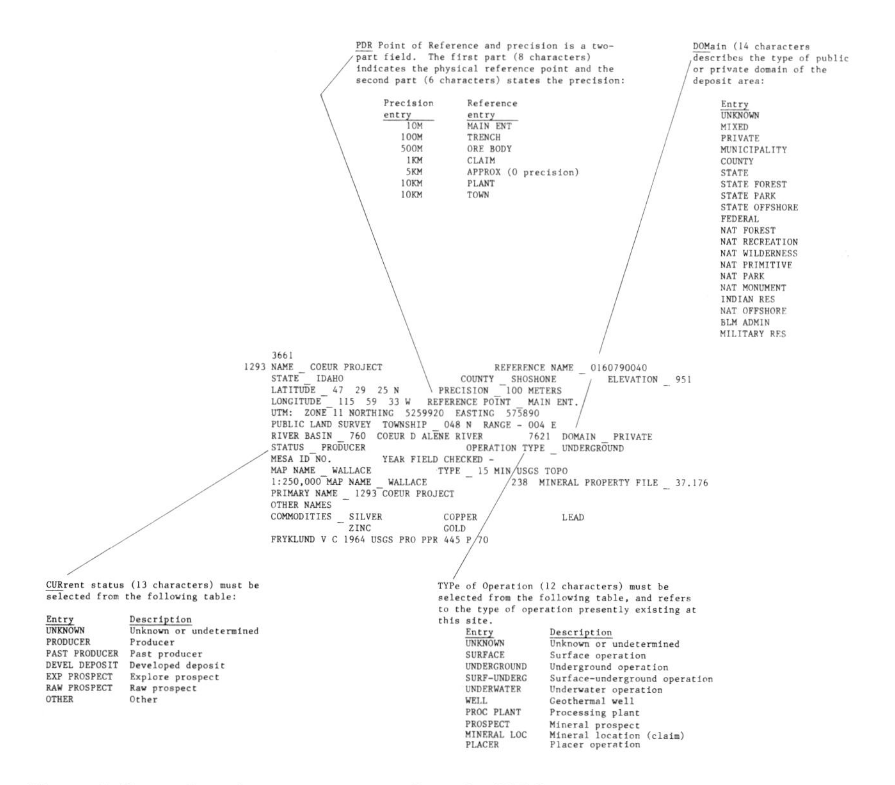

Figure 4. Examples of some output options for MILS.

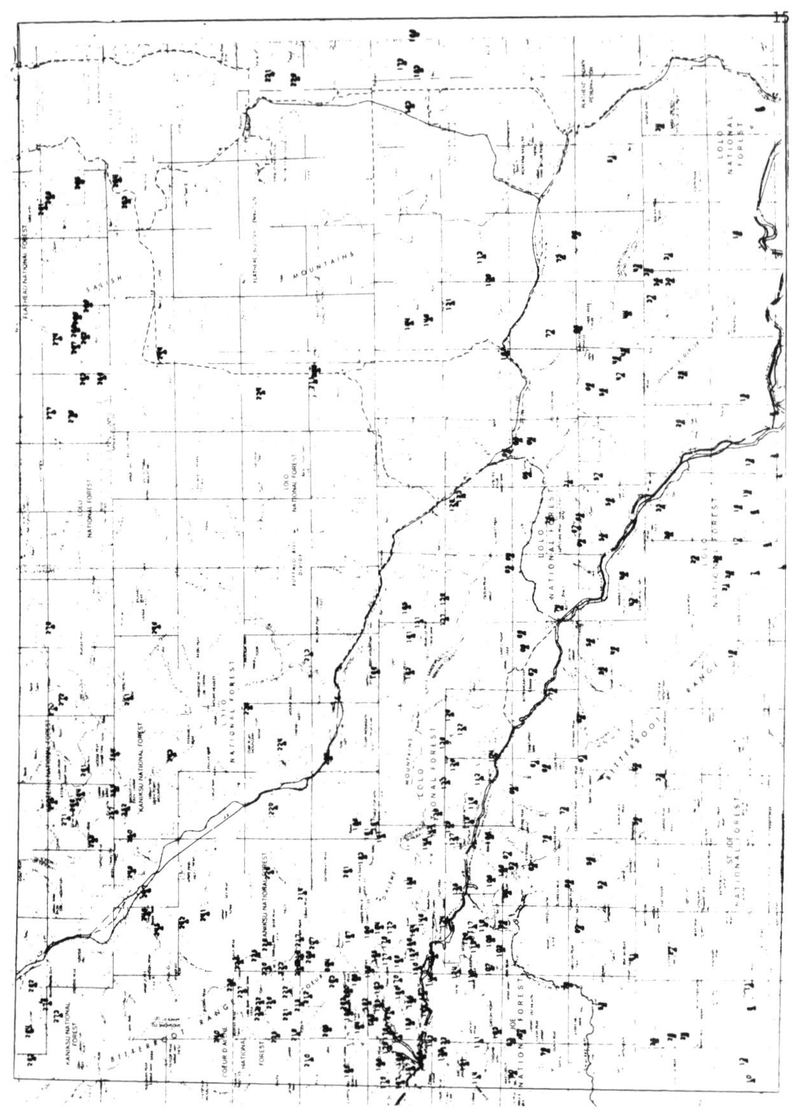

Figure 5. Clustered MILS locations for the wallace 1:250,000 quadrangle.

of the kind of things considered, table 1 reproduced from Davenport indicates the data input, and table 2 indicates the data output ranked by ascending copper price. As an example of the use of this data when copper prices are stated in comparable dollars, notice that if the copper price is at 70¢, the economic rents flowing to property No. 1 will be 39¢ per pound, whereas the economic rents associated with property No. 16 will be zero. Figure 6 graphs these data.

The MAS then provides capability for a manager of wildlands to identify whether or not the nonfuel minerals have been found in the area of the

Table 1.—Example of typical deposit information required for financial evaluation of a property

Category description and units	Year of occurrence		Annual category value
	Begin	End	
Exploration .... value, thousands ..	1978	1979	$470
Land acquisition .... do ..	1980	1980	$538
Mining preparation .... do ..	1979	1980	$1,791
Mine plant .... do ..	1979	1980	$898
Mine equipment .... do ..	1979	1979	$2,286
Do .... do ..	1980	1980	$2,846
Mine equipment reinvestment .... do ..	1984	1984	$604
Do .... do ..	1985	1985	$632
Do .... do ..	1986	1986	$955
Do .... do ..	1987	1987	$2,292
Do .... do ..	1990	1990	$1,198
Do .... do ..	1991	1991	$1,244
Mill plant and equipment .... do ..	1979	1980	$18,703
Working capital .... do ..	1981	1981	$2,366
Mine operating cost value per ton ore[1] ..	1981	1995	$1,450
Mill operating cost .... do ..	1981	1995	$1,700
Ore mined per year .... tons ..	1981	1995	4,520,000
Copper:			
Feed grade .... pct Cu ..	1981	1995	0.43
Mill recovery .... pct ..	1981	1995	93.00
Concentrate grade .... pct Cu ..	1981	1995	28.00
Smelter recovery .... pct ..	1981	1995	98.00
Smelter grade .... pct Cu ..	1981	1995	98.00
Refinery recovery .... pct ..	1981	1995	99.90
Smelter operating cost value per ton conc ..	1981	1995	$93.00
Refinery operating cost value per ton blister ..	1981	1995	$192.00
Transportation to smelter value per ton conc ..	1981	1995	$6.90
Transportation to refinery value per ton blister ..	1981	1995	$9.90
Molybdenum:			
Feed grade .... pct Mo ..	1981	1995	0.013
Mill recovery .... pct ..	1981	1995	63.00
Concentrate grade .... pct Mo ..	1981	1995	50.00
Price .... value per pound ..	1981	1995	$4.01
Gold:			
Feed grade . troy ounces per ton ..	1981	1995	0.003
Mill recovery .... pct ..	1981	1995	90.00
Concentrate grade troy ounces per ton	1981	1995	0.20
Smelter recovery .... pct ..	1981	1995	95.00
Selling price value per troy ounce	1981	1995	$173.69
Silver:			
Feed grade ...... troy ounces per ton ..	1981	1995	0.06
Mill recovery .... pct ..	1981	1995	90.00
Concentrate grade troy ounces per ton	1981	1995	3.53
Smelter recovery .... pct ..	1981	1995	95.00
Selling price value per troy ounce	1981	1995	$4.93

[1]*All tonnages are in metric tons.*

Table 2.—Example of the SAM system supply table output[1]

Sequence number	Property identification			Copper price per pound	Production of copper[2] (thousand metric tons)			
					Production		Cumulative production	
	Name of property	Latitude	Longitude		Annual	Total	Annual	Total
0000000001	Property # 1	—	—	$0.31	9	186	9	186
0000000002	Property # 2	—	—	.36	5	95	15	281
0000000003	Property # 3	—	—	.39	253	10,353	267	10,634
0000000004	Property # 4	—	—	.54	45	490	312	11,124
0000000005	Property # 5	—	—	.54	6	252	318	11,376
0000000006	Property # 6	—	—	.59	106	3,487	424	14,863
0000000007	Property # 7	—	—	.61	17	276	441	15,138
0000000008	Property # 8	—	—	.64	87	1,223	528	16,362
0000000009	Property # 9	—	—	.64	71	567	599	16,929
0000000010	Property #10	—	—	.64	39	1,315	638	18,244
0000000011	Property #11	—	—	.64	5	82	642	18,326
0000000012	Property #12	—	—	.65	86	1,891	728	20,217
0000000013	Property #13	—	—	.68	8	111	736	20,329
0000000014	Property #14	—	—	.68	12	116	748	20,445
0000000015	Property #15	—	—	.69	98	1,858	846	22,303
0000000016	Property #16	—	—	.70	20	137	865	22,439
0000000017	Property #17	—	—	.72	115	4,696	980	27,135
0000000018	Property #18	—	—	.74	8	185	988	27,320
0000000019	Property #19	—	—	.76	6	63	994	27,383
0000000020	Property #20	—	—	.79	38	307	1,032	27,690
0000000021	Property #21	—	—	.79	13	273	1,045	27,963
0000000022	Property #22	—	—	.79	31	155	1,076	28,119
0000000023	Property #23	—	—	.79	8	162	1,084	28,281
0000000024	Property #24	—	—	.80	110	1,095	1,194	29,376
0000000025	Property #25	—	—	.80	15	220	1,208	29,596
0000000026	Property #26	—	—	.81	50	3,237	1,258	32,833

Table 2.—Example of the SAM system supply table output[1]—Continued

Sequence number	Property identification			Copper price per pound	Production of copper[2] (thousand metric tons)			
					Production		Cumulative production	
	Name of property	Latitude	Longitude		Annual	Total	Annual	Total
0000000027	Property #27	—	—	.81	10	181	1,268	33,014
0000000028	Property #28	—	—	.82	53	1,103	1,320	34,117
0000000029	Property #29	—	—	.83	1	14	1,322	34,131
0000000030	Property #30	—	—	.83	82	2,637	1,404	36,768

[1] *Copper supply analysis prepared by the Minerals Availability Field Office.*

[2] *Production figures are rounded to the nearest thousand metric tons. Cumulative production figures are derived by summing unrounded production figures and then rounding to the nearest thousand metric tons.*

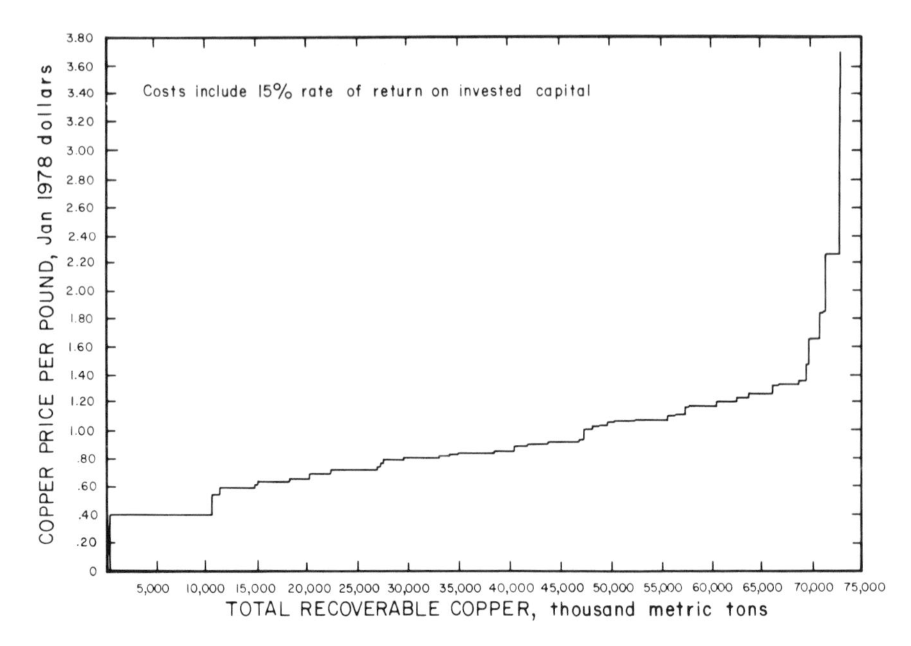

Figure 6. Example of SAM system supply curve.

wildland and to the extent that actual production or evaluation has occurred will permit access to that information. In addition, the techniques involved in project evaluation are available from the U.S. Bureau of Mines.

In the case of petroleum and coal, the availability of information is somewhat different. Coal, because of its bedded characteristics, can be inferred geologically, relatively simply over a wide geographic area. If the wildland in question is coal land, this fact will allow fairly precise geologic description of the coal beds underlying the wildland. Based upon this description, mining engineering cost estimates can be made either by experts in the U.S. Department of Energy or by commercial firms which will allow a cost estimate of the coal which can be compared with the value of coal at consuming points, less transportation, to determine whether or not the deposits would generate economic rents.

In the case of petroleum, it is unlikely that there would be any known deposits of petroleum on the wildlands which were not under development. The wildlands, if such deposits exist, could be evaluated by a petroleum engineer to determine the economic rents. It is for petroleum that the expected value for exploration of these lands is likely to be high in certain special circumstances, but that is a separate issue. The Department of Energy should be able to provide cost evaluation of known petroleum deposits if any, otherwise the wildland manager is forced into another kind of evaluation.

National Uranium Resource Evaluation.—The Department of Energy has undertaken a National Uranium Resource Evaluation (NURE) program. The output of this program is an evaluation of the uranium resources of the United States in very considerable geographic detail. The relevant report is the Grand Junction report on uranium, October 1980. This report describes in some detail the methodology used to make the assessment and then presents assessments by resource regions. Special studies are identified and the quadrangles which are fully evaluated are indicated. Thus, this is a source to which the wildland manager can turn to see whether uranium is a potential resource in his area of concern.

U.S.G.S Petroleum Potential Reserves Estimates.—The United States Geological Survey published in 1975, and updated in 1980, estimates the potential reserves in petroleum by province in the United States. These estimates are developed using a technique involving geological estimates of each area by experts in the area and then a development of probability distributions of the probable size of potential reserves in each area. The studies cover both oil and gas and can be used by the wildland manager only in the most general sense. Oil and gas occur in only a very limited area of petroleum provinces, and whether or not it occurs in the particular area under consideration is unknown until exploration activity is underway. Although these estimates are the best that are available, they are subject to severe criticism because they are essentially estimates of unknown quantities and are subject to considerable variability (Harris and Carrigan 1980a and 1980b).

Singer and Overshine (1979) attempted a similar kind of potential study for mineral deposits in broad areas, specifically in the mineral resource evaluation of Alaska. The techniques used, while applicable to broad areas, are subject to significant variability in results and are of little aid to a specific area of wildlands.

Other Techniques.—The other techniques of resource evaluation apply to very broad areas and address such issues as whether or not resources are adequate to sustain economic growth. The literature in this area is very large and need not be summarized here because the results are of no value in the valuation of the outputs of any specific land area. They are mentioned because they are the most common kind of resource estimates and, therefore, are the most commonly quoted. An introduction to the techniques of this kind of appraisal can be found in Brobst (1979) and in several pieces in U.S.G.S. (1974).

Research Recommendations

The primary objective for research in evaluation of mineral products from wildland is to develop ways to simulate the value of these lands for exploration for potential mineral deposits. Where the deposits have not been discovered but the lands have high potential for some kind of mineralization, existing valuation techniques are insufficient to guide land use decisions. Exploration activity or the opening of the lands for exploration that would determine such a value may well be inconsistent with the other values from the wildlands and the conduct of an exploration program may in fact destroy such values. Similarly, without the exploration, the land use manager is left to make his land decision without knowing whether there are mineral values foregone.

However, it is very difficult to design a research program to attack the problem. The most promising research is taht started under the uranium program, where techniques of resource evaluation and area appraisals were advanced considerably. A research program building upon the pioneering work underway in the use of geostatistics, decision models, and the geological science models of resource occurrence provides the framework for developing an ongoing research program in this area.

Literature Cited

Berg, Andrew W., and Carrillo, Fred V. 1980. MILS: The minerals industry location system of the Federal Bureau of Mines. Bureau of Mines Information Circular 8815. Washington, D.C. 24 p.

Brobst, D. A. 1979. Fundamental concepts for the analysis of resource availability. *In* Scarcity and Growth Reconsidered. Smith, D. K. (ed.). Johns Hopkins University Press, Baltimore, Md.

Davidoff, Robert L. 1980. Supply analysis model (SAM): A minerals availability system methodology. U.S. Bureau of Mines Information Circular 8820. Washington, D.C. 43 p.

Harris, D. P., and Carrigan, F. J. 1980a. A probabilistic endowment appraisal system based upon the formalization of geologic decisions, a general description. Department of Mining and Geological Engineering, College of Mines, University of Arizona, Tucson, Ariz. 114 p.

Harris, D. P., and Carrigan, F. J. 1980b. A probabilistic endowment appraisal system based upon the formalization of geologic decisions, a final report. Demonstration and compartive analysis of estimates and methods. 1980. Department of Mining and Geological Engineering, College of Mines, University of Arizona, Tucson, Ariz. 136 p.

Singer, D. A., and Overshine, A. T. 1979. Assessing metallic resources in Alaska. American Scientist, Vol. 67, No. 5. p. 582-589.

United States Geological Survey. 1974. United States Mineral Resources. Geology Survey Professional Paper 820. Washington, D.C. 722 p.

Chapter 7
Timber Valuation

William F. Hyde

This chapter examines the demand price appraisal for standing timber, known as "stumpage." The demand price is the purchaser's offer price per unit of standing timber ready for harvest. The objective here is to examine the conceptual economic basis for stumpage price appraisal as well as to review the procedures actually used for appraisal and to comment on when particular appraisal procedures are most appropriate. It will be shown that the difference in scale between local and institution-wide planning can have a substantial effect on the preferred appraisal procedure and the demand price itself.

The chapter is organized into four major parts. The first reviews the general conceptual background for appraisal of any *in situ* resource, beginning with derived demand and opportunity costs. The second part considers application of these concepts to timber in the short run when the resource in question is mature and ready for harvest, and in the long run when the timber is immature and harvest is only anticipated sometime in the future. The distinction between competitive and noncompetitive markets is important, particularly in the short-run case. Growth and relative price trends are important in the longer run. Existing practice often misunderstands the competitive/noncompetitive distinction. It also struggles with interesting data problems in the noncompetitive and the longer-run cases. A third part of the paper reviews some of the side issues which often cloud discussion of stumpage appraisal, such as risk and uncertainty, consumers' surpluses, multipliers and secondary benefits, and joint product (multiple use) values. A current annotated bibliography on stumpage price valuation is attached.

General Conceptual Model

Economic evaluation is founded on the principles of consumer sovereignty and value-in-exchange. Consumer sovereignty insures that consumers themselves, rather than some central authority, determine value in a free and open market for final goods and services. Value-in-exchange identifies the price of a good or service as equal to the price it can bring in its next highest valued alternative use.

In reality there is no truly open market free from public administration, however, for most goods and services, we assume that consumer sovereignty is the predominant price determining factor and that the impact of public intervention is small. Such is the case with timber. Its final product, usually lumber, sells in an open and competitive market where consumers have free choice.[1] Public intervention in the forms of assistance to nonindustrial private timber growers, favorable capital gains tax treatment for all timber growers, and tax deductible interest payments for home buyers (who are the final users of most lumber) may not substantially modify the market price for lumber. Regardless of the impact of these interventions, however, we accept them as given, and beyond the scope of this analysis. Therefore, this analysis begins from the reasonable assumption of competitive consumer demand for lumber.

The quantity demanded of a final good like lumber is a function of its price, the prices of its close substitutes, such as brick and building block, and the general income level of its consumers. We generally assume that the price of substitutes and the income level are external to our interests and that demand for lumber composes only a small portion of consumer budgets. Thereafter, we can express demand as a declining function of its own price—as D_L in figure 1. Whatever the quantity of timber demanded, e.g., q_L at the price p_L, additional demand, q'_L-q_L, only occurs if the price for all lumber is reduced to p'_L.

Lumber demand leads stumpage demand by a period equal to the time it takes to process stumpage into lumber. In other words, the current demand for stumpage derives from the expected future demand for lumber. This expected demand can be estimated from observations of current lumber prices, price trends and lumber futures markets. The factors of lumber production are stumpage and the harvest, transportation, and milling inputs. Assuming these factors combine in fixed proportions, the supply price for the nontimber factors can be expressed as the increasing function S_0 in figure 1. The demand price for stumpage, the remaining productive factor, clearly cannot exceed the difference between the expected future demand price for lumber and the supply price for the nontimber factors. Therefore, stumpage demand, D_S in figure 1, is expressed as the vertical distance between expected D_L and S_0. It is equal to zero where $D_L = S_0$, and exceeds zero for smaller volumes of expected lumber demand or where the expected demand price for lumber is greater than the cost of its nontimber inputs. Like the demand for lumber, the demand for stumpage is a declining function of its own price. When the lumber market is in equilibrium (lumber supply S_L equals D_L) at p_L, then we expect the cost of the nontimber factors to be p_0 and the stumpage price to be $p_L - p_0$, or p_S. This stumpage price p_S is also the economic rent accruing to management of the site on which the stumpage stands.

Because lumber markets are large and lumber is homogeneous, one unit of lumber is identical to and substitutes for another. Our focus is on the final unit of lumber exchanged. Any other unit of lumber can substitute for this marginal unit at price p_L without altering the stumpage price from p_S.

Lumber markets generally cut across several states and depend upon a large number of stumpage markets. The latter exist one per timbershed, of which there are generally several per state. This suggests that many of the changes which we observe in the quantity of lumber demanded are small, insufficient to measurably affect the lumber price. Expansion of a local housing market or of exports of a specialized lumber product are examples. Neither of these alters the generalized market lumber price. Similarly, such changes in the quantity of lumber are insufficient to measurably impact the stumpage demand price. The costs of the nontimber productive factors are more important. Stumpage prices will vary as, among these factors, transportation and harvest costs vary within a timbershed and mill processing costs vary with the quantity of stumpage demanded by the mill. Indeed, timbershed boundaries are defined by the maximum distance over which logs (cut stumpage) are transported from the timberstand to a central processing center composed of one or more mills. Further from the mill, transportation costs are greater, therefore, S_0 in figure 1 shifts upward, and the stumpage price at a given site decreases. On the timbershed boundary, stumpage price and site rent are zero.

The stumpage price becomes the critical short-run variable confronting timber landowners. If the short-run costs of offering stumpage for sale (sale administration costs and, sometimes, sale appraisal and roadbuilding costs) exceed the stumpage price, then wise producers either cut their losses and retire from the business or delay selling while awaiting additional timber growth (thereby obtaining greater expected stumpage prices). If, however, the stumpage price exceeds the short-run costs, then landowners can make a short-run profit by selling their stumpage.[2] (We observe that some landowners still withhold their stumpage from the market unless the stumpage price exceeds some personal reservation price in excess of short-run costs, a price which is related, often in an unspecified way, to the landowner's market expectations, personal requirements for cash, or timber regeneration costs.)

In general, whether landowners regenerate their forests and remain in the timber-growing business depends on whether the stumpage price plus its expected adjustment over time exceeds the costs of both growing and offering stumpage.

As an aside, this conceptual approach to valuation overlooks two issues which some consider important, distributive justice and justification for value. The distribution of wealth can affect price, and the converse is true also. Usually, however, distributive issues are set by national policy and become the responsibility of public health and welfare agencies. Where distributive objectives are appropriate to land management agencies which might sell stumpage, they are probably best dealt with as constraints on management, constraints set prior to price and quantity determination. Justifications for value, the second issue, are psychological, ethical, moral, and utilitarian questions beyond the scope of this chapter. Consumers decide these questions each for themselves. All that is needed here is to observe and report value as demonstrated by constrained consumer activity.

Application of These Concepts

The precise method of empirical timber appraisal varies with data availability. Direct estimation of the stumpage demand function may be possible in markets where stumpage price information exists. Otherwise it is unnecessary to derive stumpage prices from known lumber prices and factor costs. Applications of either the direct estimation or the derived method vary in the short and long run, or according to whether or not the standing timber being appraised is mature and harvestable. Accurate appraisal is most difficult for both direct and derived estimation where the market is noncompetitive.

The Short Run

In the short run, the issue is the value of standing timber ready for sale, particularly the value of standing mature and old growth timber. Formal appraisal is unnecessary where the stumpage market is competitive and there is no doubt about offering the stumpage for sale now. Accurate derivation of the stumpage price from the lumber price occurs in the market. Stumpage either sells at a market price determined by multiple competitive bids or else does not sell at all. Therefore, appraisal is redundant. Indeed, in competitive markets, formal appraisal is only an attempt to anticipate the market. Differences between competitive market prices and formally appraised prices imply error in the appraisal.

Formal appraisal is necessary where it is important to anticipate competitive market prices without actually offering stumpage for sale, for example where a timber landowner is uncertain whether to sell his stumpage this year or next and chooses to compare the two options. Expected second year stumpage prices reflect the current price anticipated for the landowner's stumpage adjusted for the changing demand for lumber and changing factor costs during the intervening year. Increasing sawmill inventory and a backlog of previously sold but unlogged stumpage suggest decreasing lumber prices and mill demand, therefore decreasing stumpage prices.

Formal appraisal is also necessary in noncompetitive markets, that is, where either a few purchasers exercise monopsony power or a single timber landowner offers sufficient timber in one large sale to affect the market price. The former is the usual case in many timbersheds, particularly in the Rocky Mountain west. The existence of only a few purchasers within a timbershed implies an even smaller number of bidders for any given timber sale within that timbershed. All mills and loggers will not be interested in every sale within their timbershed. Indeed, there is often only one bid, and the resulting sale price may be only a fraction of the stumpage price in similar competitive markets.

Derived demand.—Appraisal in noncompetitive markets is generally consistent with derived demand. In its standard form it follows the formula:

$$p_L - M - L = p_S \quad [1]$$

where p_L is the lumber price per thousand board feet, M is the mill operation cost, L is the harvest or logging and hauling cost, and p_S is the stumpage price per thousand board feet. The stumpage price must be converted from the lumber measure of the previous parameters to the log measure in which stumpage sells. It is public agency practice to also subtract a return for millowner and logger profit and risk from the left-hand side of the equation.

The values attaching to these parameters vary among stands within a timbershed. The lumber price varies with timber species and quality. Many mills are designed for logs within a given diameter range; therefore, mill operation costs may vary with average log size. Logging and hauling costs increase with more restrictive access in the forms of timber growing at a greater distance from the mill and on steeper, less stable slopes. Logging costs decrease, however, because of scale economies in the harvest operation as timber volume per acre increases.

Two standard appraisal procedures, known as the "investment" method and the "overturn" method, apply technical and statistical estimates, respectively, to assess the values of each parameter in equation [1]. The most common use of the investment method occurs where there is little or no experiential data, for example where the timber sale in question is of unprecedented size or where an altogether new timbershed is being opened. This method hypothesizes a model mill and logging operation and extracts costs for equation [1] which are appropriate to the hypothetical model. Returns to profit and risk, where calculated, are taken as an average return to the hypothetical capital invested in the model mill and logging operation. The overturn method is more common where experiential information is plentiful. Observations of mill and logging costs are taken from a representative industry sample. They are evaluated with more or less statistical precision in order to arrive at values for equation [1]. Returns to profit and risk, where calculated, are a function of the frequency of log to lumber turnover (or overturn) as well as of an average return on invested capital.

The problem with these procedures is that, as applied, they tend to disregard evidence that mill operation and logging costs vary with log size and sale volume as well as evidence that relative lumber prices have been increasing over time. This means that the second parameter on the left-hand side of equation [1] is, incorrectly, treated as a constant and that the third is, incorrectly, permitted to vary only with hauling distance. Correct derivation should reflect that each of these parameters, and therefore stumpage demand price, is a function of volume and, perhaps, log size.

Lumber price changes over time are particularly important. They explain, for example, the recent history of Forest Service timber sales in Western Oregon and Washington with appraisals sharply divergent from winning competitive bids. The Forest Service appraises timber sales at current value and then allows up to 5 years for the harvest operation (recently extended to 7 years in special situations). Purchasers' bids are based upon expected increasing timber prices over the next 5 years and often exceed the Forest Service appraisal by more than 100%.[3] This is no reason to discard either the investment or overturn procedure. Their correct applications can take the time, log size, and sale volume factors into account. Correct applications for noncompetitive markets, however, are infrequent. There is considerable need for good examples of both the investment and the overturn procedure which are responsive to all the relevant variables discussed above.

Direct estimation.—Direct stumpage price estimation is an alternative to derivation of the stumpage price from the demand for lumber. Direct estimation requires assessing the demand and, where relevant, supply functions for stumpage and is restricted to the extent that data for estimating these functions, competitive stumpage market price data, are available. Direct estimation is known as the "comparable" or "transactions evidence" procedure, because its data originate with comparable timber sale transactions.

Jackson and his associates (Jackson and McQuillan 1979, Merzenich 1981) have demonstrated one variant of this procedure in a series of recent applications. They simplify joint estimation of the stumpage supply and demand functions by estimating equilibrium stumpage price as a function of various factors which might shift either the demand or the supply functions for logs. Their common demand shifter is mill backlog D (both cut and uncut inventory), and their usual supply shifters have to do with harvest costs per unit S_C (e.g., harvest method, tree diameter, haul distance) and harvest volume S_V (volume per acre and either total volume or total acreage). Constraints on harvest operations C (e.g., Small Business Administration set-aside sales and contract duration) may also explain a significant share of the variance in observed stumpage prices.

$$p_S = p_S(D, S_C, S_V, C) \qquad [2]$$

There must also be a time or price trend variable on the right-hand side of equation [2] if the intent is to estimate current competitive bid prices for timber which will be harvested in the future, as is the case with the Forest Service timber.

The objective is to estimate, for noncompetitive markets, what the competitive stumpage prices would be. If data for such analysis is carefully restricted to observations of competitive sales, defined as sales with several bidders, then the analytical results can be applied in comparable noncompetitive markets to estimate their competitive market stumpage price. That is, Jackson's appraisal approach can provide coefficients for the independent variables on the right-hand side of equation [2] which, when applied to the local physical characteristics of a noncompetitive market, estimate competitive market prices, the correct appraised stumpage prices.

Correct empirical estimates from transactions evidence and for noncompetitive markets are recent, and much remains to be learned about how coefficients for the independent variables vary for different markets and over time. We must be careful to understand that competitive market coefficients serve to model noncompetitive markets. Competitive markets, themselves, need no sophisticated mathematical models, and noncompetitive market price observations are of no use in examining the social value of the resource.

The Longer Run

In time, standing timber grows both in volume and in value. The longer run price appraisal problem is one of anticipating the expected stumpage value at some specified future date after growth has occurred. Therefore, estimating growth of the timber stand is an important feature of long run projections. It is, however, outside this discussion of stumpage prices. (Interested readers might refer to the *Forestry Handbook* (Forbes 1961) and other references for physical production functions, known as timber yield curves.)

In the long run, the competitive/noncompetitive market distinction remains important. Price appraisal is easier in competitive markets where timber volumes exchanged are small. Derivation from expected future lumber prices is possible, but the general difficulty of accurate projection recommends in favor of simplicity. Direct estimates from current stumpage prices adjusted according to the rate of relative annual price change are easier. Current stumpage prices are known. Various annual rates of historical and projected increase ranging approximately from 1.5% to 3.5% have been reported. Managers who doubt their price projections can test their resource allocational decisions for sensitivity to stumpage price changes in this range. Of course, there will be short-run variations around the long-run estimates, variations resulting from short-term building and business cycle adjustments and localized adjustments in mill capacity and growing stock.

The noncompetitive case implies large volume changes sufficient to affect the demand-supply equilibrium. Such changes require estimating the impact of changing volume on local stumpage prices, as well as projecting the price change over time, as in the previous competitive case. Stumpage price changes resulting from volume shifts are unlikely for single local timbersheds in the long run. Large stumpage volume changes within a timbershed may well occur, but in the longer run they can only lead to corresponding mill capacity shifts. It is unlikely that shifts within any timbershed can affect price in the much larger lumber market. After longer run capacity adjustments, we expect the isolated local stumpage market to return to its old equilibrium price (adjusting for temporal price changes of course), because marginal mills in each timbershed must earn the same return in long-run equilibrium.

Additional Points

Several side issues enter the discussion of timber appraisal. The important issues are: (1) risk and uncertainty; (2) quality, species and product differences and; (3) aggregation or appraisal of regional or national stumpage prices. Risk and uncertainty are probably best managed by testing decisions dependent on stumpage price information for sensitivity to a range of stumpage prices: the more risk averse the decisionmaker, the lower the stumpage price range. The impacts of quality and species differences on stumpage price can be determined by statistical estimation. If the differences bear a consistent relationship to the stumpage price in question, then a measure of quality or species may be included in the stumpage price equation. If, as is less likely, the differences bear an inconsistent or unknown relationship to the stumpage price, then they suggest a different product, requiring a second, independent demand price appraisal.

To this point, our attention has focused on stumpage demand prices within a single timbershed. Sometimes, however, knowledge of regional or national stumpage prices, or of the impacts on them caused by corporate decisions or public policies is needed. These occasions, for example longer term forest

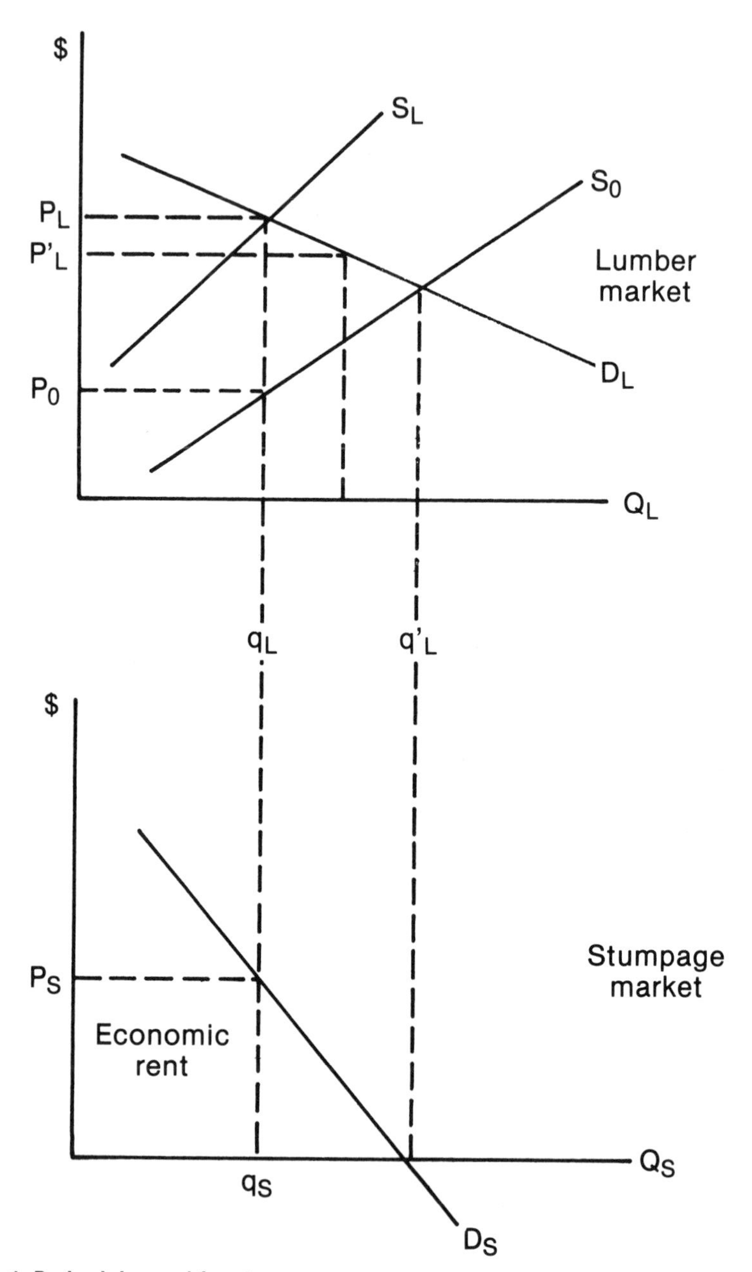

Figure 1. Derived demand for stumpage.

planning, require stumpage demand functions explaining the aggregate of many timbersheds. The potentially large price and quantity impacts which corporate and public policies may have on these aggregate functions justify multiple equation econometric models. These models are beyond the scope of this chapter, but it is useful to know that they are built on the same principles as the derived demand and direct estimation models examined earlier. The difference, aside from aggregation, is that their greater complexity may provide a more sophisticated understanding of the various factors underlying demand and supply shifts for both lumber and stumpage, now and over time.

Consumers' surpluses, a previously ignored topic, may become important to aggregate stumpage valuation adjustments resulting from public policy changes. Consumers' surpluses is the value in excess of price which consumers receive for inframarginal goods and services. Diagrammatically, it is the area above the market price and below the demand curve, the shaded area in figure 1. Corporate managers need not consider this value because they collect none of the benefits from changes in it. Public managers interested in aggregate social welfare should be concerned, but only in those unusual cases where their actions cause supramarginal shifts in aggregate stumpage prices (shifts sufficient to significantly alter estimates of consumers' surpluses).

Joint production or multiple use, and secondary benefits and multipliers are side issues which sometimes appear in discussions of, but are unimportant to, the demand price valuation of timber. Joint production of timber together with other forest outputs may affect resource allocation decisions through its impact on cost functions, but it does not affect timber demand functions. Its potential, therefore, is not meaningful to stumpage price appraisal. There are secondary benefits to any use of any resource, therefore, secondary benefits become important only when the resource in question has an abnormal secondary impact or when they refer to resources which are both newly utilized as a result of, in our case, selling additional timber, and not replacing another use of timber or some other resource. Either the case for unusual secondary benefits must be proven before these benefits are accumulated or else decisionmakers must be prepared for expensive and time-consuming calculation of similar secondary benefits for all possible alternative decisions.

Summary, Conclusions, Policy Implications

Appraisal is unnecessary in competitive markets. The market sets the final stumpage price regardless of whether appraisal and managerial effort spent on appraisal is wasted. Appraisal is necessary, however, where market projections are required and where either the buyer or seller has market power, that is where his timber harvest decision can affect the stumpage price. This is probably the more usual case, because most timbersheds have only a few buyers, and even where there are many buyers, public agencies may be dominant among the few sellers. The important feature in these noncompetitive cases is that stumpage price must be appraised as a function of quantity. (Point estimates of one price regardless of volume demanded are incorrect.) Stumpage price also should be a function of time where harvests from a single sale are allowed to occur over time. This is an important point for public agencies, because they tend to allow harvests over periods as long as 5 years, sufficient time for substantial stumpage price modification.

There are two standard approaches to stumpage price appraisal for standing mature timber—derived demand and direct estimation. The derived demand procedure appraises stumpage prices as the residual remaining after subtracting all nontimber production costs from the lumber demand price. Lumber price is known from the market. Difficulties, when they exist, arise in accurate estimation of the nontimber production costs. Competitive bids far in excess of appraisal are evidence of this difficulty in the Forest Service experience.

Direct estimation of stumpage demand price requires estimation of the stumpage demand and supply functions for the timbershed. Single step estimation of price from comparable data and as a function of both demand and supply shifters is a modification of this approach. The problem with direct estimation is the lack of sufficient empirical observations from comparable sales on the same or similar timbersheds. Choice between derived demand and direct estimation is determined by which has the better data set.

Risk and uncertainty may be incorporated in either case by testing resource allocational decisions for sensitivity to variation around the estimated stumpage price. Product, quality and species differences may be introduced through another variable in the stumpage price equations or by making a second and independent appraisal. Longer-run projections must take timber growth and the upward trend in relative stumpage prices into account.

Timber valuation is not a topic in need of great research. There is much need, however, for correct illustrative case studies, modelling competitive markets and fully responsive to variables such as volume, diameter, access, and time.

References

Adams, Darius M., and Richard W. Haynes. 1980. The 1980 softwood timber assessment market model. Forest Science, vol. 26, no. 3 (September) (supplement).

Data Resources, Inc., 1981. Demand for Pacific Northwest timber and timber products. Vancouver, Wash. Forest Policy Project of Washington State University.

These are the two best-known projections of aggregate stumpage prices.

Forbes, R. D., ed. 1961. Forestry Handbook. New York: Ronald Press. Sections 2,3.

A beginning reference for yield tables.

Gregory, G. Robinson. 1972. Forest Resource Economics. New York: Ronald Press, Ch. 8.

The textbook explanation of derived demand appraisal for timber.

Hyde, William F. 1980. Timber Supply, Land Allocation and Economic Efficiency. Baltimore, Md. Johns Hopkins University Press. Ch. 4.

Vogely, William A. 1981. Valuation of mineral resources: A state-of-the-art review. In this volume.

Comments on economic rent of the forest resource.

Jackson, David H., and Alan G. McQuillan. 1979. A technique for estimating timber value based on tree size, management variables and market conditions. Forest Science, vol. 25, no. 4. December. p. 620-626.

Merzenich, James P. 1981. The use of stumpage valuation equations in FORPLAN. (unpubl. ms. USDA Forest Service, Region 1).
Applications of direct statistical stumpage price estimation for various Northern Rocky Mountain National Forests.

Mead, Walter J. 1966. Competition and Oligopsony in the Douglas-fir Lumber Industry. Berkeley, Calif. U. California Press.
Analysis of one cause of the difference between appraised and successful bid prices for Forest Service stumpage in Western Oregon and Washington.

Weiner, Alfred E. 1981. Appraising national forest timber value: A concept reexamined. Journal of Forestry 79(6):372-376.
A concise summary of current U.S. Forest Service appraisal methods with examples. Weiner was the Forest Service chief appraisal officer.

Weintraub, Sidney J. 1959. Price-making in Forest Service timber sales. American Economic Review 49(4):628-637.
An early comment on the economic intuition of the derived demand stumpage price appraisal procedure.

Footnotes

[1]*Lumber is the predominant final product and serves as our example throughout this paper. Calculations are conceptually identical for the demand price for stumpage processed into pulpwood, posts, pilings, fuelwood and furniture. Consumers have essentially unhindered free choices in each of these markets.*

[2]*This economic explanation of the relation between stumpage prices and timber production explains private management. Public agencies may operate at variance with this explanation. The Forest Service, for example, first determines its harvest level apart from prices and costs and then appraises the stumpage price at a level designed to make the predetermined harvest attainable. (The predetermined harvest level may be either greater than or less than that determined by equating prices and marginal costs. There are examples of both cases.)*

[3]*The large difference between bid and appraised prices is unimportant in these competitive markets. (Timber sells at the bid and competitive price. The appraised price is irrelevant except as a starting point for bids.) The difference suggests, however, that the appraisal is too low. Since the Forest Service appraisal procedure is the same in both competitive and noncompetitive markets, then noncompetitive appraisals are probably also too low. This is important because the appraisal essentially sets the winning bid price in noncompetitive markets. The result may be a substantial transfer from the public treasury to noncompetitive market loggers and millowners.*

Chapter 8
Estimating Benefits of Range for Wildland Management and Planning

E. T. Bartlett

Introduction

Approximately two-thirds of the land of the United States can be considered to be wildland, and most of this can be classified as range.[1] Range includes both forested and non-forested lands which support an understory or periodic cover of herbaceous or shrubby vegetation amenable to grazing or browsing use (Range Term Glossary Committee 1974). Range provides many outputs such as recreation, water, forest products, wildlife, and related goods and services, but has traditionally been associated with providing forage for livestock. This chapter examines the methods that have been used to value benefits relating to range forage and to the ecological aspects of range resources, and identifies topics for future research.

Range Benefits

Production of range forage for livestock grazing is an important use of range; however, other herbivores use range forage. In all cases, range forage is an intermediate good used to produce other outputs such as red meat, wildlife and associated recreational benefits, and wild horses and burros. It also appears that society places value on the continuity of the range ecosystems and the plant species within those ecosystems.

The amount and quality of range forage varies between ranges and over time on the same range. In addition, the amount of forage available for grazing depends on the type of animal using that forage. The amount of range forage used depends on the characteristics of the range, the stocking rate, and the types of animals grazed.

Numerous species of wildlife occur on range and derive all or part of their habitat and nutritional requirements from native range. Some of the wildlife species compete for the range resource with domestic animals, others might be thought of as complimentary users of the range forage resource, depending on the range ecosystem and season of use. Most wildlife production studies on range have concentrated on big game species, such as deer and elk. Research is needed to determine the joint production relationships between different animal species when they are present during the same seasons or during different seasons. In fact, little work has been done to determine joint production relationships of different domestic animal species.

In addition to big game, wild horses and burros are present on many western ranges. These animals compete for forage with both livestock and wildlife. While most people have not seen a wild horse or a wild burro, there is a benefit derived from them by society. This is discussed later.

Non-use benefits of range include the continuity of the various range ecosystems and the continuing existence of species that are rare, threatened, or endangered. There are numerous other benefits from range such as recreation, esthetics, water, and forest products.

Domestic Livestock Grazing

Approximately one-half of the nation's wildland is grazed by domestic animals. Range forage has been classified in resource economics as a market good, as opposed to a non-market good. This is a valid classification in the case of private range that is allocated to users by a market system. However, on U.S. Government lands, grazing has been allocated by federal requirements to obtain grazing permits. Thus, public range forage is not allocated by a true market system, although permits are sold with ranches.

The value of range forage grazed by livestock is derived from the value of the livestock produced. Thus, the value of range forage depends on the values of products produced from range forage, the value of other types of feeds and forage that might be used to produce the products, and the efficiency of the operation. The value of the range forage is the total amount that the firm would be willing to pay for the last increment of forage, which is the value of the output attributable to the increment of the input less the costs of using that input. This amount is the value of the marginal product or marginal value productivity, and for individual firms, represents the demand for range forage.

Several empirical approaches have ben used in an attempt to identify the marginal value productivity for range forage.[2] The methods can be generally classified as: (1) comparisons with market-priced forages and feed sources; (2) capitalization of permit values; and (3) production analysis.

Comparison with Market-Priced Forages and Feed Sources.

This approach is based on determining the value of substitutes for range forage in the production process, and adjusting the value for differences in the cost of using different forage or feed sources. The most common alternative forage resource has been comparable private leased range. Numerous studies have been conducted since 1916, with the 1966 Western Livestock Grazing Survey[3] and Bergland and Andrus (1977) among the most recent.

The premise that is used to justify estimating public grazing value from private grazing values is that firms will bid for both sources to the margin, in which case the price of private grazing will equal the price of public grazing (Nielsen 1972). However, it has been shown that the rancher does not pay the full value for public grazing, and that he is not allowed to purchase federal grazing to the margin (Roberts 1963). The approach that has been used to derive an estimate of the value of federal range forage has been as follows:

$$F = \text{MVP} - E \quad [1]$$

where F is the full market value of federal forage, MVP is the market value of the forage determined from private lease rates, and E is the non-fee costs of using public ranges such as herding, improvement maintenance and transportation (Nielsen 1972). E adjusts the value to the net differences in using the public forage as opposed to the private forage.

The adjusted private lease rate was the basis for grazing fees from 1969 to 1978, and was recommended as the preferred method in 1977 by the U. S. Departments of Agriculture and Interior (Bergland and Andrus 1977). In fact, the 1977 study assumed that non-fee costs had increased at a constant rate since the 1966 survey. This assumes that the intensity of management has remained constant over this time period. In fact, many grazing systems were implemented on federal allotments which intensified management and increased non-fee costs (Bartlett and Ralphs 1978). This is not a weakness of the empirical approach, but a weakness in the application of the approach.

The private lease rate approach results in the value of range forage at the current level of use. If the value is used in cases where there are only marginal changes in the forage provided, the private lease rate approach can be used if the private range is comparable to the public forage resource (Dyer 1981). Quality of the range (forage quantity and quality, distributional factors such as water and topography) should be considered when comparing private range to public range so that the animal productivity of the two range resources is comparable.

The private lease rate approach possibly could be expanded to estimate demand for public range forage. To do so, the demand for private range forage must be derived using econometric methods. The derived demand then would be adjusted to reflect demand for public range forage. There has been no study that has attempted such an approach (Godfrey 1981), although Johnson and Hardin (1955) discussed the factors that affect the demand for pasture forage.

Other forage sources such as pasture, hay, or supplemental feeds have been suggested as points of measurement in efforts to estimate range forage value. The use of pasture lease rates would be very similar to the private lease rate described above; however, the problems involved in relating pasture values to range values would be greater. Pastures are generally much higher in productivity than range, and are managed in small units.

The value of hay has been used to estimate value of range forage (U.S.D.A Forest Service 1980, p. C-6). A formula was used that multiplied the average animal weight times the average price per ton of hay times a quality factor of pasture. Hay is exchanged in a competitive market, and, as such, reflects the changes in livestock values and other feed source values (Godfrey 1981). Empirical evidence could not be found that relates hay to range forage.[4] A general caution concerning methods that are based on alternative feed sources is that the market price of a substitute is not a good proxy for range forage value, but substitute feeds do influence the demand for range forage.

Of the valuation methods that are based on market forage or feed sources, the private lease rate approach can be used to value range forage in wildland management and planning. However, this approach should be used only if the change in forage provided is marginal, and the private leased range is comparable to the public range (Dyer 1981).

Capitalization of Permit Values

Historically, the fee for grazing public range forage has been below the value of the range forage.[5] Because the marginal value of the public forage exceeded the marginal costs of using it, the permits have been valued. The permit value is the capitalized difference between the marginal revenues and marginal costs. Roberts and Topham (1965) give the value of public range as:

$$V = F + PC \qquad [2]$$

where V is the annual value of public forage to ranchers, F is the grazing fee, P is the market value of the grazing permit, and C is the capitalization rate.

Several studies have tested the permit value equation (Gardner 1962, Roberts and Topham 1965, and Martin and Jefferies 1966). Gardner (1962) used an expectation model to estimate the difference between private and public grazing changes. The difference was capitalized to represent the expected value of the permit. Actual permit values were well below the expected permit values. Gardner argued that this was because of the restrictive rules for qualifying for a permit, and the history of reducing permitted grazing when allotments were reassigned. Roberts and Topham (1965) stated that the fee plus the discounted value of the permit was a good estimate of the value of public forage at the site.

Martin and Jefferies (1966) used regression analysis to estimate the price of ranches as a function of acres of private land, animal unit of FS permits, animal units of BLM permits, animal units of state permits, number of breeding animals, steers and heifers sold with the ranch and the year the ranch was sold. The marginal value of public range forage was the parameter on FS and BLM permits. The estimates were similar to actual permit values found by Gardner (1962), but below the expected values.

A discussion of these results is warranted. Martin and Jefferies (1966) argue that the returns from beef that results from public range use do not justify the price paid for public range permits. They hypothesize that there are other returns besides beef production to the permit investment. These include anticipated appreciation in permit value, reduced taxes through tax shelters, ranch fundamentalism, and conspicuous consumption. Ranch fundamentalism refers to those that place some value on being in the livestock business and on that way of life. Conspicuous consumption refers to those that buy ranches because "one who lives in the West should have a ranch." The argument is that permit values represent benefits in addition to those gained from grazing range forage for livestock production.

If this argument is true, why were Gardner's expected permit value so much higher than actual values? Martin and Jefferies (1966) state, "The outputs of private rental lands are just as complicated as the outputs on public leases. One should not use private rental land as a standard for comparison, with the implication that private rentals are used for beef production only." Private lease rates also may be influenced by the season in which they are grazed. It is logical that a rancher would lease additional private range only at times when his deeded and public range were limiting. Thus, the values of private leased range may be higher because of the critical nature of the forage in a particular season. In Colorado, changing the amount of spring grazing on public ranges had a much greater impact on livestock sales than changing the amount of grazing in other seasons (Cook et al. 1980).

Another explanation of expected permit values exceeding actual values is that the permit value is reduced by the tenure uncertainty associated with permits (Milliman 1962). A recent study in New Mexico showed that while FS and BLM permits increased in value from 1965 to 1979, the private grazing price index increased at a greater rate (Fowler and Gray 1980). In fact, neither BLM or FS permits increased in value at a rate equal to the U. S. consumer price index, and BLM permit value increased at a lower rate than did FS permit value. The BLM permit value has not increased since 1975, when the grazing Environmental Impact Statement process was started. Thus, uncertainty of permit tenure may influence permit values. In Oregon, Winter and Whittaker (1981) did not find that public grazing rights statistically effected private-land sale prices during 1970 to 1978. They explained the lack of permit value as being brought about by increasing grazing fees and uncertain tenure of permits.

Another factor that could influence the permit value is option value. Option value is the value in addition to the value of the resource that arises from retaining an option to use the good or service for which future demand is uncertain (Krutilla and Fisher 1975). Ranchers may stock their own range resources conservatively in normal years, and rely on the public range forage at permitted amounts or less than permitted amounts. In periods of forage shortage, they could rely on both resources to survive such periods.

To summarize, it has been shown that public range grazing fees have been below the range forage value and that value has accrued to the permit. However, it is questionable that the short-term marginal value productivity of range forage for grazing is equal to the permit value. Because permits are issued for 10 years, there is a long term value possibly related to an option value. In addition, permits may increase or decrease in value independent of the forage value. In any event, an estimate of range forage value based on permit value results in an estimate of value for the current level of forage provided. To derive demand, estimates at different levels of forage would be needed. However, it is doubtful that such a derived demand would be very useful, because changes in permitted use effects the value of the permit because of uncertainties in tenure that are implied. The examination of permit value does give rise to many questions concerning range values.

Production Analysis

Production analysis is an approach (or a group of approaches) that values an input on the basis of the production process and resulting value of the output(s). There are basically two ways to approach the problem: (1) empirically estimate the production function; or (2) use operations research to model the relationships based on budget data.

Roberts (1963) suggested that a third-degree polynomial would be appropriate for a public forage production function based on grazing intensity (eq. [3]).

$$R = bX + cX^2 - dX^3 \qquad [3]$$

where R is the total physical output times the market price of the livestock realized off the range, and X is the number of cows grazed per section (representing grazing intensity). From this, Roberts derived the MVP of grazing intensity. Most ranges are not stocked considering such a relationship, but are generally stocked at a moderate level of intensity. Range forage is only one variable input in livestock production by ranch operations, and the problems of estimating more complex problems increases greatly.

In the budgeting technique, the total gross value of the firm's output is calculated, then the costs of all variable inputs except range forage are deducted. The remaining portion of gross value is known as the residual, which is the return to, or value of, the unpriced input (Sinden and Worrell 1979). If the residual is calculated for several amounts of the unpriced input, a demand schedule can be estimated. In a sample to determine rancher budgets, general ranch information should be obtained from a relatively large sample and detailed production relationships should be determined on a small number of case ranches that are representative of the population (Plath 1956).

The results obtained by budgeting are based on an implicit production function that is contained within the budget and estimate short-run value. Martin and Snider (1980) derived short-run values of range forage in the Salt-Verde Basin of Arizona using a budgeting approach. They also estimated the average and marginal long-run values of range forage by deducting fixed costs from the residual and capitalizing the remainder. This budget study was unique because forage value was estimated; most budget studies merely report the economic characteristics of range firms. A 1965 report apparently incorporated budget analysis to determine economic impacts of changes in grazing fees and permitted use (USDA Economic Research Service 1965). While impacts on livestock sales were estimated, value of the public range forage was not examined.

Linear programming is a technique that has been used to analyze budget data. The residual of the marginal unit of input is known as the "shadow price" in linear programming. Parametric analysis, in which the amount of range forage is varied, can be used to calculate the residuals which represent the demand for the unpriced input. This technique has been used to derive demand for Forest Service forage in Colorado (Bartlett et al. 1981). The demand was estimated for various livestock prices and under two management schemes: variable herd size and constant herd size. The constant herd size resulted in a demand based on the costs of alternate feed sources; the variable herd size scheme allowed adjustment of inputs and products.

The Economic Research Service uses budgeting and linear programming to estimate the marginal value of public range forage in the western U.S.[6] Also, several studies have assessed the impacts of potential changes in public forage supply and cost on net ranch income, livestock sales, and local and regional economies (Peryam and Olson 1975, Olson and Jackson 1975, Lewis and Taylor 1977, Torell et al. 1979, Torell et al. 1980, Cook et al. 1980). None of the studies were extended to estimate the value of public range forage.

While linear programming provided a technique to rapidly analyze budget information and derive demand for range forage, results are based on the budget data and the assumptions incorporated with the linear programming model. Budgetary information is rapidly outdated because of changes in operation caused by changing market prices for outputs and technology (McConnen 1976). Values obtained with the uses of linear programming analysis are determined by changes in other inputs, and other resources are valued and reflected in the measurement of any given factor or resource (McCorkle 1956). In fact, it is difficult to compare the results of various studies unless the linear programming models have been formulated in a similar manner. A set of common assumptions and model formulation rules are needed so that valuation studies are consistent.

Godfrey (1981) mentions five assumptions that cause linear programming to be biased and not comparable to estimates derived for other benefits. Three of these assumptions relate to how the linear programming model is constructed and concern temporal availability, non-fee costs, and nutrient requirements of different animals. Both the study by Bartlett et al. (1981) and the continuing work by the Economic Research Service incorporated these factors. Another of Godfrey's assumptions was related to the theoretical validity of deriving demand from a fixed proportion production function, which he admitted is not a major problem. However, a truely fixed proportion model would result in a linear production function and horizontal demand. This is an area in which recommendations are needed to guide future use of linear programming. Finally, Godfrey (1981, p. 42) stated, "...and perhaps most importantly, the demand function derived from an LP model is generally very sensitive to changes in the price of the output(s) and/or other inputs." This is not necessarily an assumption of linear programming, but it does show that the estimates of forage demand are sensitive to the demand shifters.

Other Valuation Approaches

Other studies have been made to determine valuing of public grazing. Most of these have been done to estimate grazing fees for state owned range forage and are based on livestock prices and various other factors including carrying capacity (Huss 1955, Harris and Hoffman 1963, Campbell and Wood 1951, McDowell and Johnson 1964). Most of the results were based on what was acceptable to the lessor and lessee and were not based on empirical estimates of the value of range forage.

Approaches that are used to estimate non-market benefits such as recreation have not been applied to range forage. However, a study at Colorado State University will use a bidding game approach to estimate public range forage value. The resulting values will be compared to those estimated with a linear programming approach (Bartlett et al. 1981).

Grazing Fee Issue

Grazing fees for federal forage are to reflect fair market value of the forage (Federal Land Policy and Management Act of 1976). While the grazing fee does not impact the value of forage, the way in which the fee is determined may influence which method is the most appropriate to estimate value. The methods that have been discussed above have been used when the fee is below forage value. Several authors have advocated allocating grazing of public ranges on the basis of competitive bids (Brewer 1962, Gardner 1963, Martin and Jefferies 1966). While there is disagreement on the tenure of grazing, the contention is that the grazing rights would be exchanged in a competitive market and that grazing would be valued at the margin. In addition, bidders would consider seasonal availability of the forage, forage quantity and quality, and other characteristics of the public range. It is highly unlikely that such a competitive bid system will evolve. The present regulations for grazing permits were established with consideration of equity and the stability of the range livestock industry.

Private Range Forage

Private range forage is used by the owner or is leased in conditions that are assumed to be competitive (Godfrey 1981). The value of forage used by the owner can be estimated by production analysis. Johnson and Hardin (1955) and Jacobs (1974) provide a more complete discussion. In the case of leased range, studies have been done to estimate these rates (see discussion above). Nielsen and Workman (1971) cautioned that grazing leases include various services other than the use of the range forage. An empirically derived demand for private forage has not been reported. However, estimates of value at current levels of private range use should be adequate to represent this resource, because no large changes in grazing of private range forage are expected.

Value of Wildlife Use

Wildlife compete for the same resource base that is used by domestic livestock. Wildlife uses are classified as consumptive, non-consumptive, and indirect or vicarious users of wildlife (see the chapter in this book by Shaw). These uses have been valued by the income compensation function approach or the expenditure function approach described by Alan Randall. However, these values have not been related to the habitat that the animals need to produce the various wildlife benefits.

Because wildland management programs influence the amount of wildlife and domestic animals present on an area, there is disagreement on how the resource should be allocated to different animal species. Range forage for domestic grazing is valued on the site and at the margin. Therefore, wildlife should be valued on a comparable basis in order to provide information concerning the efficiency criterion. This is not easy, especially because little has been reported on the joint production functions of different species of animals using the same resource base.

Wild Horses and Burros

While wild horses and burros have long been a common feature of many western ranges, their value was largely ignored until the passage of the Wild Free-Roaming Horse and Burros Act of 1971. The law essentially dictates that the horses and burros will not be disturbed by people; society decided it valued their existence even though most people never actually observed the animals. The original law implied a high value, because few herd control measures were allowed (Cook 1975). Provisions in the Federal Land Policy and Management Act of 1976 and the Public Rangelands Improvement Act of 1977 modified the control measures allowed, and indicate that society values wild horses and burros less than originally thought.

Godfrey (1979) reviewed the topics and found that very little is known of the value of wild horses and burros. He determined the expenditures being made to reduce herd numbers which does not estimate the demand for the animals but might reflect some minimum value that society places on ecosystems being grazed by wild horses and burros. Johnston and Yost (1979) reviewed economic literature that related to wild horses and burros, and reported very few studies or articles on the subject. Research is needed to determine the existence value of these animals.[7]

Ecological Continuity

Krutilla and Fisher (1975) define existence values as value that individuals have for an environment regardless of the fact that they will never demand the services it provides at the site. Society values the existence of range ecosystems or the option value of saving them for use in the future. This benefit of range has not been estimated empirically, but in the future this may be possible. To date, this benefit, as well as the benefits from rare and endangered species, have been assured through legislation. Legislation has mandated agencies to provide for ecosystem continuity and diversity as well as to make efforts to insure the survival of limited animal and plant species. Given the present state-of-the-art, demand estimates and marginal values of these benefits are not expected to be forthcoming.

The relationship between ecological continuity and other range benefits should be evaluated. Environmental quality may be maintained or improved with proper and moderate livestock grazing (Council on Agricultural Science and Technology 1974). In addition, Workman and Hooper (1968) suggested that ranchers were more willing to make range improvements than agencies, because fees were lower than the value of the forage. In the management and planning of wildlands, program costs should be allocated to the benefits for which they are implemented.

Needs in Range Valuation Research

Values of benefits are needed if benefit cost analysis is to be used as an information system in wildland planning and management. Some approaches are available to estimate the value of range benefits, particularly range forage for domestic grazing. Demand estimations must be made in a consistent manner across the geographical area being planned or managed. Research is needed to insure consistent empirical results, to investigate values related to range forage, and to estimate values of other benefits.

It appears that the budgeting approach using linear programming is presently the most appropriate method to derive demand for range livestock grazing. Alternative feed and forage sources, seasonal availability of forage, livestock prices, and range capacities can simultaneously be included in the analysis. It is not evident how these parameters should be estimated or which should be allowed to vary. A study by an individual or group of scientists should be made that would result in a set of guidelines for using this approach so that values are consistent and comparable between geographical areas and across different groups or individuals that use the technique.

Non-grazing benefits that are received by permit holders should be determined. Even though fees may approach true value, there will still be other benefits, such as the option to use the resource in the future. While the measures of these values are not available and their existence is even speculative, the benefit would be gained by society. Therefore, research is needed to determine to what degree these benefits exist and what their values are.

Research is needed to estimate the value of wild horses and burros as well as wildlife. The values of these benefits must be made on a consistent basis with other resource values. The benefits associated with ecological continuity, ecological diversity and threatened and endangered species are also unvalued at present. While it would be beneficial to have values for these, other areas of research have higher priority. Congress has placed constraints on wildland managers in that they will manage continuity and diversity and will protect threatened and endangered species.

Literature Cited

Bartlett, E. T., and M. R. Ralphs. 1978. Estimation of grazing values for the 1980 RPA program. Report of the RPA evaluation work group. U.S. Department pf Agriculture, Forest Service, Washington, D.C. 29 p. [Mimeo]

Bartlett, E. T., Paul Kehmeier and R. Garth Taylor. 1981. Valuation and demand for U. S. Forest Service grazing in Colorado. Colorado State University, Department of Range Science, Fort Collins, Colo. 62 p.

Bergland, B., and C. D. Andrus. 1977. Study of fees for grazing livestock on

federal lands. A report from the Secretaries of Interior and Agriculture. Washington, D.C., U. S. Govt. Printing Office: 1977-248-888/6624.
Brewer, Michael F. 1962. Public pricing of natural resources. Journal of Farm Economics 44(1):35-49.
Campbell, J. A., and V. A. Wood. 1951. A range land rental system based on carrying capacity and the price of beef. Journal of Range Management 4(6):370-374.
Cook, C. Wayne. 1975. Wild horses and burros: A new management problem. Rangeman's Journal 2:19-21.
Cook, C. Wayne, Garth Taylor and E. T. Bartlett. 1980. Impacts of federal range forage on rancher and regional economies of Colorado. Colorado State University Experiment Station Bulletin 576S, 7 p.
Council on Agricultural Science and Technology. 1974. Livestock grazing on federal lands. Journal of Range Management 27(3):174-181.
Dutton, W. L. 1953. History of Forest Service grazing fees. Journal of Range Management 6(6):393-398.
Dyer, A. A. 1981. Public natural resource management and valuation of non-market outputs. Paper presented at Workshop 5, Committee to Evaluate Rangeland Strategies of the Bureau of Land Management, National Academy of Sciences, May 11-13, Boise, Idaho. 48 p.
Foss, Philip O. 1959. The determination of grazing fees on federally owned rangelands. Journal of Farm Economics 41:535-547.
Fowler, John M., and James R. Gray. 1980. Market values of federal grazing permits in New Mexico. New Mexico State University, Cooperative Extension Service, Range Improvement Task Force Report 2, 23 p.
Gardner, B. Delworth. 1962. Transfer restrictions and misallocation in grazing public range. Journal of Farm Economics 45(1):109-120.
Gardner, B. Delworth. 1963. A proposal to reduce misallocation of livestock grazing permits. Journal of Farm Economics 45(1):109-120.
Godfrey, E. Bruce. 1979. The economic role of wild and free roaming horses and burros on rangelands in the western United States. A final report submitted to the Intermountain Forest and Range Experiment Station, USDA Forest Service. Utah State University, Department of Economics, Logan, Utah.
Godfrey, E. Bruce. 1981. Definition of economic research needed to evaluate forage supplies on range and cropland for integrating assessments of renewable resources at national, regional, and state levels: A final report. Utah State University, Department of Economics, Logan, Utah. 58 p.
Harris, Grant A., and Wallace R. Hoffman. 1963. Determining equitable grazing fees for Washington Department of Natural Resources Land. Journal of Range Management 16(5):265-275.
Huss, Donald L. 1955. A basis for a conservation lease of rangeland on the Edwards Plateau of Texas. Journal of Range Management 8(5):208-210.
Jacobs, V. E. 1974. An economic approach to forage yield measurement and valuation. pp. 523-532. *In* Forage fertilization, Mays, D. (ed.). American Society of Agronomy, 677 S. Segoe Rd., Madison, Wisc.
Johnson, Glenn L., and Lowell S. Hardin. 1955. Economics of forage evaluation. Purdue University Agricultural Experiment Station Bulletin 623, 20 p.

Johnston, Warren E., and Glenn Yost. 1979. An annotated bibliography on selected aspects of Western range economics relating to the study of wild and free-roaming horses and burros. University of California, Davis, Department of Agricultural Economics. 33 p. [Mimeo]

Krutilla, John V., and Anthony C. Fisher. 1975. The economics of natural environments. Resources for the Future, Inc. and John Hopkins University Press, Baltimore, Md. 292 p.

Lewis, Eugene P., and David T. Taylor. 1977. Impacts of public lands policies on the livestock industry and adjacent communities. Big Horn County. Wyoming Agricultural Experiment Station Research Bulletin 116. 62 p.

Martin, William E., and Gene L. Jefferies. 1966. Relating ranch prices and grazing permit values to ranch productivity. Journal of Farm Economics 48(2):233-242.

Martin, William E., and Gary B. Snider. 1980. The value of forage for grazing cattle in the Salt-Verde Basin of Arizona. University of Arizona, Department of Agricultural Economics, Report No. 22, 41 p.

McConnen, R. J. 1976. Public land grazing and ranch economics. Montana State University, Department of Agricultural Economics and Economics, Staff Paper 76-10. 38 p.

McCorkle, C. O., Jr. 1956. The application of linear programming to research in the economies of range improvement and utilization. p. 135-151. *In* Economic Research in the Use and Development of Range Resources, A Methodological Anthology 1957. Committee on the Economics of Range Use and Development of Western Agricultural Economics Research Council.

McDowell, James I., and Jerome E. Johnson. 1964. An economic analysis of alternative methods for establishing grazing rentals on state school lands in North Dakota. North Dakota State University, Department of Agricultural Economics, Report No. 37, 30 p.

Milliman, J. S. 1962. Capitalized values and misallocation in grazing public range: A comment. Journal of Farm Economics 44(4):1097-1100.

Nielsen, Darwin B. 1972. Economic implications of variable versus single grazing fees. Journal of Range Management 25:2-7.

Nielsen, Darwin B., and John P. Workman. 1971. The importance of renewable grazing resources on federal lands in the 11 Western states. Utah Agricultural Experiment Station Circular 155.

Olson, C. E., and J. S. Jackson. 1975. Impact of change in federal grazing policies on south-central Wyoming mountain valley cattle ranches. Wyoming Agricultural Experiment Station Research Bulletin 96, 21 p.

Peryam, J. Stephen, and Carl E. Olson. 1975. Impact on potential changes in BLM grazing policies on west-central Wyoming cattle ranches. Wyoming Agricultural Experiment Station Research Bulletin 87, 17 p.

Plath, C. V. 1956. Use of surveys in economic research in forage production for grazing. Journal of Farm Economics 38:1617-1626.

Range Term Glossary Committee. 1974. A glossary of terms used in range management. Society for Range Management, Denver, Colo. 36 p.

Roberts, N. K. 1963. Economic foundations for grazing use fees on public lands. Journal of Farm Economics 45:721-731.

Roberts, N. K., and Mardell Topham. 1965. Discovering grazing values. Utah Agricultural Experiment Station Economics Series 65-3, 29 p.
Sinden, John A., and Albert C. Worrell. 1979. Unpriced Values: Decisions Without Market Prices. John Wiley and Sons, New York. 511 p.
Torell, Allen, J. R. Garrett and C. T. K. Ching. 1979. The impact of changes in public lands policies on a sample of 36 ranches in Elko County, Nevada. College of Agriculture, University of Nevada, Reno. 49 p.
Torell, Allen, William O. Champney, Chauncey T. K. Ching, et al. 1980. Economic impact of BLM grazing allotment reductions on Humboldt County, Nevada. Division of Agriculture and Research Economics, University of Nevada, Reno. 56 p.
U.S.D.A. Economic Research Service. 1965. Effects of changes in grazing fees and permitted use of public rangelands on incomes of Western livestock ranches. ERS 248. U. S. Government Printing Office, Washington, D.C. 33 p.
U.S.D.A. Forest Service. 1980 A Recommended Renewable Resources Program - 1980 Update. U.S. Govt. Printing Office, Washington, D.C. 20402.
Winter, John R., and James K. Whittaker. 1981. The relationship between private ranchland prices and public-land grazing permits. Land Economics 57(3):414-421.
Workman, John P., and Jack F. Hooper. 1968. Preliminary economic evaluation of cattle distribution practices on mountain rangelands. Journal of Range Management 21(4):301-304.

Footnotes

[1]*Wildland is defined as forest and rangelands, and excludes urban areas, industrial areas, cropland and improved pasture.*

[2]*The methods will be discussed with respect to public range. Some of the methods are applicable to private range forage and will be briefly summarized later.*

[3]*The author has not been able to locate a copy of the 1966 study, but it is summarized in Bergland and Andrus (1977).*

[4]*The author could not obtain a copy of the original study on which this formula was based. One can only assume that it was derived by some statistical method.*

[5]*For a discussion of the history of grazing fees on public range, see Dutton (1953), Foss (1959) and Bergland and Andrus (1977).*

[6]*This study is led by Dr. K. Gee and has been supported by the Forest Service USDA, and Bureau of Land Management, USDI.*

[7]*The Bureau of Land Management was at one time going to issue an RFP for such a study; however, to my knowledge, it was never issued.*

Chapter 9
Valuation of Water on Wildlands

S. L. Gray and R. A. Young

Introduction

Forest management policies can affect the quantity, quality, and/or timing of water flowing from forest watersheds, effects which may be registered at sites distant from the point where the policy operates. As examples, forest policies can change water yield, affect rate of siltation of stream beds, or dampen the flood peak on a given river. Altered water flows or qualities may affect numerous economic activities, including off-stream uses (such as crop irrigation, households and industries), and in-stream purposes (including recreation, fish and wildlife habitat, power generation and waste dilution). These impacts have an economic dimension, which may be positive (moderate supply increases; enhanced quality) or negative (flooding, reduced water supplies, or degraded quality). This chapter deals with the concepts and procedures appropriate to assigning economic values to these impacts of wildland management policies.

Background

The conflicting demands for increasingly scarce water are generally not resolvable through normal market exchange processes. The physical characteristics of water, including its mobile, flowing nature and pervasive interdependencies among uses, make it difficult to establish and enforce the property rights which provide the basis for market allocation and exchange (Gaffney 1969, Bower 1963, Ditwiler 1975). As a result, market prices which might provide a basis for policy and program analysis, are seldom observed, and decisions on development and allocation tend to be made in non-market (i.e., political and administrative) contexts. In the absence of market prices, the evaluation impacts of altered water flow regimes on wildlands requires the estimate of surrogate market, or "shadow," prices. It is within this context that forest management policies affecting the quantity, quality and timing of water supplies are to be evaluated.

The broad principles appropriate to the shadow pricing question have long been available (e.g., Marglin 1962). However, a consensus on a systematic analytical framework for water valuation has not been reached among economic analysts. An assessment of the literature suggests instead, variation in the definition of water use, analytical perspectives or accounting stances adopted by analysts, and, in many instances, inappropriate techniques applied for shadow pricing water. The result is shadow price estimates in alternative uses which may be inappropriate and non-comparable.

Scope

Policy impacts can be categorized into the following cases (Howe 1971):

1. Impacts for which market prices exist and the prices reflect scarcity values.
2. Impacts for which market prices are observable, but the observed prices fail to reflect social values (as in the case of the presence of market failures such as monopoly, or public intervention in markets via subsidies or price controls).
3. Impacts for which no market prices exist, but the conceptual and empirical bases are available for identifying surrogate or shadow prices (as for public goods, externalities).
4. Impacts for which market-like prices are not meaningful (including non-efficiency objectives).

The analysis here focues on the estimation of economic value of the resource in alternative uses, those covered by categories 1, 2 and 3 above. The question of "secondary" or "indirect" impact valuation is not dealt with.

Although there are multiple objectives in water resource development and allocation, these comments are largely confined to the efficiency objective, defensible on several grounds (Freeman and Haveman 1970).

Conceptual Framework

Economic Value

Economic value attaches to resources whenever they are scarce, (i.e., whenever users would willingly pay a price for them rather than do without). When markets operate effectively, market values (or prices) serve to allocate resources and commodities to those uses yielding greatest returns or consumer satisfaction. When they do not, the allocation decision may require the use of various techniques for estimating value. In either case, resource value has meaning only in relation to some explicit objective or set of objectives. Value is then measured as the resource's contribution to the stated objective(s) (Marglin 1962). Several objectives may be relevant for water resource development (U.S. Water Resources Council 1973), including enhancing national economic development, enhancing regional economic development, enhancing environmental quality, and enhancing social well-being. The first of these seems to be the objective of economic efficiency. The second perhaps is a combination of economic efficiency (from a regional perspective) and an income distribution objective. The third reflects the expectation that water development (and use) will enhance the quality of the physical environment. The fourth may represent a mixture of income distribution and other nonmeasurable factors comprising the general social well-being. Comments here are limited to value defined in terms of the economic efficiency objective for two major reasons. First, economic efficiency, under conditions of resource scarcity, remains an important social objective, and efficiency values thus have viable economic meaning. Second, estimates of efficiency values are necessary for assessing the trade-offs if alternative social objectives enter the objective function with non-zero weights.

Economic efficiency may be defined as an allocation of resources such that no further reallocation would provide gains in production or utility to some firms or individuals without simultaneous losses to others (i.e., Pareto optimality). The conditions necessary to this optimal resource allocation are provided in the model of the competitive market system. Numerous expositions of this theory are available, ranging from Marglin's (1962) rigorous approach, to less formal versions, such as Haveman's (1975).

On the producer's side of the market, prices represent the value or opportunity costs of resources used in alternative lines of employment. These prices guide investment decisions. On the consumer's side, prices reflect the relative valuation of a good or service, and thus convey consumer desires to producers. In short, prices in the market model reflect the social significance (value) of resources and commodities. However, few would argue that the restrictive assumptions of the model always conform to reality. Any violation of the assumptions tends to render prices less than fully effective as a measure of social significance and as a resource allocation device. Therefore, artificial estimates of resource value (or shadow prices) are necessary.

There are several cases in which these assumptions are not met and which preclude the market from allocating resources optimally. These circumstances, usually termed "market failures," include: (1) the existence of uncompensated, or non-market, interdependencies (externalities); (2) decreasing costs or increasing returns; (3) resource immobilities; (4) public goods; and (5) indivisibilities or "lumpiness" in factors or products (Herfindahl and Kneese 1974). Examples of each of these failures may be identified in water resource development and allocation issues. Each renders market prices less than fully effective as value indicators.

The preceding definition of efficiency is itself subject to criticism as a definitive choice criterion. Particularly in the field of water resource development, the Pareto no-loss condition for efficiency in resource reallocation is difficult to satisfy. These limitations have led to an extension of the traditional definition of economic efficiency and to attempts to value resources by means other than market prices. The definition is extended through the notion of compensatory side payments, whereby gainers must be able to compensate losers and still remain better off to have a particular reallocation judged efficient (Marglin 1962).

The basic concept for establishing shadow prices is the notion of willingness to pay as the indicator of value. Willigness to pay reflects the consumer's willingness to forego other consumption rather than do without the commodity in question. For example, three alternatives, A, B, and C, may exist in public water resource development. Let alternative C represent the viable "no development" alternative while A and B are "positive" alternatives in the sense that there is a willingness to pay for both rather than to go without them. A problem emerges in determining which of the two to undertake. The choice may be made on the basis of willingness to pay. If, for example, A's beneficiaries are willing to pay more for A than are B's for alternative B, or if A's beneficiaries are willing to compensate B's beneficiaries in order to get them to forego alternative B, then alternative A is more efficient. The net efficiency benefits (i.e., net willingness to pay) becomes the difference between aggregate willingness to pay for an alternative and aggregate willingness to pay to do without that alternative.

A Definition of Value

In most cases water is partly or wholly a non-market good. Thus, procedures for estimating water value can be interpreted as efforts to simulate market outcomes. Based on the previous discussion, the definition of value appropriate to the water resource is the amount that a perfectly rational and fully informed user of the good would be willing to pay for it (Marglin 1968). In accordance with the concepts of diminishing marginal productivity or utility, willingness to pay falls as increasing quantities are utilized. The willingness to pay relation is provided by the conventional demand function for a commodity or input. This measure, intended to be commensurate with market value, is a measure of exchange value. Value, as used here, is identical with "benefit," as used in benefit-cost literature (i.e., willingness of users to pay).

Willingness to pay often differs, in the evaluation of water, from what the user actually pays. In situations where water supply is rationed by non-price mechanisms, such as water rights under the appropriation doctrine, willingness to pay may exceed actual payments. The same situation may arise where a change in output represents a signficant increment to the total supply of the commodity and perfect price discrimination is not used in pricing the output. This situation is quite common in water resources developments which typically add relatively large discrete increments to supply (this is the indivisibilities case characterized by "lumpiness" in factors and/or products), and where users are charged only a single price for their increment. Revenues obtained in these cases do not reflect the full value of the resource, and willingness to pay represents an attempt to identify the schedule of surrogate market, or shadow prices.

Special Problems in Estimating the Economic Value of Water: Conceptual Issues

"With and without" principle.—This rule asserts that benefits and costs are to be measured as increments which would occur with the projects or program as compared to without. Adherence to the rule assures that measured benefits (or costs) are solely the result of the program or project, rather than measures of changes, some of which would have occurred even in the absence of the program.

The accounting stance.—In the theoretical construct of the enterprise economy, the perspective of the individual is usually emphasized. Under the private accounting stance, the individual is motivated to act in accordance with gains and losses as he perceives them. Pursuit of his own objectives, such as maximizing utility or profits, is assumed to occur independently of gains and losses occurring elsewhere in the system. The private water user may thus view benefits in quite a different manner than should agents of the public. When the responsibility for an allocation decision rests with a public agency, an alternative criterion may be appropriate. In the water resources literature, two major alternatives to the private perspective are found (i.e., alternative "objective functions" or "accounting stances"). These reflect the viewpoints, respectively, of regional planning authorities (river basin or state) and the federal government (Howe 1971).

Regional and national accounting stances differ from the previous case in that social rather than private costs or values are incorporated into the analysis because of market failure and/or public intervention into market processes. Analysis adopting a regional accounting stance, for example, may properly ignore certain extra-regional externalities (pecuniary or technological) and may take as given commodity prices influenced by the federal government's intervention in markets (such as agricultural price supports). Ideally, the national accounting stance should attempt to utilize social opportunity costs and values for all inputs and outputs, whether they are correctly, incorrectly, or not priced at all by market mechanisms. All externalities should be also identified and measured.

To avoid inappropriate comparison across alternative uses and regions, care must be taken to identify whether a local or national perspective has been adopted by the analysts, and appropriate adjustments must be made to provide consistency and comparability.

Total, average, and marginal values.—An elementary distinction among economic concepts of value is that relating to total, average, and marginal values. Total value or benefit from public provision of a good or service is measured by the total willingness to pay for a given level of output (i.e., the area under the demand curve for a particular quantity). With a downward sloping demand curve, this area thus includes both the price-quantity rectangle and the consumer surplus triangle. Thus, for a demand curve defined by $D = f(Q)$, the total value of some quantity, Q_o, of publicly supplied good is $V = g(Q) = \int_o^{Q_o} f(Q)dQ$.

The marginal value represents the contribution of an incremental addition of good or factor to a specific objective function and is defined by the first derivative of the total value function. (The marginal value function is, in effect, the demand curve for the resource.) Thus, if total value is $V = g(Q) = \int_o^{Q_o} f(Q)d(Q)$, then marginal value is $V' = f(Q)$. As will be shown later, the marginal value function is most important for purposes of efficiency in water resource development and allocation. For the development case, economic efficiency requires that development be undertaken to the point of equality between the marginal value of the output and its marginal cost. For the allocation decision (i.e., the allocation of constrained water supplies among competing uses), economic efficiency is achieved when net marginal values are equal for all uses.

The third concept, that of average value, is simply the value per unit of publicly-supplied output. That is, $\bar{V} = V/Q$ where V = total value and Q = quantity of publicly-supplied output. It is of theoretical or practical significance for water development and allocation only in special cases. It is mentioned here because its conceptual simplicity and ease of computation often lures the nonspecialist into using it indiscriminately as an approximation of marginal value. Average value is usually larger than marginal value, although in some important cases they are equal.

To state these concepts more formally, let

$$f(Y_1, Y_2, \ldots Y_m; X_1, X_2, \ldots X_n) = 0 \qquad [1]$$

be the implicit multi-product, multi-factor production function faced by an individual or by a regional or basin water planning authority (Marglin 1962). $Y = (Y_1, Y_2, \ldots Y_m)$ is a vector of outputs and $X = (X_1, X_2, \ldots X_n)$ is a vector of resources or inputs.

Let the net income be represented by

$$Z = \sum_{i=1}^{m} Y_i P_{y_i} - \sum_{j=1}^{n} X_j P_{x_j} \qquad [2]$$

for P, the prices (or shadow prices) of inputs j and outputs i, and Y_i and X_j the respective outputs i and inputs j. Maximum net return is found by setting the partial derivatives of equation [2] equal to zero.

$$\partial Z/\partial X_j = \partial (Y_i P_{y_i})/\partial X_j - \partial (X_j P_{x_j})/\partial X_j = 0 \qquad [3]$$

for ($i = 1, \ldots m$; $j = 1$). The first term in equation [3] is the value marginal product of factor j used in producing good i, and the second term is the marginal (factor) cost of j. Optimality (economic efficiency) in allocation is obtained when the marginal value product equals the marginal cost for each input j. Marglin (1962) extends this statement to a more general and conceptually complete formulation which specifies the possibilities of varying prices and input-output relations over the entire planning horizon.

Long-run versus short-run value.—A second conceptual distinction in the concept of value is that between short- and long-run value. This distinction is related to the degree of fixity of certain resources and is especially important where commodities are used for further production (i.e., are intermediate as opposed to final goods), as is typical with respect to water.

The rational producer's willingness to pay for an increment to water supply is equivalent to the net increase in the value of output attributable to the added water. The distinction between short-run and long-run value is that in the short-run, where some resources are fixed, estimates of net increases in the value of output can properly ignore the sunk costs of the fixed resources. This is not the case in the long run, where all costs must be covered. The implication here is that short-run values may be much greater than in the long-run, and it is essential to avoid comparisons of estimates based on one concept with estimates based on the other, or using estimates based on one concept where the other is appropriate. For example, a farmer's in-season choice of the quanitity of irrigation water to apply would utilize the short-run value, whereas public investment decisions in water supply facilities should adopt the long-run perspective.

Changes in value over time.—Two external forces which affect value estimates generally and which are associated with the passage of time are changes in the general price level and technological change. It should be readily apparent that changes in the general price level can have significant impacts on value estimates and, except during the rare periods of price stability, benefits and costs are thus specific to the price level prevailing at the time of the estimates. While professional wisdom suggests that future changes in the general price level should be ignored in developing benefit estimates (Prest and Turvey 1965), expected changes in relative prices should be incorporated in such estimates.

Incorporating technological change into benefit measures is complex, because associated factor and commodity price changes should also be incorporated. Historically, technological change has altered factor and commodity price relationships (i.e., the historical downward trend in real food prices resulting from technological advance). Therefore, it is inappropriate to include technological change without simultaneously projecting the associated price changes.

Non-marginal changes in supply.—Another general conceptual issue regarding the valuation question has to do with cases in which output changes are large enough to have major impacts on factor and commodity prices. Some water projects fall in this category (for example, the effect of the California Water Project on national fresh fruit and vegetable markets, additions to flat water recreation resulting from development in the Tennessee, Ohio, and Arkansas river basins, etc.). Dean and King (1970) projected substantial commodity price impacts in conjunction with planned irrigation development in central California. The point here is that equations [2] and [3] would have to be modified so that commodity demand functions replace fixed commodity prices. See Martin (1979) for a recent application.

Physical and Economic Issues in Evaluating Water

The recent increase in the perception of water as an economic resource has come about as growing population and levels of economic activity have greatly augmented demands for the resource. Quantity, as the usual economic consideration, is only one aspect of the water use picture. Water supplies and uses vary in both time and space, so that two additional dimensions of the resource—location, and timing of resource availability—are immediately obvious.

Water is a relatively bulky commodity. For off-stream uses, it is often the case that transportation and conveyance costs are large relative to value at the site of use, and may even exceed that value (Howe and Easter 1971).

Further, water quality (the character and amount of dissolved and/or suspended constituents) has important implications for utility and productivity of water. (See Peskin and Seskin (1975), Freeman (1979), and Feenberg and Mills (1980) for detailed discussions of benefit-cost analysis in water quality management.) Further, water may be found in varying qualities, depending on the nature of the soils through which it moves and on human activity. These four dimensions—quantity, quality, time, and location—form an integral part of the water problem. Therefore, their consideration may have a significant impact on the estimation of water value in alternative uses.

This discussion of special problems in evaluating water, framed in the context of these dimensions, is divided into two major categories including (1) physical aspects of supply and use, and (2) economic aspects of supply and use. Institutional and other factors are omitted from the discussion.

Physical aspects of supply and use.—In virtually any general discussion of natural resources, a distinction is drawn between stock (non-renewable) and flow (renewable) resources. With a few notable exceptions, water falls within the latter category. The resource seldom stays in one location for long periods of time. Thus it is further classified as a fugitive resource. Its general fugitive nature is responsible for some important physical interdependencies and attendant valuation problems. A particular concern is the definition of the unit of utilization.

It is common to distinguish between in-stream (non-withdrawal) and off-stream (withdrawal) uses. Uses are also categorized as consumptive (where water is lost to the system, usually by evaporation) or nonconsumptive. Generally, withdrawal uses are the major consumptive uses, but even here it is rare that the entire quantity of water withdrawn is consumed. In-stream uses, in contrast, are not generally termed consumptive uses. However, storage of water for in-stream use can result in substantial loss from evaporation or seepage, a consumptive use effect that is rarely taken into account in water valuation studies. Also, the unconsumed portion, whether for withdrawal or in-stream use, may be greatly altered in quality, time, and location.

In contrast to other resources, water is relatively unique in that its use for one purpose at a given time and location does not necessarily preclude its use elsewhere, at a later time, for the same or different purposes. Thus water "used" in the upper reaches of a river for electric power generation or recreation, etc. is usable downstream in any number of withdrawal or non-withdrawal uses. The total productive use of a unit of water may be many times greater than that at the initial point of use.

Physical interdependence and economic impacts.—There is a major problem which increases the difficulty of evaluating water. A specific water use, in most cases, cannot be viewed in isolation from potential alternative utilizations. The typical river basin will contain several alternative uses for water, and one use may affect others through any or all of the quantity, quality, time, and location dimensions.

The existence of these physical interdependencies creates peculiar difficulties in assigning theoretically sound value estimates to water in single purposes. Value of a particular unit of water in a given river system is the sum of the value marginal product in the initial use and the value of the return flow in all subsequent uses. The sum, in a system context, is net of the positive and negative effects which are engendered elsewhere or subsequently in the system. Thus, the value of a unit of water to the entire system, as opposed to a single use, becomes relevant in the systems context. This has some rather important implications for water allocation and reallocation among uses either within one system or between river basins (Butcher et al. 1972).

Appropriate allocation variable.—Formally, the valuation problem posed by physical interdependencies in water use is that of specifying the unit of measure of the variable X (quantity of water) in equation [2]. In certain situations (e.g., in-stream use such as recreation), evaluation of water resource development decisions may not require a measure of value per unit of water "used." This is true as long as one use is complementary or supplementary to (i.e., does not compete with) another. A realistic example of such cases would be a storage project whose primary purpose is creating water supply for hydroelectric power or provision of flood control which may facilitate flat-water based recreation. Up to a rather high level of recreation use, there will likely be no adverse effects on the primary purpose. Thus project evaluation can proceed by summing annual recreation benefits and primary benefits without establishing a value per unit of use. However, once a competitive relationship is established, it is necessary to impute a recreational value to units of water to assess this trade-off.

Another problem is posed by in-stream utilization. While navigation, recreation, power generation, and waste load assimilation do not withdraw or consume (evaporation and seepage aside) water in the usual hydrological sense, in-stream uses clearly can foreclose other economic uses at a particular location and at later times. Water released from storage for power generation, waste dilution, or to maintain minimum flow, may preclude withdrawals for irrigation, municipal, or industrial use. Again, water use becomes competitive, and rational economic evaluation requires a procedure for assigning values to units of water.

For cases involving withdrawal use, some unit measure of use is clearly called for in the course of evaluating alternative allocations. The choice of the appropriate measures usually has been between the withdrawal versus the depletion (consumption) concepts. The arguments presented by Olson (1966) and d'Arge (1970) are representative of these contrasting approaches. Olson argues that water scarcity in the West supports the consumption concept but that withdrawal is the relevant concept in the humid regions of the country, where consumptive use is a relatively small portion of total diversions. In contrast, d'Arge contends that the selection of the appropriate variable depends on the interdependencies existing among users and on the availability of benefits estimates. His conclusion is that consumption is the relevant variable for public planning purposes; however, withdrawal and consumption may be equivalent.

Consideration of the appropriate variable will depend on the accounting stance, and the distinction between the perspective of the individual water-using entity and that of the public or social viewpoint. It appears that, given present institutional arrangements, the individual (private sector) perspective considers only withdrawal, because that is the quantity of water for which expense is incurred. Under a different set of institutional arrangements, the individual might find a market such that his return flows are valued and thus cause him to alter his perspective.

The points made by d'Arge concerning the importance of the type of interdependence and that from the public perspective consumption is the relevant variable are persuasive. However, conventional measures of consumption (in terms of evaporation) may be misleading for public economic analysis in some special instances. For example, irrigation return flows in portions of the Southwest may be so degraded in quality through salt pickups as to be unusable. Additionally, because decades may be required before excess irrigation water can percolate back to the ground water table, return flows may not be available for reuse in any reasonable planning horizon. In such cases, the withdrawal variable may be a much closer approximation to actual use than is consumption measured as evaporation.

The choice of the variable used to represent water "use" involves the nature and degree of physical and economic interdependence and the persepective of the decision maker. Also, a definition of use must be selected which is applicable to both in-stream and withdrawal uses. Thus, it appears appropriate that the definition be general. Therefore, any alteration in quantity, quality, time, or location for economic benefit constitutes "use" for which an appropriate economic value may need to be derived.

Stochastic water supplies.—Still another physical aspect of water supply and use which can cause problems in value estimation is stochasticity or uncertainty in supply. Under conditions of stochastic supplies, the amount of water which actually becomes available for use may differ from that expected at the time of initial planning. As a result, production is less efficient than it would have been in the presence of accurate forecasts, and economic value is reduced. Where actual water supplies are less than expected, net value accruing to water is also less than expected, because no appropriate planned reduction in output occurred in advance. Where supplies exceed those anticipated, the resulting increase in benefits would be less than it could be if associated with a planned increase in output. These considerations reflect a two-part relationship to measure the value of alternative levels of water supply under uncertainty. See Hufschmidt and Fiering (1966) for detailed discussion of this point.

Economic Aspects of Water Affecting Valuation

The second major set of factors leading to special difficulties in evaluating water are termed somewhat artibrarily as "economic." These include value productivity at a given site, temporal variability of demands, valuations related to location and quality, and comparability of value estimates.

Site productivity.—Site productivity refers to the value productivity of water used at a particular geographic location for a specific class of use. Two facets of this concept should be noted. These are the consumer utility (economic value of the final commodity) produced by the water supply and the physical productivity of water in producing a commodity. These concepts are analogous, respectively, to the concepts of product price and marginal physical productivity in the theory of the firm.

With the exception of withdrawals for residential consumption and in-stream uses for recreation, water is an intermediate good used in the production of other commodities. For the majority of cases, within each class of use (withdrawal or in-stream) there are a number of products, each with a different productivity and price. Thus, one would expect many different water value estimates within a single use category associated with measuring the returns from each product or crop.

The value of water in the stream or at the point of diversion also will vary substantially over distance. This may be because of the cost of transportation to the point of final consumption (or the cost of transporting the consumer to the location of use). Similarly, value would vary with geographic variation in demand resulting from population distribution, tastes and preferences, income differences, etc.

The second aspect of site productivity concerns the factors which influence the physical productivity at a particular location for each type of use. Examples of these factors include soil and climatic characteristics affecting the physical productivity of irrigation water, esthetic characteristics of a particular site which influence its value for recreation, and the vertical drop available at any given dam site for hydropower production.

Physical productivity of water is also dependent upon the investment in other resources used in conjunction with water. Examples in this include the height to which a power dam is constructed, the development of picnic facilities, campsites, boat launches, etc. in conjunction with water supplies for recreation, and investment in efficient water application systems in irrigation. Capital investments in storage and distribution facilities usually exhibit large-scale economies. This is a principal basis for public action in the water supply field, but is also responsible for substantial variation in estimated water value at a given site.

Temporal variability in demand for water.—Demand for water over time may vary substantially. Because the concept of value used here is based on user's demand, temporal variability in demand can have significant consequences on value estimates. The variation may tend from the very short-run to the long-run. In the former, examples include the demand for residential water and for hydropower, both exhibiting predictable daily fluctuations in demand. In the longer run, most other demands vary seasonally, such as those for water used in irrigation, navigation, recreation, and waste load assimilation. Also, secular trends in population, income, and technology have a long-run impact on the demand for water. Seasonal and cyclical variations in precipitation influence the demands for certain water uses. Demands, in these cases, are supply dependent, which suggests that water demand varies stochastically just as water supply does.

As suggested previously, the estimated short-run value may be significantly greater than estimated long-run value. Therefore, for resource allocation purposes, attempts to establish water values which are comparable requires a common planning period. Annual increments of time are the usual choice because of data availabilty and resource constraints. However, if the previous contention that physical and economic interdependencies should be accounted for in value estimates is valid, a period as long as a year may mask, rather than highlight, the competitive and complementary relationships.

Valuation as related to location and quality.—An important physical characteristic of water is that it is a relatively bulky commodity for which transportation costs are typically large relative to value at the site of use. This implies that water values will vary with location much more than will the values of less bulky goods.

Also, water must frequently undergo some form of processing (filtration, chlorination, pressurization, etc.) before use. Thus, there will be differences in value between the raw (unprocessed) water compared to the value of processed water.

The Issue of Comparable Values

A well-known precept in economics is that comparable prices require that the characteristics of a commodity are comparable in place, time, and form. Similarly, specifying strictly commensurable shadow prices for alternative uses of water requires that values per unit of water be conceptually equivalent in terms of time, location, and quality.

It is useful to distinguish between two concepts of water value. Most estimates of value in the literature are conceptualized so as to apply to a specific site of use (conventionally, for withdrawal use, at the user's point of intake), with quality and time dimensions implicitly or explicitly specified. These estimates of water value, termed "site values," are appropriate for most allocation decisions relating to water development and use for specific withdrawal purposes. However, for decisions concerning reallocation between uses, including in-stream as well as off-stream uses, site values might be overestimated relative to values in-stream, if transportation costs are ignored. In such cases, it appears that value should be measured in the stream or water body, presumably at a site suitable as a point of use or for diversions. Similarly, because of variation in the quality of water required for alternative uses, the least common denominator for specifying water quality is the raw (unprocessed) water in the water body. This latter concept of water value is referred to as "in-stream value." Under this concept, both processing and transportation costs must be deducted from site values of withdrawal uses in order to obtain value estimates which are comparable (Flinn and Guise (1970) present a sophisticated modeling effort which incorporates these distinctions).

The problem is less tractable when dealing with time. As noted previously, some common time span is essential for comparing values because of the likely discrepancy between short- and long-run values. However, the longer the time period upon which an analysis is based, the less the potential complemenatrities are likely to be illustrated, and the more competitive the uses will appear. However, short-run analysis taking these interrelationships into account becomes much more complex and expensive.

The advent of the digital computer has facilitated the development of dynamic models which can encompass the temporal, spatial, and quality dimensions of the problem simultaneously, as well as permitting representation of the multiple product, stochastic supply, and interdependency characteristics mentioned earlier. The initial major innovations in the area emerged largely from the activities of the Harvard Water Program reported in Maass et al. (1962) and Hufschmidt and Fiering (1966). Currently, most value estimates do not include adequate consideration of these factors.

Techniques for Determining the Economic Value of Water

Observation of Transactions Relating to Water

Two cases of observation of transactions are addressed here. The first, termed direct observation, describes the transaction solely in terms of the exchange of money for water. In the second, or indirect case, the transaction may deal with a bundle of resources, including land as well as water.

Free-market transactions.—Market transactions for water are not common. However, where they do exist, the observed price must be carefully interpreted. It is noted that the flexibility of tenure under the riparian rights doctrine is quite limited, because property rights in water, which form the basis necessary for exchange, are lacking. Under the appropriation doctrine, several types of direct market transactions in water can be described. The least complex has been termed the "irrigation water rental market" (Anderson 1961). The owner maintains the title to the perpetual annual stream of water supplies but sells his right to receive the water for a specified period of time. The observed prices in rental markets are based on private, short-run demands and may be of limited utility in evaluating long-term public investment or reallocation decisions.

Transactions in permanent water rights are not common because of institutional constraints designed to avoid third-party effects (Ditwiler 1975), and state restrictions prohibiting the transfer of rights except when the land to which the right pertains is involved in the transaction (Hartman and Seastone 1970). Where such permanent transfers are found (e.g., within mutual ditch companies, or conservancy districts) they may be between users for the same or different purposes. Observed transaction prices of transfers between similar uses are conceptually correct measures of the long-term private value of the resource in that purpose. However, even here some cautions in interpretation are warranted. First, stochastic supplies introduce the possibility of a discount for uncertainty. If the right has a junior standing and does not receive full supply in water-short periods, the observed price will understate the value of a guaranteed supply. Second, the price of a right is for a right to a perpetual series of annual flows, not the price of a unit volume of water. To derive the value of a specified unit volume, an appropriate capitalization formula and the proper interest rate must be applied to the price of the right.

The value of water rights has also been estimated indirectly where the right is transferred as a part of a real property transfer. Statistical regression analysis applied to a sample of such transactions characterized by variation in water supply per unit of land permits inferences to be drawn as to the value of the water right (Hartman and Anderson 1963, Renshaw 1958b, Milliman 1959).

Freeman (1979) presents a detailed review of the problem of employing property values to study the benefits of non-marketed goods and services, particularly with respect to environmental quality. Feenberg and Mills (1980) also deal with this question with respect to water quality.

Other examples of free-market transactions in water are scarce. One which should be noted is the sale of bottled spring or distilled water for household purposes, largely for drinking. The price of this water sets an upper limit on the value of water in urban and residential uses.

"Administered" prices as measures of value.—A second type of observed transaction in water is that in which water supplies in withdrawal uses are sold under an "administered" price system. In this case, the public agency or utility which supplies water may sell it at a specified price through a metered system. The consumer is free to adjust his consumption to reflect his marginal valuation at the specified price. Statistical analysis of cross-section (Howe and Linaweaver 1967) or time-series (Young 1973) data pertaining to the consequent relationship between consumption and price can be used for inferring water value to the final user.

In much the same way, prices may be imposed upon individual users of irrigation water (although most irrigation water is not measured or priced at the margin). These prices, while they may be set artificially low for purposes of subsidizing irrigation, are crude representations of the short-run value of water if a user may purchase all quantities desired at that price, and if the assumption of profit-maximizing behavior holds. The term "crude" is descriptive of approximate value, because it is value at the point of use, not at the point of diversion, which is most often measured. If the costs of acquiring and transporting water are borne by people other than the users, then, from society's perspective, the value of water in irrigation will be much lower (or even negative) at the point of diversion.

Deriving Value Estimates from the Production Function

The classical approach to estimating values of non-marketed commodities is to estimate the demand function for the good in question. The case of estimating municipal water demand was treated in the previous section. In most other uses, water is an intermediate good, in which case the demand function is the marginal value product function, the first derivative of the production function in value terms. This technique has been most widely employed in valuing water in irrigation use, where numerous experiments have studied crop response to water application and other factors (Hexem and Heady 1978). The general approach is to derive a schedule representing the short-run value of the marginal product under the experimental conditions. While the technique has appeal as a means of estimating short-run private values, limitations are encountered in using it for estimating the long-run social value of water. Public intervention is often present in the market for particular irrigated crops, either through direct price control or price manipulation by supply control. Most studies employ the prices received by farmers in valuing outputs. In such cases, private willingness to pay would exceed an appropriate measure of the social value of the marginal unit at the point of use. Perhaps more important, the short-run production function, estimated with all factors but water fixed, may not provide an appropriate measure of the long-run marginal product.

Cobb-Douglas type functions fitted to farm account data with irrigation water as an explicit variable have been employed in developing estimates of long-run marginal value productivity. A number of such studies have been done in India and Pakistan (Khan and Young 1979).

In industries other than irrigated agriculture, a scarcity of data necessary to estimate demand or production relationships and the fact that water accounts for a very small portion of production costs have generally forced analysts to turn to one of the alternative estimating procedures discussed below.

Residual Imputation

Resource valuation is essentially a problem of assigning a "price" to resources or commodities in the absence of markets to perform the function. Residual imputation achieves this by allocating the total value of output among each of the resources used in a single productive process. This is a straightforward method for estimating the value of water when used as an intermediate good. If appropriate prices can be assigned to all inputs but one, then the residual of the total value of product is imputed to the remaining resource (Heady 1952).

The technique is based upon two major givens: (1) The market prices of all resources, except the one to be valued, are equal to the returns at the margin (value of the marginal product), and (2) the total value of output can be divided into shares such that each resource is paid according to its marginal productivity and the total value of output is completely exhausted. Consider a simple example where three factors, capital, labor, and water, are used in the production of a single output Q. The problem is to impute a value to the water resource. Based on the two givens,

$$\mathrm{TVP}_Q = (\mathrm{VMP}_L \times L) + (\mathrm{VMP}_K \times K) + (\mathrm{VMP}_W \times W), \qquad [4]$$

where TVP_Q is the total value of output Q; VMP_i represents the value marginal product of any resource, i; and L, K, and W refer, respectively, to quantities of labor, capital, and water employed. If the value of marginal products of labor and capital have been accurately determined, then the value of water at the margin (VMP_W) may be computed by rewriting equation [4] as follows:

$$\mathrm{TVP}_Q - ((\mathrm{VMP}_L \times L) - (\mathrm{VMP}_K \times K)) = \mathrm{VMP}_W \times W. \qquad [5]$$

Then, substituting according to the first given,

$$\mathrm{TVP}_Q - (P_L \times L) - (P_K \times K) = \mathrm{VMP}_W \times W. \qquad [6]$$

Equation [6] is solved for VMP_W to estimate P_W. The assumptions underlying residual imputation as formulated above are that no residual remains, and further, that the exact return to each resource can be imputed.

The question arises as to whether or not factor payments according to marginal productivities will just exhaust total product. The answer is provided by a principle known as Euler's Theorem which states that, under certain conditions, resources paid according to marginal productivity will result in complete exhaustion of total product (Henderson and Quandt 1978). The postulates cited previously are satisfied by production functions homogeneous of the first degree. The Cobb-Douglas function which implies constant returns to scale is one which satisfies Euler's Theorem and has been used in empirical estimation of marginal value products (Sadan 1969).

Residual imputation is subject to limitations which should be recognized by the user. Two particular cases are noted here: (1) the problem of omitted variables; and (2) problems of estimation when price supports or subsidies or other exogenous influences are exerted on production.

First, factor payments in accordance with marginal productivity will just exhaust total product only if resources are used to a point at which marginal and average productivity are equal. Resource use at a level less than that necessary for the equality to hold will result in factor payments greater than total product. Resource use at a level greater than is necessary to produce the equality will result in an excess of total value of output over total factor payments. Thus, only at a very specific level of resource use (i.e., at a point exhibiting constant returns to scale) are the conditions of residual imputation met. Thus, the method is valid as long as the requirements of the competitive model (including the equilibrium condition that marginal cost equals average cost) are met.

Second, there is the very serious operational difficulty encountered through the use of prices as indicators of value marginal products for all resources but one. If resources are not allocated so that all factor inputs are employed to the level where prices are equated with value marginal products, the imputational process may result in either under- or overestimation of the value of the resource in question.

Even where the production function exhibits constant returns to scale and prices reflect marginal value products, there may be omitted variables. For example, crop production budgets designed to estimate the value of irrigation water often omit management, and sometimes even land and family labor costs. Omission of these factor costs means that the returns to such resources are being imputed to the residual resource, resulting in an overstated value estimate. This is an instance of the more general problem arising when resources other than that selected as the residual (i.e., water) are not priced in the market. Errors in assigning opportunity costs to these factors would lead to errors in imputing water values. Second, if commodity prices are distorted through public intervention, as in agriculture, the VMP's and the residual imputation procedure are subject to bias. If production prices are high (lower) than market equilibrium, then the residual is over- (under-) stated.

This procedure is most applicable to estimating the value of water in production processes (such as irrigated crop production), where the water resource is a substantial contributor to total product. In industrial uses, where water rarely represents more than 1 or 2 percent of total input costs, the difficulty in properly shadow pricing the other factors, particularly capital, management, and risk bearing, creates particular problems in deriving accurate estimates of a residual value of water.

Mathematical programming procedures can be used to derive theoretically similar imputations of the value of water. Burt (1964) pioneered this approach with application to irrigation water, deriving a long-run net benefit function from parametric variation of a water supply constraint in a linear programming (L.P.) model of a California agricultural region. Depending on the formulation of the L.P. model, long-run or short-run value estimates can be derived. Young and Bredehoeft (1972) and Daubert et al. (1980), among others, have used L.P. models to impute short-run values to irrigation water.

Two additional techniques closely related to the residual imputation approach warrant discussion. They are the "change in net income" and "value added" approaches.

Change in net income.—This method (CINI) defines the increment in net producer income associated with adding water to a production process as willingness to pay for the incremental water. The approach is that adopted for valuing irrigation water benefits by the U.S. Water Resources Council (1979). (Retaining the notation introduced in equation [2] above and letting the subscripts 0 and 1 attached to the input and output variables refer, respectively, to values without and with an investment or program adding to water supply.) The water resource is designated X_1. Assuming that the increase in crop production following from the added water supplies is not large enough to influence crop prices, the change in net income associated with a discrete addition to water supply per unit of time is:

$$\Delta Z = Z_1 - Z_0 = \left(\sum_{i=1}^{m} Y_{1i} P_{y_i} - \sum_{j=2}^{n} X_{1j} P_{x_j} \right) - \left(\sum_{i=1}^{m} Y_{0i} P_{y_i} - \sum_{j=2}^{n} X_{0j} P_{x_j} \right) . \quad [7]$$

The second term in equation [7], in effect, represents the annual net returns to the fixed land resources in the "without" project situation.

The unit value of water may be obtained by dividing the expression in equation [7] by the incremental quantity of water (i.e., ΔX_1).

The CINI approach requires the same assumptions of the residual imputation procedure, namely, that resources be optimally allocated, that factor and product prices correctly reflect social values, and that all inputs be properly represented in the calculations. The CINI technique also can be interpreted as an approximation to the optimal allocation conditions expressed in equation [3] for the case where the incremental water input is discrete rather than an infinitesimal amount.

The CINI method can be used to measure effects of changes in water quality on the value of water (Pincock 1968, Moore et al. 1974, Kleinman and Brown 1977, Oyarzabal and Young 1978).

Value-added approach.—Studies have attempted to measure the value of water from a regional perspective using regional interindustry models. Such studies typically adduce a concept of "value added," or more generally, of income of primary resources per unit of water withdrawal as a criterion for allocating the resource. Value added is equivalent to the net payments to primary resources (land, mineral resources, labor, management services, water) added by the relevant entity. The prototype of such studies was developed by Nathaniel Wollman (1963) for the purpose of allocating water from a proposed inter-basin transfer in New Mexico.

In symbols, the technique can be explicated as follows:

$$\mathrm{GRP} = X_1 P_x + \sum_{j=2}^{R} X_j P_{x_j} + \sum_{j=R+1}^{m} X_j P_{x_j} . \qquad [8]$$

Equation [8] allocates gross regional product (GRP) among water (X_1), other primary resources (X_j; $j = 2 \ldots R$) and purchased or imported inputs (X_j; $j = R + 1 \ldots m$). $X_1 \ldots X_r$ are the primary resources represented in value added. P_{x_1} is the unknown value of water.

The value added (VA) imputation proceeds by calculating

$$\mathrm{VA} = \mathrm{GRP} - \sum_{j=R+1}^{m} X_j P_{x_j} \qquad [9]$$

and imputing a value of P_{x_1} by dividing VA by X_1.

The VA approach is similar in concept to the residual imputation technique described above. However, it is readily seen that in terms of equation [6], equation [8] imputes the productivity of all primary resources, not just water, to the water resource. Implicitly, resources $X_2 \ldots X_r$ are assigned a zero shadow price, rather than being assigned a conceptually correct opportunity cost.

While maximizing the return to the region's primary resources may be an attractive criterion to regional planning agencies, the approach may not be generally applicable. In another New Mexico study, d'Arge (1970) justified the value-added criterion for water allocation by assuming water to be absolutely scarce relative to all other resources. This is asserted to justify the implication that the social opportunity cost of labor and other primary resources is zero. If this is true, then the maximum social productivity of the scarce water resource would equal maximum total value added. However, it is doubtful that water is ever so scarce, even in the western United States, to warrant the assumption of zero opportunity cost of labor and other resources. Thus, it is questionable that even a regional planning authority should ignore the alternative cost of primary resources other than water in its allocation decisions. It is likely that a state or basin agency evaluating a water project on the basis of benefits measured in terms of a value-added concept will unfairly inflate the returns to a public investment program in comparison to the potential gains from private use of the same investment funds. Typically, primary resources other than water are also scarce and valuable in alternative uses, at least from the national and private perspective. If so, primary regional income per unit of water use as a measure of value results in estimates which may be several times too high from either the private or the national accounting perspective. Thus, the use of the regional value-added criterion appears appropriate only under quite limited conditions (if ever).

Wollman's (1963) study is one such example. In that case, finances for new water supplies were provided largely by federal funds, and the decision to develop the new water supplies was already made. Investment costs to the State were quite small, and the problem of the state water administration was to allocate the potential increment among alternative uses rather than measure benefits of new supplies. Wollman's estimates of sector values were overstated, but probably the sectors were correctly ranked. Therefore, his policy recommendations were appropriate. However, it must be emphasized that there are only limited conditions under which the numerical estimates of value are applicable.

Alternative cost.—The fourth major technique of value estimation discussed here is based on the concept of "alternative cost" (Steiner 1965). Alternative, in the alternative cost context, refers to a substantively different means of accomplishing the same project purpose. Value of benefit is based on the cost of the most likely feasible alternative. The definition is deceptively simple, because there are a number of possible cases, including private alternatives to public projects, public alternatives to each component of dual purpose projects, etc. Herfindahl and Kneese (1974) provide more detailed exposition.

Consider the case in which a private alternative (e.g., a railroad system for commercial transport) to a public development (e.g., navigation for the same purpose) exists. Suppose that the same level of "output" (transportation) would be forthcoming regardless of which alternative is selected. In this case, the concern is to provide the output at the lowest cost (i.e., the choice criterion becomes one of comparative costs). The technique has particular appeal, because estimation of a demand schedule often is very difficult, if not impossible. However, no demand function needs to be estimated in this case, because one level of output will result from either alternative. Gross willingness to pay would be determined by the highest cost alternative. However, the net willingness to pay, or net benefits, is estimated by the reduction in cost associated with the least cost alternative. Thus, maximum willingness to pay is determined by the cost of the least expensive alternative. This same argument would hold for two public alternatives for providing the same output and in the case in which two public alternatives are complementary products of a common project.

In a situation in which a higher cost private alternative exists which would be implemented in the absence of a public alternative, the evaluation process is not quite so simple. If neither alternative need be built to a fixed scale, then the problem arises from estimating a demand schedule covering the output range, between the private level of output and the public level of output (assuming demand is not totally inelastic). The benefits from public provision of output are bounded by the higher private cost. If the demand curve is elastic, benefits from public provision would include the consumer surplus triangle. Therefore, the cost of the private alternative represents the upper limit of willingness to pay (benefits) for the public alternative.

The primary advantage of the technique is that, for cases in which demands are relatively inelastic, maximum willingness to pay can be estimated without estimating demand functions. In those situations where the output of each of two alternatives is water, as in the case of private development of ground water for irrigation versus public supply, the least cost alternative can represent a legitimate estimate of the social value of water. In other situations, however, straightforward comparison of costs is not sufficient, and an additional step in value estimation is required. These cases involve a particular output obtainable from different technical processes. Some of these processes may make little or no use of water as an input to production, while others rely quite heavily on water as an input. In such situations (e.g., transportation, power production, and waste treatment), estimation of water values is a two-step process. First, the alternative costs of accomplishing a given purpose must be estimated. Second, for those alternatives using relatively large amounts of water in the production process, a value per unit of water must be imputed.

Consider the estimation of the value of water in waste load assimilation, which requires not only that the cost of the best alternative means of accomplishing the same purpose be determined (i.e., the cost of treating effluent to achieve an improvement in water quality), but also that an appropriate portion of residual (net) benefits be attributed to the water resource. In this example involving a combination of the alternative cost technique and residual imputation, the variables whose values must be determined include total annual treatment costs as a function of treatment efficiency, the level of pollutant removed by treatment at different levels, the marginal cost of treatment, and the quantity of water required to dilute the effluent to prescribed levels. Then an appropriate value can be imputed to units of water used for assimilating wastes (Merritt and Mar 1969, Gray and Young 1974).

User surveys.—The final category concerns methods for determining the demand for water when no exchange transaction or diversions for production occurs, that is, when the "use" activity involves neither consumption nor diversion. In such cases, usually associated with recreation and esthetic enjoyment of water in natural surroundings, water has a public or collective good character. Here, analysts have come to rely on user surveys to derive estimates of the value of the recreation experience, and more particularly, of the value of the contribution of environmental resources, such as water, to that experience. Two general lines of approach can be identified—the travel cost method and contingent event evaluation (bidding games) (Knetsch 1974). Randall's contribution in this book provides a detailed development of the conceptual framework.

The basic concept underlying the travel cost approach is that an increase in access cost associated with distance will affect recreation activities in the same way as would an increase in access cost resulting from a rise in admission fees. If experimentation regarding admission fees were possible, a demand curve could be derived. In the absence of such a possibility, inferences to demand have been derived by surveying users so as to relate recreational activity to costs of travel. It also must be assumed that recreation is the only purpose of the trip.

Even if the stated assumptions hold, the travel cost approach may be limited in its applicability to water resource evaluation. First, it is important that predicted recreational usage from a new facility be net of losses in adjacent sites. Because the travel cost approach measures existing demand, its extension to new sites is appropriate only if the new sites are comparable in recreation quality. Grubb and Goodwin (1968) and Burt and Brewer (1971) report elaborate investigations of multiple reservoir recreation systems which largely overcome this difficulty. Where major changes in the recreation experience are planned, some alternative procedures must be sought. Of more significance for the present discussion is the fact that travel cost estimates represent total values, rather than the marginal values needed for problems of allocating between competing uses. The total value attributable to water-based recreation is a suitable measure of recreational benefits for water development decisions.

Where a marginal value per unit of water is sought, the question arises as to how to measure the quantity of water in this largely nonconsumptive case. In the few cases where this has been attempted, the usual approach has been to approximate marginal value by finding the average value of benefits, by dividing total benefits by total reservoir volume (Wennergren 1965).

For the short-run problem of allocating water between recreation and alternative uses, it appears that none of the measures previously discussed would be appropriate. One method which appears to have promise is the user survey of contingent event evaluation or bidding games (Randall et al. 1974). The general approach asks users to value alternative levels of supply of a public good. While the method is subject to the limitations of the "free rider" problem, attempts at its use have yielded plausible responses when properly employed. Davis (1963) found that the responses obtained from travel cost and direct questioning approaches were not significantly different. Greenley et al. (1981) surveyed users to measure benefits associated with water quality improvement and preservation in the South Platte River Basin of Colorado. Daubert and Young (1981) applied the method to flowing streams, measuring the willingness to pay of several classes of recreationists for alternative stream flow levels. While user survey methods appear to have promise, they must not be accepted uncritically.

Review of Applications of Analytical Methods—Withdrawal Uses

Crop irrigation.—Scores of estimates of irrigation water values have been published. However, they lack consistency regarding estimates of the value of water in irrigation. The primary reason for this is the fact that at least five distinct concepts of irrigation water value emerge from the literature. Each may be appropriate for water allocation decisions in particular circumstances. These five concepts are very short-run, short-run, and long-run values from the private perspective, long-run values from the regional perspective, and long-run values from the national perspective. Irrigation water values, within the context of these concepts, may be estimated by observation of market transactions, residual imputation techniques (including the change in net income approach), and alternative cost techniques.

The first of these is seldom found in the literature because water markets are rare. Many political jurisdictions do not permit free market transfers of water. In most instances, observable market transactions relate to the very short- or short-run values in the water rental market context.

The second analytical technique, in various forms, enjoys the most widespread use in estimating irrigation water values. Residual imputation techniques have been applied to all of the five concepts identified above. Very short-run values (Green 1968), short-run values (Huszar et al. 1970, Miller and Boersma 1966, Hartman and Whittlesey 1961, Sorenson and Clark 1970, Gisser 1970, Gray and Trock 1971) and long-run values (Burt 1964, Anderson et al. 1966, Lindeborg 1970, Shumway et al. 1970, Skold and Epp 1966, McLeod 1968, Butcher et al. 1971, Matson et al. 1969, Howe and Easter 1971, Grubb 1966, Brown and McGuire 1967, Beattie et al. 1971, Fox and Rollins 1969, O'Connell 1972) have been estimated, given the private perspective, from residual imputation procedures.

The technique has also been used fairly extensively in estimating long-run values from the regional perspective. Examples of various residual imputation techniques employed in this regard include the use of input-output models (Hartman and Seastone 1970, 1966, Bradley and Gander 1968, Tijoriwala et al. 1968, Skold and Greer 1969), linear programming models (Young 1970) and combinations of the two (Kelso et al. 1973, Lofting and McGauhey 1968, Gray 1970). Application of these techniques represents attempts to measure direct contributions to regional income per acre-foot of water in irrigated agriculture.

Attempts to use direct regional value added as a measure of irrigation water value must be undertaken with care and must be reviewed with equal caution. From the regional perspective, care must be taken to account for components of value added contributed by all primary factors other than water, including returns to the management function. Failure to do so may result in imputed values for water which are too large. Regional value added estimates may also be significantly larger than national value. Kneese (Wollman et al. 1963), for example, provides the basis for indicating the extent to which regional value added can overstate national water value. His data show that when a charge for family living allowance (opportunity cost of family farm labor) is deducted from net farm income, the estimated value of water is only about 30 percent of the estimated direct regional value added per acre-foot.

Estimates of long-run values from the national perspective, which are appropriate to federal agency involvement in allocation and development decisions, are surprisingly rare. From this perspective, long-run value requires that the effects of any external interference on agricultural resource and product markets be taken into account in the estimation of resource values. For example, on the output side, commodity prices in several important instances have been historically supported and stabilized, although this policy has become less prevalent. On the factor supply side, quantities of resources may be restricted and prices for factors set artificially low. In such cases, the long-run social value of water must be based upon imputed market prices for the affected commodities and factors. Accommodating these publicly administered incentives, penalties, rules and opportunities is currently required for value estimation at the national level (U.S. Water Resources Council 1973). An example of an attempt to take commodity price support and stabilization programs and the social value of resources into account in imputing a value to water is found in Bain et al. (1966).

"Alternative cost" as a method of valuation of irrigation water has not received much attention in the literature but appears to have merit in several cases. In the relatively humid eastern U.S., for example, it appears reasonable that a private alternative to public provision of supplies exists in the form of withdrawal from lakes, streams, and aquifers. Privately developed supplies may well be less expensive than public supplies in these areas. Therefore, if the resource is not economically scarce, the private cost of water may be a reasonable approximation of the social value.

Also, in the western U.S., the private cost of ground water as an alternative to public provision is of some interest. Although the issue is complicated by finite ground water supplies and the possibility for external or third-party costs associated with pumping, the private cost of ground water could serve as a lower bound estimate of the social value of water (Keleta 1976). For situations other than those involving consideration of reallocation from irrigation, it appears that further consideration of the alternative cost method of estimating irrigation water values is appropriate.

Industrial use.—Three basic approaches to water value estimation have been applied to industrial uses: value added, residual imputation, and alternative cost.

The value-added approach (Powell 1956, Kneese 1959, Lofting and McGauhey 1968, Wollman et al. 1963, d'Arge 1970) involves the estimation of the ratio of value added to the water used in the process (utilization typically measured as consumptive use). Value added is an appealing approach to value estimates because of its relative simplicity. However, the approach is not appropriate, because it omits consideration of the opportunity costs of primary resources other than water. Value added per unit of water consumed in manufacturing may have extremely high values simply because some industries have very large value added but require very small quantities of water. Regional value added per acre-foot of water consumed often ignores the opportunity cost of other primary factors. In essence, these other resources are assumed to have zero opportunity costs, and their values are thus attributed to water. Also, the use of average value added per acre-foot can yield a significantly different allocation policy than would the use of an incremental value-added concept (d'Arge 1970).

The alternative cost approach to valuing industrial water involves the use of the cost of intake or internal recycling to represent the ceiling on the price which the firm would be willing to pay for water. The cost of intake variant (Renshaw 1958b, Bramer and Motz 1969) assumes that the cost of intake represents a measure of the value of water in the productive process. However, such costs represent the average cost of operating the delivery system and are only indicative of the industry's ability to pay for water. They do not reflect incremental costs, and thus are of limited value for private or public water allocation decisions.

The second variant is the internal recycling cost (Olson 1966), in which the marginal cost of recycling at each quantity of water demanded is used to indicate the maximum willingness to pay or value of water to the firm. The limited estimates available suggest values estimated by the alternative cost variants which are well below those estimated by the value-added criteria and which, for reasons mentioned previously, are much more believable.

The final approach to valuing water in industrial use is that of residual imputation (Wollman et al. 1963). This approach, as discussed previously, is conceptually correct but has not been widely used. Despite its shortcomings, the residual imputation technique in the context of estimating industrial water values is worthy of further study.

Municipal use.—The value of municipal water is defined by consumer's demand for the final commodity. While a fairly substantial body of literature exists relating the demand for water to alternative pricing policies for municipal use, such studies illustrate the willingness to pay for water out of the tap and thus relate to value from the private perspective (Hanke 1970, Linaweaver et al. 1967, Seidel and Baumann 1957, Gardner and Schick 1964, Conley 1967, Howe and Linaweaver 1967, Young 1973, Hansen et al. 1979, Hansen and Narayanan 1981, Danielson 1979, Gardner 1977, Billings and Agthe 1980, Foster and Beattie 1979, 1981, Griffin et al. 1981). From the social perspective, the appropriate estimate of value is that for raw water rather than tap water, where willingness to pay includes the value of treated water which also has been stored and transported to location of use. Social value of water in municipal use requires that costs of storage, treatment and transportation be deducted from the private value. Again, additional research is necessary to assess the long-run social value of water used for municipal purposes.

Review of Applications of Analytical Methods—Non-withdrawal or In-stream Uses

Recreation.—Estimates of the value of water in recreation require prior synthetic imputed values for the recreation services. The latter has occupied the attention of analysts for the past couple of decades, while attention to the former has been relatively recent. Additional development of the appropriate theory in this area is addressed by Alan Randall in another chapter of this book. The purpose here is only to cite some of the existing attempts to value water in recreation under circumstances in which recreation is competitive with other uses. This means that value estimates must be expressed in terms of some unit volume of water. Variations in the measure of volume lead to widely divergent value estimates in the relatively few studies which have addressed the issue. Some studies concerned with standing bodies of water use the entire volume of the water body; others have used the volume of the minimum conservation pool; others have used an arbitrary volume near the surface, for example, depths up to 15 feet; others have used the evaporation and seepage losses. Finally, a concept which is attractive but quite difficult to use is that the volume of water removed from a reservoir will eventually reduce the value of recreation, and the appropriate measure of water value is the change in the value of recreation per unit of water.

Regarding the estimation of value of the recreational experience, relevant literature includes Clawson (1959), Brown et al. (1964), Wennergren (1965), Grubb and Goodwin (1968), Lerner (1962), Wollman et al. (1963), Hyra (1978), Gordon et al. (1972), Knetsch (1974), Charbonneau and Hay (1978), Stevens and Kalter (1970).

Specific attempts to measure the value of water in recreation include Coppedge and Gray (1968), Wennergren (1965), Renshaw (1958b), Sirles (1968), McNeely and Badger (1968), Walsh et al. (1980). Daubert and Young (1981) estimated willingness to pay for alternative levels of in-stream flow, in free-flowing streams, using the contingent valuation method for measuring public good demand (Bradford 1970, Randall et al. 1974, Brookshire et al. 1976). Despite the growing number of efforts in this area of inquiry, much research remains to be done determining the appropriate conceptual and empirical basis for estimating the value of water in recreation uses. Also more in-stream value estimates from a range of sites are necessary to get a range of possible values. Refinements in questionnaires and conceptualizations are definitely needed.

Fish and wildlife habitat.—Problems of measuring the net dollar value of output and of choosing the appropriate measure of water use pertinent to the previous section are also pertinent to determining the value of water used in providing fish and wildlife habitat. Attempts to measure the value of water on a unit basis in this use are virtually non-existent. Therefore, translations of values estimated for specific activities (fishing, hunting, sports fisheries, etc.) must be used to provide very crude approximations of water value per unit of use. Such approximations are useful only in providing order-of-magnitude estimates. Literature in the former regard includes Brown et al. (1964), Gordon (1968), Crutchfield (1962), Hammond (1964), Charbonneau and Hay (1978), Gordon et al. (1972), Hammack and Brown (1974), Hyra (1978). Attempts at specific valuation of water on a per unit basis (Sieker 1955, Renshaw 1958b) are dated but provide interesting procedures. In sum, techniques for valuing water use in this category need further refinement.

Hydroelectric power generation.—Water for hydropower generation, like water for navigation, has been traditionally considered a free good. As a result, while there are numerous studies pertaining to economic justification of public hydroelectric power developments (Eckstein 1958, Krutilla and Eckstein 1958, Hufschmidt and Fiering 1966, Sewell et al. 1968), little has been done regarding efforts to value water for this purpose. This method for doing so, however, is a combination of alternative cost and residual imputation (Hastay et al. 1971, Young and Gray 1972, Whittlesey and Gibbs 1978).

Waste load assimilation and water quality.—Additional water provides a non-withdrawal benefit by diluting the pollution load, and reducing the damages suffered by users of degraded water.

Several alternative methods of assessing the value of water for waste load assimilation have been reported. The most direct means is to estimate the relative damages associated with varying levels of water quality (Kneese and Bower 1968, Colorado River Board of California 1970). Because of the well-known difficulties involved with direct damage estimation and the estimate of dollar values of effects on consumption and production, the earliest approaches to the problem employed an alternative cost approach. The cost of treating effluent to achieve the same quality level as would be reached by the dilutive effects of additional water was used as a measure of value (Russell 1970, Merritt and Mar 1969, Gray and Young 1974). As long as effluent levels are within the bounds which can be handled by primary levels of treatment, the alternative cost method appears to be appropriate for estimating values in waste load assimilation. However, as waste levels increase to the point at which secondary and tertiary levels of treatment are required to meet quality standards, alternative costs would become relatively large, and actual damage reduction would become the appropriate concept of value.

In recent years, efforts to measure damage functions (from which dilution benefits can be derived) have appeared. The problem of measuring damages is made especially difficult by the vast variety of substances which can pollute waterways. Various substances can cause different damages in a given water use, and across water uses. In principle, the more narrowly the polluting substance is defined, the more precise the damage estimate is. At present, most analysts are forced to aggregate individual pollutant substances into broad groups, such as organic matter, dissolved solids (salinity), or heavy metals.

The most attention has been given to salinity, particularly in the Colorado River Basin. Damage functions in irrigation were first attempted by Pincock (1968). After refinements in the theory of salinity damage functions, primarily by Yaron and Bresler (1970), Moore et al. (1974) formulated a linear programming version of the residual imputation method to measure salinity damages in the Imperial Valley, California. Kleinman and Brown (1977) updated this work, and extended it to the other portion of the lower Colorado River Basin. Oyarzabal and Young (1978) treated the same subject in a study of the Mexicali Valley, Mexico.

Several statistical analyses of salinity damages and damage reductions to households and industries have been attempted in the past decade. Tihansky (1974) reviewed early approaches. Eubanks and d'Arge (1977) studied the life of various household appliances in the Los Angeles area, as these lives were shortened by salinity in water supplies. The total costs of reduced useful life are converted into a household damage function, which is aggregated to derive a regional damage function. McGuckin and Young (1981) performed a similar study for communities on the Arkansas River in eastern Colorado, which is the most saline reach of river in the U.S.

Because recreational value of water can also be reduced by pollution, the travel cost and direct questioning approaches have been used to study these effects (Ericksen et al. 1978, Greenley et al. 1981, Greenely et al. 1982). Freeman (1979) provides a detailed analysis of the problem. Bouwes and Schneider (1979) used a travel cost approach incorporating a water quality rating variable in the model. Feenberg and Mills (1980) demonstrate property values and travel cost methods for measuring benefits of water quality improvement.

Brown and Plummer (1979) dealt with the question of damages arising from suspended solids (i.e., silt) washing from recently timbered forest lands.

Navigation.—Water has been treated as a free good in its use for navigation purposes. Two attempts have been made to derive a value of water in this use (Renshaw 1958a, Young and Gray 1972). However, the alternative cost approach to valuation of water transport and a residual imputation procedure for imputing a value to water appears to be the appropriate valuation procedure. There do not appear to be any significant impacts of forest management policies on water for navigation.

Research Priorities

The first suggestion is to encourage closer ties between social scientists researching the questions of wildland resource valuation and biological and physical scientists who are studying the impact of forest management on water flows and quality. There is a large body of knowledge developed on the latter subject (U.S. Forest Service 1979), as well as on water valuation, but the productivity of both groups of researchers would likely be enhanced by interdisciplinary research into problems.

A second and closely related suggestion is to conduct water valuation studies within a systems context. While the conceptual basis for valuation in this regard exists, and some empirical estimation has been attempted, much more is needed in the identification and measurement of physical interdependencies among uses and the implications of their existence on water valuation. This issue will likely increase in importance as resource scarcity increases and reinforces the need for ties between economic management and hydrologic modeling in the value estimation process.

A third suggestion deals with the area of nonmarketed collective type outputs, particularly those dealing with water-based recreation, fishery and wildlife habitat, and water quality. Value estimates in this area are meaningful and useful. Additional replications of previous studies are needed, and further theoretical and methodological refinements are necessary for these valuations to reach an appropriate level of acceptance by applied practitioners of resource valuation and by policy-makers in resource management agencies. It will be desirable, for example, to study in-stream flow values for recreationists under a range of hydrologic, economic, and environmental conditions. Water quality enhancement and degradation, particularly with regard to siltation impacts directly on recreationists and on fisheries, deserves considerably more examination.

Literature Cited

Anderson, Dale O., Neil R. Cook, and Daniel D. Badger. 1966. Estimation of irrigation water values in Oklahoma. Processed Series P-528, Oklahoma Agricultural Experiment Station

Anderson, R. L. 1961. The irrigation water rental market, a case study. Agricultural Economics Research 8(2).

Bain, J. S., R. E. Caves, and J. Margolis. 1966. Northern California's water industry. Johns Hopkins Press, Baltimore, Md.

Beattie, B. R., E. N. Castle, and W. G. Brown. 1971. Economic consequences of interbasin transfer. Oregon Agricultural Experiment Station Bulletin 116.

Billings, R. B., and D. E. Agthe. 1980. Price elasticities for water: A case of increasing block rates. Land Economics 56(1):73-84.

Bouwes, N. W., and R. Schneider. 1979. Procedures in estimating benefits of water quality change. American Journal of Agricultural Economics 61(3):535-539.

Bower, Blair T. 1963. Some physical, technological and economic characteristics of water and water resources administration. Natural Resources Journal 3(2).
Bradford, D. F. 1970. Benefit-cost analysis and demand curves for public goods. Kyklos 23:775-791.
Bradley, Iver E., and J. P. Gander. 1968. The economics of water allocation in Utah: An input-output analysis. Bureau of Economic and Business Research, Center for Economic and Community Development, University of Utah.
Bramer, H. D., and D. J. Motz. 1969. The economic value of water in industrial uses. Cyrus W. Rice and Co., National Technical Info. Service Doc. No. PB 189248.
Bredehoeft, J. D., and R. A. Young. 1970. The temporal allocation of ground water: A simulation approach. Water Resources Research 6(1).
Brookshire, D. S., B. C. Ives, and W. D. Schultze. 1976. The valuation of aesthetic preference. Journal of Environmental Economics and Management 3:325-346.
Brown, G. M, Jr., and C. B. McGuire. 1967. A socially optimal pricing policy for a public agency. Water Resources Research 3(1).
Brown, G. M., Jr., and Mark Plummer. 1979. Recreation valuation. Appendix to "An economic analysis of nontimber use of forest land in the Pacific Northwest," Forest Policy Project Report. Washington State University, Pullman, Wash.
Brown, William, A. Singh, and E. N. Castle. 1964. An economic evaluation of the Oregon salmon and steelhead sport fishery. Oregon Agricultural Experiment Station Research Bulletin 78, Corvallis, Oreg.
Burt, O. R. 1964. The economics of conjunctive use of ground and surface water. Hilgardia 36(2). California Agricultural Experiment Station, Berkeley, Calif.
Burt, O. R., and D. Brewer. 1971. Estimation of net social benefits from outdoor recreation. Econometrica 39(5):813-827.
Butcher, Walter, C. Crosby, and N. Whittlesey. 1972. Long run costs and policy implications of adjusting to a declining water supply in eastern Washington, Part I. Washington State Water Resources Research Center Report No. 9, Pullman, Wash.
Charbonneau, J. J., and M. J. Hay. 1978. Determinants and economic values of hunting and fishing. Transactions, 43rd North American Wildlife and National Resources Conference 43:391-403.
Clawson, Marion. 1959. Methods of measuring demands for and value of outdoor recreation. Reprint No. 10, Resources For The Future, Inc., Washington, D.C.
Colorado River Board of California. 1970. Need for controlling salinity in the Colorado River. Los Angeles, Calif. Unnumbered report.
Conley, B. C. 1967. Price elasticity of demand for water in southern California. Annals of Regional Science 7.
Convery, F. J., and C. W. Rader. ca. 1976. The valuation of water flowing from federal forest watersheds in the south: An inquiry. Unnumbered mimeo report. School of Forestry and Environmental Studies, Duke University.

Coppedge, R. O., and J. R. Gray. 1968. Recreational value of water in major reservoirs in New Mexico. Agricultural Experiment Station Bulletin, New Mexico State University, Las Cruces, N. Mex.

Crutchfield, J. 1962. Valuation of fishery resources. Land Economics 38(2).

Danielson, L. E. 1979. An analysis of residential water demand using micro-time series data. Water Resources Research 14(4):263-274.

d'Arge, R. 1970. Quantitative water resource basin planning: An analysis of the Pecos River Basin, New Mexico. Report No. 8, Water Resource Research Institute, New Mexico State University, Las Cruces, N. Mex.

Daubert, John T., R. A. Young, and H. J. Morel-Seytoux. 1980. Measuring external diseconomies from ground water use in conjunctive ground and surface water systems. *In* Dan Yaron and C. S. Tapiero (editors) Operations research in agriculture and water resources, p. 525-536. Elsevier-North Holland, Amsterdam.

Daubert, J. T., and R. A. Young. 1981. Recreational demands for maintaining instream flows: A contingent valuation approach. American Journal of Agricultural Economics 63:666-676.

Davis, R. K. 1963. The value of outdoor recreation. Ph.D. thesis, Harvard University, Cambridge, Mass.

Dean, Gerald W., and Gordon A. King. 1970. Projection of California agriculture to 1980 and 2000: Potential impact of the San Joaquin Valley west side development. Giannini Foundation Research Report No. 312. University of California, Berkeley, Calif.

Ditwiler, C. D. 1975. Water problems and property rights: An economic perspective. Natural Resources Journal 75(4):661-680.

Eckstein, Otto. 1958. Water resource development: The economics of project evaluation. Harvard University Press, Cambridge, Mass.

Ericksen, Ray K., and R. G. Walsh, et al. 1978. Recreation benefits of water quality: Rocky Mountain National Park, South Platte River Basin, Colorado. Technical Rep. No. 12, Colorado Water Research Institute, Fort Collins, Colo.

Eubanks, L., and Ralph C. d'Arge. 1977. Municipal and industrial consequences of salinity in the Colorado River service area of California. *In* J. C. Anderson and A. P. Kleinman (editors) Salinity management options for the Colorado River. Utah Water Research Lab. Rep. P-78-003, Logan, Utah.

Feenberg, D., and E. S. Mills. 1980. Measuring the benefits of water pollution abatement. Academic Press, New York, N.Y. 180 p.

Flinn, J. D., and J. W. Guise. 1970. An application of spatial equilibrium analysis to water resources allocation. Water Resource Research 6(2).

Foster, H. S., Jr., and B. R. Beattie. 1979. Urban residential demand for water in the United States. Land Economics 55(1):43-58.

Foster, H. S., Jr., and B. R. Beattie. 1981. On the specification of price in studies of consumer demand under block price scheduling. Land Economics 57(4):624-629.

Fox, Alan, and Norman Rollins. 1969. The value of irrigation water for the production of vegetables and potatoes in upstate New York. Department of Agricultural Economics Reserach Paper 311, Cornell University, Ithaca, N.Y.

Frank, M. D., and B. R. Beattie. 1979. The economic value of irrigation water in the western U.S.: An application of ridge regression. Department of Agricultural Economics, Texas A&M University, College Station, Texas.

Freeman, A. M., III. 1966. Adjusted benefit-cost ratios for six recent reclamation projects. Journal of Farm Economics 48(5):1002-1009.

Freeman, A. M., III. 1979. The benefits of environmental improvement: Theory and practice. Johns Hopkins University Press for Resources For the Future, Baltimore, Md. 272 p.

Freeman, A. M., III, and R. H. Haveman. 1970. Benefit cost analyses and multiple objectives: Current issues in water resource planning. Water Resources Research 6(6):1533-1539.

Gaffney, Mason. 1969. Economic aspects of water resource policy. American Journal of Economics and Sociology 28(2).

Gardner, B. D., and S. Schick. 1964. Factors affecting consumption of urban household water in northern Utah. Utah Agricultural Experiment Station Bulletin 449, Logan, Utah.

Gardner, Richard. 1977. An analysis of residential water demand and water rates in Minnesota. Water Resources Research Center Bulletin 96, University of Minnesota, Minneapolis, Minn.

Gisser, Mischa. 1970. Linear programming models for estimating the agricultural demand function for imported water in the Pecos River basin. Water Resources Research 6(4).

Gordon, D., D. W. Chapman, and T. C. Bourne. 1972. Economic evaluation of sport fisheries: What do they mean? Transactions American Fisheries Society 293-331.

Gordon, Douglas. 1968. An economic analysis of Idaho sport fisheries. Idaho Cooperative Fisheries Unit, University of Idaho. Unnumbered report.

Gray, R. M., and Warren Trock. 1971. A study of the effects of institutions on the distribution and use of water for irrigation in the lower Rio Grande basin. Texas A&M Water Research Institute Technical Rep. No. 36, College Station, Texas.

Gray, S. L. 1970. Economic effects of diverting the Columbia River. Unpublished Ph.D. dissertation, Washington State University, Pullman.

Gray, S. L., and R. A. Young. 1974. The economic value of water for waste dilution: Forecasts to 1980. Journal of the Water Pollution Control Federation 46(7):1653-1663.

Green, John W. 1968. An economic analysis of irrigation in the Oklahoma panhandle. Unpublished Ph.D. dissertation, Oklahoma State University, Stillwater, Okla.

Greenley, Douglas, Richard Walsh, and R. A. Young. 1981. Option value: Empirical evidence from a case study of recreation and water quality. Quarterly Journal of Economics 96(4):657-674.

Greenley, Douglas, Richard G. Walsh, and R. A. Young. 1982. Option value, preservation value and recreational benefits of improved water quality. Westview Press, Boulder, Colo.

Griffin, A. H., W. E. Martin, and J. C. Wade. 1981. Urban residential demand for water in the U.S.: Comment. Land Economics 57(2):252-256.

Grubb, Herbert W. 1966. The importance of irrigation water to the economy of Texas. Texas Water Development Board Report No. 11, Austin, Texas.

Grubb, Herbert W., and James T. Goodwin. 1968. Economic evaluation of water-oriented recreation in the preliminary Texas water plan. Texas Water Development Board Report No. 84, Austin, Texas.

Hammack, Judd, and G. M. Brown, Jr. 1974. Waterfowl and wetlands: Toward bioeconomic analysis. Johns Hopkins Press for Resources For the Future, Baltimore, Md.

Hammond, M. C. 1964. Ducks, grain and American farmers. Waterfowl Tomorrow. U.S. Department of the Interior. U.S. Government Printing Office, Washington, D.C.

Hanke, S. H. 1970. Dynamics of household water demand. Water Resources Research 6(3).

Hansen, Roger D., and R. Narayanan. 1981. A monthly time series model of municipal water demand. Water Resources Bulletin 17(4):578-585.

Hansen, Roger D., et al. 1979. Municipal water use. Utah Science 40(2):51-53.

Hartman, L. M., and R. L. Anderson. 1963. Estimating irrigation water values, a regression analysis of farm sales data from northeastern Colorado. Technical Bulletin 81, Colorado Agricultural Experiment Station, Fort Collins, Colo.

Hartman, L. M., and D. A. Seastone. 1966. Regional economic interdependencies and water use. *In* A. V. Kneese and S. C. Smith, Water research. Johns Hopkins Press, Baltimore. Md.

Hartman, L. M., and D. A. Seastone. 1970. Water transfers: Economic efficiency and alternative institutions. Johns Hopkins Press, Baltimore. Md.

Hartman, L. M., and Norman Whittlesey. 1961. Marginal values of irrigation water: A linear programming analysis of farm adjustments to changes in water supply. Colorado State University Experiment Station Technical Bulletin No. 70, Fort Collins, Colo.

Hastay, Millard, et al. 1971. The Columbia River as a resource: Socioeconomic considerations of diversion and value of Columbia River water, Part A. State of Washington Water Research Center, Pullman, Wash. Unnumbered report.

Haveman, Robert. 1975. Economics of the public sector, 2nd ed. Knopf, New York, N.Y.

Heady, E. O. 1952. The economics of agricultural production and resource use. Iowa State University Press, Ames, Iowa.

Heady, E. O., A. Morton, and D. A. Christensen. 1981. Programmed effects of surface water price levels on U.S. agricultural water use and production patterns. Western Journal of Agricultural Economics 6(1):113-127.

Henderson, James M., and Richard E. Quandt. 1978. Microeconomic theory: A mathematical approach, 3rd ed. McGraw-Hill Book Company, New York, N.Y.

Herfindahl, O. C., and A. V. Kneese. 1974. Economic theory of natural resources. Merrill, Columbus, Ohio.

Hexem, Roger W., and E. O. Heady. 1978. Water production functions for irrigated agriculture. Iowa State University Press, Ames, Iowa.

Howe, C. W., and F. P. Linaweaver. 1967. The impact of price on residential water demand. Water Resources Research 3(1).

Howe, C. W., and W. K. Easter. 1971. Interbasin transfers of water: Economic issues and impacts. Johns Hopkins Press, Baltimore, Md.

Howe, C. W. 1971. Benefit-cost analysis for water systems planning. Water Resources Monograph No. 2, American Geophysical Union, Washington, D.C.

Hufschmidt, Maynard M., and Myron B. Fiering. 1966. Simulation techniques for design of water resource systems. Harvard University Press, Cambridge, Mass.

Huszar, Paul, M. D. Skold, and R. A. Danielson. 1970. Evaluation of irrigation water and nitrogen fertilizer in corn production. Colorado State University Experiment Station Technical Bulletin 107, Fort Collins, Colo.

Hyra, Ronald. 1978. Methods of assessing instream flow for recreation. Washington, D.C., U.S. Fish and Wildlife Service Instream Flow Information Paper No. 6.

Keleta, Ghebreyohannes. 1976. Economics of cost-sharing for public irrigation projects. M.S. thesis, Department of Economics, Colorado State University, Fort Collins, Colo.

Kelso, M. W., W. E. Martin, and L. E. Mack. 1973. Water supplies and economic growth in an arid environment. University of Arizona Press, Tucson, Ariz. 328 p.

Khan, M. Jameel, and R. A. Young. 1979. Farm resource productivities and agricultural development policy: A case study of the Indus Basin, Pakistan. Land Economics 53(3):388-396.

Kleinman, A. P., and F. Bruce Brown. 1977. Economic damages in agriculture in the Lower Colorado River Basin. *In* J. C. Anderson and A. P. Kleinman (editors) Salinity management options for the Colorado River, p. 117-249. Utah Water Research Laboratory Report P-78-003, Logan, Utah.

Kneese, A. V. 1959. Water resources development and uses. Kansas City Federal Reserve Bank Occasional Report.

Kneese, A. V., and B. T. Bower. 1968. Managing water quality: Economics, technology, institutions. Johns Hopkins Press, Baltimore, Md.

Knetsch, Jack L. 1974. Outdoor recreation and water resource planning. Water Resource Monograph No. 3, American Geophysical Union, Washington, D.C.

Krutilla, J. V., and O. Eckstein. 1958. Multiple purpose river basin development. Johns Hopkins Press, Baltimore, Md.

Lerner, Lionel. 1962. Quantitative indices of recreational values in western agricultural economics research. Council, Committee on Economics of Water Resources Development, Report No. 11, Economics in Outdoor Recreation, Berkeley, Calif.

Linaweaver, F. P., Jr., et al. 1967. A study of residential water use. Federal Housing Administration Technical Series 12, U.S. Department of Housing and Urban Development.

Lindeborg, Karl. 1970. Economic values of water in four areas along the Snake River in Idaho. Idaho Agricultural Experiment Station Bulletin 513, Moscow, Idaho.

Lofting, E. M., and P. H. McGauhey. 1968. Economic evaluation of water, Part IV: An input-output and linear programming analysis of California water requirements. Contribution No. 116, Water Resources Center, University of California, Berkeley, Calif.

Maass, Arthur, et al. 1962. Design of water resource systems. Harvard University Press, Cambridge, Mass. 527 p.

Marglin, Stephen. 1962. Objectives for water resource development: A general statement. *In* A. Maass, et al., Design of water systems. Harvard University Press, Cambridge, Mass.

Marglin, Stephen A. 1968. Public investment criteria. MIT Press, Cambridge, Mass.

Martin, William E. 1979. Returns to public irrigation development and the concomitant cost of commodity programs. American Journal of Agricultural Economics 61(5):1107-1114.

Matson, A. J., et al. 1969. Investigation of irrigation development in the Big Sioux Basin and the East Dakota Conservancy District, Parts I and II. Department of Economics, South Dakota Experiment Station, Brookings.

McGuckin, J. Thomas, and R. A. Young. 1981. Economic feasibility of desalination of brackish household water supplies. Journal of Environmental Economics and Management 8(1):79-91.

McLeod, Dennis M. 1968. An economic analysis of water resource development for irrigation in North Dakota. Interim North Dakota State Water Resources Development Plan, North Dakota State Water Commission, Bismark, N. Dak.

McNeely, John, and Daniel Badger. 1968. Demand for selected recreational activities in south central Oklahoma. Oklahoma State University Technical Bulletin No. T-106, Stillwater, Okla.

Merritt, L. B., and B. W. Mar. 1969. Marginal values of dilution water. Water Resources Research 5(6).

Miller, S. F., and L. L. Boersma. 1966. An economic analysis of water, nitrogen and seeding relationships on corn production in woodburn soils. Oregon Agricultural Experiment Station Bulletin 98, Corvallis, Oreg.

Milliman, J. W. 1959. Land values as measure of primary irrigation benefits. Journal of Farm Economics 41(2).

Moore, C. V., P. Sun, and J. H. Snyder. 1974. Effect of Colorado River water quality on irrigated agriculture. Water Resources Research 10(1):137-146.

O'Connell, P. F. 1972. Valuation of timber, forage and water from National forest lands. Annals of Regional Science 6(2):1-14.

Olson, Sherry M. 1966. Some conceptual problems in interpreting the value of water for humid regions. Water Resources Research 2(1).

Oyarzabal-Tamargo, F., and R. A. Young. 1978. International external diseconomies: The Colorado River salinity problem in Mexico. Natural Resource Journal 18(1):77-89.

Peskin, H. M., and E. P. Seskin. 1975. Cost-benefit analysis and water pollution control. Urban Institute, Washington, D.C.

Pincock, M. Glade. 1968. Assessing impacts of declining water quality on gross value output of agriculture: A case study. Water Resources Research 5(1):1-12.

Powell, S. T. 1956. Relative economic returns from industrial and agricultural water uses. Journal of the American Water Works Association 48.
Prest, A. R., and R. Turvey. 1965. Cost-benefit analysis—A survey. Economic Journal 75(4):683-735.
Randall, A., B. Ives, and C. Eastman. 1974. Bidding games for valuation of environmental improvement. Journal of Environmental Economics and Management 1(4):132-149.
Renshaw, Edward. 1958a. Cross sectional pricing in the market for irrigated land. Agricultural Economics Research 5(2).
Renshaw, Edward 1958b. Value of an acre foot of water. Journal of the American Water Works Association.
Russell, Clifford. 1970. Public policy, technology and industrial water use. Part II. *In* C. W. Howe, C. S. Russell, and R. A. Young, The impacts of technical change, public policies and changing market conditions on water use patterns in selected sectors of the U.S. economy. U.S. National Water Commission Report EES-71-001.

Sadan, Ezra. 1969. An estimation of return to irrigation water in Israel with reference to seawater desalting proposals. California Agricultural Experiment Station, Giannini Foundation Research Report No. 305, Berkeley, Calif.
Seidel, H. F., and E. R. Baumann. 1957. A statistical analysis of water works data for 1955. Journal of the American Water Works Association 49.
Sewell, W. R. D., et al. 1968. Forecasting the demand for water. Department of Engineering, Mines and Resources, Ottawa, Ontario, Canada.
Shumway, D. R., G. R. King, H. O. Carter, and G. W. Dean. 1970. Regional resource use for agricultural production in California, 1961-65 and 1980. Giannini Foundation Monograph No. 25, Berkeley, Calif.
Sieker, J. H. 1955. Planning for the recreational use of water: A plea. Water: The 1955 yearbook of agriculture. U.S. Government Printing Office, Washington, D.C.
Sirles, J. E. 1968. Application of marginal analyses to reservoir recreation planning. Water Resources Research Institute Report No. 12, University of Kentucky, Lexington, Kentucky.
Skold, M. D., and A. Epp. 1966. Optimal farm organization for irrigated farms in south central Nebraska. Res. Bulletin 222, Nebraska Agricultural Experiment Station, Lincoln, Nebraska.
Skold, M. D., and A. J. Greer. 1969. The impact of agricultural change on a local economy in the Great Plains. Colorado State University Experiment Station Technical Bulletin 106, Fort Collins, Colo.
Sorenson, J. N., and R. T. Clark. 1970. Marginal value of irrigation water and a case study of transfer in southeastern Wyoming. Wyoming Agricultural Experiment Station Bulletin 511, Laramie, Wyoming.
Steiner, Peter O. 1965. The role of alternative cost in project design and selection. Quarterly Journal of Economics 79(3).
Stevens, T. H., and R. H. Kalter. 1970. Technological externalities, outdoor recreation and the regional economic impact of Cayuga Lake. Agricultural Economics Research Report 317, Cornell University, Ithaca, N.Y.

Tihansky, Dennis P. 1974. Economic damages from residential use of mineralized water supply. Water Resources Research 12(2):145-154.

Tijoriwala, A. K., W. E. Martin, and L. G. Bower. 1968. Structure of the Arizona economy: Output interrelationships and their effect on labor and water requirements. Arizona Agricultural Experiment Station Technical Bulletin No. 180, Tucson, Ariz.

U.S. Forest Service. 1979. An approach to water resources evaluation of non-point, silvicultural sources (A Procedural Handbook). U.S. Environmental Protection Agency, Environmental Research Laboratory, Athens, Ga. (EPA 600/8-80-012)

U.S. Water Resources Council. 1973. Principles and standards for planning water and related land resources. Federal Register 38(174):Part III, September 10. 167 p.

U.S. Water Resources Council. 1979. Procedures for evaluation of national economic development (NED) benefits and costs in water resource planning (Level C); Final Rule. Federal Register 44(242):72892-72976.

Walsh, R. G., et al. 1980. An empirical application of a model for estimating the value of instream flow. Colorado Water Resources Research Institute Completion Report No. 101, Colorado State University, Fort Collins, Colo.

Wennergren, Boyd. 1965. Value of water for boating recreation. Utah State University Agricultural Experiment Station Bulletin 453, Logan, Utah.

Whittlesey, Norman, and K. C. Gibbs. 1978. Energy and irrigation in Washington. Western Journal of Agricultural Economics 3(1):1-10.

Wollman, Nathaniel, et al. 1963. The value of water in alternative uses. University of New Mexico Press, Albuquerque, N. Mex.

Yaron, D., and E. Bresler. 1970. A model for economic evaluation of water quality in irrigation. Australian Journal of Agricultural Economics 14(1):53-62.

Young, R. A. 1970. Public policy, technology and agricultural water use. Part III. Unpublished report to National Water Commission. Resources For The Future, Inc., Washington, D.C.

Young, R. A., and S. L. Gray. 1972. Economic value of water: Concepts and empirical estimates. Technical Report to National Water Commission. National Technical Information Service, PB-210-356, U.S. Department of Commerce, Springfield, Va.

Young, R. A., and J. D. Bredehoeft. 1972. Digital computer simulation for solving management problems of conjunctive ground and surface water systems. Water Resource Research 8(3):533-556.

Young, R. A. 1973. The price elasticity of demand for water: A case study of Tucson, Arizona. Water Resources Research 9(6):1068-1072.

Young, R. A. 1978. Economic analysis and federal irrigation policy: An appraisal. Western Journal of Agricultural Economics 3(2):257-267.

Chapter 10
Benefit Estimation for Scenic and Visibility Services

Alan Randall

In terms of the general conceptual model of benefit cost analysis,[1] any wildlands management program changes the X vector of "man-controlled inputs." This modifies the attributes of the environment, changing the S vector of services it provides. Scenic and visibility services are likely to be among those influenced. These changes are perceived by people, whose utility or level of satisfaction is affected. Given their preferences and the constraints which face them, individuals place economic values, positive or negative, on the increments or decrements in service flows which result from changes in the X vector.

The general model for BCA estimates total project benefits by aggregating the net benefits of providing specific elements, s_k, of the S vector (Ch. 2, eqs. [4] and [5])[2]. This form of aggregation requires one of the following: that the various s_k be separable in production (supply) and consumption (demand); that the S vector be partitioned into separable subvectors and benefit estimation be performed at the subvector level or that an experimental design matrix be developed to estimate the effect on benefit levels of varying one service while holding the level of the other (nonseparable) service constant, and vice-versa. Alternatively, benefit estimation for the whole S vector would need to be performed holistically.

Thus, the research design for estimating specific kinds of benefits and the aggregation procedure for determining total net benefits must be established simultaneously (and with explicit consideration of the separability question).

Scenic services are defined in terms of the perceived characteristics of the scene or vista. Visibility refers to the clarity of the visual medium, that is, its ability to transmit visual images without distortion or discoloration.

It is usually reasonable to think of scenic and visibility services as being completely separable in production. Many actions affect scenic services (e.g., decisions pertaining to timber harvesting), visibility (e.g., pollution of the air), but not both. Where an action has scenic and visibility impacts (e.g., an ugly smoke stack creates plume blight while polluting the air, or a controlled forest burn has short-term visibility effects and causes scenic damage of longer duration), it is reasonable to assume these effects are additive, which is consistent with the assumption of separability in production.

In contrast, scenic and visibility services are clearly nonseparable in consumption. The enjoyment of a vista depends in part on the clarity of the air through which it is seen. Small changes in the scenic content of the vista (e.g., the addition of patches of snow or small clouds against a blue sky) influence preference rankings of color photographs which otherwise differ only in visual air quality (Latimer 1979, Daniel 1979, Craik 1979, Malm et al. 1980, Latimer et al. 1980).

Separability is a crucial concern in research design for benefit estimation and aggregation. Identification of separable relationships and development of strategies to handle nonseparability are important tasks in pragmatic benefit estimation.

Integrated Analysis: Action, Impact, Perception, Preference, and Economic Costs of Damage or Benefits of Improvement

Integrated benefit analysis defines the (proposed) action, quantifies its impact upon the flow of environment services in objectively measurable terms, records human perceptions of the impact and preferences (with respect) to alternative levels of provision of the impacted environmental services, and estimates the economic costs of damage (for adverse impacts) or benefits from favorable impacts. This chain of empirical analysis is entirely consistent with the general conceptual model for benefit cost analysis.[3] If the analyst also considers the cost of the proposed action and the costs of mitigating adverse impacts, the necessary information for a complete benefit cost analysis will have been generated.

In the case of scenic amenities, a recent study of the esthetic impact of alternative cooling systems for nuclear power plants (Adams et al. 1980) may serve as an example of integrated analysis. Landscape characteristics were "objectively" measured by reducing three-dimensional scenes to two-dimensional color photographs and measuring with geometric instruments the percentage of the photograph area occupied by objects with various scenic characteristics (e.g., evergreen forest, flowing water, clear still water, and man-made intrusions). Individuals ranked each photograph for its visual esthetic appeal, and the statistical correlation between visual esthetic scores and measured scenic characteristics was judged to be satisfactory.

The economic benefits of obtaining preferred scenic conditions or avoiding less preferred scenic conditions were established using contingent valuation. Individual household willingness to pay was found to be statistically predictable, given information on household demographic characteristics, the difference in the individual's visual esthetic scores among the alternative scenes, and the individual's attitudes toward nuclear power and pollution control (attitude variables especially pertinent to the nuclear cooling tower issue). Adams et al. (1980) suggest their results may be generally applied to estimate the benefits of preferred cooling tower designs, with relatively little expense devoted to primary data collection. Landscape characteristics, with and without the proposed action, must be measured, and information about the demographic characteristics of the regional population must be available.

For atmospheric visibility benefits, a recent study in the national park lands of the Southwest (Schulze et al. 1981a) provides an example of integrated benefit analysis. Visibility conditions in the region, as measured by optical instruments, were related to regional air pollutant emissions. Alternative scenarios were then developed, in terms of regional emissions and their impact on regional visibility. Alternative visibility conditions were represented with color photographs, and a method of calibrating color photographs with instrument-measured visibility was developed. Human subjects reported their perceived visibility ratings for a set of such photographs. The researchers concluded that human perception of changes in visual air quality, whether viewed via color slides, color prints, or on-site, are predictable on the basis of instrument-measured color contrast.

The economic benefits of obtaining improved visibility, or avoiding reductions in visibility, were determined at the household level using contingent valuation. Visitor and non-visitor benefits were estimated, and aggregate benefits of preserving visibility in the Southwest park lands were compared to the economic costs. Benefits substantially exceeded costs, and non-visitor benefits (i.e., option and existence values) accounted for the bulk of the total benefits.

Rowe and Chestnut (1981) provide a detailed discussion of integrated benefit assessment for atmospheric visibility. While Schulze et al. (1981a) uses contingent valuation for benefit estimation, Rowe and Chestnut discuss the potential for using various expenditure function methods, as well as contingent valuation.

Integrated analysis is clearly the ideal, because it maximizes the opportunity to generate information relevant to management planning as well as benefit information, and to discover which kinds of information are most useful for these purposes (c.f. the Schulze et al. (1981a), finding that the instrument-measured color contrast was a good predictor of human perception of, and preference among, alternative levels of visibility).

However, integrated analyses may be too costly for routine benefit estimation. It seems desirable to make a major effort at integrated analysis for each fundamentally new kind of benefit estimation problem (i.e., each new kind of environmental service or new grouping of nonseparable services and, perhaps, each new application in a generically different environment). These integrated analyses often will suggest serviceable short-cuts for subsequent, less expensive studies (Adams et al. 1980).

Impacts, Perceptions, Attitudes and Preferences

At a purely conceptual level, perceptions, attitudes, and preferences are essential intermediate links in the chain from action to impact to economic value. If one can conceptualize the objectively measurable reality of an environment, perceptions are the reality that the individual observes via his senses (sight, hearing, smell, touch, etc.). In terms of the general model for

BCA, attributes *A* and services *S* constitute the objectively measurable reality, while it is the perceived characteristics of *S* which enter individual utility functions. Preferences refer to individual rankings of alternative goods and services. Thus, over the same domain, the preference function and utility function are synonymous. In the traditional economic model, preferences, constraints, and relative costs determine choice.

However, perceived characteristics, constraints, and relative cost are not sufficient to determine choice. Individual attitudes explain why different persons with similar perceptions and facing similar constraints and relative costs may make quite dissimilar choices. Attitudes vary among individuals and may change over time. Presumably, individual perceptions and attitudes are together sufficient to predict individual preferences. There is substantial conceptual and empirical literature on perceptions attitudes, and preferences, in general (Ajzen and Fishbein 1977, Fishbein and Ajzen 1975) and with particular preference to environmental amenities including scenic and visibility services (Craik and Zube 1976). For the immediate purpose of benefit estimation, the pertinent question is whether conceptual and empirical efforts in the study of perceptions, attitudes, and preferences constitute an essential step in economic valuation.

The study of perceptions, attitudes, and preferences has been helpful in validating the benefit estimation efforts of economists. There is evidence that people perceive impacts, are capable of ranking alternative perceived environments according to preference, and develop attitudes with respect to environmental characteristics (Daniel et al. 1979). There is evidence of regular relationships among perceptions, preferences, attitudes, choice, and individual economic valuations (Lea 1978). Such evidence tends to encourage economic efforts at benefit estimation. Willingness to pay or to accept compensation, as revealed in contingent markets, must be viewed as a contingent choice (i.e., a behavioral intention contingent upon the circumstances posited). Therefore, it is important to know something about the reliability with which intentions are translated into actual behavior (Ajzen and Fishbein 1977, Hebert et al. 1979).

Careful study of perceptions and preferences also can identify the measurable environmental characteristics people perceive and prefer, and which help determine the value of economic benefits (Schulze et al. 1981a). The perception and preference aspects of that study clarified the relationship between economic benefits and perceived characteristics, suggesting the characteristics upon which economic analysts may effectively focus and which optical physicists may most usefully measure.

Perceived quality indices, e.g., the perceived environmental quality index, the visual esthetic quality index, the scenic beauty estimator, etc. (Latimer 1979, Craik 1979, Daniel 1979), if carefully calibrated with both observable characteristics and human preferences, are valuable in monitoring the effectiveness of programs for environmental management (Craik 1979). More generally, the relationships between characteristics, perceptions, attitudes, preferences, behavior, and economic values provide essential information for environmental management (Fox et al. 1979). The manager manipulates the *X* vector of "human-controlled inputs" in order to modify characteristics, all for the purpose of creating beneficial impacts. Knowledge about these links permits the manager to augment the most pertinent beneficial characteristics while mitigating the most important adverse characteristics, within the limits imposed by the opportunity costs of alternative actions.

Recent developments in economic theory suggest a role for information about perceptions, preferences, etc., in explaining individual variation in willingness to pay for environmental services. As the "new" theory of consumption (Becker 1965, Lancaster 1966, Stoll 1980) recognizes, individuals desire goods not as physical objects but for the characteristics they provide and the activities that individuals can produce by combining them with other goods and with their time. Thus, consumption technology—the way in which individuals are able to perceive and use the characteristics which goods provide—plays an important role in determining the economic values which individuals place on goods. Because consumption technologies differ among individuals, that is, different individuals perceive and use the same goods differently, it is reasonable for individuals in otherwise identical economic circumstances to place quite different values on the same good or service. This general observation applies with particular force to scenic and visibility services. Information about perceptions, preferences, etc., may play a helpful role in statistical analysis of individual value data for scenic and visibility services, providing a data base for statistical efforts to identify regularities in cross-sectional value estimates.

Estimation of Economic Benefits

A general framework for economic benefit estimation has been provided elsewhere in this book.[4] The benefits (positive or negative) of an action are defined as the consequent change in the Hicksian compensating measure of consumer's surplus. There are cases in which market price or demand information may be used directly in benefit estimation. Where the action results in a relatively small increment or decrement in divisible goods traded in infinitely large markets, the unit price multiplied by quantity change is an adequate indicator of benefits (Randall and Stoll 1980). For larger changes in quantity, where Marshallian demand information is available, the integral under the demand curve and across the quantity change provides an approximation of the appropriate measure of consumer's surplus in certain restricted, but quite commonly encountered, cases (Willig 1976, Randall and Stoll 1980).

Considerable effort and ingenuity have been invested in developing and implementing methods for estimating the economic value of goods and services which are not directly traded in markets. The "mainstream" techniques may be divided into two categories: those which approach consumer's surplus via the income compensation function, and those which use an expenditure function approach. The first-mentioned techniques directly obtain consumer's surplus information from subjects in interview, survey, or experimental situations. For the most part, these methods are directly congruent with theoretical concepts of benefit valuation. However, concerns may arise as to whether the interview, survey, or experimental mechanisms used are adequate to ensure accurate revelation of consumer's surplus values. The expenditure function approach uses data generated by actual choices, thus circumventing many of these doubts about data quality. However, the path from behavioral observation to benefit estimation is indirect and requires stringent analytical assumptions,[5] some of which may be in varying degrees implausible and restrictive. The strengths of one group of techniques are mirrored by the weaknesses of the other group, and vice-versa.

Because the income compensation function approaches involve the creation of contingent or experimental markets, there are relatively few restrictions on their range of applicability. They may be used to estimate benefits of providing services beyond the currently observed range, and to evaluate services far removed from existing markets (the extreme examples being option and existence values, which are not necessarily related to current patterns of use). Expenditure function approaches, in contrast, require data generated in markets for some good or service closely related to the environmental amenities of interest.

The conceptual framework for non-market benefit estimation is well developed for partial equilibrium evaluation of one-shot programs to increase or decrease the level of provision of a single environmental service. However, there remain unresolved difficulties in general equilibrium analysis and in analysis of situations where several actions to augment environmental amenities are under simultaneous consideration. In this latter case, there is some fragmentary empirical evidence (consistent with theoretical considerations) that benefits from a specific action will be greater when that action is the only one under consideration or the first considered, than if the action is the last-considered of several proposed actions (Majid et al. 1983). Work in progress at the Universities of Chicago and Kentucky has shown that benefits to Chicago residents from improved visibility at the Grand Canyon are greater when the Grand Canyon program is the only one under consideration than when that program is an "add-on" to programs improving visibility in the Chicago region and the eastern half of the continental United States.[6]

These results suggest that the benefits of a package of programs implemented simultaneously would be overestimated by studies which estimated the benefits of each program separately, and that the benefits of a single program which impacts several elements of the S vector may be similarly overestimated by valuing each element separately and then summing the values of each. Unfortunately, the current state-of-the-art has not solved this problem. Holistic valuation of the benefits of the whole package of changes would resolve this problem but introduce many problems of estimation.

Use and Value

Early attempts at non-market benefit estimation concentrated on services used ("consumed") at the site where they were provided—services enjoyed at recreation sites in the case of the travel cost method, and amenities at the place of residence in the case of the property value method. More recently, it has been recognized that individuals may benefit from environmental services without using them on-site (Weisbrod 1964, Krutilla and Fisher 1975). The probability of use in some future time may generate expected consumer's surplus; risk adverse persons may enjoy an option value, i.e., a value in addition to expected consumer's surplus, from assurance of an option for future use (Weisbrod 1964, Schmalensee 1974, Graham 1981); a positive quasi-option value may be generated by the prospect of future gains in information from postponing irreversible change to environmental resources about which little is known (Arrow and Fisher 1974); and genuine benefits may accrue to individuals comforted by the assurance that environments they never expect to visit continue to exist (existence value).

There is general agreement among resource economists that genuine benefits from environmental services may be derived independently of current on-site use. Total "preservation value" was found to be many times greater than on-site use value for visibility in the Southwestern park lands (Schulze et al. 1981a), and several times larger than on-site user values for increments to a regional park system in Australia (Majid et al. 1983).

Preservation value is usually considered to include use value, option value, and existence value. Given that option price (OP), option value (OV), and expected consumer surplus (ES) are defined such that OP = ES + OV, there is a long-standing controversy as to whether OV might be negative in some cases (Schmalensee 1972). Graham (1981) may have made considerable progress in settling this controversy by developing a general framework for benefit cost analysis under uncertainty, in which OP and ES appear as special cases of no overriding importance. While most writers define existence value as the value of benefits created independently of use,[7] that definition appears insufficiently precise. Existence value surely requires knowledge, description, and perhaps depiction (which suggests some kind of use). Clearly, it is necessary to carefully develop the concept of existence value, perhaps along the lines that existence values may be derived from a kind of use, but not personal on-site use.

There is support for the notion that total preservation value of environmental services may often exceed on-site use value. The difference between total preservation value and on-site use value will be larger, the fewer and poorer are the substitutes for the environmental service in question and the larger the costs of replacing that environment. Accordingly, benefit estimation should be addressed to total preservation value as well as on-site use value.

Selection of Benefit Estimation Methods

As a general rule, current knowledge offers little support for the use of expenditure function methods to estimate those kinds of benefits which are not derived from on-site use. There is some hope that subscriptions to environment-oriented publications, and financial contributions to specific environmental causes may eventually serve as data sets for expenditure function analysis to estimate the non-visitor benefits of various environment services. Meanwhile, income compensation function approaches offer perhaps the only feasible methods of estimating these kinds of benefits. Studies of option price (Greenley et al. 1981) and total preservation value (Schulze et al. 1981a, Majid et al. 1983) have used contingent valuation methods. If some of the more-or-less incentive-compatible experimental methods can be effectively adapted for collection of value data, they could be used to determine option price and/or total preservation value.

The on-site user benefits of scenic amenities and visibility services produced on forest land are enjoyed by visitors to that land and nearby sites, and residents of places near forest land. Because contingent valuation and experimental techniques are adaptable to most any situation for which contingent and experimental markets can be created, these techniques are adaptable for estimating on-site benefits of scenic and visibility services on forest land. The existing research literature (e.g., Schulze et al. 1981b), the guidelines for evaluation for water resources projects (U.S. Water Resources Council 1979), and the Visibility Benefits Assessment Guidebook (Rowe and Chestnut 1981) provide substantial guidance for the application of contingent valuation methods.

Applicable benefit estimation techniques which use the expenditure function approach include the travel cost method and hedonic analysis of property value data. Standard travel cost methods are oriented toward user values of specific sites. These techniques are not well adapted to identifying the separate contributions of different sites to the total benefits from a multi-destination trip, and various site characteristics—including scenic characteristics and the level of visibility—to total trip benefits. Standard travel cost techniques, therefore, are, more appropriate for estimating the benefits of scenic attractions at sites which serve as specific trip destinations than for valuing general regional scenic characteristics or regional visibility.

A "hedonic travel cost approach" has recently been developed, in an attempt to adapt the travel cost method for evaluating specific site characteristics (Brown and Mendelsohn 1980). This approach inverts the standard travel cost approach to data collection, by examining travel costs from a single origin to multiple destinations. If travel costs, socioeconomic characteristics of the individual traveler, and the characteristics of alternative destinations could be quantified, a hedonic price function could be estimated. This would permit estimation of benefits from providing specific characteristics. A recent review has labeled this technique "promising," but draws attention to the limitations imposed by its analytical assumptions (Rowe and Chestnut 1981).

There is considerable literature reporting hedonic price analyses of property value data to estimate the economic value of housing characteristics and neighborhood amenities, including scenic amenities and atmospheric visibility. Most reported research has focused upon urban and residential property markets, suggesting that hedonic techniques are best adapted to those environments (Brown and Pollakowski 1977, Harrison and Rubenfeld 1978, Witte et al. 1979). Nevertheless, the growth of vacation and second home subdivisions near privately and publicly owned wildlands suggests the possibility of hedonic analysis. In particular, the paired comparisons technique (Brookshire et al. 1979, 1982) may be appropriate. Two potential applications for estimating scenic values are: (1) homes in, or overlooking, pristine forest environments may be paired with homes in environments exhibiting a greater degree of human intrusion; and (2) homes in or near publicly owned wildlands with management plans committed to long-term preservation may be paired with homes near publicly or privately owned lands where there is a positive possibility of significant human intrusion (e.g., logging) in the near or medium term. These techniques, of course, offer no possibility of capturing the total economic benefits from forest land scenic amenities. However, they may capture the benefits which accrue to owners of nearby residences and vacation homes, and these benefits are likely to be strictly additive to benefits enjoyed by traveling visitors and vacationers.

Because visibility, in the wildlands context, tends to be a regional rather than local phenomenon, the prospects of successfully using travel cost or hedonic property value techniques for estimating visibility benefits seem rather poor. That is, considerable difficulty might be expected in separating the economic effects of regional differences in visibility from those of regional variation in scenic and other amenities.

To briefly summarize, contingent valuation techniques appear to be most widely applicable for estimating economic benefits of scenic amenities and atmospheric visibility in wildlands environments. However, continued improvements in these techniques, and an increasing accumulation of empirical evidence suggesting but not conclusively proving their reliability, will only partially deal with concerns about the hypothetical nature of contingent markets and the lack of incentive-compatibility of these methods. There appear to be limited possibilities for using travel cost and hedonic property value methods to value scenic amenities in wildlands environments. However, the advantages of these methods—primarily their reliance on data recording actual choices—come at the cost of limited applicability and the need for analytical assumptions, which are in some degree questionable. The potential for using travel cost and hedonic property value methods to estimate visibility benefits in wildlands environments seems more limited than that with respect to scenic amenities.

Benefit Aggregation

Across the User Population

It is often convenient to estimate benefits for some subpopulation of amenity users (e.g., a survey sample or group of experimental subjects, a sample of visitors to particular sites, or a sample of homeowners or renters in particular localities). Benefit estimator equations (or bid equations) can be estimated, relating individual benefits to sociodemographic characteristics and the attributes of available substitute amenities (Water Resources Council 1979). These can be used to project benefits from a subpopulation to the entire users population, or transfer the findings of carefully conducted site-specific studies to other similar situations. Sociodemographic data and substitute amenity descriptors pertinent to the entire population (or the similar situation) are applied to the previously estimated bid equations.

Across Services

The avoidance of aggregation errors across service categories (multiple counting of some benefit items and failure to count others) requires complete consistency between the research procedures for estimating benefits of particular services and the procedures for aggregating benefits across service categories. This requirement emphasizes previous comments on the problems of separability among service categories, and the built-in tendency of individual service benefit estimates, when aggregated, to overestimate total package benefits.

The Magnitude of Benefits

Individual research situations vary with respect to amenity and visibility service levels, the array of substitute and complement environmental services, and the size and characteristics of the relevant demander populations, making it difficult to extrapolate benefit estimates from one situation to others. Further, the relatively few high quality empirical research studies reported in the literature are often incomparable with respect to the precise definition of the amenities valued, research methods, and analytical assumptions.

There is perhaps more evidence about the size of visibility benefits than scenic benefits. Brookshire et al. (1982) found mean annual benefits of visibility improvements[8] in the Los Angeles metropolitan area on the order of $200 per household (contingent valuation) and $300-$400 per household (hedonic analysis) of property values. Because the two methods were not strictly comparable, and theoretical considerations predicted larger value estimates from hedonic analysis, these results were interpreted as consistent with each other. Programs to prevent a decline in visibility at the Grand Canyon were estimated, in contingent valuation studies, to generate mean annual preservation benefits per household of about $86 in four urban areas, Albuquerque, Chicago, Denver, and Los Angeles (Schulze et al. 1981a). Benefits, similarly defined, were more than $100 in Chicago, when the Grand Canyon program was the only one considered, but only about $20 when Grand Canyon visibility was considered after subjects had made (hypothetical) decisions about local and regional programs affecting Chicago. These local and regional programs generated mean annual benefits on the order of $250-$350 per household depending on the program considered.[9]

Hedonic analyses of property value data have estimated mean annual benefit from air quality improvements in the range of $80-$600 per household in urban areas (Brookshire et al. 1979, Harrison and Rubenfeld 1978, Loehman et al. 1980). The value of shoreline (scenic) amenities in urban environments was found to be of similar magnitude (Brown and Pollakowski 1977). Willingness to pay for the esthetic improvement provided by mechanical draft—as opposed to natural draft—nuclear cooling towers ranged from $40 to $120 annually, per household (Adams et al. 1980).

A contingent valuation study of the aesthetic (scenic) benefits from surface mine reclamation in a wooded, mountainous, rural environment found mean annual benefits of about $70 per household (Randall et al. 1978).

These empirical results are, at best, suggestive of the range of mean annual benefits per household for various programs providing scenic and visibility services.[10] As research efforts in these directions accumulate, one would expect to find observations for specific programs higher and lower than those reported above.

Aggregate program benefits depend on household benefits and the number of households affected. Schulze et al. (1981a), contending that the Grand

Canyon is a national treasure and that empirical results from households as distant as Chicago supported such a procedure, aggregated across the national population. Total benefits for preserving Grand Canyon visibility, thus calculated, exceed $7 billion annually, and were orders of magnitude greater than benefits to Grand Canyon visitors. Randall et al. (1978) discussed the problem of selecting the proper population for aggregation and present an example showing the significant effect of that choice on the size of aggregate benefits. Analysts need to take care to select the appropriate population for aggregation and to document and justify their decisions. The national population may well be concerned with a few well-known national treasures such as the Grand Canyon. Nevertheless, there will be many cases where the population demanding scenic and visibility services at a specific site, or in a specific wildlands management district, is much more restricted.

Amenity Benefits: A Hierarchy of Evidence

Despite the economist's best empirical efforts, there will remain cases where it is impossible to provide complete estimates of economic benefits. In such cases, it is essential to provide as much documented evidence of benefits as possible, even though some of that evidence falls short of conveying dollar benefit numbers.[11] In research underway at the Universities of Chicago and Kentucky, a hierarchy of evidence concerning benefits has been developed.[12] Starting at the bottom, this hierarchy includes:

1. The production of amenity services may be documented.
2. It may be documented that amenity services necessarily have positive economic benefits. Because an increase in the level of amenities at a given site (while nothing else changes) cannot reduce the scope of an individual's opportunity set, the choice to "consume" an amenity when available provides definite evidence that the amenity contributes positively to utility and thus to economic benefits. For scenic attractions, a positive level of visitation provides such evidence. For visibility, which varies hour-by-hour, day-by-day, and on a seasonal basis, careful regression analysis of time-series data may document that visitation at particular sites and participation in particular activities are significantly and positively correlated with visibility. These kinds of results provide definite evidence that improved visibility increases utility and thus generates positive economic benefits.

   Significant positive relationships were found between visibility and a wide range of activities in an urban environment:[13] recreational aviation, visitation at high-rise observation decks, outdoor recreation, participation sports, and spectator sports. There appear to be sound prospects of documenting similar kinds of evidence in wildlands areas. Activities of interest may include site visitation and the use of hiking trails, scenic lookouts, ski lifts, and aerial tramways.
3. Where fees are charged for participation in various activities, total revenue in excess of variable costs of service places a lower bound on economic benefits. Entrance fees, camping fees, and fees for use of

boat docks, ski lifts, aerial tramways, etc., may provide opportunities for estimating lower bounds on the benefits of scenic attractions. Statistical time-series relationships between revenues and visibility may permit estimation of a lower bound on visibility benefits.

4. The change in aggregate consumer's surplus associated with a change in the level of amenity remains the most complete evidence of economic benefits.

The operating rule should be to assemble and document the best and most complete set of evidence of economic benefits possible. That implies documentation of the kinds of evidence which rank lower in this hierarchy, in cases where accurate consumer's surplus estimates are not feasible. This kind of documentation is essential to avoid the erroneous implication that those services for which dollar-valued benefit estimates are unavailable are, therefore, of zero value.

Literature Cited

Adams, R. C., J. W. Currie, J. A. Hebert, and R. Shikiar. 1980. The visual aesthetic impact of alternative closed cycling systems. Main report. Richland, Wash. Batelle Pacific Northwest Laboratory. NUREG/CR-0989.

Ajzen, I., and M. Fishbein. 1977. Attitude-behavior relations: A theoretical analysis and review of empirical research. Psychological Bulletin 84:888-918.

Arrow, K. J., and A. C. Fisher. 1974. Environmental preservation, uncertainty, and irreversibility. Quarterly Journal of Economics 88:312-319.

Becker, G. S. 1965. A theory of the allocation of time. The Economic Journal 75:493-517.

Brookshire, D., R. d'Arge, W. Schulze, and M. Thayer. 1979. Methods development for assessing air pollution control benefits. EPA-600/6-79-0016. Vol. 2: Experiments in valuing non-market goods: A case study of alternative benefit measures of air pollution control in the south air basin of Southern California. United States Environmental Protection Agency, Washington, D.C.

Brookshire, D., M. Thayer, W. Schulze, and R. d'Arge. 1982. Valuing public goods: A comparison of survey and hedonic approaches. American Economic Review.

Brown, G., and H. O. Pollakowski. 1977. Economic valuation of shoreline. The Review of Economics and Statistics 59:272-278.

Brown, G., and R. Mendelsohn. 1980. The hedonic-travel cost method. Final report prepared for Division of Program Plans, United States Department of Interior, University of Washington, Seattle, Wash.

Clawson, M., and J. L. Knetsch. 1966. Economics of outdoor recreation. Johns Hopkins University, Baltimore, Md.

Craik, K. H. 1979. The place of perceived environmental quality indices (PEQIS) in atmospheric visibility monitoring and preservation. p. 116-122. *In* D. Fox, R. J. Loomis, and T. C. Greene (eds.) Proceedings of the

Workshop in Visibility Values. [Fort Collins, Colo.] USDA Forest Service General Technical Report WO-18. Washington, D.C.
Craik, K. H., and E. H. Zube (eds.). 1976. Perceiving environmental quality: Research and Applications. Plenum Press, New York, N. Y.
Currie, J. M., J. A. Murphy, and A. Schmitz. 1971. The concept of economic surplus and its use in economic analysis. Economic Journal 81:741-799.
Daniel T. C. 1979. Psychological perspectives on air quality and visibility in parks and wilderness areas. p. 84-92. *In* Proceedings of the Workshop on Visibility Values. D. Fox, R. J. Loomis, and T. C. Green, editors. [Fort Collins, Colo.] USDA Forest Service General Technical Report WO-18. Washington, D.C.
Daniel, T. C., E. H. Zube, and B. L. Driver. 1979. Assessing amenity resource values. USDA Forest Service General Technical Report RM-68. Rocky Mountain Forest and Range Experiment Station, Fort Collins, Colo.
Fishbein, M., and I. Ajzen. 1975. Belief, attitude, intention and behavior. Addison-Wesley Publishing Company.
Fox, D., R. J. Loomis, and T. C. Greene. (tech. coord.). 1979. Proceedings of the workshop in visibility values. [Fort Collins, Colo.] USDA Forest Service General Technical Report WO-18. Washington, D.C.
Graham, D. A. 1981. Benefit cost analysis under uncertainty. American Economic Review 71:715-725.
Greenley, D. A., R. G. Walsh, and R. A. Young. 1981. Option value: Empirical evidence from a case study of recreation and water quality. Quarterly Journal of Economics 95:657-673.
Harrison, D., and D. L. Rubinfeld. 1978. Hedonic housing prices and the demand for clean air. Journal of Environmental Economics and Management 5:81-102.
Hebert, J., R. Shikiar, and R. Perry. 1979. Valuing environment via bidding games: A psychological perspective. Batelle Pacific Northwest Laboratory, Richland, Wash.
Krutilla, J. V., and A. C. Fisher. 1975. The economics of natural environments: Studies in the valuation of commodity and amenity resources. Johns Hopkins University Press, Baltimore, Md.
Lancaster, K. J. 1966. A new approach to consumer theory. Journal of Political Economy 74:132157.
Latimer, D. A. 1979. Analysis of scenic degradation caused by air pollution. p. 69-73. *In* Proceedings of the Workshop in Visibility Values. D. Fox, R. J. Loomis, and T. C. Greene, editors. [Fort Collins, Colo.] USDA Forest Service General Technical Report WO-18. Washington, D.C.
Latimer, D. A., T. C. Daniel, and A. Hugo. 1980. Relationships between air quality and human perception of scenic areas. Systems Applications Incorporated. San Rafael, Calif.
Lea, S. E. G. 1978. The psychology and economics of demand. Psychological Bulletin 85:441-460.
Loehman, E., D. Boldt, and K. Chaikin. 1980. Measuring the benefits of air quality in the San Francisco Bay area. Part I: Study design and property value study. Draft final report. SRI International, Menlo Park, Calif.

Majid, I., J. Sinden, and A. Randall. 1983. Benefit evaluation of increments to existing systems of public facilities. Land Economics 59:377-392.

Malm, W. C., K. K. Leiker, and J. V. Molenar. 1980. Human preception of visual air quality. Journal of Air Pollution Control Association 30:122-131.

Randall, A., O. Grunewald, S. Johnson, R. Ausness, and A. Pagoulatos. 1978. Reclaiming coal surface mines in central Appalachia: A case study of the benefits and costs. Land Economics 54:472-489.

Randall, A., and J. R. Stoll. 1980. Consumer's surplus in commodity space. American Economic Review 70:449-455.

Rowe, R. D., and L. G. Chestnut. 1981. Visibility benefits assessment guidebook: Final Report. U. S. Department of Interior, Environmental Protection Agency, Research Triangle Park, N. C. EPA-450/5-81-001.

Schmalensee, R. 1972. Option demand and consumer's surplus: Valuing price changes under uncertainty. The American Economic Review 62:813-824.

Schulze, W. D., D. S. Brookshire, E. G. Walther, and K. Kelley. 1981a. The benefits of preserving visibility in the national parklands of the southwest. Methods development for environmental control benefits assessment, 8. U. S. Department of the Interior, Environmental Protection Agency.

Schulze, W. D., R. C. d'Arge, and D. S. Brookshire. 1981b. Valuing environmental commodities: Some recent experiments. Land Economics 57:151-172.

Stoll, J. R. 1980. The valuation of hunting related amenities: A conceptual and empirical approach. Ph.D dissertation, Department of Agricultural Economics, University of Kentucky, Lexington.

U.S. Water Resources Council. 1979. Procedures for elevation of national economic development benefits and costs in water resources planning (level c): Final rule. Federal Register 44 (242, part ix) December 14.

Weisbrod, B. A. 1964. Collective-consumption services of individual consumption goods. Quarterly Journal of Economics 78:471-477.

Willig, R. D. 1976. Consumer's surplus without apology. American Economic Review 66:587-597.

Witte, A. D., H. J. Sumka, and H. Erekson. 1979. An estimate of a structured hedonic price model of the housing market: An application of Rosen's theory of implicit markets. Econometrica 47:1151-1173.

Footnotes

[1]*Randall, The conceptual basis of benefit cost analysis, Chapter 2, this volume.*

[2]*Ibid. Note that the organization of this volume, which addresses various categories of wildlands services in separate chapters, implies a similar aggregation procedure.*

[3]*Ibid. See especially, equations [1-5] and figure 1.*

[4]*Randall, Chapters 2 and 4, this volume.*

[5]*The assumptions noted here are not merely the customary economic assumptions of utility maximizing behavior, diminishing marginal productivity and utility, consumer sovereignty as the basis for individual valuation, and an interpersonal aggregation system rooted in the existing pattern of distribution. These methods require additional*

assumptions and restrictions in order to permit derivation of the expenditure function and the inverse Hicksian demand curve; for example, integrability conditions must be satisfied, restrictive conditions are often placed on substitution and complementarity relationships, and analytical convenience often limits the choice of functional form. The point is that the basic data usually require relatively little manipulation to yield value estimates via income compensation function approaches but considerably more manipulation when expenditure function approaches are used. These additional analytical steps introduce additional complexities which are usually circumvented with the use of restrictive assumptions.

[6]*USEPA Cooperative Agreement 807768-01-0, G. S. Tolley, Principal Investigator. A working paper reporting this result was presented at the 1981 meeting of the American Economic Association: Alan Randall, John P. Hoehn and George S. Tolley, "The Structure of Contingent Markets: Some Results of a Recent Experiment."*

[7]*See Stoll (1980) for a definition of existence value in a "new" demand theory framework.*

[8]*In each of the studies reported below, the degree of visibility improvement to be valued is quantified in some way. The reader is referred to the original reports for answers to the question, "how much visibility improvement?"*

[9]*See footnote 6.*

[10]*Rowe and Chestnut (1981) provide a more complete survey of empirical benefit estimates.*

[11]*Randall, Benefit cost....., Chapter 3, this volume.*

[12]*See footnote 6.*

[13]*Ibid.*

Chapter 11
Benefits of Outdoor Recreation and Some Ideas for Valuing Recreation Opportunities

Perry J. Brown

Introduction

Planning for outdoor recreation resources has evolved over the years from only site planning to site, area, and regional planning. As outdoor recreation planning has expanded geographically, it also has become more integrated. Regional plans provide guidance for area plans which, in turn, provide guidance for site plans. Also, outdoor recreation planning is one functional component of multiresource planning, where recreation resources are planned integratively with wildlife, grazing, timber, cultural, and other resources.

These changes from isolated site plans to geographically broader and to functionally integrated plans have raised concerns about the ability to adequately set goals for recreation and to assess the benefits and costs of outdoor recreation programs. Questions also are being asked about the benefits to be achieved by investment in outdoor recreation resource management. Satisfactory answers to such questions depend on the ability to identify and assess relevant benefits and costs.

From a planning perspective,[1] information is needed on the benefits of outdoor recreation programs (including definitions), how the worth of these benefits can be measured, and how they are related to valued precepts of individuals and society. Considerable thought has been focused on this problem, especially regarding economic measures of benefit (Clawson and Knetsch 1966, Sinden and Worrell 1979). However, there is a recognition among many scientists studying outdoor recreation that very little is known about the benefits of outdoor recreation. Therefore, this chapter identifies the kinds of benefits associated with outdoor recreation, suggests possible routes for the production of individual and social benefits, and presents some ideas for research to identify benefits and to measure the worth of input factors in their production. Because the focus is on identifying benefits of outdoor recreation, costs associated with production of benefits are not examined and net benefits are not discussed. In an economic efficiency framework, only the benefit side of the equation is considered.

Precepts, Goals, Benefits

To enable discussing benefits reference is needed to judge whether or not something is beneficial. This reference comes from the valued precepts of individuals and society.[2] These precepts are exposed as moral statements about the way things ought to be, in statements of preference for one thing over another, and in the setting of goals. In planning, valued precepts are transformed into ends to be sought, or goals.

Articulating a goal helps to identify benefits, because a benefit is something which leads toward a goal (Young 1970).[3] Benefits of outdoor recreation are the advantageous outcomes which recreationists and society realize from people participating in recreation activities.

Because decisions about providing outdoor recreation opportunities usually are made in a social context greater than just outdoor recreation concerns, outdoor recreation needs to be considered in the context of multiple goals and other goods and services. This usually demands identifying the quantitative facts about benefits and costs which, in turn, permits expression of value of outdoor recreation opportunities relative to other goods and services whose value has been similarly quantified.

In outdoor recreation planning, one needs to have information about precepts, goals, and benefits. Planners need to know the precepts of their clients, they need to know how these precepts can be articulated as goals, they need to know the benefits and costs of actions, and they need to know how these benefits and costs can be measured in commensurable manner with those for non-recreation uses of natural resources.

Searching for, analyzing, and interpreting these kinds of information enables the planner to define the purposes (goals) of planning and to identify the means (actions) of achieving those purposes. These four kinds of information do not prescribe the processes of planning or valuation, nor are they all needed for each individual technical activity in planning. For instance, knowledge of precepts is necessary for developing goals responsive to the needs perceived by clients, but once those goals are set, other technical aspects of planning, such as allocation of resources, can be done without considering the client's precepts further. For allocation of resources, given one or more goals, one needs to know the benefits and costs associated with each alternative allocation and commensurable values for the benefits and costs among the alternative allocations.

Obtaining the necessary information is extremely difficult, and the ability to make rational decisions is complicated, because commensurable indexes for the value of benefits and costs associated with many goods and services have not been developed, and because clients vary from one goal to the next goal. Determining the value of benefits in commensurable terms of relatively intangible things, such as outdoor recreation, clean air, family cohesion, etc., is difficult at best, and of questionable utility. Even if the benefits could be compared in commensurable terms, the various actions and programs benefit different people. The problem then becomes whose precepts are to be served (Rivlin 1971).

Improved information and better methods of identifying and measuring benefits and costs are needed. In the absence of a perfectly rational decision making system, there are political, executive, and administrative systems that can use benefit and cost information. These systems, which interact to allocate scarce resources among competing goals, need the best available information on benefits and costs, including their value.[4]

One helpful framework is the outdoor recreation benefit production process. Viewing outdoor recreation concerns in a production framework helps to sort the various inputs, actions, and outputs involved in outdoor recreation management and consumption.[5]

Outdoor Recreation Benefit Production

It has been asserted that the underlying purpose of outdoor recreation management (or any other resource management) is to provide benefits to individuals and society (Wagar 1966). How these benefits are produced can be described by several production processes which are linked together (Driver and Brown 1975, Driver and Rosenthal 1982). These production processes help identify the relevant inputs, production activities, and outputs of recreation resource management and of recreation resource consumption. Particularly helpful is clearer specification of the products of management and of the consumers' use of management outputs. Such specifications are necessary to determine what outputs are affected by different actions and which kinds of benefits and costs arise from different outputs.

Five different production processes can be described: production of recreation opportunities, primarily by resource managers; production of recreation experiences by recreationists; production of societal benefits by directly producing recreation opportunities and by secondary activities and processes associated with recreation opportunities; production of individual recreationist and societal benefits derived from having recreation experiences; and production of societal benefits from recreation use (fig. 1).

The production of recreation opportunities involves manipulating basic resources of land, labor, and capital through various management activities to produce sites and areas with specific characteristics where certain activities are possible and where realization of certain specific experiences is probable.[6] Management activities such as planning, allocating, constructing, zoning, and regulating can be involved in this process. Even without any managerial input, some recreation opportunities are produced by the land itself.

There are numerous ways to specify recreation opportunities. For example, the Forest Service has classified recreation opportunities as dispersed and developed, as different kinds of facilities, and as activity opportunities. More recently it has adopted the Recreation Opportunity Spectrum (Driver and Brown 1978, Clark and Stankey 1979, Stankey and Brown 1981) as a planning and management concept and has begun to specify six types of recreation opportunity from the primitive to the modern urban. Within each of

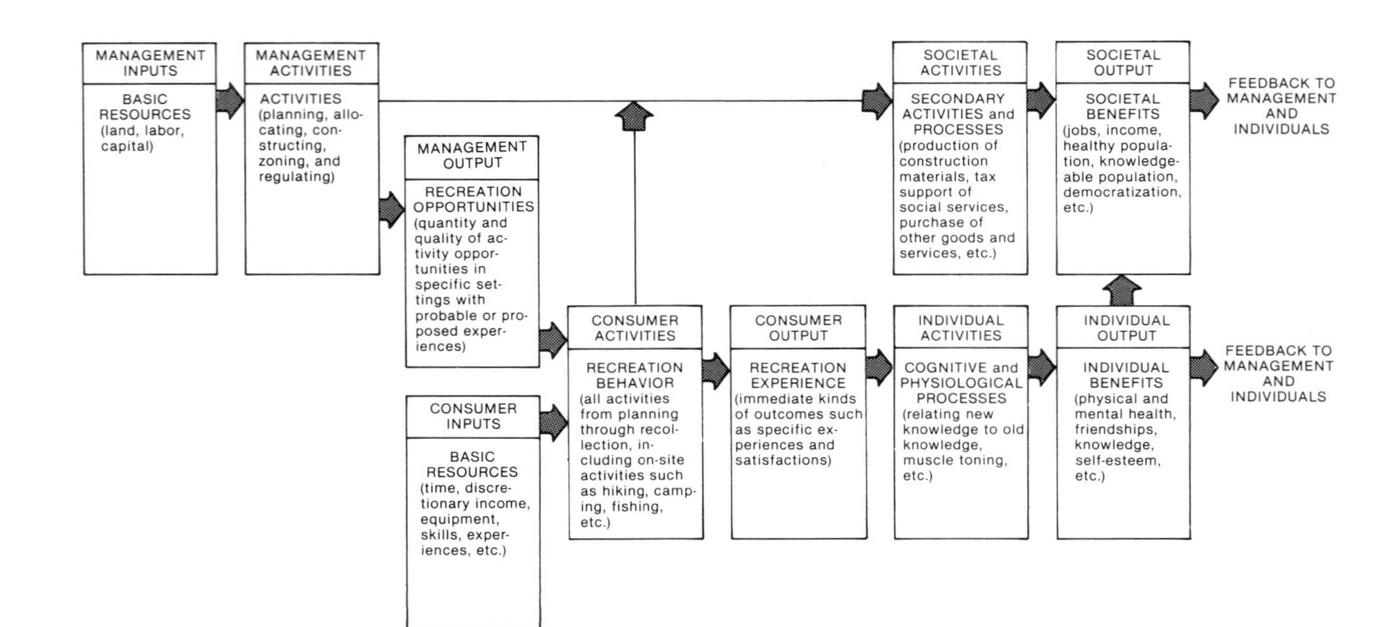

Figure 1. Overall process and subprocesses for producing outdoor recreation benefits.

these classes of opportunity, appropriate activity opportunities, setting conditions, and probable specific experiences are identified. These six broad types of opportunity and the more specific refinements of them are particularly important in multiple resource planning, because they define the product of outdoor recreation management (Hendee 1974, Driver and Brown 1975). It is to the production of these opportunities which management organizations allocate resources, and it is the value of these opportunities which needs to be determined for efficient multiple resource planning. But, these outputs of management often have been poorly specified, causing problems in their production and in measurement of their value.

Recreation opportunities are intermediate products which lead to benefits, basically through three different processes. In their production, there is direct employment of managers, construction workers, maintenance personnel, and others, resulting in contribution to income. Purchase of goods and services used in recreation opportunity production often leads to secondary employment and income. Finally, the workers directly producing recreation opportunities and those involved in producing input goods and services use their income to purchase personal goods and services and to contribute to the tax base, thus causing a multiplier effect by the original production activity. This process defines the production of benefits by directly producing recreation opportunities. The kinds of benefits it leads to are generally economic with also some contribution to social services and personal psychological rewards.

While benefits can be produced, net benefits either to individuals or to society are not automatically produced by providing recreation opportunities if resources are fully used for other activities and if individuals would prefer to work in other activities. In that case, providing recreation opportunities simply shifts benefits, resulting in no net gain, and possibly even net losses. However, there are cases where resources are underused and where providing outdoor recreation opportunities has increased net benefits.

Recreation opportunities also contribute to production of benefits when they are used by recreationists. In one case they are used as an input to the recreationist's production of recreation experiences. In this case, the value of the recreation opportunity is its value as an input factor in the recreationist's production of experiences. Because other factors of production, such as time, travel, and equipment, vary considerably for recreationists, the value of the recreation opportunity, as a proportion of total value, depends upon the value of other input factors. Additionally, the contribution of recreation opportunities to total benefits is less than the contribution of the experience, because the recreation opportunity is a necessary but not sufficient factor in the production of experiences, which are themselves intermediate outputs between recreation opportunities and benefits. That is, experiences are of higher value than are recreation opportunities which are a factor in the production of experiences. Attempts to value outdoor recreation should specify whether the outdoor recreation opportunity or the outdoor recreation experience is being considered. In multiple resource allocation, the value of the recreation opportunity is usually of interest.

Recreation experiences are produced when a recreationist uses a recreation opportunity. In this situation the recreationist engages in a behavior at a site to realize a specific experience or set of outcomes (Driver and Tocher 1970,

Brown et al. 1973, Hendee 1974, Driver and Brown 1975, Driver and Brown 1978). The outcomes are specific experiences such as experiencing other people, experiencing nature, experiencing exercise, experiencing skill development, experiencing esthetic pleasures, etc. Taken together, a salient package of specific experiences defines the overall recreation experience (Driver and Tocher 1970).

As already mentioned, the value of the recreation experience more closely approximates the total value of the benefits of recreation than does the recreation opportunity, but because some benefits arise through synergistic processes, not all of the value can be accounted for from a single recreation experience. For example, the benefit of good physical health may be contributed to by each recreation experience, but it can only be achieved by frequent experiences. An occasional strenuous recreation experience can possibly contribute to a decline in physical health.

The aggregate effect of individual recreation benefits often is societal benefits. For example, if individuals are more physically healthy, the society will be more physically healthy, possibly resulting in a lowering of health-related costs.

In the second case of benefits being produced by recreation use, figure 1 shows that there is a direct link between recreation use and societal benefits, just as there was such a link to societal benefits from producing recreation opportunities. Recreationists seek information, buy equipment, and purchase gasoline, food, and other goods and services. All of this activity contributes to the benefits received by society from recreation use. These benefits are primarily economic but also might encompass education, social service, and specific psychological benefits. While most serious study of outdoor recreation has focused on the benefits attributable to a site or to the recreation experience, the societal benefits attributable to recreation use might be considerable.

Kinds of Benefits from Outdoor Recreation

There are many ways to classify benefits of outdoor recreation. One of the simplest is to divide them into two categories, individual and social (including economic). However, this classification is too broad. In contrast, to discuss each specific benefit is probably too detailed and redundant to be meaningful. Therefore, an intermediate classification system is proposed. Its major advantage is in suggesting the specific kinds of benefits which might be emphasized by focusing on the major concerns of different scientific disciplines.

Economic benefits generally are those associated with production, consumption and exchange of goods and services. They can be individual in that they make a person better off, and they can be social such as those associated with economic development. Social benefits generally are those which accrue to groups of people (societies). Some of them are family benefits, social cohesion benefits, and community use benefits. Cultural benefits generally are those which deal with the thought characteristics of a society. These may take the form of developing ethics and other predilections which regulate the way societies behave. Physiological benefits generally are those dealing with health and functioning of the human body. They are most associated with physical conditioning and stress reduction. Psychological benefits generally are those which are perceived by an individual as enhancing his well-being. They include option and existence benefits often associated with wilderness and wildlife, and affiliation, environmental perception, developmental, and health benefits.

Economic benefits from outdoor recreation and the development of techniques for measuring their worth are discussed in the chapter by Wilman. The remainder of this chapter deals with social, cultural, physiological and psychological perspectives of the benefits arising from outdoor recreation resource management and use.

Benefits of Outdoor Recreation

Relatively few benefits of outdoor recreation have been defined very well or have had their value measured (Kelly 1981). Probably the most extensively researched are the psychological and physiological benefits, although there is limited information about other types of benefits.

Among the social benefits, family cohesion benefits have been shown by West and Merriam (1970) and Orthner (1976), and family learning benefits are not well documented except in studies of socialization (Kelly 1977). Social cohesion is an assumed benefit of outdoor recreation participation because of the often observed phenomenon that recreation takes place in groups (Cheek 1981). Some other social benefits of outdoor recreation, such as those accruing from a community's use of recreation areas for community events, are not known, while some other social benefits to communities arising from tourism and attraction of industries because of recreation opportunities have been more fully identified (Rajender et al. 1967).

Cultural benefits of outdoor recreation have not been well studied. The educational benefits and resulting ''good citizenship'' often ascribed to outdoor recreation (HCRS 1979) are reputed but undocumented. The development of ethics through group activity and activity in ''natural'' environments is common to organized recreation use; yet, little is known about the development of such ethics by those who recreate outside of these organized groups.

Some physiological benefits are better known because of their direct implications for human health. The reduction in risk of cardiac problems by regular strenuous exercise is well documentecd, and some other effects such as hearing sensitivity increases after long wilderness visits have been noted (Thorstenson et al. 1975). Less well defined are physiological changes which occur because the types of pressures on recreationists that exist in recreation settings are often different from those in usual daily environments.

Psychological benefits, which include both enhanced personal functioning and purely perceived benefits, overlap some of the kinds of benefits already discussed. Most of the work involved in identifying these benefits has focused on identifying the immediate antecedents to them. That is, it has focused on identifying the specific experiences (outcomes, immediate benefits, etc.) associated with outdoor recreation activities. These specific experiences have been assumed to lead to specific, identifiable benefits such as perceptions of and actual better self concept, greater social status, increased physical and mental health, greater knowledge about people and environments, relief from job, home, family, and physical stresses, increased work productivity, and so forth.

Numerous researchers have been involved in identifying these specific experiences for many activities. For example, Potter et al. (1973), More (1973), and Brown et al. (1977) identified experiences of hunting; Driver and Knopf (1976) and Driver and Cooksey (1977) identified experiences of fishing; Brown and Haas (1980) identified experiences of backpacking; Haas et al. (1980) identified experiences of cross-country skiing; Schreyer and Nielson (1978) identified experiences of whitewater floating; and Ulrich and Addoms (1981) have begun to identify experiences associated with passive and off-site use of residential parks.

Little work has actually proceeded on translating these specific experiences into benefits. However, some work in therapeutic recreation suggests that some translations are possible. Heaps and Thorstenson (1974) showed that after self-reliance oriented experiences in wilderness environments, students develop improved self concepts, and that after month-long wilderness experiences, anxiety significantly decreases and hearing sensitivity significantly increases (Thorstenson et al. 1975). Furthermore, the psychological need satisfying properties of recreation, as shown by Tinsley and Kass (1979) among others, suggests the possibility that recreation produces important therapeutic need satisfaction benefits in areas other than demonstrated by Heaps and Thorstenson (1974).

This very brief review of the benefits of outdoor recreation reveals that the relationship of these presumed benefits to outdoor recreation has not been systematically identified. Similarly, measurement of the value of many of these benefits has been virtually non-existent. However, there has been some measurement of the value of input factors for producing benefits using econometric and psychometric techniques. Economic measures have been used to establish the worth of recreation sites (Dyer and Whaley 1968) and recreation experiences (King and Walka 1980). Both travel cost and contingency valuation methods have been used (King and Davis 1980) in these exercises. Economic measures also have been used in estimating the economic importance and impacts of tourism (Rajender et al. 1967), with regional analysis models (e.g., input-output, economic base) used in these impact analyses.

Psychometric measures have been used to establish the value of specific experiences (Haas et al. 1980). Generally, this has involved either ranking or rating the value of the experiences (Driver and Knopf 1976). These methods, while increasing understanding about the relationships among different specific experiences within the overall experience, do not insure knowledge of how valuable each specific experience is relative to each other specific experience and do not enable comparison of the value of other resource uses whose value has not been measured psychometrically. More widespread use of psychometric methods for determining the value of resource management benefits and use of psychometric ratio scaling would overcome these problems. Alternatively, further development of economic measures to value these experiences would also enable necessary comparisons.

One of the interesting possibilities for enhancing measurement of the value of input factors for producing benefits has been using psychometric means to identify the relevant attributes of recreation opportunities and experiences, and then using econometric techniques to estimate the worth of these opportunities and experiences (King and Dyer 1980, King and Walka 1980). Use of psychometric methods to identify the attributes of the product which are important to consumers may help define the product in consumer-relevant terms. Then, it is presumed that the consumer will be able to more accurately estimate his willingness to pay (assign worth) for the product, and that worth of products will vary among products.

Future Research

Research is needed to help identify the benefits that arise from outdoor recreation and the value that these benefits have relative to the goals of society. Two means of identifying these benefits would be useful. Determining how outdoor recreation benefits are produced through the five production processes described earlier probably will lead to discovering most of the relevant benefits. At the same time, reviewing the literature for benefits that are proven or hypothesized, hypothesizing benefits from specific experiences, and brainstorming benefits might identify additional benefits not arising from examining the production processes. Once benefits are hypothesized, experimental and quasi-experimental research in areas such as physiology, sociology, anthropology, and psychology will need to be used to establish their link to outdoor recreation.

For purposes of defining land management goals and determining the impacts of outdoor recreation resource management, the benefits of management and use of resources should be identified.

Current technical efforts in land management planning require a different line of research. These efforts are focused on making decisions about how to use forest and range land to provide a specific array of products demanded by society. One category of these products is outdoor recreation opportunities. For these opportunities, the benefits do not need to be specified to derive information useful to make an allocation. What is needed is the ability to estimate the value of various recreation opportunities in producing recreation benefits. These values need to be measured in terms commensurable with the values for other resource products such as timber stumpage and forage value. At present, this means that the value of our outdoor recreation products needs to be estimated in monetary terms. However, because many outdoor recreation opportunities are not well defined and they are non-marketed, there are special problems in making a commensurable valuation. Research can help define better the products of management and the products demanded by recreationists, and it can help to measure the worth of these products so that this worth can be used in estimating net benefits as part of the resource allocation decision process.

Since outdoor recreation opportunities are defined in terms of activity opportunities, setting attributes, and probable experiences, research should focus on the relationships among these three variables to more precisely specify the products we are trying to value. For these well defined opportunities, techniques for estimating their worth need to be refined so that values are commensurable with estimates of worth of other natural resource products, and so that estimates of worth are reliable. To generate useful land management planning information, the need is to continue integrating research in both psychometric and econometric techniques.

Literature Cited

Brown, Perry J., A. Allen Dyer, and Ross S. Whaley. 1973. Recreation research - so what? Journal of Leisure Research 5(1):16-24.

Brown, Perry J., and Glenn E. Haas. 1980. Wilderness recreation experiences. Journal of Leisure Research 12(3):229-241.

Brown, Perry J., Jacob E. Hautaluoma, and S. Morton McPhail. 1977. Colorado deer hunting experiences. p. 216-225. *In* Transactions of the Forty Second North American Wildlife and Natural Resources Conference. Wildlife Management Institute, Washington, D.C.

Cheek, Neil H. 1981. Social cohesion and outdoor recreation. p. 49-53. *In* Social benefits of outdoor recreation. John R. Kelly, editor. Leisure Behavior Research Laboratory, University of Illinois, Champaign-Urbana.

Clark, Roger N., and George H. Stankey. 1979. The recreation opportunity spectrum: A framework for planning, management, and research. USDA Forest Service General Technical Report PNW-98. Pacific Northwest Forest and Range Experiment Station, Portland, Oreg.

Clawson, Marion, and Jack L. Knetsch. 1966. Economics of outdoor recreation. Johns Hopkins Press, Baltimore, Maryland.

Driver, B. L., and Perry J. Brown. 1975. A social-psychological definition of recreation demand, with implications for recreation resource planning. p. 63-88. *In* Assessing demand for outdoor recreation. National Academy of Sciences, Washington, D.C.

Driver, B. L., and Perry J. Brown. 1978. The opportunity spectrum concept and behavioral information in outdoor recreation resource supply inventories: A rationale. p. 24-31. *In* Integrated inventories of renewable natural resources: Proceedings of the workshop. Gyde H. Lund et al., technical coordinators. USDA Forest Service General Technical Report RM-55. Rocky Mountain Forest and Range Experiment Station, Fort Collins, Colorado.

Driver, B. L., and Raymond W. Cooksey. 1977. Preferred psychological outcomes of recreational fishing. p. 27-40. *In* Catch and release fishing as a management tool: A national sport fishing symposium. R. A. Barnhart and T. D. Roelofs editors. Humboldt State University, Arcata, California.

Driver, B. L., and Richard C. Knopf. 1976. Temporary escape: One product of sport fisheries management. Fisheries 1(2):21-29.

Driver, B. L., and Donald H. Rosenthal, compilers. 1982. Measuring and improving the effectiveness of public outdoor recreation programs. George Washington University, Washington, D.C.

Driver, B. L., and S. Ross Tocher. 1970. Toward a behavioral interpretation of recreational engagements, with implications for planning. p. 9-31. *In*

Elements of outdoor recreation planning. B. L. Driver, editor. University Microfilms, Ann Arbor, Michigan.
Dyer, A. Allen, and Ross S. Whaley. 1968. Predicting use of recreation sites. Utah Agricultural Experiment Station Bulletin No. 477. Logan, Utah.
Haas, Glenn E., B. L. Driver, and Perry J. Brown. 1980. A study of ski touring experiences on the White River National Forest. p. 25-30. *In* Proceedings North American Symposium on dispersed winter recreation. College of Forestry, University of Minnesota, St. Paul, Minnesota.
Heaps, Richard A., and Clark T. Thorstenson. 1974. Self-concept changes immediately and one year after survival training. Therapeutic Recreation Journal 8(2):60-63.
Hendee, John C. 1974. A multiple-satisfaction approach to game management. Wildlife Society Bulletin 2(3):104-113.
Heritage Conservation and Recreation Service. 1979. The third nation-wide outdoor recreation plan. Washington, D.C.
Kelly, John R. 1977. Leisure socialization: Replication and extension. Journal of Leisure Research 9(2):121-132.
Kelly, John R., editor. 1981. Social benefits of outdoor recreation. Leisure Behavior Research Laboratory, University of Illinois, Champaign-Urbana.
King, David A., and Lawrence S. Davis. 1980. Recreation benefit estimation: A discussion summary. Journal of Forestry 78(1):27-28.
King, David A., and A. Allen Dyer. 1980. Integrating economics and psychological approaches to determining wildland recreation values. Report to Rocky Mountain Forest and Range Experiment Station, USDA Forest Service Contract No. 16-770-CA. School of Renewable Natural Resources, The University of Arizona, Tucson, Arizona.
King, David A., and Ann W. Walka. 1980. A market analysis of trout fishing on the Fort Apache Indian Reservation. Report to Rocky Mountain Forest and Range Experiment Station, USDA Forest Service Contract No. 16-736-GR. School of Renewable Natural Resources, The University of Arizona, Tucson, Arizona.
More, Thomas A. 1973. Attitudes of Massachusetts hunters. p. 72-76. *In* Human dimensions in wildlife programs. J. C. Hendee and C. Schoenfeld, editors. Wildlife Management Institute, Washington, D.C.
Orthner, Dennis K. 1976. Patterns of leisure and marital interaction. Journal of Leisure Research 8(2):98-111.
Potter, Dale, John C. Hendee, and Roger N. Clark. 1973. Hunting satisfaction: Game, guns, or nature? p. 62-71. *In* Human dimensions in wildlife programs. J. C. Hendee and C. Schoenfeld, editors. Wildlife Management Institute, Washington, D.C.
Rajender, G. R., Floyd K. Harmston, and Dwight M. Blood. 1967. A study of the resources, people, and economy of Teton County. Division of Business and Economic Research, University of Wyoming, Laramie.
Rivlin, Alice. 1971. Systematic thinking for social action. The Brookings Institution, Washington, D.C.
Schreyer, Richard C., and Martin L. Nielsen. 1978. Westwater and Desolation Canyons: Whitewater river recreation study. Institute for the Study of Outdoor Recreation and Tourism, Utah State University, Logan.

Sinden, John A., and Albert C. Worrell. 1979. Unpriced values. John Wiley and Sons, New York.

Stankey, George H., and Perry J. Brown. 1981. A technique for recreation planning and management in tomorrow's forests. *In* International Union of Forestry Research Organizations 17th Congress Proceedings, Kyoto, Japan, September 1981. 6:63-73.

Thorstenson, Clark T., Richard A. Heaps, and Robert Snow. 1975. The effect of a twenty-nine day wilderness survival experiences on anxiety and hearing sensitivity. Therapeutic Recreation Journal 9(3):117-120.

Tinsley, Howard E. A., and Richard A. Kass. 1979. The latent structure of the need satisfying properties of leisure activities. Journal of Leisure Research 11(4):278-291.

Ulrich, Roger S., and David L. Addoms. 1981. Psychological and recreational benefits of a residential park. Journal of Leisure Research 13(1):43-65.

Wagar, J. Alan. 1966. Quality in outdoor recreation. Trends in Parks and Recreation 3(3):9-12.

West, Patrick D., and Lawrence C. Merriam, Jr. 1970. Outdoor recreation and family cohesiveness. Journal of Leisure Research 2(4):251-259.

Young, Robert C. 1970. Establishment of goals and definition of objectives. p. 261-272. *In* Elements of outdoor recreation planning. B. L. Driver, editor. University Microfilms, Ann Arbor, Michigan.

Footnotes

[1]*Planning is conceived both as defining purposes (goals) and choosing means to achieve the purposes.*

[2]*A "precept" is a principle intended as a general rule of action. Precepts are valued in that relative worth, utility, or importance is given to them. Often, these precepts are referred to as values of individuals or society. In the discussion in this chapter, "value" is used to mean the relative worth, utility, or importance of something. The more restricted definition of value as monetary worth of something is not used. For this more restricted definition the term "worth" is used.*

[3]*The assumption here is that goals are selected to represent a desired state of well-being, with well-being defined in terms of the valued precepts, and that a benefit is something which promotes well-being.*

[4]*See the chapter by Randall which discusses the use of benefit-cost analysis in providing information for decision making.*

[5]*The subsequent discussion is focused on benefits and excludes discussion of costs and net benefits.*

[6]*Recreation opportunity has been defined as the chance to engage in a specific recreation activity in a specific setting to realize a predictable recreation experience (Driver and Brown 1978).*

Chapter 12
Problems in Wildlife Valuation in Natural Resource Management

William W. Shaw

Introduction

Although resource valuation most often implies economic assessment, wildlife values have been addressed in ecological, sociological, psychological, and political science as well. Despite the considerable attention that has been given to this topic, there is still widespread skepticism concerning the utility of existing wildlife valuation methodologies. Some of the confusion over wildlife valuation is simply an extension of the debate over recent developments in economic methods for assessing noncommodity and existence values. These issues are discussed in other chapters. But two additional problems hinder the widespread application of quantitative assessment methods for wildlife—the need to define the wildlife-based products of wildland management and the need to identify the users who benefit from these products.

Taking this broad perspective, resource value assessment can be viewed as a three-staged process (fig. 1). There are two logical antecedents to applying wildlife values information in specific resource management situations. One should be able to define the product, and one should be able to identify who uses the product and consequently receives the benefits being valued. In the case of wildlife, neither of these tasks has been adequately completed. Lacking a good foundation of knowledge concerning who benefits and what the benefits are, the utility of even the most sophisticated approaches to value assessment is limited by the inability to estimate how completely they have captured all categories of benefits and/or users. Therefore, the principal weakness in any quantitative assessment of wildlife values is not the validity or precision of these measures (although this is the focus of much debate), but rather the uncertainty concerning the importance of those human values that are not addressed by any particular assessment methodology. Appropriately, much of the research that is relevant to wildlife valuation has focused on these related questions instead of value assessment. For these reasons, this

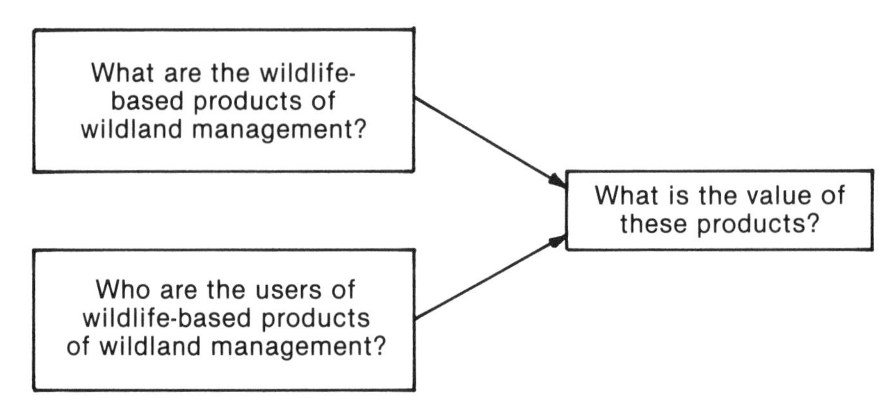

Figure 1. The wildlife valuation process.

chapter addresses three questions: What are the wildlife-based products of wildlands? Who are the people who benefit from wildlife resources? How well can the values of wildlife be assessed in quantitative terms?

Defining the Wildlife-Based Product of Wildlands

One of the earliest systems for cataloging wildlife was developed by King (1947). He proposed six categories of wildlife values—recreational, esthethic, educational, biological, social, and commercial. Since that time, many other organizational schemes have been developed. Steinhoff (1980) found 12 different major systems for cataloging wildlife values. Systems have been developed based on attitudinal typologies (Kellert 1979, 1980), recreational activities (Hendee 1969), recreational experiences (Hendee 1974, More 1973) or broad categories of users or uses (Shaw 1974). The ways in which people benefit from wildlife are extremely diverse, and the fact that no one system for organizing these benefits has received widespread acceptance suggests that there is still considerable confusion concerning the definition of the wildlife-based products of resource management.

Three major issues complicate the task of defining the wildlife-based output of natural resource systems:

1. The role of wildlife in outdoor recreational experiences is not thoroughly understood.
2. The ecological significance of specific wildlife populations is not thoroughly understood.
3. There is confusion concerning the relationships among the different potential measures of wildlife-based outputs of land management.

The Role of Wildlife in Recreational Experiences

A major area of recreation research has focused on defining the recreational output of wildlands in terms of opportunities for different types of human experiences (Driver and Brown 1978, Driver and Rosenthal 1979, Driver and Harris 1981). The conceptual problem in assessing wildlife management outputs in these terms lies in defining the contribution of wildlife to various types of outdoor recreational activities. For some types of recreation, like hunting and bird watching, wildlife are the focal point. In these situations, it seems reasonable to assume that recreational opportunities are the ultimate output of the resource management system. Research in these cases has focused on defining the types of wildlife or habitats that contribute most to the experiences (Brown et al. 1977, Witter and Shaw 1979). But for other types of outdoor recreation, the role of wildlife is less clear. Activities such as hiking and camping may not be dependent on the presence of wildlife, but in many situations, wildlife affect the quality of these experiences. In these situations, the difficult valuation question concerns what, if any, value should be imputed to wildlife resources from these secondary uses?

The Ecological Significance of Wildlife

Some important reasons for preserving wildlife are based on its ecological functions. Human survival is inextricably linked to the continued performance of the myriad of energy flow and material cycling processes of the earth's ecosystem. Wild animals are an essential component in this complex system. What is not well understood, however, is the ecological importance of specific types of wildlife or specific populations of wild animals (Martinka 1980). Ecosystems are complex systems with many homeostatic mechanisms that can compensate for some variations in the ecological components. Consequently, it is very difficult to quantify the ecological effects of different resource management alternatives. This issue has been the object of considerable research by the Fish and Wildlife Service, which has developed a habitat evaluation procedure (HEP) (Fish and Wildlife Service 1980). However, this methodology is relatively new and not fully proven.

Ecological science has not yet determined what parameters best indicate critical environmental conditions and at what point critical thresholds are crossed. The problem is compounded because conventional methodologies of benefits assessment are not well equipped to deal with the overlap and interactions between different possible levels of analysis. For example, ecological processes can be described on a molecular level (caloric transfer and material cycling), an organismic level (effects on individual organisms), a population level, a community level, or on an ecosystem level. Different levels of analysis reveal valid human costs or benefits, but they are not independent measures. Each is related to the others, and consequently, total benefit or cost is not a simple sum of these different approaches.

Furthermore, a basic conceptual issue surrounding wildlife-based products is whether benefits such as those involving the ecological functions of wildlife can be assessed with any methodology based on human behavior alone. Are ecological values of wildlife adequately understood by people and reflected in their behavior? If so, then the debate is simply whether existence values can be adequately assessed using economic methodologies. But these ecological values are not exactly analogous to things like wilderness, which have been the object of most existence value assessments. This is because some of these ecological functions are not simply valued for enriching the human experience. In principle, some of the ecological roles of wildlife are essential to human survival. Some attempts have been made to deal with this problem using risk and uncertainty models to develop decision criteria for endangered species preservation (Bishop 1978). These approaches clarify decision options but do not result in explicit valuation of the resource.

Relationships Among Different Wildlife-based Outputs of Wildlands Systems

The confusion about defining the products of wildlife management involves not only deciding what the meaningful categories are but also defining their relationships to each other. This poses an important conceptual dilemma that must be faced in any attempt to measure total value of wildlife resources (Schweitzer 1981).

> "For example, if a recreation experience is viewed as the end-value consumer product, it can be directly valued on the basis of how much a group of recreationists would or do pay for use; a value can (at least conceptually) also be imputed to animals because they are one factor in the production of recreation experiences; and a value can further be imputed to habitat because it is one factor in the production of animals. In principle, all of these assessments depend only upon knowing the market behavior of recreationists and the technical nature of production. In contrast, if the very existence of a particular animal population is of direct utility to society, some economic expression of utility must be directly determined from the behavior or potential behavior of the utility-receivers. It cannot be imputed from expenditures focused on viewing or consuming animals; the activities of on-the-ground users do not provide an adequate basis for valuation."

The question is whether the ecological services attributable to wild animals are reflected in human behavior and, consequently, assessible using the anthropocentric methods of economics. If all values of wildlife are not reflected in human behavior, in what terms should they be expressed? Present understanding of the wildlife-based products of wildlands has not conclusively answered these questions.

Defining the Users of Wildlife Resources

Closely related to the problem of defining the wildlife-based products of wildland management is the need for good information concerning the users of wildlife resources. Users have been classified according to recreational activities (USDI 1977), levels of interest or appreciation (Langenau 1976, Lyons 1980), location of use (urban vs. rural; Brown and Dawson 1978), whether or not the activity leads to removal of animals (consumptive vs. nonconsumptive; Hendee 1969), and whether or not the use involves actual contact with wild animals (direct vs. indirect; Langenau 1976, Lyons 1980). Although each of these organizational schemes has some utility in understanding wildlife values, no single approach has been widely accepted.

The lack of knowledge about users of wildlife resources becomes apparent when wildife users are classified into three basic categories—hunters and other direct consumptive users, direct nonconsumptive users, and indirect or vicarious users.

Consumptive Wildlife Users[1]

Consumptive wildlife users (principally hunters and fishermen) are relatively easy to identify and study. Sport hunting and fishing requires the purchase of a license. This provides a readily obtainable sampling base for user studies. Although there are problems associated with identifying unlicensed sportsmen, understanding of the consumptive users of wildlife resources is relatively good. Thus, it is known that about 20 million people participated in sport hunting involving more than 478 million days, and that they spent $5.8 billion on these activities in 1975 (USDI 1977). Furthermore, there is a good understanding of various socio-demographic characteristics associated with hunters and fishermen and of their attitudes and motivations (Hendee and Potter 1975, Bevins et al. 1968, Klessig and Hale 1972, More 1973). This information often is available at state as well as national levels. The main knowledge lacking about sportsmen concerns the benefits they receive and the factors that most affect these benefits. Another area receiving considerable attention involves the determinants of hunting and fishing behavior and how education can influence this behavior (International Association of Fish and Wildlife Agencies 1981).

Direct Nonconsumptive Users of Wildlife

Considerable information concerning the numbers and characteristics of direct nonconsumptive users of wildlife (bird watchers, wildlife photographers, etc.) has become available in recent years. The 1975 National Survey of Hunting, Fishing, and Wildlife-Associated Recreation, for example, revealed that 49 million Americans spent 1.6 billion days engaged in wildlife observation in that year (U.S. Fish and Wildlife Service 1977). Numerous other studies are beginning to provide a basis for understanding nonhunting wildlife enthusiasts (Payne and Degraaf 1975, Witter and Shaw 1979, Shaw and King 1980, Fazio and Belli 1977, Brown 1978, Langenau 1976). More (1979) conducted a comprehensive review of the literature related to demand for nonconsumptive uses of wildlife, and concluded that that research is in the early stages of identifying participation rates and user characteristics. Little information is available concerning behavior and motivations for nonhunting wildlife enthusiasts.

Secondary users of wildlife also include people who benefit from seeing or hearing wildlife while engaged in other (not wildlife-oriented) activities. Very little is known about people who enjoy the presence of wildlife while engaged in various outdoor recreational activities, working around the home, commuting to work, or other activities that may occur in the presence of wild animals.

Indirect or Vicarious Users of Wildlife

A third category of wildlife users has been termed indirect or vicarious users. This refers to people who benefit from wildlife without any direct contact with the animals. Very little is known about these types of benefits from wildlife or about what segments of the American public enjoy them. However, there are considerable indications that this category of wildlife user is a major one—perhaps involving more people than any other user type. The national attitudinal studies by Kellert (1979), for example, revealed that 89 percent of the Americans surveyed favored protection of the bald eagle even if it resulted in increased cost for energy development. Any assessment of total values of wildlife resources would be seriously deficient if these indirect users were not considered.

Economic Value Assessment

The problems associated with defining the products of wildlife management and identifying the users of these products have not precluded the application of economic methodologies to wildlife valuation. Leitch and Scott (1977) compiled an annotated bibliography covering 691 publications related to economic values of fish and wildlife and their habitats. Although this source included articles concerned with general outdoor recreation and natural resource economics, many of the reports that were reviewed deal specifically with wildlife valuation. These applications of economics range from basic expenditure studies to the more complex analyses entailed in assessing recreation, option, and existence values. Additionally, several publications have presented general overviews of the wildlife valuation problems (Langford and Cocheba 1978, Midwest Research Institute 1979, Shaw and Zube 1980, Dwyer 1980, Schweitzer 1981).

From an economics perspective, the most difficult issues of wildlife valuation are concerned with the application of two developing methodologies—assessment of the noncommodity values associated with recreation, and assessment of existence values associated with indirect or vicarious uses. Although both of these methodologies are the subject of considerable debate among economists, significant progress has been made in recent years. Recreation and existence value assessment methods are discussed in detail elsewhere in this book (see chapters by Randall). Frequently cited examples of application of recently developed economic methodologies to wildlife valuation include Hammack and Brown (1974), Martin et al. (1974), Bishop (1978), Brown et al. (1978b, 1980).

There appear to be two levels of debate concerning the utility of wildlife valuation attempts. The first is principally addressed by economists. Because the wildlife-based products of wildland management are not exchanged through a market system, economists must utilize other indices of user benefits (travel cost methods, survey based methods, etc.). There continues to be considerable discussion over the precision and validity of these approaches (Schweitzer 1981).

In addition, there is still a major unresolved conceptual issue limiting the application of these approaches in multiple resource situations. Because of the limitations in understanding of the wildlife-based products of land management and of the people who benefit from them, the portion of the total value of wildlife that has been assessed cannot be estimated. Because benefits from wildlife that accrue in the form of existence and option values do not involve direct human use, their assessment is more difficult than assessment of direct uses of resources. There is concern that most applications of economics to wildlife resources only address a small portion of the total value of wildlife resources. If this is the case, then even major refinements in methods for quantifying values of direct uses of wildlife will be relatively insignificant in terms of assessing total values of wildlife.

This issue does not invalidate economic wildlife assessment methodologies, but it has important implications for how wildlife values information should be used in natural resource planning and management. In many natural resource management situations, valuation of specific types of wildlife or wildlife uses can be useful, such as comparisons among different recreation outputs for alternative management strategies. Furthermore, in many cases, simply being able to estimate minimum value of wildlife can be useful, even though it may admittedly address only part of the total value involved. But until better estimates can be made of the total value of wildlife including indirect as well as direct uses, caution is necessary in using wildlife value estimates in a context that implies estimation of total value.

Literature Cited

Bevins, Malcolm I., Robert S. Bond, Thomas J. Corcoran, Kenneth D. McIntosh, and Richard J. McNeil. 1968. Characteristics of hunters and fishermen in six Northeastern states. Northeast Region Research Publication, Agricultural Experiment Station, University of Vermont, Bulletin 656. Burlington.

Bishop, Richard C. 1978. Endangered species and uncertainty: The economics of a safe minimum standard. American Journal of Agricultural Economics 60(1):10-18.

Brown, Gardner M., Jr., J. John Charbonneau and Michael J. Hay. 1978a. The value of wildlife estimated by the hedonic approach. Working Paper No. 6. Division of Program Plans, U.S. Fish and Wildlife Service.

Brown, Gardner M., Jr., J. John Charbonneau, and Michael J. Hay. 1978b. Estimating values of wildlife: Analysis of the 1975 Hunting and Fishing Survey. Working Paper No. 7. Division of Program Plans, U.S. Fish and Wildlife Service.

Brown, Perry J., J. E. Hautaloma, and S. M. McPhail. 1977. Colorado deer hunting experiences. Transactions of the North American Wildlife and Natural Resources Conference 42:216-225.

Brown, Tommy L., and Chad P. Dawson. 1978. Interests, needs and attitudes of New York's metropolitan public in relation to wildlife. Cornell University, Natural Resources Research and Extension Series No. 13. 51 p.

Driver, B. L., and Perry J. Brown. 1978. The opportunity spectrum concept and behavioral information in outdoor recreation resource supply inventories: A rationale. *In* Integrated inventories of renewable natural resources. Proceeding of the workshop [Tucson, Arizona, Jan. 8-12, 1978]. Gyde H. Lund, et al., technical coordinators. USDA Forest Service General Technical Report RM-55, 482 p. Rocky Mountain Forest and Range Experiment Station, Fort Collins, Colo.

Driver, B. L., and Charles C. Harris. 1981. Improving measurement of the benefits of public outdoor recreation programs. p. 525-538 *In* Proceedings,

Division 4 of XVII World Congress, International Union of Forestry Organizations, Kyoto, Japan.
Driver, B. L., and D. H. Rosenthal. 1979. Measuring and improving the effective ness of public outdoor recreation programs. A report on a recreation output measures workshop, December 11-14, Harpers Ferry, West Virginia. Department of Human Kinetics and Leisure Studies, George Washington University, Washington, D.C. 79 p.
Dwyer, John F. 1980. Economic benefits of wildlife related recreation experiences. *In* Wildlife Values. 1980. William W. Shaw and Ervin H. Zube, editors. Center for Assessment of Noncommodity Natural Resource Values. Institutional Series Report #1, School of Renewable Natural Resources, University of Arizona, Tucson. 117 p.
Fazio, James R., and L. A. Belli. 1977. Characteristics of nonconsumptive wildlife users in Idaho. Transactions N. American Wildlife and Natural Resource Conference 42:110-128.
Hammack, Jubb, and Gardner Mallard Brown Jr. 1974. Waterfowl and wetlands: Toward bioeconomic analysis. Resources for the Future, Inc., Johns Hopkins Univ. Press, Baltimore, Maryland. 95 p.
Hendee, John C. 1969. Appreciative versus consumptive uses of wildlife refuges: Studies of who gets what and trends in use. Transactions North American Wildlife and Natural Resource Conference 34:252-256.
Hendee, John C. 1974. A multiple-satisfaction approach to game management. Wildlife Society Bulletin 2(3):104-113.
Hendee, John S., and Dale R. Potter. 1975. Hunter and hunting: Management implications of research. p. 137-161. *In* USDA Forest Service General Technical Report SE-9. Southeastern Forest Experiment Station, Asheville, N.C.
International Association of Fish and Wildlife Agencies. 1981. Hunter education in the United States and Canada with Recommendations for Improvement. 51 p. + Appen.
Kellert, Stephen R. 1979. Public attitudes toward critical wildlife and natural habitat issues. USDI Fish and Wildlife Service and Yale School of Forestry and Environmental Studies. 138 p.
Kellert, Stephen R. 1980. Contemporary values of wildlife in American society. *In* Wildlife Values. William W. Shaw and Ervin H. Zube, editors. Center for Assessment of Noncommodity Resource Values, Institutional Series Report #1. University of Arizona, Tucson, Ariz. School of Renewable Natural Resources. 117 p.
King, R. T. 1947. The future of wildlife in forest land use. Transactions North American Wildlife Conference 12:454-467.
Klessig, Lowell L., and James B. Hale. 1972. A profile of Wisconsin hunters. Technical Bulletin No. 60. Wisconsin Department of Natural Resources, Madison, 24 p.
Langenau, E. 1976. Nonconsumptive uses of the Michigan deer herd. Ph. D. dissertation, Michigan State University, East Lansing, Mich.. 94 p.
Langford, William A., and Donald J. Cocheba. 1978. The wildlife valuation problem: A critical review of economic approaches. Canadian Wildlife Service. Occasional Paper number 37. 37 p.
Leitch, Jay A., and Donald F. Scott. 1977. A selected annotated bibliography

of economic values of fish and wildlife and their habitats. Department of Agricultural Economics, North Dakota Agricultural Experiment Station, Fargo, North Dakota. Agricultural Economics Miscellaneous Report No. 27. 132 p.

Schweitzer, Dennis L. 1981. The state-of-the-art of valuation of wildlife and fish resources for the National Forest System. *Draft* internal report, Rocky Mountain Forest and Range Experiment Station, USDA Forest Service, Fort Collins, Colo. 50 p.

Shaw, William W. 1974. Meanings of wildlife for Americans: Contemporary attitudes and social trends. Transactions North American Wildlife and Natural Resources Conference 39:151-155.

Shaw, William W., and David A. King. 1980. Wildlife management and nonhunting wildlife enthusiasts. Transaction North American Wildlife and Natural Resources Conference 45:219-225.

Shaw, William W., and Ervin H. Zube, editors. 1980. Wildlife values. Center for assessment of noncommodity natural resource values. School of Renewable Natural Resources, University of Arizona, Tucson, Ariz. Inst. Rep. No. 1. 117 p.

Steinhoff, Harold W. 1980. Analysis of major conceptual systems for understanding and measuring wildlife values. *In* Wildlife Values. William W. Shaw and Ervin H. Zube, editors. Center for Assessment of Noncommodity Natural Resource Values, Institutional Series Report #1. School of Renewable Natural Resources. University of Arizona, Tucson, Ariz. 117 p.

U.S. Department of Interior, Fish and Wildlife Service. 1977. 1975 National survey, hunting, fishing and wildlife associated recreation. 100 p.

U.S. Department of Interior, Fish and Wildlife Service. 1980. Habitat as a basis for environmental assessment. Ecological Service Manual 101.

Witter, Daniel J., and William W. Shaw. 1979. Beliefs of birders, hunters, and wildlife professionals about wildlife management. Transactions N. American Wildlife and Natural Resources Conference 44:298-305.

Footnotes

[1]The consumptive/nonconsumptive distinction does not imply anything about the impacts of these users on the resource. The terminology is simply a widely used and convenient manner for distinguishing between those activities which may lead to direct removal of individual animals by the user and those which do not.

Chapter 13
Recreation Benefits From Public Lands

Elizabeth A. Wilman

Introduction

Public forest lands can produce wood, water, forage, wildlife habitat, and recreational opportunities. As the demands for each of these products grow, the necessity to make rational resource allocation decisions increases. This need has been formally recognized in the multiple-use legislation of the 1960s and the rangeland management acts of the 1970s. Interpretation of this legislation has suggested economic efficiency as a resource allocative objective (Krutilla and Haigh 1978, Haigh and Krutilla 1980).

The purpose of multiple-use management, in an economic efficiency context, is to maximize net benefits to the American people from the production of current and future timber harvests along with a time stream of service outputs. These service outputs include the vegetative and land and water characteristics of the forest which are instrumental in supporting wildlife populations, providing forage for cattle, sustaining a municipal or irrigation water supply, providing flood reduction, and supplying essential inputs for outdoor recreation consumers such as hunters, fishermen, hikers, backpackers, and others. One of the main functions of forest management is to manage the vegetative, land, and/or water components so as to produce the desired combination of timber and other service outputs. Perhaps the main problem in carrying out this function is determining what the desired combination is.

Many of the resource service outputs, for historical, legal, or technical reasons, have no market price, or prices unrelated to their economic values. This, together with the lack of methodologies for assessing changes in the economic value of these nonmarket resource service ouptuts resulting from changes in vegetation characteristics, has impeded this assessment. This chapter presents an approach to the measurement of changes in the value of nonmarket recreation service outputs. In addition, one particular case, recreational deer hunting sites, is examined as an example.

Demand for Recreation Service Outputs

A forest or wildland environment can be looked at as providing a set of recreation sites. Recreation demands often have been assessed in terms of the demands for visits to these sites. However, the demand for visits to recreation sites also can be viewed as being derived from the demands for the recreation service outputs that these sites provide. As Randall noted, the output of these recreation services is a function uniquely determined by environmental attributes or characteristics. In this chapter, the terms characteristic, attribute and recreation service output are used interchangeably. These characteristics and the recreation service outputs can be altered by management practices. The supply of the characteristic, or recreation service output, also is changed. Given the demand for the recreation service output, a shift in supply causes the demand curve for a visit to be shifted and the value of a visit to be changed.

As a guide to determining the relevant recreation service outputs or characteristics to consider in assessing demands, it is useful to consider psychological studies which examined the components of satisfaction (or utility) that recreationists obtain from recreational activities.

For example, Haas et al. (1979) looked at the satisfactions of wilderness users in three Colorado study areas. Vegetative characteristics (meadows, forests, etc.), water-related characteristics, and wildlife characteristics all were rated by recreationists as contributing to the satisfactions they derived from the wilderness recreation experience. This implies that such recreationists would have demands for these characteristics, that would affect their demands for, and choices of, recreation sites. To the extent that management practices alter these characteristics (or the recreation service outputs provided), they change the availability of (or cost of obtaining) these characteristics. This imposes some costs or benefits on the consumer. These costs or benefits may be assessed either by looking at the demands for characteristics, as compared to the changed cost of obtaining them, or by looking at the changed demands for site visits.

In the case of deer hunting, there has been some debate in the literature regarding the characteristics which deer hunters demand. Today's sport hunters may receive any of a wide variety of satisfactions from hunting activities (Knopf et al. 1977, Potter et al. 1977, Stanley et al. 1977, More 1977). Although the expectation of success is a necessary component of hunter satisfaction, there are other significant aspects also.

The role of "bagging game" in producing the satisfaction that hunters derive from the hunting experience was described well by More (1977). He suggested that hunting, like many other sports, is a goal-oriented or challenge sport. As with other goal-oriented sports, enjoyment comes from the process of attempting to solve the problem, or attain the goal, rather than from the goal itself. However, periodic attainment of the goal is necessary to provide feedback to the hunter on his success in solving the problem.

In general, hunters require a probability of success greater than zero and less than one, although the preferred probabilities within this range may vary.

To enhance the satisfaction they derive from the challenge itself, other scenic, esthetic, and social aspects of the experience may contribute to it to greater or lesser degrees. However, these other factors probably do not contribute to satisfaction in a linear fashion, but instead interact with the success probabilities.

If expectations of hunting success are always crucial to providing hunter satisfactions, forest resource characteristics which affect hunting success will have some value to recreational hunters. In addition, other factors affected by forest management practices are important to the hunter. The esthetic character of the forest environment may be one factor. To the extent that it is possible to provide high probabilities of hunting success and/or esthetically desirable vegetation patterns in areas whose land forms or aspect make them already more desirable, the benefits derivable from the improved bag probabilities or more esthetic vegetation patterns may be increased.

Managing Lands for Recreation Service Outputs

In the past, timber management has been the main focus for forest managers. However, because timber outputs and recreation service outputs are often jointly produced, the same variables can be manipulated to affect both timber production and the characteristics which constitute the recreation service outputs. The effects on the scenic and esthetic characteristics may need to be considered, and/or effects on wildlife habitat or population levels. Now, the form and degree of manipulation of forest vegetation characteristics on public lands must be motivated by the more general objective of producing an efficient combination of outputs. In economic terms, this can be stated as the objective of maximizing the net economic value that can be obtained from available resources, including the value of outputs which do not have market prices. Given this objective, there is a need to assess the effects that forest management practices can have on the production of nonmarket recreation service outputs, including those which involve wildlife habitat and population levels.

Both Boyce (1977, 1980) and Thomas (1979) developed relationships which express the suitability of an area as wildlife habitat in terms of its land and vegetative characteristics. For example, Boyce, in studying deer habitat in hardwood forests in the southern Appalachians, found that forage availability and the size of openings permitting the utilization of forage were key factors. Specifically, Boyce related three factors as an index of deer habitat suitability: (1) the proportion of the area in seedling habitat; (2) the proportion of the area in mature (pole 10) habitat; and (3) the opening size distribution.

Thomas's work focused on the Blue Mountains of Oregon and Washington. He found that forage and cover are key deer habitat factors that can be manipulated to affect deer populations. The forage-cover ratio was used as the primary management variable, although it was pointed out that the environmental setting or land type on which the management action is applied can affect the response that the deer population will have. Thomas developed response relationships for both deer and elk populations to changes in the forage-cover ratio for various land types, which can be described in terms of slope, aspect, elevation, type of vegetation which can be supported, and tree stocking potential.

Effects on wildlife populations which result from a management treatment directly affecting the vegetation depend upon the ecological linkages between the vegetative pattern and the particular population. However, if the wildlife populations are valuable to users such as hunters, then a vegetative pattern that provides good wildlife habitat will also be valuable.

The esthetic and scenic characteristics of the forest also must be considered. However, it is not necessary to separate the degree to which a characteristic is habitat-related from the degree to which it is esthetic. Rather, what is important is that characteristics whose value to the user can be directly or indirectly affected by forest management activities not be excluded from consideration.

Techniques for Measuring Recreation Values

If a set of forest management practices affects the vegetative characteristics which constitute recreation service outputs, then one of the necessary elements of a benefit-cost assessment is the benefits (or costs) to recreationists.

In general, there are two types of approaches that can be used to derive these benefits (or costs). One is the direct questioning income compensation approach. This approach is discussed in chapter 4 by Randall. The second—the expenditure function approach—uses other market-generated information (or information generated by observations on the choices recreationists actually make) to derive values for recreation sites or characteristics of recreation sites which can be used to derive benefits (or costs).

The second approach is examined here. It involves setting up a utility maximization model as Randall does. Such a model describes how individual recreation consumers make decisions about the amounts of different site quality characteristics they will consume, along with the number and/or length of the visits they will make. In the case of recreation, the household itself helps to produce the outputs it consumes. Therefore, the approach can also be characterized as a household production function approach.[1] Almost all models whose intent is to estimate recreation site benefits or benefits from changes in site quality can be described in household production function terms.

The Travel Cost Approach

The primary approach in recreation benefit estimation that has relied on observations of choices made by individuals to reveal their demands has been the travel cost approach. Hotelling[2] first suggested that travel costs might be viewed as necessary expenditures to consume the services of a recreation site, and that assuming that there were a group of consumers with the same demand curve, variation in their required travel expenditures would allow identification of their common demand curve and estimation of the consumer's surplus benefits each of them would enjoy based on their proximity to the site.

The basic travel cost approach is detailed by Clawson,[3] and Clawson and Knetsch (1966). Expressing this approach in a consumer utility maximizing framework, the consumer's utility function can be written as:

$$U(x,n), \qquad [1]$$

where x is a numeraire good, and n is visits to the site. The consumer's cost function is

$$C = x + nc, \qquad [2]$$

where x has a price of 1, and c is the travel cost associated with a visit to a site. The first-order conditions give

$$\frac{U_n}{U_x} = c. \qquad [3]$$

That is, in choosing the number of visits to the site, the consumer equates the marginal utility received from a visit to the marginal cost of another visit, which is the travel cost. Over a cross section of consumers with the same utility function but facing different travel costs to get to the site, sufficient points on the marginal utility (or demand) function may be observed to identify it. The area under the demand curve and above the consumer's travel cost gives the consumer's surplus or the benefits the consumer derives from visiting the site. Aggregating all consumers gives the aggregate site demand curve and the consumer's surplus estimate of benefits derived from the site.

Some problems arise in application of the method. One involves time costs. There are time as well as monetary costs involved in visits to the site. If consumers have the same opportunity costs of time, and the length of time on site does not vary, then only travel time costs are relevant (Wilman 1980). However, because the method is based on variation in travel costs, allowance must be made for the time costs of travel. Although attempts have been made to include such costs (Cesario 1976, McConnell and Strand 1981), their magnitude has not been well documented.

A second problem involves the functional form used in estimating the demand curve. Linear models, semilog models, quadratic models and double log models have been used. Both Ziemer et al. (1980) and Vaughan et al.,[4] in comparing the first three of these, found the semilog specification best. However, there is evidence that this model is not always adequate. Smith

(1975) found that while both the semilog and double log forms were acceptable according to the conventional R^2 criteria, the Cox likelihood ratio test indicated that neither was reasonable in describing wilderness behavior. Cheshire and Stabler (1976) found evidence that the semilog form overpredicts visits at extreme distances and underpredicts at middle distances. They suggested an asymptotic logarithmic form which involves an extra parameter—a constant added to the distance before the logarithmic transformation is performed. They also suggested that double log forms are illogical because they fail to account for either the upper limits (a limit to the distance at which there will be positive visits) and a lower limit (a limit to the visits that will be taken at zero cost).

Although models such as probit, logit, and Tobit have not received much attention in the recreation benefits literature, they provide alternatives, particularly when the data includes whether or not any visits occur at a particular distance, as well as the number of visits that occur. In general, such models require data disaggregated to the level of the individual recreation consumer, or at least an indication of the visit levels of individual consumers at various distances. Probit or logit models are most appropriate when consumers would take at most one visit per time period at any given distance. In this case, the question is reduced to that of whether or not a visit will occur.[5] The probit and logit models differ in terms of the form of the probability function. The probit model is based on a cumulative normal function, and the logit on a cumulative logistic function. The advantage of these models is that the upper and lower limits discussed by Cheshire are implicit in the functional forms. They differ mainly in that the probit function has flatter tails and hence probabilities of participation can be reduced from 0.5 to 0 more rapidly (Pindyck and Rubinfeld 1976).

When a consumer may take many visits, a Tobit model may be more appropriate (Tobin 1958). Briefly it may be written as

$$E(n/c, n > 0) = \beta c + \sqrt{\sigma}\lambda, \qquad [4]$$

where the left side is the expected level of n, given $n > 0$

β = the coefficient on the travel cost variable

$\sqrt{\sigma}$ = the coefficient of λ and the standard deviation of the error term from $n = \beta c + \epsilon$

$$\lambda = \frac{f}{1\text{-}F}$$

where f = the density function for the normal distribution

$1\text{-}F$ = the cumulative density function for the normal distribution (or the probability $n > 0$).

The Tobit model can be estimated by maximum likelihood techniques. However, a simpler method for computation purposes was suggested by Heckman (1974). Probit analysis can be used to obtain estimates for λ, and then ordinary least squares, or more correctly generalized least squares, can be used to estimate equation [4].[6] Although equation [4] is used for estimation purposes, if both sides are multiplied by $(1-F)$, the left side gives the unconditional expected visit level traditionally estimated in travel cost curves.

Other potential problems involve multiple destination trips and congestion at recreation sites. In the first case, it is difficult to derive a value for the site apart from the remainder of the bundle. In the second case, the services of the site vary with the number of consumers using it. In both of these cases, determining the effect on recreation site benefits involves modeling individual behavior. Both cases need some study using disaggregated data on individuals in order to develop and test models that will incorporate such effects. Without such efforts it is impossible to know if there are appropriate adjustments that can be made to the travel cost model (Smith 1981).

A Model of Recreational Choice

This section presents a model which describes the way individuals make their recreation decisions. Among the things which enter the individual's utility function are the levels of the quality characteristics.

Observation suggests that recreationists do not necessarily confine their visits to one site. To some degree this may be because of variability in the availability of time. However, variability in site choices would appear to be greater than can be explained solely by variability in time availability.

Other possible explanations originate in the recreationist's utility function rather than his cost function. A recreationist may wish to consume more than one quality characteristic and may choose to visit multiple sites to obtain multiple characteristics at the level he desires. Alternatively, there may be imperfect perception of the characteristic levels of a site, or a demand for consumption of a variety of different sites. Even if only one quality characteristic entered the utility function, more than one site might be visited.

All of the above factors are considered in the model presented. However, initially the model is simplified by assuming there is only one relevant characteristic, and that time constraints are not important. Therefore, the only reasons for a hunter to visit more than one site are that his perceptions of quality are imperfect or that he has some small demand for variety. In either case, only a small random element is introduced into his site choice calculus; for practical purposes it is assumed that all visits are to the same site. The utility function for the individual consumer is expressed as:

$$U(x,n,q), \qquad [5]$$

where x = a composite of other goods and services
n = the number of visits
q = the level of the quality characteristic.

The consumer also faces a cost function for obtaining x, n, and q. This can be expressed as:

$$x + C(n,q), \tag{6}$$

where x (the numeraire good) has a unit price, and $C(n,q)$ is the cost function for n recreation visits of quality q.

It is useful at this point to introduce the concept of an expenditure (or bid) function (also see Randall, Ch. 4). This function, $b = b(n,q)$, essentially relates the individual's willingness to pay for recreation services to the level of n and q he consumes. Assuming the individual has a limited amount of money to spend, Y, then if he bids the amount b for n and q, he will have only $Y - b$ left to spend on x. If otherwise he would be able to obtain a level of satisfaction (or utility) U_0 from his consumption, he certainly would not bid an amount for (n,q) that would reduce his overall utility below U_0. The bid is further defined as the full bid amount which would leave the consumer just at utility level U_0 (no better or worse than without (n,q)). Using this bid concept we may write the utility function as

$$U_0 = U(Y - b,n,q), \tag{7}$$

where b is the consumer's bid amount or the willingness to pay to consume n visits of quality q.

From the expenditure (or bid) function $b = b(n,q)$ the marginal bid functions (or compensated demand functions) for q and n can be derived.

If the "n,q" bundle were being sold on the private market so that the seller could always extract the full bid amount, one could observe the bid amounts by observing market prices. However, when the consumer faces a cost function produced outside the private market, there is no guarantee that the costs incurred by the consumer will equal full bid amounts. It is only certain that the costs will not exceed those amounts. Therefore, a set of identical consumers facing different costs, in general, will not yield observations along one bid function. This may not matter in some cases. If the marginal utilities of n, x and q are independent of x (the amount of other goods and services), then the value of changes in n or q can be evaluated, although the total value of either n or q cannot. Alternately, if the change in the cost faced by the consumer is very small relative to the price of x, and thus results in a very small income effect on its consumption, the marginal bid function (or compensated demand function) may be fairly closely determined. The general household production function has been used by several authors (Bockstael and McConnell 1978, Brown et al. 1978, McConnell 1979, Brown and Mendelson 1980, Eubanks and Brookshire 1981).

Because the data which are used to estimate these models are composed of cross-sectional observations on the (n,q) choices individuals make, there are two additional kinds of considerations.

First, because the utility function and the cost function simultaneously affect the (n,q) choice, is it possible to separate the two influences as is necessary to obtain estimates of the consumer's surplus change resulting from a management action? Because the choice of n (or q) is determined by equating the marginal bid or willingness to pay for x (or q) with the marginal cost, separating the two influences essentially means identifying the marginal bid and marginal cost curves. To identify either one of these, it is required that there be independent variation in the other. Four models are presented below. They differ in the kinds of assumptions that are made to identify the marginal bid and marginal cost curves. Models such as the multiple-site travel cost model can be derived in special cases.

The second consideration involves incorporating management changes into the model. How this is done depends upon how the particular identifying assumptions are made, although in general terms, the direct effect is to change the marginal cost of obtaining q for some subset of visitors.

Model A

Here it is assumed that neither U_q nor U_n is affected by changes in x. That is, the utility function can be written as $U(x) + U(n,q)$. This model identifies a marginal bid function for n (although q is allowed to adjust to changes in n), and a marginal cost curve for n (with adjustment in q). This is achieved by positing an independent shift variable for the utility function, which is related to socioeconomic variables such as income, and by assuming a form for the cost function which will allow the marginal cost of a visit to change independently of the marginal cost of q. A management change which alters the marginal cost of q shifts both the marginal bid or willingness-to-pay curve, and the marginal cost curve.

First consider the individual, with utility and cost functions (eq. [7] and [6] respectively), to choose levels of x and q, given a fixed level of n. This gives the following equilibrium condition:

$$C_q = \frac{U_q}{U_x}, \qquad [8]$$

where C_q = the partial derivative of $C(n,q)$ with respect to q, and represents the marginal cost of q (with n constant)

U_q = the partial derivative of $U(n,q)$ with respect to q, and represents the marginal utility of Q (with n constant)

U_x = the derivative of $U(x)$ with respect to x, and represents the marginal utility of x.

The right side gives a marginal bid price for the consumption of q with a fixed n. For different levels of n, different marginal bid prices for q would result. Now consider the marginal bid price for n, given that q is always allowed to adjust to its new optimal level as n changes. This marginal bid price is given by the right side of equation [9].

$$C_q f_n + C_n = \frac{U_q}{U_x} f_n + \frac{U_n}{U_x}, \qquad [9]$$

where $q = f(n)$ is the relationship between the optimal q and n
f_n = the change in q as a result of a change in n
U_n = the marginal utility of n (q constant)
C_n = the marginal cost of n (q constant).

Although it is true that because equation [8] still holds, equation [9] can be reduced to $C_n = U_n/U_x$, the full cost and utility changes resulting from a change in n are given by equation [9].

To identify the marginal bid function for n, given that adjustments in q are possible, it would be necessary to have a number of consumers with the same marginal bid functions, but different marginal cost functions.

To ensure that the marginal bid function for n (given that adjustments in q are possible in response to changes in n) is the appropriate function to derive, it is necessary that only changes in C_n are used to identify the marginal bid function. This can be done if C_n varies independently of C_q, or if q is fixed, responding neither to changes in C_q nor to the changes in n resulting from changes in C_n. If C_q as well as C_n changes, and q is not fixed, then $fn = dq/dn$, which determines the direction of the bid curve, changes as C_n changes and integration over the marginal bid curve becomes very difficult.

A not unrealistic form of the cost function, which allows changes in C_n to occur independently of changes in C_q is:

$$C = n(h + K(q)), \qquad [10]$$

where h is the fixed cost of a visit, unrelated to the level of q chosen. For example it could be the minimum cost to get from a given origin to one of a set of sites. $K(q)$ is that part of the cost of a visit which depends upon q. The marginal cost of n is now

$$C_n = h + K(q), \qquad [11]$$

and the marginal cost of q is

$$C_q = n\, K_q. \qquad [12]$$

If the variation in the C_n function is caused by variation in h, C_n can vary without causing simultaneous variation in C_q. Therefore, the marginal bid function for n (allowing adjustments in q to take place according to $q = f_n$) can be identified.

Given that there is variation in the C_n function independent of variation in the C_q function, then variation in the C_q function, which causes variation in the f_n function of equation [9], has the effect of shifting both the marginal bid function for n and the marginal cost function.

For estimation purposes it is useful to think of a two-stage model. In general, stage I involves regressing Total Cost on n, I_q, and h to obtain P_n. (Often P_n is directly observable, and stage I can be omitted.) In stage II, the simultaneous model in equations [14] and [15] is estimated using the observed or calculated P_n.

Stage I

$$\text{Total Cost } P = m(n,I_q,h), \text{ from which prices } P_n \text{ are derived.} \quad [13]$$

Stage II

$$\text{Marginal Bid } P_n = j(n,I_q,S), \quad [14]$$

$$\text{Marginal Cost } P_n = i(n,I_q,h), \quad [15]$$

where P_n = visit price (or cost)
S = socioeconomic demand shifters (Income, Education, Age, etc.)
I_q = an index of the availability of q.

For example, I_q could equal

$$\sum_{\text{all } i} \frac{q_i \times C_i}{1 + d_i - h},$$

where q_i = the quality level at site i
$d_i - h$ = the distance to site i, over and above h
C_i = the capacity (or perhaps acreage) of i.

Variation in h identifies the marginal bid function, variation in S identifies the marginal cost function. The I_q term acts as the shift variable which represents variation in the f_n and C_q functions. Both the marginal bid and marginal cost curves will be shifted by changes in C_q.

It might be noted that the choice of n (and q) is only observed if the travel cost price (or supply price, P_n) is such that the choice of n would be positive. Whether or not a positive visit level occurs depends upon h and I_q. With a constant I_q, the probability of a visit is a function of h. This implies, following Heckman (1974), that the model to be estimated should be formulated as

Stage II

$$\text{Marginal Bid } P_n = j(n,I_q,\lambda,S), \quad [16]$$

$$\text{Marginal Cost } P_n = i(q,I_q,h), \quad [17]$$

where λ is the density function for the normal distribution divided by the cumulative probability function (i.e., the probability of participation).

The term λ is a function of h and I_q. For a given I_q, the probability of a visit varies with h. The resultant marginal bid function will take into account not only changes in P_n caused by changes in n but also caused by changes in the probability of a visit.

Once equations [16] and [17] have been identified, integration over n (where λ changes as n changes) will yield a consumer's surplus estimate for the visitor from a given origin, conditional on his visitation. However, allowing that the probability of participation changes across origins, the consumer's surplus for a person from a given origin will be

$$\mathrm{CS} = \int_0^{n^*} (j(n,I_q,\lambda,S) - i(n,I_q,h))\overline{(1-F)}dn, \qquad [18]$$

where: $\overline{(1-F)}$ is the average probability of the nth visit across all origins, having at least n visits.

Changes in I_q will result in shifts in the marginal bid curve, the marginal supply curve, and in the consumer's surplus. If the consumer's surplus change is all that needs to be known and if the marginal bid curve and the marginal cost curve both shift upward by constant amounts (ΔP and ΔC) as a result of the change in I_q, the consumer's surplus change can be written as

$$\begin{aligned}\Delta\mathrm{CS} &= (\Delta P - \Delta C)\overline{(1-F^*)}\,n^* \\ &\quad + \int_{n^*}^{n'} (j(n,Iq,\lambda,S) - i(n,Iq,h))\overline{(1-F)}dn.\end{aligned} \qquad [19]$$

The first term on the right side gives the consumer's surplus change at the existing expected visit level $(1\text{-}F^*)n^*$, and the second term gives the change due to the increase in the expected visit level to $(1\text{-}F')n'$. If n does not change, the first term is all that is required.

The multiple-site travel cost model—termed the Cesario-Knetsch model—can be derived as a special case of model A (Cesario and Knetsch 1976, Knetsch et al. 1976, Bouwes and Schneider 1979, Johnson et al. 1981). The Cesario-Knetsch model has been formulated as

$$n_{ij} = f(c_{ij}, s_{ij}, S_j, q_i), \qquad [20]$$

where n_{ij} = expected trips to (or trips per capita from origin j) to site i
c_{ij} = the cost of a visit to site i from origin j
s_{ij} = an index of the availability of origin j of substitute opportunities for site i
S_j = a vector of socioeconomic and demographic variables for origin j
q_i = a quality vector for site i.

As a special case of model A, $c_{ij} = h$ and n_{ij} is the product of (1-F) and n. The term s_{ij} is a composite term combining information on the prices and quantities of the set of available sites. It serves essentially the same role as the I_q variable in equations [17] through [19]. The term λ is excluded, its effects being included through the choice of functional form. In the specification it is assumed that c_{ij} changes independently of s_{ij}, and that a site demand curve can be estimated with q constant. This is the same as assuming $f_n = 0$ in equation [9]. If there are no constraints on the form of the utility function, $f_n = 0$ requires that q be fixed. That is, over some range the marginal cost of q faced by a set of identical consumers must be vertical at q_1, as shown in figure 1. In this case, only one of the terms s_{ij} or q_i is required to describe the marginal cost of q.

Given these assumptions, the multiple-site travel cost model can be used to derive a demand curve for n, given a constant q (q_1), and to assess the value of a site with that q_1. If a set of identical consumers faced a different vertical marginal cost curve for q (i.e., at q_2 in fig. 1), the choice of q would be different, as would the consumer's surplus estimate. With q_2 rather than q_1, the demand curve for n would shift, reflecting the higher quality level obtainable.

If the assumptions for the Cesario-Knetsch model are met, it can be relatively straightforwardly applied. This application is detailed in Johnson et al. (1981). As shown here, it can be regarded as a special case of model A with rather strict assumptions governing the cost function. As will be shown later

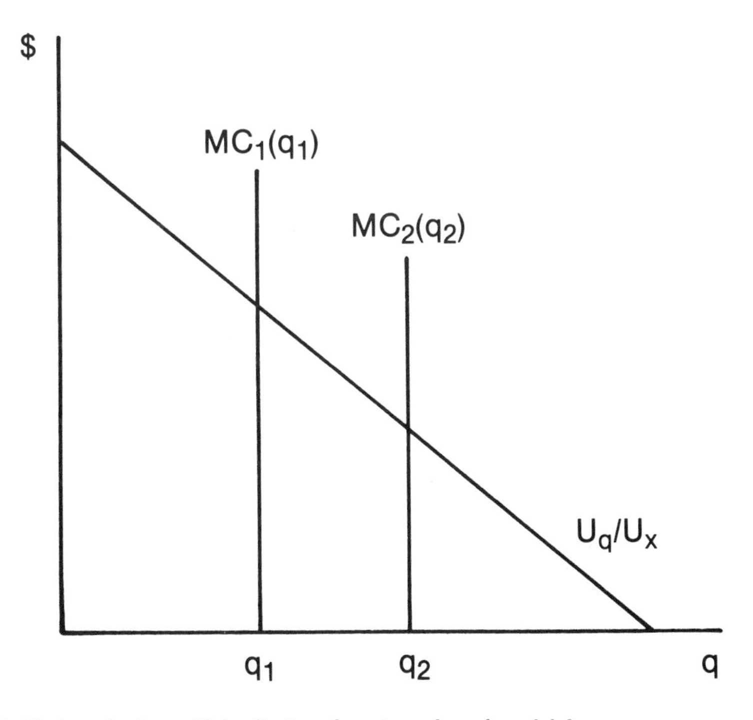

Figure 1. Choice of *q* in multiple-site travel cost version of model A.

with the presentation of model D, special assumptions governing the form of the utility function can also produce this model.

The above model presents a method of assessing consumer's surplus changes as a result of varying costs of obtaining levels of q.

Model B

Again it is assumed that U_q and U_n are unaffected by changes in x, or $U(x,n,q) = U(x) + U(n,q)$. In this model, the marginal bid and marginal cost functions for q, with n fixed, are identified. The management change then shifts the marginal cost curve for q, changing the consumer's surplus.

This time consider the consumer to choose x and n, given q. This results in the following equilibrium condition:

$$C_n = \frac{U_n}{U_x} \,. \qquad [21]$$

The right side gives a marginal bid function for the consumption of n with fixed q. Next, consider the marginal bid function for q, given that n is always allowed to adjust to its new optimal level as q changes. This marginal bid price is the right side of equation [22].

$$C_n g_q + C_q = \frac{U_n}{U_x} g_q + U_q \,, \qquad [22]$$

where $n = g(q)$ is the relationship between the optimal n and q
g_q = the change in n as a result of the change in q.

To identify the marginal bid function for a q given that adjustments in n are possible, it is necessary that there be a number of consumers with varying marginal cost functions for q, but the same marginal bid function. At the same time, it is necessary that the $g(q)$ function not change. This requires either that C_q vary independently of C_n, or that n be fixed.

It is difficult to conceive of a reasonable form for the cost function that would allow C_q to vary with C_n remaining constant. However, there may be cases where the alternative, the constant n assumption, can be used. This can result if n is constrained in some way, as, for example, if only one visit is allowed.

If the constraint $n \leq N$ is added to the cost function the consumer faces, equation [22] becomes

$$(C_n + \gamma)g_q + C_q = \frac{U_n}{U_x} g_q + \frac{U_q}{U_x} \,, \text{ if } n < N \text{ and } \gamma = 0, \qquad [23]$$

$$C_q = \frac{U_q}{U_x} \,, \text{ if } n = N \text{ and } \gamma > 0. \qquad [24]$$

When the constraint is binding and $\gamma > 0$, all that is required is variation in C_q for the marginal bid function for q to be identified.

For estimation purposes this model might be specified as:

Stage I

$$\text{Total Cost } P = m(n,q,I_q,h). \quad [25]$$

Stage II

$$\text{Marginal Bid } P_q = j(n,q,\lambda,S), \quad [26]$$

$$\text{Marginal Cost } P_q = i(n,q,I_q). \quad [27]$$

Again, it is true that the q choice is observed only if a positive visit level occurs and the bid function should contain a λ term.

A management change will change I_q and will shift the marginal cost curve for q, changing the consumer's surplus amount. If n is constant, the change in consumer's surplus is the first term on the right side of equation [19].

Model C

This approach involves specifying a particular form of the utility function that allows the choice of q to be made independently of the choice of n. In this case, two approaches are possible. Given the form of the cost function used in model A, an average demand curve for a visit can be estimated. Exogenous variation in the marginal cost of q will shift this curve and change the consumer's surplus estimate for an average day. Alternately (because the q choice is independent of n), the model in equations [25] through [27] can be estimated.

In model C, the utility function is written as:

$$U(x) + nU(q). \quad [28]$$

This form assumes that the utility derived from each visit is the same regardless of the number of visits taken. Assuming the cost function to be as in equation [10], the first order conditions for q given n include

$$(1/U_x)(Uq) = K_q. \quad [29]$$

In this case, the choice of q does not depend on the level of n. Therefore, the marginal bid function for n need not consider adjustments in q in response to changes in n. The first order conditions for n include

$$(1/U_x)(U(q)) = h + K(q). \quad [30]$$

However, because neither $U(q)$ nor $h + K(q)$ varies with the level of n, this condition does not determine the level of n, but rather whether any visits will take place. If $U(q)/U_x \geq h + K(q)$, visits will occur, but the level will be indeterminate. If equality rather than inequality held, the cost of a visit would provide some useful information on its utility, or the bid amount a consumer would be willing to pay for that visit. In general, the equality will not hold. However, for a subset of visitors it will hold. For the marginal visitor $U(q)/U_x = h + K(q)$ will hold. This means that for a group of visitors with identical utility functions the highest $h + K(q)$ observed will be an observation on the bid amount. The bid amount for a visit of a given quality q (and hence a given $K(q)$) can be observed by observing the highest h incurred by a visitor in the group of consumers with identical preferences.

The change in the bid amount resulting from a shift in $K(q)$ (i.e., through a change in the I_q term, as in model A) can be determined by observing a wider set of identical consumers. Observing the maximum h at alternative levels of $K(q)$ will allow the estimation of the bid amounts per visit at different $K(q)$ levels.

This leads to the manner in which the average demand curve for a visit could be estimated. Suppose there are N days in a season during which a recreationist could visit the site with q, at cost $h + K(q)$. If he visits n times, this is equivalent to an n/N probability for each visit. This probability is a function of $(U(q)/U_x) - K(q) - h$. If q and $K(q)$ are constant across individuals with identical utility functions, then the different n/N observations are a function of h. A probit, logit, or similar function can give the probability of a visit as a function of h. The area under the function above $h + K(q)$ gives the consumer's surplus for an individual with that level of cost.

A shift in $K(q)$, and, therefore, a change in q, shifts the function and the $h + K(q)$, resulting in a change in the consumer's surplus.

Alternately, the marginal bid and marginal cost curves for q may be identified, and the consumer's surplus for a visit of quality q estimated as the area under the marginal bid curve and above the marginal cost curve.

However, again the visit—and hence the quality choice—is only observed if $U(q)/U_x \geq h + K(q)$. For given $U(q)/U_x$, $K(q)$, and q, whether or not the visit occurs depends on h. Therefore, the probability of observing the visit and the quality choice q depends upon h. The model to be estimated should be formulated as in equations [25] through [27].

Model D

Model C can be further extended to account for different utility functions across visits. This may also imply different marginal utility functions for q across visits, but it need not. Here, it is assumed that the marginal utility of q remains constant. In this case, the utility function for q is:

$$U(x) + U_1(q) + U_2(q) + U_3(q) + U_4(q) + \ldots U_n(q), \qquad [31]$$

with the cost function remaining as in equation [10].

For each visit it will be true that

$$K_q = \frac{U_{iq}}{U_x} \qquad [32]$$

and that

$$U_i(q)/U_x \geq h + K(q). \qquad [33]$$

If one observes a set of visits for a given consumer, the total utility obtained from those visits can be expressed as:

$$n\,\overline{U(q)} = U_1(q) + U_2(q) + \ldots U_n(q). \qquad [34]$$

Because the ith visit is observed only if $U_i(q)/U_x \geq h + K(q)$, the maximum observed $h + K(q)$ for a given i will give an estimate of $U_i(q)/U_x$. The average maximum $h + K(q)$ gives an estimate of $\overline{U(q)}/U_x$.

The method of estimation in this case is the same as in the previous example. This can be seen by considering the estimation process as if one were estimating the bid curve for each i separately. The probability of the first visit would be estimated as a function of h (given constant q and Kq). This would lead to a function such as $f(1)$, shown in figure 2.

Assuming $N = 3$, $f(2)$ and $f(3)$ can be similarly estimated. If $h + K(q)$ for the jth individual is as shown in figure 2, the areas above $h + K(q)$ and under $f(1)$, $f(2)$, and $f(3)$ respectively can be estimated. These areas give the consumer's surplus estimates CS(1), CS(2), and CS(3). The total consumer's surplus is CS(total) = CS(1) + CS(2) + CS(3). However, the same estimate could be obtained if the average function $\bar{f}$ was estimated.

The function $\bar{f}$ can be estimated by fitting a probit, logit, or similar function using the average probability of a visit ($n/N = (P(1) + P(2) + \ldots P(N))/N$), where n/N is a function of h. The area under this function and above $h + K(q)$ gives the consumer's surplus for the average visit. Multiplying by N will then given an estimate of the total consumer's surplus over the n visits.[7] A management change that changes I_q will shift the $\bar{f}$ curve and change the consumer's surplus estimate.

Model D is also consistent with the Cesario-Knetsch multiple-site travel cost model. As long as the marginal utility of q does not change across visits, the choice of q will not be affected by the choice of n. Therefore, a demand curve for n can be estimated given a constant q. A shift in the S_j of equation [20] is equivalent to a shift in the I_q and will result in a different q choice. This will shift the demand curve for n as well as $h + K(q)$, and result in a new site value.

Because the choice of q is still independent of n, the alternate approach of estimating the marginal bid and marginal cost functions for q can also be used here (i.e., eqs. [25], [26] and [27]).

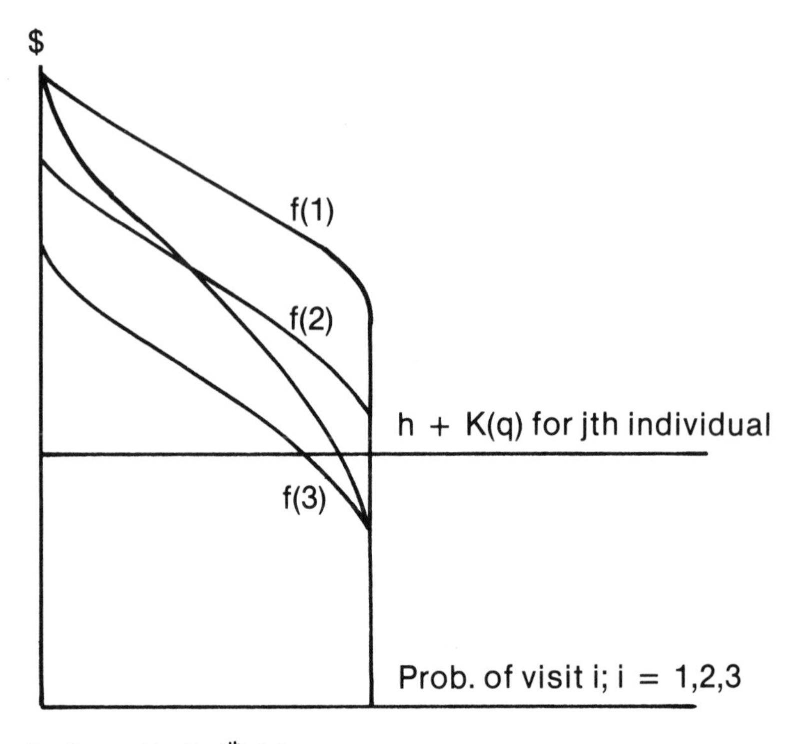

Figure 2.—Demand for the ith visit.

If, in model D, the different utility function across visits also implied different marginal utilities for q (that is, the q choices differed in a non-random manner) then marginal bid and marginal cost functions would have to be estimated and identified separately for each visit i. To identify a marginal bid function for the ith visit it would be necessary to observe the ith visits for a set of identical consumers facing different I_q.

A Hunting Model With Season Length and Bag Limitations

In previous models that apply to recreation service outputs in general, the quality variable q was treated as a characteristic which can be consumed over and over as more visits are taken. However, in a model of hunting behavior, it seems appropriate that a relevant quality variable be the probability of bagging a deer at a given site. Given the restriction that only one deer can be bagged, the quality level chosen will affect the number of visits the hunter expects to make, according to the following relationship:

$$V(q,n) = 1 + (1-q) + (1-q)^2 + (1-q)^3 + \ldots + (1-q)^{n-1}, \qquad [35]$$

where V = the expected number of visits
n = the number of visits the hunter would make if he did not bag a deer

q = the probability of bagging a deer at the site visited during a visit of a given length (i.e., one day).

Given that V is determined by equation [34], the utility function becomes

$$U(x, V(q,n), q) \quad [36]$$

and the cost function

$$x + C(V(q,n), q). \quad [37]$$

With a budget constraint, Y, the utility function can be written as

$$U(Y - b, V(q,n), q), \quad [38]$$

where b is the willingness to pay to consume $V(q,n)$ and q.

Now the question is which of the models is the best suited to the hunting case. First consider model A. With a fixed n, the first order conditions for q are

$$C_v V_q + C_q = \frac{U_v V_q}{U_x} + \frac{U_q}{U_x}. \quad [39]$$

Now the marginal bid price for n, with q being allowed to adjust as n changes, is

$$(C_v V_q + C_q) f_n + C_v V_n = \left(\frac{U_v V_q}{U_x} + \frac{U_q}{U_x}\right) f_n + U_v V_n. \quad [40]$$

To estimate the bid function for n, variation in the marginal cost of n should not cause the function f_n to vary. The cost function with a fixed cost, h, is written as

$$C = V(q,n)(h + K(q)). \quad [41]$$

The marginal cost of q, given a constant n, is now

$$C_q = V_q(h + K(q)) + V(q,n) K_q. \quad [42]$$

The marginal cost of n, allowing q to adjust, is

$$C_n = V_q(h + K(q)) f_n + V(q,n) K_q f_n + V_n(h + K(q)). \quad [43]$$

In this case, variation in h will cause variation in both the marginal cost of n and the marginal cost of q. Therefore, the assumption of variation in C_n independent of variation in C_q is not tenable. The only other possibility is to assume q to be fixed, as in the Cesario-Knetsch simplification of this model. However, in many cases, this will not be a very believable assumption, given a wide variety of sites available to a hunter from any given origin.

Although model A does not seem too useful here, model B may have some applicability. In the case of a fixed length hunting season, n will be constrained to be less than or equal to the season length N.

With the constraint that n be less than or equal to N, the cost function can be written as

$$C = V(q,n)(h + K(q)) + \gamma(N - n). \qquad [44]$$

The equilibrium conditions for n are now

$$(1/U_x)(U_v V_n) = V_n(h + K(q)) \; \gamma = 0 \; N > n, \text{ or} \qquad [45]$$

$$n = N. \qquad [46]$$

When the constraint is binding, n is not affected by variation in C_q, C_n, or q. This means that the marginal bid and marginal cost curves for q do not need to be concerned with adjustments in n, resulting in

$$(1/U_x)(U_q V(n,q) + U(q)Vq) = KqV(n,q) + (h + K(q))Vq\,. \qquad [47]$$

For econometric estimation purposes, this can be written as in equations [25] through [27] with $n = N$, the season length.

The C model may also be appropriate for the hunting case. The utility function is written as

$$U(x) + V(n,q)U(q) \qquad [48]$$

and the cost function as

$$x + V(n,q)(h + K(q)). \qquad [49]$$

For each visit, the consumer would choose q so that

$$(1/U_x)(U_q V(n,q) + V_q U(q)) = K_q V(n,q) + V_q(h + K(q)). \qquad [50]$$

Given that a deer has not been bagged on a previous visit, a visit will occur if

$$(1/U_x)(U(q)) \geq h + K(q). \qquad [51]$$

Because neither the right side nor the left side of equation [51] vary with n, the level of n will be indeterminate and, therefore, not affected by q. Only whether or not any visits occur is affected by q. Model C is similar to model B in that it can be estimated via the set of equations [25], [26], and [27].

Because in model D n is not indeterminate, this model does not appear to be useful in the hunting example.

Summary of the Models

There are a number of models that can be used to value changes in recreation service outputs. Which one is appropriate depends upon which identifying assumptions best fit the particular case being studied. In model A, the marginal bid function for n is identified, and shifts with changes in the marginal cost of q, I_q. A simpler version of model A is the Cesario-Knetsch multiple-site travel cost model. In model B, n is fixed, and the marginal bid and marginal cost curves for q are identified. The marginal cost curve shifts as a result of management changes that affect the availability of q. In model C, the choice of q is unaffected by n. Again, marginal bid and marginal cost curves for q may be estimated. But, given that the marginal cost of n can change independently of the marginal cost of q, it is also possible to estimate an average visit demand curve which will shift with changes in I_q. Model D generates similar estimation models to model C. However, the Cesario-Knetsch model also can be estimated from D, given that the marginal cost of n can change independently of the marginal cost of q.

The deer hunting model with a bag constraint adds the complication that visits are a function of q and n. Therefore, it is not possible for the marginal cost of n to change without changing the marginal cost of q. This means that models A and D are inappropriate. Model C or model B can be applied, depending upon whether the assumption of a constrained n, or a constant $U(q)$ across visits is most tenable.

In the deer hunting case, not all of the variables are directly observable. $V(n,q)$, for example, represents the expected number of visits. This number will not be observed. Instead, the actual number will be observed. However, because the actual number should only vary randomly around the expected number, this should cause no estimation problems. The n variable is not observed for all hunters. It is observed only for those who do not bag an animal. However, given groups of hunters with similar costs and preferences, the observed n values can be generalized.

Some Extensions Using Model C

Because the assumptions underlying model C are reasonable, some further complications can be introduced to make the model more realistic. First, the length of visit is allowed to be a choice variable instead of being fixed. Second, time costs (t_1 for travel time, l for a day on site) are introduced.

With a simpler model than C, the effect of introducing visit length and time costs would be quite simple. Suppose there is no site quality choice, and the utility of a day is simply the constant D. Because the utility function does not distinguish days and visits, the hunter will choose either one long visit or a number of day visits, depending upon which option yields the greater net benefits. Let A be the net benefits of one long visit and B, the net benefits generated by many day visits.

$$A = D \cdot v - (h + t_1 + l) - (v - 1)(r + l) \quad [52]$$

$$B = D \cdot v - (h + t_1 + l)v , \quad [53]$$

where v is the number of days visited and r is the cost of staying overnight.

Subtracting B from A yields $-(h + t_1 + l) - (v-1)(r + l) + (h + t_1 + l)v$. This will be positive where $A > B$ or when $r + l < h + t_1 + l$, and one long visit will be chosen. At $r + l = h + t_1 + l$, the hunter will be indifferent between one long visit and 1-day visits.

When the quality variable, q, is introduced, and the observed number of days visited, $V(q,n)$, is a function of q, the switchover point is not as easily derived. Then, D is replaced by $U(q)$, and the choice of q will be different for 1-day visits versus one long visit, because the marginal cost of q is different under the two circumstances. However, again the hunter will choose one long or a number of day visits, depending upon which option yields the greatest net benefits.

Let A' be the net benefits generated by one long visit and B' be the net benefits generated by 1-day visits:

$$A' = U(q_1)\, V(q_1,n) - (h + t_1 + k(q_1) + t_2(q_1) + l)$$
$$- (V(q_1,n) - 1)(r + l) \quad [54]$$

$$B' = U(q_2)\, V(q_2,n) - (h + t_1 + k(q_2) + t_2(q_2) + l)\, V(q_2,n), \quad [55]$$

where q_1 is chosen with one long visit, and q_2 is chosen with many 1-day visits.

Subtracting B' from A', $U(q_1)\, V(q_1,n) - U(q_2)\, V(q_2,n)$ can be approximated by

$$½(k(q_1) + t_2(q_1) - k(q_2) - t_2(q_2) + (k(q_1) + t_2(q_1))\, V(q_2,n)$$
$$- (k(q_2) - t_2(q_2))\, V(q_2,n)) + U(q_2)\, V(q_1,n) - U(q_2)\, V(q_2,n). \quad [56]$$

With $\overline{K(q) + t_2(q)} = ½(K(q_1) + K(q_2) + t_2(q_1) + t_2(q_2))$, $A' - B'$ is now

$$- (h + t_1 + \overline{k(q) + t_2(q)} + l) - (V(q_1,n) - 1)(r + l)$$

$$+ (h + t_1 + \overline{k(q) + t_2(q)} + l)\, V(q_2,n) + U(q_2)\, V(q_1,n)$$
$$- U(q_2)\, V(q_2,n). \quad [57]$$

Although this may not generally provide a good deal of information about the switch point, it will do so in specific cases. For example, if V_q is very small so that $V(q_1,n) \cong V(q_2,n)$, then the switchover point is $r + l = h + t_1 + \overline{k(q) + t_2(q)} + l$.[8]

Other Characteristics

Earlier discussion of components of hunter satisfaction emphasized that characteristics other than the probability of bagging game can influence hunter satisfactions (e.g., esthetic and scenic characteristics). Therefore, it is necessary to consider a model which includes such characteristics. One addition, a scenic characteristic, denoted s, is assumed. This characteristic also enters the hunter utility function. In all likelihood, $Uqs \neq 0$ and $Usq \neq 0$. Following More's observation, it is also likely that bagging game still is the major objective of hunters, and that although utility might be derived from q alone, no utility would be derived from s alone (More 1977). It seems reasonable to write the utility function as

$$(U_1(q) + U_2(q,s))\, V(q,n). \qquad [58]$$

The switchover point derived for model C is also appropriate here. With $J(q,s)$ and $t_3(q,s)$ added to the switchover point is

$$r + l = h + t_1 + \overline{k(q) + J(q,s) + t_2(q) + t_3(q,s)} + l\,, \qquad [59]$$

where both s and q are arguments in the cost function, but the cost function exhibits the characteristic that the marginal cost of q can change without changing the marginal cost of s.

First consider the case where only 1-day visits occur. Assuming that it is q whose marginal bid and cost function are of concern, first consider whether changes in q will affect s. The choice of s given q is determined by

$$(1/U_x)\, V(q,n)U_{2s} = V(q,n)(J_s + t_{3s}). \qquad [60]$$

In general, changes in q will affect the choice of s. Allowing s to adjust to changes in q gives the marginal bid equals marginal cost relationship for q as

$$\begin{aligned}(1/U_x)(V(q,n)U_{2s}\,Y_q + V(q,n)(U_{1q} + U_{2q}) + V_q(U_1(q) + U_2(q,s)))\\ = V(q,n)(J_s + t_{3s})Y_q + V(q,n)(k_q + J_q + t_{2q} + t_{3q})\\ + V_q(h + t_1 + k(q) + J(q,s) + t_2(q) + t_3(q,s) + l)\,, \qquad [61]\end{aligned}$$

where Y gives the relationship between s and q, $s = Y(q)$ and $Y_q = ds/dq$.

Because k_q and t_{2q} can vary independently of the J_s and t_{3s} functions, equation [61] can be used as a basis for determining the marginal bid and cost functions for q, allowing s to adjust.

It is possible that $Y_q = 0$. This could come about if $U_2(s,q) = qU_2(s)$ and $J(s,q) + t_3(s,q) = qJ(s) + qt_3(s)$. The first order conditions for s would become

$$(1/U_x)\,(V(q,n)qU_{2s} = (V(q,n))q(J_s + t_{3s}). \qquad [62]$$

Because $(V(q,n))\cdot q$ cancels, $Y_q = 0$ and equation [61] becomes

$$(1/U_x)(V(q,n)(U_{1q} + U_2(s)) + V_q(U_1(q) + qU_2(s)))$$

$$= V(q,n)(k_q + J(s) + t_{2q} + t_3(s)) + V_q(h + t_1 + k(q) + qJ(s) + t_2(q) + qt_3(s) + l). \qquad [63]$$

When the situation changes from the 1-day visit regime to the one long visit regime, the same approach can be used for valuing visits taken under this regime.

Information Required for Estimation

The information required in the C hunting model with varying visit length, time costs, and multiple characteristics is fairly detailed. It requires knowledge of the choices of hunters in terms of characteristics such as q and s. The cost of a visit and the q and s choices made during that visit in terms of both time and money also must be known. To be able to use variation in this cost to identify the visit demand curve or the marginal bid curve for q or s, the exogenous factors I_q, I_s, and h must be measured.

The third of these is relatively straightforward, but the first two require a relatively detailed knowledge of the characteristics of sites and their geographic dispersion relative to the various origins of consumers. The measure suggested for I_q is

$$I_q = \sum_{\text{all } i} \frac{q_i \times C_i}{1 + d_i - h}, \qquad [64]$$

where q_i = the level of q at site i
C_i = the capacity of site i
$d_i - h$ = the distance to site i, over and above h.

This measure is required for each characteristic whose bid curve is to be identified, or for which a management change which could affect its relative availability to some users is to be evaluated.

On the demand side, an estimate is needed of the proportion of the population that is consuming at different costs. Ideally, some information should be available on socioeconomic characteristics and preferences of both consumers and nonconsumers. However, this often may be prohibitively costly. As an alternative, data for different socioeconomic or preference groups can be obtained from sources such as the national hunting and fishing survey, and information collection for a given study can focus on the choices, preferences, and socioeconomic characteristics of consumers.

Conclusions

Information on the values of recreation service outputs is important for multiple-use decision making. For normal recreation service outputs, where things such as bag limits do not impose unusual conditions, a number of models can be used to assess the benefits or costs of a management action that affects the level of the characteristic (or recreation service output) and, in turn, its marginal cost. These include models which are similar to the traditional travel cost model, in that the demand curve estimated is the demand curve for visits. and the management change causes that demand curve as well as the cost curve for a visit to shift. Model A, model C, and model D all can be used in this manner. With certain assumptions, both model A and model D can be used as the Cesario-Knetsch multiple-site travel cost model. Also included are models where the marginal bid and marginal cost curves for the characteristic are estimated. Model B, model C and model D can be used in this manner.

The hunting model has a fixed season length and the added complication of a bag limit. These constraints limit the number of models that are applicable. Model C would appear to be the best choice for this case. Some additional refinements may be introduced to make C fit the hunting case better. These include time costs, varying visit length, and multiple visits.

Although some basic approaches can be implemented to value changes in recreation service outputs, more research is needed. Together with the direct questioning (or income compensation) approach discussed by Randall, the expenditure function approach (relying on market data or observations on actual behavior) which underlies the models developed in this chapter can be a valuable tool for assessing these values.

Literature Cited

Bockstael, N., and K. McConnell. 1978. The estimation and use of the household production function for wildlife recreation. University of Rhode Island, Department of Natural Resources, Staff Paper No. 15, Kingston, R.I.

Bouwes, Nicholaas W., Sr., and Robert Schneider. 1979. Procedures in estimating benefits of water quality change. American Journal of Agricultural Economics 61(3):535-539.

Boyce, Stephen G. 1980. Management of forests for optimal benefits (DYNAST-OB). USDA Forest Service Research Paper SE-204. Southeastern Forest Experiment Station, Asheville, N.C.

Boyce, Stephen G. 1977. Management of eastern hardwood forests for multiple benefits (DYNAST-MB). USDA Forest Service Research Paper SE-168. Southeastern Forest Experiment Station, Asheville, N.C.

Brown, Gardner M., Jr., and Robert Mendelson. 1980. The hedonic-travel cost method. Final Report prepared for the Division of Program Plans, U.S. Department of the Interior.

Brown, Gardner M., Jr., John Charbonneau, and Michael J. Hay. 1978. The value of wildlife estimated by the hedonic approach. U.S. Department of the Interior, Fish and Wildlife Service. Working Paper No. 61. Washington, D.C.

Cesario, Frank J. 1976. Value of time in recreation benefit studies. Land Economics 52:32-41.

Cesario, Frank J., and Jack Knetsch. 1976. A recreation site demand and benefit estimation model. Regional Studies 10:97-104.

Cheshire, P. C., and M. J. Stabler. 1976. Joint consumption benefits in recreation site surplus: An empirical estimate. Regional Studies 10:343-351.

Clawson, Marion, and Jack L. Knetsch. 1966. Economics of outdoor recreation. Resources for the Future. Johns Hopkins University Press, Baltimore, Md.

Eubanks, Larry S., and David S. Brookshire. 1981. Methods for valuing non-market resources: Theoretical and empirical comparisons. Prepared for the meeting of the Econometric Society, December 21, 1981.

Haas, Glen E., Deborah J. Allen, and Michael J. Manfredo. 1979. Some dispersed recreation experiences and the settings in which they occur. p. 21-26. *In* Assessing amenity resource values. Terry C. Daniel, Ervin H. Zube, and B. L. Driver, editors. USDA Forest Service General Technical Report RM-68. Rocky Mountain Forest and Range Experiment Station, Fort Collins, Colo.

Haigh, J. A., and J. V. Krutilla. 1980. Clarifying policy directions: the case of national forest management. Policy Analysis (Fall).

Heckman, James J. 1974. The common structure of statistical models of truncation, sample selection and limited dependent variables and a simple estimator for such models. Annals of economic and social measurement 5(4):475-479.

Johnson, Reed, John V. Krutilla, Michael D. Bowes, and Elizabeth A. Wilman. 1981. A methodology for estimating the consequences of forest management on recreation benefits. Multiple Use Forestry Project, Resources for the Future.

Knetsch, Jack L., Richard E. Brown, and William J. Hansen. 1976. Estimating expected use and value for recreation sites. *In* Planning for tourism development: Quantitative approaches. C. E. Gearing, W. W. Stewart, and T. Var, editors. Praeger Publishers, New York, N.Y.

Knopf, Richard C., B. L. Driver, and John R. Bassett. 1977. Motivations for fishing. p. 191-204. *In* Transactions of the thirty-eighth North American Wildlife and Natural Resources Conference.

Krutilla, J. V., and J. A. Haigh. 1978. An integrated approach to national forest management. Environmental Law 8(2):375-384.

McConnell, Kenneth E. 1979. Values of marine recreational fishing: measurement and impact of measurement. American Journal of Agricultural Economics 61(5):921-925.

McConnell, Kenneth E., and Ivar Strand. 1981. Measuring the cost of time in recreation demand analysis. American Journal of Agricultural Economics 63(1):151-156.

More, Thomas A. 1977. Attitudes of Massachusetts hunters. p. 230-234. *In* Transactions of the thirty-eighth North American Wildlife and Natural Resources Conference.
Pindyck, R. S., and D. L. Rubinfeld. 1976. Econometric models and economic forecasts. McGraw-Hill, New York, N.Y.
Potter, Dale R., John C. Hendee, and Roger N. Clark. 1977. Hunting satisfaction: Games, guns, or nature? p. 220-229. *In* Transactions of the thirty-eighth North American Wildlife and Natural Resources Conference.
Smith, V. Kerry. 1975. Travel cost demand models for wilderness recreations: a problem of non-nested hypothesis. Land Economics 51:103-111.
Smith, V. Kerry. 1981. Congestion, travel cost recreation demand models and benefit evaluation. Journal of Environmental Economics and Management 8(1):92-96.
Smith, V. Kerry, and Raymond J. Kopp. 1980. The spatial limits of the travel cost recreation demand model. Land Economics 56:64-72.
Stankey, George H., Robert C. Lucas, and Robert Ream. 1977. Relationship between hunting success and hunting satisfaction. p. 235-241. *In* Transactions of the thirty-eighth North American Wildlife and Natural Resources Conference.
Thomas, Jack Ward. Wildlife habitats in managed forests: The Blue Mountains of Oregon and Washington. 1979. Agricultural Handbook No. 533. USDA Forest Service, published in cooperation with the Wildlife Management Institute and the U.S. Department of the Interior, Bureau of Land Management, Washington, D.C.
Tobin, James. 1958. Estimation of relationships for limited dependent variables. Econometrica 26:24-36.
Wilman, Elizabeth A. 1980. The value of time in recreation benefit studies. Journal of Environmental Economics and Management 7(3):272-286.
Ziemer, Rod F., Wesley N. Musser, and R. Carter Hill. 1980. Recreation demand equations: functional form and consumer surplus. American Journal of Agricultural Economics 136-141.

Footnotes

[1]*Although we use the terminology "household production function" because that is what is used in the economics literature, the point of view is essentially that of an individual consumer. This is because hunting is an individual decision. Other decisions, such as buying a car, may better be characterized as household decisions.*

[2]*See the letter from H. Hotelling in R. A. Prewitt, "The Economics of Public Recreation: An Economic Study of Recreation in the National Parks." (Washington, D.C., The National Park Service, 1949).*

[3]*See M. Clawson, "Methods of Measuring the Demand for and Value of Outdoor Recreation." (RFF Reprint No. 10 (1976), pp. 343-351).*

[4]*William J. Vaughan, Clifford S. Russell and Michael Hazilla, "A Note on the Use of Travel Cost Models with Unequal Zonal Populations: Comment." Land Economics 58(3):400-407, 1982.*

[5]*Michael D. Bowes and John B. Loomis, "A note on the use of Travel Cost Models with unequal zonal populations: Reply." Land Economics 58(3):408-410. 1982.*

[6]*The generalized least squares estimation is appropriate to correct for the heteroscedasticity introduced by the truncation problem. At higher travel costs the probability of a visit is less and variance in the observed visits will also be less. Weights are derived which are used in the generalized least squares estimation to correct for heteroscedasticity.*

[7]*The estimate will be imperfect because some negative amounts (i.e.,* abc *in fig. 2) will be counted in this average.*

[8]*A test to determine when observations are inconsistent with a given model is used by Smith and Kopp (1980). In this case, it is also possible to use a logit or probit model to determine the point at which the probability of taking one long visit is equal to the probability of taking one day visits.*